WOMEN'S EARLY AMERICAN
HISTORICAL NARRATIVES

Sharon M. Harris is the Lorraine Sherley Professor in Literature at Texas Christian University, co-editor of *Legacy: A Journal of American Women Writers*, and president and founder of the Society for the Study of American Women Writers. Her publications include *American Women Writers to 1800: An Oxford Anthology*; *Rebecca Harding Davis: Writing Cultural Autobiography*; and *Selected Writings of Judith Sargent Murray*. She has contributed numerous articles to journals and books, among them *Legacy, Early American Literature*, and *The Oxford Companion to Women's Writing in the United States*. Professor Harris previously taught at the University of Nebraska, Lincoln, and at Temple University.

Women's Early American Historical Narratives

Edited with an Introduction and Notes by
SHARON M. HARRIS

PENGUIN BOOKS

PENGUIN BOOKS
Published by the Penguin Group
Penguin Group (USA) Inc., 375 Hudson Street,
New York, New York 10014, U.S.A.
Penguin Books Ltd, 80 Strand,
London WC2R 0RL, England
Penguin Books Australia Ltd, 250 Camberwell Road, Camberwell,
Victoria 3124, Australia
Penguin Books Canada Ltd, 10 Alcorn Avenue,
Toronto, Ontario, Canada M4V 3B2
Penguin Books India (P) Ltd, 11 Community Centre, Panchsheel Park,
New Delhi - 110 017, India
Penguin Books (N.Z.) Ltd, Cnr Rosedale and Airborne Roads, Albany,
Auckland, New Zealand
Penguin Books (South Africa) (Pty) Ltd, 24 Sturdee Avenue,
Rosebank, Johannesburg 2196, South Africa

Penguin Books Ltd, Registered Offices:
80 Strand, London WC2R 0RL, England

First published in Penguin Books 2003

1 3 5 7 9 10 8 6 4 2

Copyright © Sharon M. Harris, 2003
All rights reserved

ISBN 0 14 24.3710 7
CIP data available

Printed in the United States of America
Set in Sabon

Contents

Introduction

"I mean never to forget," Eliza Yonge Wilkinson declared in a letter she wrote about her experiences during the British invasion of Charleston in 1779. In a series of twelve letters, Wilkinson recorded in what she termed "my historical manner" her transformation from a young woman who had romanticized the English to one who had to flee them as "the approaching enemy!"[1] Whether in private documents or formal public records, history writing was integral to the formation of the new republic in the Revolutionary and post-Revolutionary years. Histories were taught in schools and read widely among the literate class, in published books and in the burgeoning periodical literature published in the United States. The writing and reading of historical narratives was considered essential in the construction of an "American" identity, as the ancient and recent pasts became the interpretive field upon which the integrity of the new nation would be built.

The ten women writers in *Women's Early American Historical Narratives*, who published historical narratives between 1790 and 1830, were instrumental in changing a field that had long been dominated by male authors. In subsequent years, women's historical texts would proliferate.[2] In the early federal period, when the subject was America itself, most historians focused on the New England region. Histories of New England by Samuel Purchas (1625), Nathaniel Morton (1669), Thomas Prince (1735–1736), John Callender (1739), and John Winthrop (1790) were the most prominent histories available to early-nineteenth-century readers. Thus Hannah Adams's *A Summary History of New England* (1799) contributed to an important but certainly not yet crowded field of study. With the movement toward independence, the country's leaders felt a great need to articulate the United States' place in world history. Calls for an "American literature" as a means of distinguishing the accomplishments of North Americans are well known, and history writing was an important part of that response. Throughout the Revolution and in the years immediately after, histories of the United States and its struggle for independence from England began to emerge, including texts such as Jeremy Belknap's *History of New Hampshire* (1784–1792), David Ramsay's *History of the Revolution of South-Carolina* (1785), William Gordon's *The History of the Rise, Progress and Establishment of the Independence of the United States of America* (1788), Benjamin Trumbull's *Complete History of Connecticut* (1797), and John Marshall's *Life of George Washington* (five volumes, 1804–1807). While such texts certainly influenced the women who were entering the field of history writing, and who cited many of them in their narratives, it was a British woman historian—Catharine Macaulay—who had the greatest influence on women historians both English and American. The mid-century publication of Macaulay's monumental eight-volume *History of England from the Accession of James I to That of the Brunswick Line* (1763–1783) was a model for the comprehensive historical tome, and it was highly regarded on both sides of the Atlantic. While all of the authors included in this collection would most likely have known Macaulay's work, Mercy Otis Warren actually corresponded with her British counterpart, benefitting from an exchange of ideas about history writing and about the progress of republicanism at the end of the eighteenth century.

History writing offered women a way to express both their intellectual abilities and their opinions on religious, cultural, and political events without risking the condemnation that women novelists sometimes faced for engaging in too imaginative endeavors. It is no coincidence that women novelists (some of whom were also writing histories) almost without exception proclaimed their work to be "based in fact" or "a true story." The very writing of such an intellectual endeavor as a historical narrative placed women within the realm of the rational, intellectual being so important to the Enlightenment's vision of the ideal citizen.

But for women, it offered something equally important: the right to express publicly their opinions on the controversial issues of the era. Some did so with trepidation, but others reveled in the freedom to articulate their positions, to use interpretations of the past to comment on their beliefs about the present and the future. None of the historians included here—nor many of their male counterparts—were writing traditional military histories. It was an era in which history was intended to define a new nation through character, actions, and a vision for the new republic.

If Hannah Adams follows the traditional pattern of apologizing for coming before the public, some of the best histories are those in which the authors *do* define their own positions, and do so without apology. Judith Sargent Murray's four-part "Observations on Female Abilities" (1798) traces women's contributions to world culture from ancient times to the present. In her concluding comments, she connects the merit earned by women in history to her contemporaries. This connection allows Murray to bring to fruition her real purpose in writing the historical essays: to argue for female independence in the present age. "The Sex," she asserts, "should be taught to depend on their own efforts, for the procurement of an establishment in life" (85). Mercy Otis Warren, whose *History of the Rise, Progress, and Termination of the American Revolution* (1805) is one of the most philosophical histories of her time, did not hesitate to assert her anti-Federalist position, even though she was writing in the heyday of New England Federalism. She moves beyond the specifics of the Revolution to contemplate the nature of a republic and the character traits necessary in its citizens if it is to survive. For Warren, history is a study of the vagaries of human nature ("of character") and the reason why people act as they do. Though she recognizes noble feelings are evident at certain times, she envisions tyranny, ambition, and avarice as the primary instigators of human action. Whereas Murray, like most of the writers included herein, looked to the near future as a time of progress and hope—especially in terms of women's opportunities in the new nation—Warren writes from a seat of concern over the corruption and pursuit of wealth that seemed to characterize the newly freed states. Thus she venerates "those pious and independent gentlemen" who settled the Massachusetts Bay Colony "not as adventurers for wealth or fame, but for the quiet enjoyment of religion and liberty" (115). It is the consequences of recent history that constitute Warren's greatest concern. For Sarah Pogson, history writing allows her to present in *The Female Enthusiast* (1807) a comparative study of her sense of the failure of the French Revolution and the success of the American Revolution. Margaretta Faugeres used her historical narratives, such as "July the Fourteenth" (1793), to celebrate Bastille Day and the radical achievements of the French Revolution. Taking a much more conservative position than that of Faugeres, Pogson recognizes the need for war, but the honorable characters do not desire it; the implication is that radical leaders like Jean-Paul Marat actually desired the bloodletting of battle and personal glory. On the other hand, Pogson's dramatic history, like Warren's traditionally styled narrative, presents a keen understanding that the dangers of internal conflict may be more damning than foreign attack. Sarah Pierce's sacred history, *Sketches of Universal History* (1811), captures an important element of history writing of the period—the idea that historical instruction should be mixed with moral instruction. Whether termed political or educational, a historical narrative's sense of moral ideals was deemed integral to the recording of history. The passage of time and the acceptance of women writing histories also allowed for more radical expressions of political opinions. Thus, Emma Willard, writing her *History of the United States* in the late 1820s, is blatantly opinionated. She openly expresses her perspectives on political matters, including her support of Andrew Jackson's campaigns against the Seminoles in Florida, and peppers her remarks with vituperative depictions of Native Americans. It was a pattern of political outspokenness she would follow throughout her writing career.

What is unusual about much of the history writing of this period is that many of the authors were writing about very recent history, about *lived* history. This sense of personal knowledge and experience—and the literary talents of some of the historians—leads to narratives that successfully capture the excitement of the Revolutionary period, much more so than the accounts of the distant past. Mercy Otis Warren is particularly adept at portraying the tension and excitement that pervaded the decision to declare independence. Warren also reveals the daily hardships of war—not just of the battles fought but also of the poverty and the privateering inherent in such an extended engagement. Likewise, Emma Willard creates very dramatic depictions of struggles between the British and American troops. Writing for students at her school, the Troy Female Seminary, Willard knew how to make history lively and entertaining for young women readers. Thus, at the beginning of the nineteenth century, history writing was evolving from straightforward accounts of the past into a genre that allowed the author to demonstrate literary talents as well.

History writing is a genre unto itself, but it includes numerous subgenres, several of which are represented in these selections. Certainly, the traditional historical narrative, presented as a factual account of a particular period or event in history, is the most common. But historical narratives in the early period often blended with other genres. Ann Eliza Bleecker's "History of Maria Kittle" (1793), for example, is an account of events during King George's War, but it draws on the popular captivity narrative genre to convey the story. Margaretta Faugeres produced historical narratives in several forms, including the poetic historical narratives represented in "The Hudson" (1793) and her poems on the French Revolution. In *Observations on the Real Rights of Women* (1818), Hannah Mather Crocker used a modified version of the popular chronicle form of rendering history, which was common in periodicals at the turn of the century, to make connections between the biblical past and the Revolutionary present. Anne Newport Royall, on the other hand, blends history writing with another emerging popular genre, travel writing, in *Sketches of History, Life, and Manners, in the United States* (1826). Because travel writing was intended to be a rendering of one's perspectives on the regions visited, Royall's is the most intimate of the narratives. But even when she is in "present time," what interests her are the historical elements of a city and its inhabitants: the heroic feats of Dick Pointer during the Battle of Point Pleasant; the personal ancedotes of Virginia residents relating to the Revolutionary era; the house in Baltimore in which General Lafayette lodged, and so on. Sarah Pogson, on the other hand, offers an imaginative historical account of Charlotte Corday's murder of Jean-Paul Marat during the French Revolution. Probably the least factual of the selections in this volume, it is an excellent example of how a writer might interpret history.

Historical dramas and novels bring history to a broader popular audience in ways that traditional narratives rarely do. Many of the women in this collection who wrote what we might term "traditional histories" also produced dramatic histories: Margaretta Faugeres's powerful drama *Belisarius* (1795) reflects ideas similar to those she posited in "The Hudson" about the necessity of war at times to establish peace and to resist foreign intrusion; and Mercy Otis Warren was best known in her own time for her many dramas, such as *The Group* (1775), which depicts the passions of wartime actions. Sarah Pierce was also known to have included historical dramas about biblical women in her students' studies at the Litchfield Female Academy.

Another important subgenre of history writing was the history textbook. Both Sarah Pierce's *Sketches of Universal History* and Emma Willard's *History of the United States* were written out of a frustration with the classroom materials available to their female students. Each offers important insights into the educational processes of the time and the role that the study of history played in that process. This educational aspect of history writing was so important in the early federal period that Judith Sargent Murray incorporated it into her collection, *The Gleaner* (1798). The one hundred columns—originally produced for the *Massachusetts Magazine*—that make up *The Gleaner* in its book form include historical essays such as "Observations on Female Abilities," historical dramas about the Revolutionary period, and a number of essays that supplement the imbedded novel *The Story of Margaretta*. These essays recount the processes undertaken by the title character's mother to educate her daughter at home. Mary Vigillius's means of teaching her daughter history is to write, in the form of letters, short historical narratives and then have her daughter reply in writing with her analysis of the subject. The goal of this written exchange is very much like that created by Pierce in her textbook: to use history as a means of teaching critical thinking. Pierce uses a question-and-response method that moves beyond rote learning to critical inquiry: "What does this teach us?" or "What do we learn from this portion of history?" It was a process intended to inculcate in young women a lifelong interest in history. Pierce's students kept diaries of their daily activities, and thus we have knowledge of how history reading became a part of their education. One student, Charlotte Sheldon,[3] notes that she read "to the 30th page" in one history and weeks later that she was reading a history of Spain. She also reads historical novels such as Sophia Lee's *The Recess* (1783–5), a study of Mary Queen of Scots. Another student, Lucy Sheldon,[4] notes that when classes were cancelled on a Tuesday afternoon, "I employed myself in reading Adams history of Rome."

These subgenres raise two important points about women's history writing: women's interest in the genre itself as a means of public expression and, equally, the challenges for women in gaining access to sources necessary to traditional history writing. Though interest in imaginative historical writing processes was undoubtedly the primary reason some women chose these subgenres of history writing, access also was a factor. Histories produced in this period drew heavily on earlier-published materials; although all the women historians included here met the high demands of literacy necessary to history writing, they had no access to higher education. They had to rely on family libraries or other means of gaining the requisite knowledge to write a historical text.

As with the histories written by their male counterparts, the women historians vary widely in terms of how carefully they identify their sources. Both Murray and Crocker give little hint as to their sources; Pierce's subtitle asserts the text was "Compiled from Several Authors," but she identifies none. Adams, who was well educated and of the elite class but had few financial reserves, was very explicit about her sources, citing many of the major histories of the period. She was known to haunt the local bookshops, using their materials in-shop because she could not afford to buy the books she needed for her work; she also used correspondence as a means of drawing information from other writers or civic leaders. Royall used a more direct approach; she interviewed leading citizens in each of the cities she visited, drawing on their knowledge of the region and its history, blending traditional written histories and oral histories. She is also the only one to overtly cite a woman author, Anne Grant, as a source. Though she cites only a few sources, the most aggressive researcher was undoubtedly Warren. She read widely among documents from British and American sources, having had access to a local minister's library. Moreover, because she was acquainted from early in her life with so many of the leaders of the Revolution, she had access to much of the private correspondence of her family members and others, including friends such as Abigail and John Adams. As she told Abigail when she requested access to the Adamses' private papers, "I have a Curiosity to know a Little More about Certain public Characters and perticular transactions."[5] There was no standard for citations or kinds of resources used in history writing in the early federal period, and these authors employ the range of practices used at the time.

What all of these histories, traditional or imaginative, have in common is being written in an era when the very idea of "republicanism" was being defined for the new nation. The values of the Enlightenment, issues of equality of the sexes, public and private virtue, and rationalism were all integral to the emerging definitions. The histories written at this time not only reflect the concepts of republicanism that were being posited but also helped to shape those concepts. Lester Cohen has argued that the republicanism of the early federal period involved a "complex intersection of ideology, ethics, history, culture, religion, and language." The structures of intellectual and social existence were intimately linked in "what Mercy Otis Warren called the beautiful 'fabric' of republicanism."[6] Anne Newport Royall's insistence on the distinctiveness of each region's people as well as of its history, for instance, reflects the importance given to the early federal period's definition of republicanism that, though states were joined into one union, they retained their unique identities and perspectives.

The concepts of virtue and reason were invested with complex gendered notions that women writers had to address. This was, as Thomas Paine asserted, "The Age of Reason," meaning that in the Enlightenment philosophy of the era, passion must be subordinated to reason and private interests to the public good. But Enlightenment philosophies were highly gendered, including the idea that women's brains were incapable of intellectual thought. By writing histories and demonstrating their intellectual abilities, women historians were engaged in breaking down such biases, often castigating extreme emotions in favor of reasoned behavior. The most ardent advocate of women's intellectualism was Judith

Sargent Murray. Asserting that any difference between the sexes was due to differences in opportunities, not abilities, she scorned the idea that "a woman's form must needs enroll, / A weak, a servile, an inferior soul; / And that the guise of man must still proclaim, / Greatness of mind, and him, to be the same."[7] Thus "Observations on Female Abilities" uses women's historical accomplishments to demonstrate their innate abilities. Hannah Adams casts the Salem witch craze of 1692 as an emotional extremism brought about by people who were "not sufficiently enlightened by reason and philosophy" (103), and Emma Willard notes that earlier witchcraft charges had been dealt with without the "phrensy" that erupted in Salem (284). It was important to separate this horrific event in America's past from the *reasoned* decision to separate from England. But some authors, especially those as interested in religion as history, put cautionary qualifiers on the concept of reason. Sarah Pierce, for instance, asserted that "Reason is capable of approving, appropriating, and applying the information conveyed to us by the word of God; but not of anticipating it" (216).

It it was the concept of virtue, however, that was most important in the discussion of republicanism. The historian Gordon Wood asserts that public moral character became the highest ideal in the social radicalism of the Revolution.[8] Public and private character were, according to these texts, inseparable. For women writers, it was a particularly complex issue. Although attitudes were beginning to change, the idea still circulated that for a woman to take a public role—such as writing—was to "de-sex" herself and to leave herself subject to public condemnation. Thus it is not surprising that virtue is a rampant theme in these historical narratives, necessarily so because of its importance to the ideals of republicanism but equally, if not more so, for its gendered implications. Even unwitting public attention could be criticized; thus Bleecker carefully renders her account of Maria Kittle's captivity in terms of Kittle's ability to maintain her virtue in spite of the dangers of captivity and war. The positive side of the issue for women was that among the virtues that members of the new republic should gain was education about and a concern for public policies. The most famous instance of this concern was rendered in Benjamin Franklin's *Autobiography*, when he charts his way to achieving "moral perfection" through the attainment of thirteen carefully delineated virtues. Many of the histories include these kinds of virtues in their depictions of colonial and Revolutionary leaders as a means of demonstrating the progress toward an ideal republic.

Most women of the period, even outspoken proponents of women's equality such as Murray and Crocker, accepted the ideas of women's physical weakness and inherent differences between the sexes. But reason and virtue were intellectual and moral traits, not physical ones, and women, they argued, were certainly capable of attaining these traits. Thus writing and public expression should be a woman's venue as well as a man's. Even a cautionary figure such as Adams negotiates these double binds by asserting that an astute writer could aid the promotion of public virtue. Warren agreed and took the idea to its most impressive heights: the emphasis upon moral character structures her history and encapsulates the uncertainties that she felt about the future of the republic. Though her history, like other accounts of the Revolution by U.S. citizens, is presented from the Patriots' perspective, not all Americans live up to these ideals and those who do not are the greatest threat to the new nation. Warren's writing reveals her fears that corruption will undo all that has been accomplished. Hers was a rare voice of caution among women's texts, but she was not alone in this perspective. Though perhaps more expansive in her concerns, she was joined by contemporary historians such as David Ramsay and John Marshall, who also lamented the widespread corruption that was becoming increasingly apparent. By emphasizing these traits, historians did not merely record colonial and Revolutionary events but also established the criteria by which such events were to be interpreted.[9] While Warren believes that America offers a better model of virtue than England, Willard, a far more ardent nationalist, asserts that the United States stands for national virtue and all of the "old and wily nations" for national vice (283).

In part because of the time and in part because of the genre, nationalistic zeal is epidemic in these narratives. Most Americans considered themselves situated in a unique historical moment and believed that the creation of the United States on republican values was exemplary of human progress. It was a moment to be recorded in histories, as part of history. Faugeres's "The Hudson" is an excellent example. Though she does address the devastation of war, the poem is largely in praise of nationalistic endeavors during the war and reflects the postwar era's increased interest in trade and commerce in a much more positive light than Warren does. She suggests that by the 1790s the New York region, and thereby the country, had returned to fertile abundance. This is an important movement in the poem and in reconstructing American history. The British had planned to conquer the rebellious colonies early in the war by invading through Canada via Lake Champlain and the Hudson River. Thus Faugeres's poem moves from the devastation of war and invasion to the reclaiming of the Hudson as a national treasure.

Pogson goes so far as to assert that, unlike France, America is a land of safety for women, regardless of their class, as long as they are virtuous (186). Royall adds an important element to the vision of the new nation. While most histories still concentrated largely on the Northeastern region of the United States, Royall roams over the entire country, focusing on regions in the southern and mid-Atlantic states as well, giving a sense of the wealth of resources and the rich history that is the United States. It is Willard's proferred pattern for teaching history, however, that reflects the greatest attention to a nationalist agenda. She begins with the local, moves to the national, and then to the global. She asserts that a student can learn about U.S. history by having his father's or mother's birth date cast in relation to being "so much before or after the date of American independence" (279). This systematic process of learning history and geography, she continues, will "contribute much to the improvement of our national literature, and consequently to the growth of wholesome national feeling" (280). Unlike Warren, who suggests there were examples of corruption even among Americans, Willard asserts that, contrary to European history, the American Revolution presented no examples of "bold and criminal ambition, which has 'waded through blood to empire'" (282). If most historians were predicting continued progress for America, Warren elucidated the fact that the end of the war was the beginning of the struggle to create a nation that would live up to the ideals for which it went to war—and, she asserted, that may be the greater battle.

Indeed, battles over the structure and values of the new nation did emerge in the post-Revolutionary years, and the histories produced in those years reflect these political differences, as well as religious and racial differences. The political perspectives of the writers are fairly evident in the texts themselves. Bleecker supported the Revolution, but felt that the costs of war destroyed the Edenic prewar life she had been privileged enough to live. In several of these histories, France becomes a touchstone for perspectives on the American cause. The French General Lafayette, who supported America's cause, is highly regarded by all of the historians. But France's roles during the American Revolution and then in its own Revolutionary moment were much more controversial. Faugeres had the most radical political vision of the ten authors included here. Her fervent support of the French Revolution, including the Jacobins, was also rendered in her poetical historical works. In poems such as "On seeing a Print, exhibiting the Ruins of the Bastille" (1793), she proclaimed: "Ah! see the *Bastille*'s iron walls thrown down, / That bulwark strong of *Tyranny*; / See her proud turrets smoke along the ground, / Crush'd by the giant arm of *Liberty*!" (51). Faugeres and her husband, a French immigrant physician, had publicly proclaimed their commitment to the French Revolution by marrying on Bastille Day. On the other end of the political spectrum concerning the French Revolution was Sarah Pogson. Radicalism as enacted by Jean-Paul Marat was too extreme for her taste, and his murder at the hands of the political moderate Charlotte Corday is deemed a tragic necessity. Emma Willard was more in line with Pogson. She felt that France was not so much in favor of America's actions as "she feared and hated her enemy"—that is, England—and asserts that if America had not defended itself, France would have sought to conquer it as well (283).

Murray's politics, on the other hand, focused on gender equality, while Warren was perhaps most out of step with the majority because of her anti-Federalist politics. Warren solicited her friend Judith Sargent Murray's help in finding subscribers for her history, in spite of the fact that Murray was a Federalist. Certainly the difficulty Warren faced was due in part to the appearance of Ramsay's and Marshall's Federalist histories shortly before her own was published; but as Murray reminded her, it was difficult to garner support in a city like Boston, which was overwhelmingly Federalist. Most Federalists believed the new Constitution would shield against impending corruption, but Warren feared that the Constitution impinged on popular sovereignty, an argument she had first presented in the Constitutional debates of 1788. She also had to face criticism from friends such as John Adams, who felt that his role in the Revolution, especially in the early years, was not sufficiently represented. But Warren stood her ground and defended her right to her own historical perspective, even though it cost her the friendship of John and Abigail Adams for many years. As she wrote to John Adams, "It was not the design of my historic work to write a panegyric on your life and character."[10]

Just as volatile and important to these historians was the issue of religion and its relation to history writing itself. As Lawrence Buell has argued, histories written in this period were "enlivened by perpetual conflict between filiopietistic and critical instincts." The debate was not simply about which would prevail—the newer, liberal forces such as the Armenian-Unitarians or the conservative Congregationalists—but "over the facts, means, and authority of the New England past."[11] Many of the male historians were also ministers, and each brought his own religious perspective to his account of history. Likewise, for many female historians, the most important subgenre of history was sacred history—indeed, they would have prioritized it as the premier field of history with political histories subordinated to it. Hannah Adams had written several comparative religious histories prior to undertaking a history of New England. *A Summary History of New England* is, in fact, a history of the religious development of the region and its influence on the Revolution. Even texts that are not overtly religious often are rooted in religious ideals. Murray's commitment to the liberal Universalist religion, for example, is reflected in her demands for an egalitarian vision of the relation between the sexes and the roles for women in the new nation.

But it is Hannah Mather Crocker and Sarah Pierce who delve

most fully into the writing of sacred histories. Crocker uses Christian history, Enlightenment reason, and democratic rights to argue for women's rights in the new republic. One of the most debated issues from biblical history was the interpretation of Eve's actions in the Garden of Eden. It was the basis on which many religious leaders demanded the subordination of women in all aspects of life. In an essay titled "On the Equality of the Sexes" (1790), for which "Observations" was an expansion of its ideas, Murray had argued that Adam was much more to blame for the fall of humankind than Eve: "It is true some ignoramuses have, absurdly enough informed us, that the beauteous fair of paradise, was seduced from her obedience, by a malignant demon, *in the guise of a baleful serpent*; but we, who are better informed, know that the fallen spirit presented himself to her view, *a shining angel still*; for thus, saith the criticks in the Hebrew tongue, ought the word to be rendered." [12]

Crocker offers an equally provocate interpretation. She asserts that the consequences of Eve's transgression were "for a certain space of time"; with the advent of Christianity, "[w]e shall consider woman restored to her original right and dignity" (230). She further asserts that the command not to eat from the Tree of Knowledge was given prior to woman's creation, so she must have received her information from Adam. Though Eve is responsible for her "impudence," Adam may not have conveyed the significance of the command. Crocker insists ultimately on "the joint transgression of our first parents" (233). Pierce, on the other hand, is much more conservative. For Pierce, "universal" history *is* sacred history (by which all of the authors in this book mean Christianity). Unlike those of Murray and Crocker, Pierce's rendition of Eve and the fall maintains the traditional condemnation of Eve: she was seduced because of her ambition and vanity (217). That Pierce accepts the condemnation of women for Eve's seduction is especially important when we consider that she was an educator who used her *Universal History* in the classroom. Virtually all of the women depicted in Pierce's history are examples of women's vanity, love of riches, and impiety: Lot's wife (220), Sarah; Abraham's wife (221–2); Jezebel and her daughter Athaliah (233–4); Lycurgus's sister-in-law (225); and so on.

Just as a historian's political alignments and religious perspectives helped shape her historical narrative, so, too, did the author's racial politics become evident in her writings. Surprisingly little attention is given to abolition in these histories, in spite of the fact that debates over manumission were being held in most of the states. Only Margaretta Faugeres and Emma Willard remark upon abolition. Faugeres had written on the subject elsewhere.[13] In an essay, she had argued that the preference for *gradual* manumission could destroy the lives of slaves. Full abolition, she felt, should be an element of the new republic. Like many of the early abolitionists, she argued that a country that had sought its own emancipation against tyranny had no right to enslave others. In the conclusion of "The Hudson," she briefly asserts:

> But while they throng the domes of *Liberty*,
> May they her sacred precepts ne'er profane;
> Nor while they boast themselves 'the virtuous *free*'
> One *slave* beneath the cruel yoke retain? . . . (49)

Willard, on the other hand, writing more than thirty years later, advocated freeing slaves only if they were to be colonized outside the United States, in Liberia—a popular idea at the time among individuals who felt that slavery as a system was harmful to *white* citizens because it molded them into the role of tyrants. Willard's position had little to do with a concern about those who were enslaved. Indeed, removal was necessary so as not to expose "the country to the dangers apprehended from a numerous free black population" (302).

It was the subject of how Native Americans fit into U.S. history, however, that created the greatest difficulties for historians of the period. Some envisioned indigenous peoples as the forces of evil; others were concerned, to a degree, about U.S. actions against them, but none of the historians could reconcile tribal nations' histories and rights with the privileges they felt were inherently due to whites within the colonial or early federal periods. Accounts of the colonial period, such as the early sections of Adams's *A Summary History of New England*, often elide the complexities of relations between the Native Americans and colonists, either by

ignoring the issue or by suggesting that Native Americans instigated the wars. Adams does note that relations between the Pil-
grims and native peoples were friendly at first but claims that the
deaths of so many Native Americans in the first years of English
settlement were due to intertribal wars and a "contagious distemper" that had existed, she insists, before the colonization project
began. Bleecker's history is specfically about a colonist's capture by
Native Americans, so it is perhaps not surprising that she depicts
them as inherently devious and savage—even those who had maintained peaceful relations with the colonists. But this attitude prevailed throughout her body of writings and was typical of the
period. Though an early abolitionist, Faugeres writes little about
Native Americans. What she does convey in these brief passages is
the stereotypic portrayal of indigenous peoples as "savage bands"
(40). In the post-Revolutionary years, such portrayals were often
justified by the assertion that many Native Americans had sided
with the British during the war; this argument ignores the reasons
why they might have chosen to fight against the Americans, and
it ignores the fact that some Native Americans also supported the
Patriots.

Certainly the historian most conflicted over the issue of Native
Americans is Mercy Otis Warren. Native Americans who, in 1778,
aligned themselves with "British renegades" are depicted as having
committed "unheard of cruelties" against the Patriots (125). But
Warren does recognize the "conflagration" against Native Americans by the military; perhaps, she suggests, it was justified as retaliation for their siding with the enemy. Her struggle with her ideas
about Native Americans is best conveyed in her declaration that
they are "savages" and yet cultivated in many ways—in their
homes, gardens, etc. She criticizes General John Sullivan for destroying all the native peoples' homes and agricultural lands, and
she is haunted by the savagery with which Native Americans have
been treated by the encroaching Europeans: "The rivers of blood
through which mankind generally wade to empire and greatness,
must draw out the tear of compassion, and every sympathetic
bosom will commiserate the sufferings of the whole human race,
either friends or foes . . . under the splendid canopy reared by their
own guilty hands" (130). While Warren cannot develop a sense of

native peoples' own cultures, she does believe they have the capacity to be "civilized," meaning, of course, converted to white Americans' ideals. Ultimately, Warren laments the extermination of Native Americans. Though Anne Royall mentions native peoples only in passing, she, too, presents them as skulking and savage but notes that their actions were "actuated by revenge, for the treatment they met with" from the U.S. military (252).

Emma Willard, on the other hand, fairly well celebrates the extermination of Native Americans by Andrew Jackson's troops. She recounts the 1818 war between the United States and the Seminoles in Florida solely as agression on the part of the Seminoles and their compatriots. The exception is an attack on a Creek village—but the Creeks had aligned themselves with Jackson against the Seminoles. Willard was adamant in her belief in the supremacy of the white race, and she added an appendix to the *History* in which she voices her opinions that Native Americans could not be "civilized."

For all of the attention to political alignments, race matters, and religion that pervade the histories written in the early federal period, the most important influence—one that is deeply linked to these issues and to the construction of republicanism and virtue as well—is the fact that these historians were women seeking new opportunities for themselves and their sex within the new republic. Whether radical or conservative, whether writing about other women or not, these ten women viewed themselves specifically as *women* historians, and the subject of women pervades their texts, be it overtly or subtly. All of the women, to greater or lesser degrees, were of the elite class by virtue of their education and social position. But the degrees *did* matter. None were wealthy, with the exception of Bleecker, but most of them were financially stable, at least to the extent that anyone could be during the Revolutionary years. In all of these texts, the authors' class biases are evident. Warren, for instance, remarks on class distinctions that, to her, are natural: the "vulgar" lower classes are easily duped; they are deceived, for instance, by Thomas Hutchinson's gentlemanly deportment, which they mistake for sanctity. Behind this comment, of course, is the longstanding antagonism between the Warren family and Hutchinson, a Loyalist (and a historian as well as a political leader). She also resents that some people without "the advantages of the best education" gained wealth during the war and, with little attention "to the principles of the revolution, took the lead in manners" (137). Anne Royall, on the other hand, came from a very different background than the others. Her widowed mother worked as a housekeeper; Anne would eventually marry her mother's employer, but his children from an earlier marriage contested her right to inheritance, and she was left to earn her own living. Not surprisingly, she observes more closely than the others the lives of the poor, including women imprisoned in Baltimore for inability to pay their debts. Since she herself was often bordering on economic impoverishment, she recognizes the class differences within the emerging U.S. culture. As she moves from region to region, she records each area's class structures, such as Albany's three distinct classes of government officials and professionals, the shopkeepers and clerks, and "foreigners, who rank with blacks and sailors" (271).

In conjunction with class, these women historians present significant instances of the developing role of women in the new nation. Some were more cautious in their assertions. Hannah Adams, a single woman who had to support herself, offers the more conventional women's prefatory remarks of apology for any seeming "arrogance" and for her "incapacity" in assuming the role of historian. Sarah Pogson also struggles with what role a woman may take in acts of war. Her rendering of Charlotte Corday hedges on making Corday a heroine, but to take on a political act of aggression and murder is, for a woman, to de-sex herself, even when it is done from a sense of duty: "To crush the murderer. . . . / I sacrifice—I quit—myself / And all the softness of a woman's name" (169).

Adams's assertion that women cannot write about war and military maneuvers is belied by the detailed accounts of war rendered by Warren and Willard. They are not writing military histories per se, but they do deem their sex inherently capable of recording the acts—benevolent and brutal—of war. Only two of the ten—Murray and Crocker—devote themselves to chronicling women in history, and their texts are important documents in the emerging arguments for women's equality. Crocker's compendium of important women in history echoes Murray's "Observations," but Crocker emphasizes biblical women. By including a two-chapter history of women from antiquity to the present, Crocker can blend her tripartite ideals—Christianity, women's rights, and democracy. Writing in the heyday of True Womanhood ideology, Crocker carefully points out in the introduction to *Observations on the Real Rights of Women* that she is not looking for a dispute between the sexes, and in an appendix she includes notations about important male figures from Moses to Samuel Johnson. Thus her overt argument for women's rights is tempered by her separate-sphere belief that it would be "morally incorrect, and physically improper" for women to trespass "on masculine ground" (231). But several of the other writers emphasize their gender in their texts. Faugeres, for example, notes in the opening lines of "The Hudson" that it is "a *Female*" poet who is crafting this narrative tour of recent history. Like Murray, Faugeres wants to present herself as a capable female writer. It is Murray, however, who presents the most explicit demands for women's equality. She argues that it is man's tyranny against women that has resulted in their humiliation and that must be eliminated. These are the extremes to which women have been subjected; thus, educating them and giving them equal opportunities become the *rational* middle ground of action in her astutely crafted argument. By using the past as a touchstone, Murray envisions "a new era in female history," a pattern that will be embraced by the next generation's commitment to women's rights.

NOTES

1. *approaching enemy* Quoted in Sharon M. Harris, *American Women Writers to 1800* (New York: Oxford University Press, 1996), 360–61.
2. *texts would proliferate* See Nina Baym's *American Women Writers and the Work of History, 1790–1860* (New Brunswick: Rutgers University Press, 1995).
3. *Charlotte Sheldon* See Harris, *American Women Writers*, 75–78.
4. *Lucy Sheldon* Quoted in Albert von Frank, "Sarah Pierce and the

Poetic Origins of Utopian Feminism in America," *Prospects: An Annual Journal of American Cultural Studies* 14 (1989): 56.

5. *perticular transactions* Quoted in *Adams Family Correspondence*, 4 vols, ed. L.H. Butterfield (Cambridge, MA: Harvard University Press, 1963): 2:377.

6. *'fabric' of republicanism* Lester H. Cohen, "Mercy Otis Warren: The Politics of Language and the Aesthetics of Self," *American Quarterly* 35.5 (1983), 381.

7. *to be the same* From Murray's "On the Equality of the Sexes," quoted in Harris, *American Women Writers*, 150.

8. *radicalism of the Revolution* Gordon S. Wood, *The Radicalism of the American Revolution* (New York: Knopf, 1992).

9. *to be interpreted* For more on Warren's engagement with the criteria of interpretation, see Cohen, 213–14.

10. *your life and character* Quoted in *Correspondence between John Adams and Mercy Warren* (1878; rpt. New York: Arno Press, 1972), 449.

11. *the New England past* Lawrence Buell, *New England Literary Culture: From Revolution through Renaissance* (Cambridge, MA: Cambridge University Press, 1986), 214–15.

12. *ought the word to be rendered* Murray, "On the Equality of the Sexes," 155.

13. *Faugeres had written on the subject elsewhere* See "Fine Feelings exemplified in the Conduct of a Negro Slave," *Posthumous Works*, 268–70.

Suggestions for
Further Reading

I. SELECTED RELATED WORKS
BY THE AUTHORS

Adams, Hannah. *An Alphabetical Compendium of the Various Sects Which Have Appeared in the World from the Beginning of the Christian Era to the Present Day.* Boston: B. Edes & Sons, 1784.

———. *A History of the Jews from the Destruction of Jerusalem to the Nineteenth-Century.* 2 vols. Boston: J. Eliot, Jr., 1812.

———. *A Narrative of the Controversy between the Rev. Jedidiah Morse D.D., and the Author.* Boston: John Eliot, 1814.

Murray, Judith Sargent. *Selected Writings of Judith Sargent Murray.* Ed. Sharon M. Harris. New York: Oxford University Press, 1995.

———. *Forming a New Era in Female History: Three Essays by Judith Sargent Murray.* Ed. Bonnie Hurd Smith. Cambridge, MA: Judith Sargent Murray Society, 1999.

Pogson (Smith), Sarah. *Essays: Religious, Moral, Dramatic and Poetical.* Charleston, SC: Archibald E. Miller, 1818.

Royall, Anne Newport. *The Black Book: or, A Continuation of Travels in the United States.* 3 vols. Washington, D.C.: Printed for the Author, 1828–29.

———. *Letters from Alabama.* Washington, D.C.: Printed for the Author, 1830.

Warren, Mercy Otis. *The Group.* Boston: Edes & Gill, 1775.

———. *Poems, Dramatic and Miscellaneous.* Boston: I. Thomas & E. T. Andrews, 1790.

II. SELECTED SECONDARY CRITICISM

Baym, Nina. *American Women Writers and the Work of History, 1790–1860.* New Brunswick: Rutgers University Press, 1995.

Dunlop, Marianne, ed. *Judith Sargent Murray: Her First One Hundred*

Letters. Gloucester, MA: Sargent-Murray-Gilman-Hough House Associates, 1995.

Harris, Sharon M., ed. *American Women Writers to 1800*. New York: Oxford University Press, 1996.

Hoffman, Ronald, and Peter J. Albert, eds. *Women in the Age of the American Revolution*. Charlottesville: U of Virginia P, 1989.

Kerber, Linda K. *No Constitutional Right to Be Ladies: Women and the Obligations of Citizenship*. New York: Hill and Wang, 1998.

———. *Toward an Intellectual History of Women: Essays*. Chapel Hill: U of North Carolina P, 1997.

James, Bessie Rowland. *Anne Royall's USA*. New Brunswick, NJ: Rutgers University Press, 1972.

Richards, Jeffrey. *Mercy Otis Warren*. New York: Twayne, 1995.

Skemp, Sheila. *Judith Sargent Murray: A Brief Biography with Documents*. Boston: Bedford, 1998.

Vella, Michael W. "Theology, Genre, and Gender: The Precarious Place of Hannah Adams in American Literary History." *Early American Literature* 28 (1993): 21–41.

Note on the Texts

The texts for this collection are based on first editions, with the exception of Willard's history, for which the second edition was used. Ann Eliza Bleecker's and Margaretta V. Bleecker Faugeres's selections are from *The Posthumous Works of Ann Eliza Bleecker in Prose and Verse. To which is added, A Collection of Essays, Prose and Poetical, by Margaretta V. Faugeres*, ed. Margaretta V. Faugeres (New York: T. & J. Swords, 1793). Judith Sargent Murray's four-part essay is from her collected essays, *The Gleaner*, 3 vols. (Boston: I. Thomas & E. T. Andrews, 1798). Hannah Adams's selections are from *A Summary History of New-England, from the First Settlement at Plymouth, to the Acceptance of the Federal Constitution. Comprehending a General Sketch of the American War* (Dedham, Mass.: Printed for the Author by H. Mann & J. H. Adams, 1799). Mercy Otis Warren's selections are from *History of the Rise, Progress and Termination of the American Revolution. Interspersed with Biographical, Political and Moral Observations*, 3 vols. (Boston: Manning & Loring for E. Larkin, 1805). Sarah Pogson's play is from *The Female Enthusiast: A Tragedy in Five Acts* (Charleston, SC: Printed for the Author by J. Hoff, 1807). Sarah Pierce's selections are from *Sketches of Universal History* (vols. 1 and 2, New Haven, CT: Barber; vol. 3, New Haven: Woodward, 1811–1917). Hannah Mather Crocker's selections are from *Observations on the Real Rights of Women, with Their Appropriate Duties, Agreeable to Scripture, Reason and Common Sense* (Boston: Printed for the Author, 1818). Anne Newport Royall's selections are from *Sketches of History, Life, and Manners, in the United States. By a Traveller* (New Haven, CT: Printed for the Author, 1826). Emma Willard's selections are

from *History of the United States, or Republic of America*, 2nd
ed., revised and corrected (New York: White, Gallagher, & White,
1829). Eighteenth- and nineteenth-century spellings and punctu-
ation have been retained, except for the long "s"; typographical
errors have been silently emended.

Women's Early American
Historical Narratives

ANN ELIZA BLEECKER
(1752–1783)

Anna Elizabeth Schuyler was born around October of 1752. The sixth and last child of Margareta Van Wyck Schuyler and Brandt Schuyler, she became part of the prosperous Dutch mercantile class in New York City. Brandt died shortly before Anna Elizabeth's birth, and Margareta married Anthony Ten Eyck in 1760. Their only daughter, Susanna (1762–?), is the addressee of the letter that constitutes Bleecker's epistolary historical narrative of the captivity experiences of Maria Kittle. On March 21, 1769, Anna Elizabeth married John James Bleecker, a member of another of the elite Dutch families of New York. They settled in Tomhanick, eighteen miles northeast of Albany. They had two daughters, Margaretta and Abella, the latter of whom died in 1777 during the American Revolution when Bleecker was forced to flee with her children as the British General Burgoyne's[1] troops invaded the region around Tomhanick. Like her mother, Margaretta became a writer (see Margaretta V. Bleecker Faugeres, page 36).

Ann Eliza, as she identified herself in her work, had been interested in writing from a young age. With her husband's encouragement, she began to write in earnest after her marriage. A prolific letter writer, Bleecker was also the author of informative and humorous "newspapers," which she sent to family members; of poetry; and of two historical narratives, "The History of Maria Kittle" (1779) and "Henry and Anne" (c. 1783).

Although critics have long identified "The History of Maria Kittle" as fiction, the narrative is, in fact, based on the

*real-life events[2] in the life of Maria Kittle (or "Kittlehuyn")
and her family, who had lived in the same region as Bleecker.
Drawing on captivity narrative traditions and her own literary interests in biblical symbolism and narrativity, Bleecker
presents Maria Kittle's captivity as a commentary on
women's wartime experiences, on the privileges and challenges of white womanhood, and on the relations between
Europeans and Native Americans in the eighteenth century.
Bleecker died in 1783; all of her work was published posthumously. When she herself was an adult, Bleecker's daughter
Margaretta published her mother's work. "The History of
Maria Kittle" was first serialized in the* New-York *Magazine
(Sept. 1790–Jan. 1791). In 1793, Margaretta collected some
of her mother's writings, including "Maria Kittle," and pub-
lished them in book form,* The Posthumous Works of Ann
Eliza Bleecker, in Prose and Verse. To which is added, A Col-
lection of Essays, Prose and Poetical, by Margaretta V.
Faugeres.

THE HISTORY
OF
MARIA KITTLE.

In a Letter to Miss Ten Eyck.

Tomhanick, December, 1779.

Dear Susan,

However fond of novels and romances you may be, the unfortunate adventures of my neighbours, who died yesterday, will make
you despise that fiction, in which, knowing the subject to be fabu-
lous, we can never be so truly interested. While this lady was expiring, Mrs. C——V——,[3] her near kinswoman, related to me her
unhappy history in which I shall now take the liberty of interesting your benevolent and feeling heart.

MARIA KITTLE was the only issue of her parents who cultivated
a large farm on the banks of the *Hudson*, eighteen miles above *Albany*. They were persons of good natural abilities, improved by
some learning; yet, conscious of a deficiency in their education,
they studied nothing so much as to render their little daughter
truly accomplished.

MARIA was born in the year 1721. Her promising infancy presaged a maturity of excellencies; every amiable quality dawned
through her lisping prattle; every personal grace attended her attitudes and played over her features. As she advanced through the
playful stage of childhood, she became more eminent than a Penelope[4] for her industry; yet, soon as the sun declined, she always retired with her books until the time of repose, by which means she
soon informed her opening mind with the principles of every useful

science. She was beloved by all her female companions, who though easily discovered her superior elegance of manners, instead of envying, were excited to imitate her. As she always made one in their little parties of pleasure on festival days, it is no wonder that she soon became the reigning goddess among the swains. She was importuned to admit the addresses of numbers, whom she politely discarded, and withdrew herself awhile from public observation. However, the fame of her charms attracted several gentlemen of family from *Albany*, who intruded on her retirement, soliciting her hand. But this happiness was reserved for a near relation of hers, one Mr. KITTLE, whose merits had made an impression on her heart. He, although not handsome, was possessed of a most engaging address; while his learning and moral virtues more particularly recommended him to her esteem. Their parents soon discovered their reciprocal passion, and highly approving of it, hastened their marriage, which was celebrated under the most happy auspices.

MARIA was fifteen when married. They removed to his farm, on which he had built a small neat house, surrounded by tall cedars, which gave it a contemplative air. It was situated on an eminence, with a green inclosure in the front, graced by a well cultivated garden on one side, and on the other by a clear stream, which rushing over a bed of white pebble, gave them a high polish, that cast a soft gleam through the water.

Here they resided in the tranquil enjoyment of that happiness which so much merit and innocence deserved: the indigent, the sorrowful, the unfortunate were always sure of consolation when they entered those peaceful doors. They were almost adored by their neighbours, and even the wild savages themselves, who often resorted thither for refreshments when hunting, expressed the greatest regard for them, and admiration of their virtues.

In little more than a year they were blessed with a daughter, the lovelier resemblance of her lovely mother: as she grew up, her graces increasing, promised a bloom and understanding equal to her's: the Indians, in particular, were extremely fond of the smiling ANNA; whenever they found a young fawn, or caught a brood of wood-ducks, or surprised the young beaver in their daily excursions through the forests, they presented them with pleasure to her; they brought her the earliest strawberries, the scarlet plumb, and other delicate wild fruits in painted baskets.

How did the fond parents' hearts delight to see their beloved one so universally caressed! When they sauntered over the vernal fields with the little prattler wantoning before them collecting flowers and pursuing the velvet elusive butterfly, MARIA's cheek suffusing with rapture, "Oh my dear," she would say, "we are happier than human beings can expect to be; how trivial are the evils annexed to our situation! may God avert that our heaven be limited to this life!"

Eleven years now elapsed before Mrs. KITTLE discovered any signs of pregnancy: her spouse silently wished for a son, and his desires were at length gratified; she was delivered of a charming boy, who was named, after him, WILLIAM.

A French and Indian war[5] had commenced sometime before; but about eight months after her delivery, the savages began to commit the most horrid depredations on the English frontiers. Mr. KITTLE, alarmed at the danger of his brothers, who dwelt near *Fort-Edward*, (the eldest being just married to a very agreeable young woman) invited them to reside with him during the war.

They were scarce arrived when the enemy made further incursions in the country, burning the villages and scalping the inhabitants neither respecting age or sex. This terribly alarmed Mrs. KITTLE; she began to prepare for flight, and the next evening after receiving this intelligence, as she and Mr. KITTLE were busily employed in packing up china and other things, they were accosted by several Indians, whose wigwams were contiguous to the village of *Schochticook*,[6] and who always seemed well affected to the English. An elderly savage undertook to be prolocutor, and desired the family to compose themselves, assuring them they should be cautioned against any approaching danger. To inforce his argument, he presented MARIA with a belt interwoven with silk and beads, saying, "There, receive my token of friendship: we go to dig up the hatchet, to sink i' in the heads of your enemies; we shall guard this wood with a wall of fire—you shall be safe." A warm glow of hope deepened in MARIA's cheek at this—Then ordering wine to be brought to the friendly savages, with a smile of diffidence, "I am afraid," said she, "necessity may oblige you to abandon us, or neglect of your promise may deprive us of your protection."—"Neglect of my promise!" he retorted with some acrimony. "No, MARIA, I am a true man; I shoot the arrow up to the Great Captain every new moon: depend upon it, I will trample down the briars round your dwelling, that you do not hurt your feet." MARIA now retired, bowing a grateful acknowledgement, and leaving the savages to indulge their festivity, who passed the night in the most vociferous mirth.

Mrs. KITTLE, with a sort of exultation, related the subject of their conference to her husband, who had absented himself on their first appearance, having formed some suspicion of the sincerity of their friendship and not being willing to be duped by the dissimulation: "And now," added MARIA smiling, "our fears may again subside: Oh my dear! My happiness is trebled into rapture, by seeing you and my sweet babes out of danger." He only sighed, and reaching his arm round her polished neck, pressed her to his bosom. After a short pause, "My love," said he, "be not too confident of their fidelity; you surely know what a small dependence is to be placed on their promises: however, to appear suspicious might be suddenly fatal to us; we will therefore suspend our journey to *Albany* for a few days." Though MARIA's soul saddened at the conviction of this truth; though her fears again urged her to propose immediate flight, yet she acquiesced; and having supped with the family, this tender pair sunk asleep on the bosom of rest.

Early the next morning Mr. KITTLE arose, first impressing a kiss on MARIA's soft cheek, as she slumbered with her infant in her arms. He then awaked his brother, reminding him that he had proposed a hunting match the preceding evening. "It is true," replied PETER, "but since hostilities have commenced so near us as the Indians inform, I think it rather imprudent to quit the family."—"Come, come," replied the other, "do not let us intimidate the neighbours by cloistering ourselves up with women and children."—"I reject the thought," rejoined PETER, "of being afraid." Then having dressed himself, while his brother charged their pieces, they left the house, and traversed the pathless grass for many hours without perceiving anything but small birds, who filled the fragrant air with melancholy. "PETER," said Mr. KIT-TLE, casting his eyes around the lovely landscape, "what a profusion of sweets does Nature exhale to please her intelligent creatures! I feel my heart expand with love and gratitude to heaven every moment, nor can I ever be grateful enough. I have health and competence, a lovely fond wife whose smile would calm the rudest storm of passion, and two infants blossoming into perfection; all my social ties are yet unbroken—PETER, I anticipate my heaven—but why my brother, do you turn pale? what dreadful idea stiffens your features with amazement? what in God's name ails you, PETER? are you unwell? sit down under this tree awhile."—To the interrogatories PETER replied, "Excuse my weakness, I am not unwell, but an unusual horror chilled my blood; I felt as if the damps of death prest already round my soul; but the vapour is gone off again, I feel quite better." Mr. KITTLE cheered his brother attributing his emotion to fear; who, by this time, having re-assumed his composure entered into discourse with cheerfulness, refusing to return home without having killed anything.

Then rising, they proceeded through lofty groves of pine, and open fields that seemed to bend under the heavy hand of Ceres.[7] At last, disappointment and fatigue prevailed on them to return home. They had gone farther than they apprehended, but passing long the bank of the river within a few miles of Mr. KITTLE's, they spied a fat doe walking securely on the beach, which PETER softly approaching, levelled his piece with so good an aim that the animal dropped instantly at the explosion. This seeming success was, however, the origin of their calamities; for immediately after, two savages appeared, directed in their course by the firing. Setting up a loud yell, they ran up to the brothers and discharged their fire-arms. Mr. KITTLE started back, but PETER received a brace of balls in his bosom. He recoiled a few steps back, and then sunk down incompassed by those deadly horrors of which in the morning he had a presentiment. Mr. KITTLE stood awhile aghast like a person just waked from a frightful dream; but on seeing the Indian advancing to tear the scalp from his dying brother, he suddenly recollected himself, and shot a bullet through his head: then grappling with the other, who was loading again, he wrestled his firelock from him, and felled him to the ground with the butt-end of it. This was no time for reflection or unavailing laments; the danger was eminent: so leaving the savages for dead, with a mournful silence, Mr. KITTLE hastened to throw the deer from off his horse, and laid his bleeding brother across him.

When our souls are gloomy, they seem to cast a shade over the objects that surround us, and make nature correspondent to our feelings: so Mr. KITTLE thought the night fell with a deeper gloom than usual. The soft notes of evening birds seemed to be the responses of savage yells. The echo of his tread, which he never before regarded, now rung dismally hollow in his ears. Even the rustling of the winds through the leaves seemed attended with a solemnity that chilled him with cold tremors. As he proceeded with his mournful charge, his feelings were alarmed for his dear MARIA; he dreaded the agitation and distress this adventure would throw her in: but it was unavoidable!

The sound of his horses feet no sooner invaded the ears of MARIA, than seizing a light she sprung with a joyful impatience to the door, and was met by her partner pale and bloody, who endeavoured to prevent too sudden a discovery of this calamity. But at the first glance she comprehended the whole affair, and retiring a few steps, with the most exquisite agony, in her countenance, "Oh Mr. KITTLE!" she cried, clasping her hands together, "it is all over—we are betrayed—your brother is killed!"—"Too true, oh, too fatally true!" replied he, falling on his knees beside her as she sunk down, "my angel! the very savages that solemnly engaged to protect us have deprived him of life; but I am yet alive, my MARIA, be comforted—I will instantly procure carriages, and before morning you and your innocents shall be beyond the reach of their malevolence."

By this time the family had crouded about them, and with grievous wailings were inquiring the particulars of this sad adventure. Mr. KITTLE having related every circumstance with brevity, ordered the corpse to be laid in a remote chamber, desiring at the same time a horse to be saddled for him. Then, more oppressed by his wife's griefs than his own, he led the disconsolate fair to her chamber, where being seated, she sighing demanded where he intended to go at that time of night. "Only," said he, "to the village of *Schochticook* to hire a couple of waggons; I shall return in an hour I hope, with a proper guard to secure our retreat from this hostile place." MARIA was silent; at length she burst into a flood of tears, which his endearments only augmented. Then expostulating with him, "Is it not enough," cried she, "that you have escaped one danger, but must you be so very eager to encounter others? besides, you are spent with sorrow and fatigue—let one of your brothers perform this silent expedition."—"It is impossible," replied the tender husband; "how can I dare to propose a danger to them from which I would shrink myself? Their lives are equally precious with mine: but God may disappoint our fears, my love!" He would have continued, but his spouse, rising from her seat, interrupted him—"At least, my dear, before you leave us give your lovely babes a farewell embrace, that if fate should— should separate us, *that* yet shall sweeten our hours of absence." Here she found herself clasped in her comfort's arms, who exclaimed, "My MARIA! I love you passionately, and if the least shadow of danger did appear to attend this night's travel, for your sake, for my blessed children's sake I would decline it: but I have left the Indians lifeless, who no doubt attacked us from some private pique; nor will they be discovered until morning."—"Well then," MARIA answered, "I no longer oppose you; forgive my fears." Meanwhile, as she stept to the cradle for her suckling, the fair ANNA, who was listening at the door anxious to hear her parents' sentiments on this occasion, quitted her station and flew to them swift as light; dropping on her knees before her father, and looking up in his face with the most attractive graces and the persuasive eloquence of simplicity. Her neck and features were elegantly turned, her complexion fairer than the tuberose, and contrasted by the most shining ringlets of dark hair. Her eyes, whose brilliancy was softened through the medium of tears, for a while dwelt tenderly on his countenance. At length, with a voice scarce audible, she sighed out, "Oh papa! do not leave us; if any accident should happen to you, mamma will die of grief, and what will become of poor ANNA and BILLY? who will care for me? who will teach me when my papa, my mamma's papa is gone?"—"My sweet child," replied he, embracing her and holding her to his bosom, "there is no danger! I shall return in an hour, and before to-morrow you shall be safe on the plains of *Albany*, and my heart shall exult over the happiness of my family."

Mrs. KITTLE now approached with her playful infant in her arms; but its winning actions extorted nothing but groans from her pained bosom, which was more stormy than Ontario-Lake, when agitated by fierce winds. Mr. KITTLE perceiving this uncommon emotion, gently took the child from her, and repeatedly kissed it, while new smiles dimpled its lovely aspect. "Oh!" said he to himself, "this gloom that darkens MARIA's soul is supernatural!— it seems dreadfully portentous!—Shall I yet stay?" But here a servant informing him that his horse was ready, he blushed at his want of fortitude; and having conquered his irresolution, after the most affecting and solemn parting, he quitted his house never to review it more!

MARIA then walked sadly back again, and having assembled the family in a little hall, they closed and barred the doors. Mrs. COMELIA KITTLE, MARIA's sister-in-law, was far advanced in her pregnancy, which increased her husband's uneasiness for her; and they were debating in what manner to accommodate her at *Albany*, when the trampling of feet about the house, and a yell of complicated voices, announced the Indians arrival. Struck with horror and consternation, the little family crowded together in the center of the hall, while the servants at this alarm, being in a kitchen distant from the house, saved themselves by a precipitate flight. The little BILLY, frightened at such dreadful sounds, clung fast to his mother's throbbing breast, while ANNA, in a silent agony of amazement, clasped her trembling knees. The echo of their yells yet rung in long vibrations through the forest, when, with a thundering peal of strokes at the door, they demanded entrance. Distraction and despair sat upon every face. MARIA and her companions gazed wildly at each other, till, upon repeated menaces and efforts to break open the door, COMELIA's husband, giving all for lost, leisurely advanced to the door. COMELIA seeing this, uttered a great shriek, and cried out, "O God! what are you doing, my rash, rash, unfortunate husband! you will be sacrificed!" Then falling on her knees, she caught hold of his hand and sobbed out, "O pity me! Have mercy on yourself, on me, on my child!"—"Alas! my love," said he, half turning with a look of distraction, "what can we do? let us be resigned to the will of God." So saying he unbarred the door, and that instant received a fatal bullet in his bosom, and fell backward writhing in agonies of death; the rest recoiled at this horrible spectacle, and huddled in a corner, sending forth the most piercing cries: in the interim the savages, rushing in with great shouts, proceeded to mangle the corpse, and having made an incision round his head with a crooked knife, they tugged off his bloody scalp with barbarous triumph. While this was perpetrating, an Indian hideously painted, strode ferociously up to COMELIA, (who sunk away at the sight, and fainted on a chair) and cleft her white forehead deeply with his tomahawk. Her fine azure eyes just opened, and then suddenly closing for ever, she tumbled lifeless at his feet. His sanguinary soul was not yet satisfied with blood; he deformed her lovely body with deep gashes; and, tearing her unborn babe away, dashed it to pieces against the stone wall; with many additional circumstances of infernal cruelty.

During this horrid carnage, the dead were stripped, and dragged from the house, when one of the hellish band advanced to MARIA, who circling her babes with her white arms, was sending hopeless petitions to heaven, and bemoaning their cruelly lost situation: as he approached, expecting the fatal stroke, she endeavoured to guard her children, and with supplicating looks, implored for mercy. The savage attempted not to strike; but the astonished ANNA sheltered herself behind her mamma, while her blooming suckling quitting her breast, gazed with a pleasing wonder on the painted stranger.—MARIA soon recognized her old friend that presented her with the belt, through the loads of shells and feathers that disguised him. This was no time, however, to irritate him, by reminding him of his promise; yet guessing her thoughts, he anticipated her remonstrance. "MARIA," said he, "be not afraid, I have promised to protect you; you shall live and dance with us around the fire at *Canada*: but you have one small incumbrance, which, if not removed, will much impede your progress thither." So saying he seized her laughing babe by the wrists, and forcibly endeavoured to draw him from her arms. At this, terrified beyond conception, she exclaimed, "O God! leave me, leave my child! he shall not go, though a legion of devils should try to separate us!" Holding him still fast, while the Indian applied his strength to tear him away, gnashing his teeth at her opposition; "Help! God of Heaven!" screamed she, "help! have pity, have mercy on this infant! O God! O Christ! can you bear to see this? O mercy! mercy! mercy! let a little spark of compassion save this unoffending, this lovely angel!" By this time the breathless babe dropt its head on its bosom; the wrists were nigh pinched off, and feeling him just expiring, with a dreadful shriek she resigned him to the merciless hands of the savage, who instantly dashed his little forehead against the stones, and casting his bleeding body at some distance from the house, left him to make his exit in feeble and unheard groans.—Then indeed, in the unutterable anguish of her soul, she fell prostrate, and rending away her hair, she roared out of her sorrows with a voice louder than natural, and rendered awfully hollow by too great an exertion. "O barbarians!" she exclaimed, "surpassing devils in wickedness! so may a tenfold night of misery enwrap your black souls, as you have deprived the babe of my bosom, the comfort of my cares, my blessed cherub, of light and life—O hell! are not thy flames impatient to cleave the center and engulph these wretches in thy ever burning waves? Are there no thunders in Heaven—no avenging Angel—no God to take notice of such Heaven defying cruelties?" Then rushing to her dead infant with redoubled cries, and clapping her hands, she laid herself over his mangled body; again softened in tears and moans, she wiped the blood from his ghastly countenance, and prest him to her heaving bosom, alternately caressing him and her trembling ANNA, who, clinging to her with bitter wailings, and kissing her hands and face, entreated her to implore the savages for mercy. "Do, my angel mamma," she urged, "do beg them yet to pity—beg them yet to save you for my poor, poor papa's sake!—Alas! if we are all killed, his heart will break!—Oh! they can't be rocks and stones!—Don't cry mamma, they will spare us!"—Thus the little orator endeavoured to confide her afflicted mother; but their melancholy endearments were soon interrupted by the relentless savages, who having plundered the house of every valuable thing that was portable, returned to

MARIA, and rudely catching her arm, commanded her to follow them; but repulsing them with the boldness of despair, "Leave me, leave me," she said, "I cannot go—I never will quit my murdered child! Too cruel in your mercies, you have given me life only to prolong my miseries!"—Meanwhile the lovely ANNA, terrified at the hostile appearance of the enemy, left her mamma struggling to disengage herself from the Indians, and fled precipitately to the house. She had already concealed herself in a closet, when Mrs. KITTLE pursuing her, was intercepted by flames, the savages having fired the house. The wretched child soon discovered her deplorable situation, and almost suffocated by the smoke, with piercing cries called for help to her dear, dear mother.—Alas! what could the unhappy parent do? whole sheets of flames rolled between them, while in a phrenzy of grief she screamed out, "O my last treasure! my beloved ANNA! try to escape the devouring fire—come to me my sweet child—the Indians will not kill us—O my perishing babe! have pity on your mother—do not leave me quite destitute!" Then turning to the calm villains who attended her, she cried, "Why do you not attempt to rescue my sweet innocent? can your unfeeling hearts not bear to leave me one—a solitary single one?" Again calling to her ANNA, she received no answer which being a presumption of her death, the Indians obliged MARIA and her brother HENRY to quit the house, which they effected with some difficulty, the glowing beams falling around them and thick volumes of smoke obscuring their passage. The flames now struck a long splendor through the humid atmosphere, and blushed to open the tragical scene on the face of Heaven. They had scarce advanced two hundred yards with their reluctant captives, when the flaming structure tumbled to the earth with a dreadful crash. Our travellers by instinct turned their eyes to the mournful blaze; and MARIA, bursting afresh into grievous lamentations, cried, "There, there my brother, my children are wrapt in arching sheets of flames, that used to be circled in my arms! they are entombed in ruins that breathed their slumbers on my bosom! yet, oh! their spotless souls even now rise from this chaos of blood and fire, and are pleading our injured cause before our God, my brother!" He replied only in sighs and groans, he scarcely heard her; horror had froze up the avenues of his soul; and all amazed and all trembling, he followed his leaders like a person in a troublesome dream.

The distant flames now cast a fainter light, and the northern breeze bent the columns of smoke over the south horizon. Sad and benighted they wandered through almost impenetrable swamps, forded the broad stream of *Tomhanick* and the rapid river of *Hosack*; they pushed through deserted settlements, where the yelling of solitary dogs increased the solemnity of midnight, not halted till the stars, emitting a feebler lustre, presaged the approach of day. MARIA, overcome by sorrow and fatigue, immediately sunk helpless at the foot of a tree, while the savages (who were six in number) kindled a fire, and prepared their meal, (in a calabash) which consisted only of some parched maize pulverized and enriched with the fat of bears flesh. Observing MARIA had fallen asleep, they offered not to disturb her, but invited HENRY KITTLE to partake of their repast. He durst not refuse them; and having swallowed a few mouthfuls of their unpalatable food, and accepted of a pipe of tobacco, he desired leave to repose himself, which being readily granted, they soon followed his example, and sunk asleep, leaving two centinels to guard against surprise, which precaution they always make use of.

I am sorry, dear SUSAN, to quit MARIA in this interesting part of her history; but order requires that we should now return to her spouse, whom we left on his way through the wood.

The village of *Schochticook* is situated on a circular plain, surrounded by high hills, rising in form of an amphitheatre. Mr. KITTLE had just gained the verge, when, chancing to cast his eyes around, he perceived the whole southern hemisphere suddenly illuminated with a bright blaze; however, being accustomed to the forest's being often fired to clear it from the under-wood, he was not much surprised, but proceeded to descend the hill. On his arriving with the account of his brother's murder, the place was put in the highest commotion; the men fitting up their arms, and the women clamouring about them, highly importunate to be removed to *Albany*; but the night being very dark, this manoeuvre was deferred till morning; nor could Mr. KITTLE prevail on a single person to return with him during the darkness; he felt himself strangely agitated at this disappointment, and refusing to repose himself, with great impatience he watched the first orient beams of Phosphor,[8] which appearing, he set off for home with two waggons and a guard of three Indians. As he approached his late happy dwelling, his bosom dilated with the pleading hope of soon extricating his beloved family from danger; he chid the slowness of the carriages, and felt impatient to dissipate the apprehensions of MARIA, to kiss the pendant tear from her eye, and press his sportive innocents to his bosom. While these bright ideas played round his soul, he lifted up his eyes and through an opening in the woods beheld his farm: but what language can express his surprise and consternation at seeing his habituation so suddenly desolated! a loud exclamation of amaze burst from the whole company at so unexpected a view—the blood revolted from Mr. KITTLE's cheek—his heart throbbed under the big emotion, and all aghast, spurring on his horse, he entered the inclosure with full speed.—Stop here unhappy man! here the fibres of thy heart crack with excruciating misery—let the cruel view of mangled wretches, so nearly allied to thee, extort drops of blood from thy cleaving bosom!—It did—it did. Uttering a deep groan he fell insensible from his horse, while his attendants, hastening towards him, were shocked beyond conception at the dismal spectacle; and, starting back with averted eyes from the dead, were thunder struck, not having power to move or speak. After awhile two Indians (who being used to sanguinary scenes, recovered themselves first) took a blanket, and walking backward to the mangled COMELIA, threw it over her naked body; the others then timidly advanced, and Mr. KITTLE opening his eyes, groaned again bitterly; then raising himself on his knees, with a look of unutterable anguish, he called upon his dear MARIA. Alas! no voice but the solemn repetition of his own cries was articulated to him: then rising with an air of distraction, he stalked round the bloody fence, and examined the dead bodies; first uncovering the pale visage of COMELIA, he surveyed in silence her distorted features; but perceiving it was not MARIA, he gently laid the cloth over again, and turning furiously, caught up his ghastly infant, whose little body was black with contusions, and his skull horribly fractured. Almost fainting under his mournful load, and staggering at the dreadful discovery, he deposited it again on the bloody earth, and clapping his hands together repeatedly with violence, "O hell! hell!" he cried, "you cannot inflict torments so exquisite as those I now suffer! how am I crushed to the center! how deeply am I degraded below worms of the sod! O my children! my children! where are you now? O my wife! my MARIA! the beloved of my bosom, are you too fallen a sacrifice? Why do I survive these miseries, my God? how can mortality support them? Burst—burst my shrinking heart, and punish a wretch for not having died in the defence of such lovely and innocent beings! Oh why was I absent in this fatal hour? why did not their groans vibrate on my soul that I might have flown to their aid?" Thus wildly lamenting and wandering among the smoking ruins, he picked up some of the calcined bones of his once beautiful ANNA. At this sight despair shook his soul afresh, new agonies convulsed his features, and dropping the sad evidence of his miseries, he extended his arms to Heaven, and roared out, "Revenge! great God! revenge if thou art just and kind as represented! Oh! that I had the power of an archangel to thunder eternal horrors on the guilty wretches who have blasted the bud of my happiness, who have darkened the brightest eyes that ever opened on the light!"

The men here interfering, to console him, observed the bones were probably those of his brother PETER; but on finding this skeleton entire, Mr. KITTLE insisted that it must have been MARIA and ANNA, who, having hid themselves, had doubtless perished in the flames. Again, in the furious extravagance of passion, he tore the hair from his head, and casting himself prostrate on the ashes, he gathered the crumbling bones to his bosom, while the big drops of anguish issued at every pore, till life, unable longer to sustain the mental conflict, suspended her powers, and once more deprived him of sensation. His companions having laid him on a waggon, now conferred together in what manner to proceed, and apprehending an attack from the savages, they unanimously concluded to lay the dead bodies on the remaining carriage, and make the best of their way to *Schochticook*, which they accordingly performed with great silence and expedition.

You may judge, my dear, what a panic the appearance of this mournful cavalcade struck over the inhabitants of this defenceless village. Mr. KITTLE was gently laid on a bed, and being let blood, his respiration became less obstructed, though he continued senseless till his unfortunate family were interred. Six weeks elapsed before he recovered any degree of strength; but even then he appeared pale and emaciated, like a second LAZARUS,[9] his disposition was entirely changed, his looks were fierce, his attitudes wild and extravagant, and his conversation, which formerly was sensible, commanding attention by a musical voice, now was incoherent, and his cadence deep and hollow, rather inspiring terror than any pleading sensation. Thirsting for revenge, and perceiving that solitude only tended to corrode his moments with the blackest melancholy, he soon after entered the British service in the capacity of gentleman volunteer, and signalized himself by his prudence and intrepidity, attracting the particular notice of his officers, who being affected with his misfortunes, proffered their services to him with so much friendship and candour, as obliged him to accept of them, and yet lightened the obligation.

But doubtless, my dear, your generous sensibility is alarmed at my silence about Mrs. KITTLE; I think we left her reposing under a tree: she was the first that awaked as the sun began to exhale the crystal globules of morning, when half rising, and reclining on her elbow, she surveyed the lovely landscape around her with a deep sigh; they were on an eminence that commanded an unlimited prospect of the country every way. The birds were cheerful; the deer bounded fearless over the hills; the meadow blushed with the enamel of FLORA[10] but grief had saddened every object in her sight; the whole creation seemed a dark blank to the fair mourner. Again recollection unlocked the sluices of her eyes, and her soft complaints disturbed her savage companions, who rising and kindling up the dying embers, began to prepare their victuals, which they invited her to partake of. This she declined with visible detestation; and turning to her brother, with the dignity of conscious merit in distress, "No," said she, "I never will receive a morsel from those bloody hands yet dropping with recent murder!—let me perish—let the iron hand of famine first pinch out my vitals and send me after my children!" Notwithstanding this, HENRY added his solicitations that she should accept some refreshment, reminding her of the consequence of her fatal resolution, which could be deemed no otherwise than suicide. Finding this had no effect, he tried to touch her feelings on a softer key—"Remember, MARIA," said he, "you have a tender husband yet living; would you wish to deprive him of every earthly consolation? Would you add affliction to affliction, and after he has performed the sorrowful obsequies of his children, to crush all his remaining hope by the news of your voluntary death? No, live my sister! be assured he will soon get us exchanged, when soft sympathies shall wash away your sorrows; and after a few years, who knows but the smiles of a new lovely progeny may again dawn a paradise of happiness on you." MARIA was affected, and half raising her eyes from the earth, she replied, "O my brother! how consoling do your words sink on my heart! though my reason tells me your arguments are improbably and fallacious, yet it soothes the tempest of my soul—I will try to live—perhaps I may again behold my dear, dear, dear husband!" Here a flood of tears interrupted her.

As this conversation was held in English, the savages were inquisitive to know the subject of it, at the same time enjoining them both never to utter a syllable in their presence expect in their own uncouth dialect, which as they perfectly understood, they could not exclude themselves from. HENRY then informed them that his sister, objecting to their method of preparing food, had desired him to prevail with them to indulge her in dressing her meals herself. This they readily granted, and farther to ingratiate themselves in the prisoners' favour, they dispatched a young Indian to hunt for partridges or quails in the groves adjoining them: He instantly returned with a brood of wood-pigeons, scarcely fledged, which he presented to HENRY, who cleaned and broiled them on sticks, with an officious solicitude to please his sister, which she observed with a look of gratitude, and taking a pigeon from the stick, began to eat more from complaisance than from inclination. HENRY was delighted at her ready acquiescence, and their repast being ended, they proceeded on their tiresome journey with less repining than the preceding night. MARIA was exempted from carrying a burden, yet she found the fatigue almost intolerable. They continually passed through a scene of conflagration, the savages firing every cottage in their way, whose mournful blaze catching the dry fields of grain, would scorch off hundreds of acres in a few moments, and form a burning path for their de-stroyers. As the sun advanced to his zenith, its rays beat fiercely on our travellers, augmented by the crackling flames around them; when meeting with a cool stream of water, MARIA was com-manded to sit down (being over-heated) while the rest approached the rivulet: the Indian that guarded MARIA was stopping down to drink, when a loud rustling among the leaves and trampling of bushes attracted his attention; he listened awhile seemingly much alarmed, then starting up suddenly, he flew to MARIA, and caught hold of her hair, aiming his hatchet at her head: the consequence was obvious, and her fate seemed inevitable; yet, with a stoical composure, she folded her arms across, and waited the fatal stroke with perfect resignation; but while the weapon was yet sus-pended over her, chancing to look around, he perceived the noise to proceed from a large deer, whose antlers were entangled in the branches of a thicket. Though an uncivilized inhabitant of the for-est, he blushed at his precipitancy, and returning the instrument of death to his girdle, after some hesitation made this apology: "MARIA, this sudden discovery is well for you; I thought we had been pursued, and we never suffer our prisoners to be re-taken; however, I was imprudent to attempt your life before there was a probability of your being rescued:" then desiring her to rise and drink, he quickly shot the deer, his associates helping him to skin it. Instead of quenching her thirst she sat down pensive on the flowing margin, casting her eyes carelessly on the stream: she knew not whether to esteem her late deliverance from death a happy providence or a protraction of misery. Observing the spot-ted trout, and other fish, to dart sportively across the water, she could not help exclaiming, "Happy! happy animals! you have not the fatal gift of reason to embitter your pleasures; you cannot an-ticipate your difficulties by apprehension, or prolong them by rec-ollection; incapable of offending your Creator, the blessings of your existence are secured to you: Alas! I envy the meanest among ye!" A gush of tears concluded her soliloquy; and being called to attend the company, she arose, and they began their journey for the afternoon. HENRY desiring to have a piece of venison (having left it behind, seldom incommoding themselves with more than the hide and tallow) they returned and obliged him with a haunch, which was very fat: at the next interval of travel he dressed it for himself and MARIA. In the evening they crossed the river somewhat below *Fort-Edward*, in a canoe left hid under some bushes for that purpose. They observed the most profound silence until they entered the woods again; but it was very late before they halted, which they did in a deep hollow, surrounded by pines whose tops seemed to be lost in the clouds. It was necessary here to light a fire, for the wolves howled most dreadfully, and the whole forest rung with the cries of wild beasts of various sorts. The confines of hell could not have given MARIA more dismal ideas than her present situation: the horrid gloom of the place, the scowling looks of her murderous companions, the shrill shrieks of owls, the loud cries of the wolf, and mournful screams of panthers, which were redoubled by distant echoes as the terrible sounds seemed dying away, shook her frame with cold tremors—she sunk under the oppression of terror, and almost fainted in HENRY's arms; however, on perceiving the beasts durst not approach the light, but began to retire, she became a little more assured, and helped HENRY to erect a booth of pine branches, making a bed of the same materials in it while he prepared their supper: having eaten, and kindled a large fire in the front of her arbour, she laid down and soon fell in a deep sleep. She felt herself refreshed by this unexpected repose, and the next morning, with some alacrity, continued her journey, hoping at last to arrive at some Christian settlement. Arriving at *Lake-Champlain*, they raised a wigwam on the bank, expecting the coming of Indians from the opposite shore to carry them over.

Here our unfortunate captives were stript of their habits, already rent to pieces by briers, and attired each with remnants of old blankets. In this new dress Mrs. KITTLE ventured to expostulate with the savages, but it was talking to the stormy ocean; her complaints served only to divert them; so retiring amoung the bushes, she adjusted her coarse dress somewhat decently, and then seating herself silently under a spreading tree, indulged herself in the luxury of sorrow. HENRY, sensible that they expected more fortitude from him, and that if he sunk under his adverse fortune he should be worse treated, affected to be cheerful; he assisted them in catching salmon, with which the lake abounds; an incred-

ible quantity of wild fowl frequenting the lake also, he laid snares
for those on the lesser sort, (not being allowed fire-arms), and succeeded so well that his dexterity was highly commended, and
night coming on, they regaled themselves on the fruits of their industry. The night was exceedingly dark, but calm; a thick mist
hovered over the woods, and the small ridgy waves softly rolled to
the shore, when suddenly a large meteor, or fire exhalation,
passed by them with surprising velocity, casting on every side
flowers of brilliant sparkles. At sight of this phaenomenon the Indians put their heads between their knees, crying out in a lamenta-
ble voice, "Do not! do not! do not!" continuing in the same
attitude until the vapour disappeared. HENRY, with some surprise,
demanded the reason of this exclamation, to which they replied,
"What he had seen was a fiery dragon on his passage to his den,
who was of so malevolent a temper, that he never failed, on his arrival there, to inflict some peculiar calamity on mankind." In
about five minutes after the earth was violently agitated, the waves
of the lake rumbled about in a strange manner, seeming to emit
flashes of fire, all the while attended with most tremendous roar-
ings, intermixed with loud noises, not unlike the explosion of
heavy cannon. Soon as the Indians perceived it was an earth-
quake, they cried out, "Now he comes home!" and casting themselves in their former posture, filled the air with dismal howlings.
This was a terrible scene to MARIA, who had never been witness
to so dreadful a convulsion of Nature before; she started up and
fled from her savage companions towards an eminence at some
distance, where dropping on her knees, she emphatically implored
the protection of Heaven: however, she was followed by an Indian
and HENRY; the latter, highly affected with her distresses taking
hold of her trembling hand, "But why, my sister!," said he, "have
you fled from us? is the gloom of a forest more cheering than the
sympathising looks of a friend?" "No, my brother!" replied
MARIA; "but the thought was suggested to me, that the supreme
God perhaps was preparing to avenge himself of these murderers
by some awful and uncommon judgment, and I fled from them as
LOT did from *Sodom*,[11] lest I might be involved in the punishment
of their guilt." They conversed in English, which displeasing the
Indian, he ordered them to return to the wigwam, threatening to

bind MARIA fast if she offered to elope again. The shock being over, silence again spread through the realms of darkness, when a high wind rose from the north and chilled our half-naked travellers with excessive cold. The savages (whose callous skins were proof against the inclement weather) not caring to continue their fires, lest they should be discovered and surprised by some English party, they passed here a very uncomfortable night; but the wind subsiding, and the sky growing clear, the sun rose peculiarly warm and pleasant, streaming ten thousand rays of gold across the lake. MARIA had scarcely performed her orations, when the savages, forming a circle round her and HENRY, began to dance in a most extravagant manner, and with antic gestures that at another time would have afforded mirth to our travellers. Having continued their exercise some time, they incontinently drew out boxes of paint, and began to ornament their captives with a variety of colours; one having crossed their faces with a stroke of vermillion, another would intersect it with a line of black, and so on until the whole company had given a specimen of their skill or fancy.

Soon after two canoes arrived, in which they passed over the lake, which was uncommonly serene and pleasant. They proceeded not far on their way before they were obliged to halt for two days, on account of MARIA's inability to travel, her feet being greatly swoln and lacerated by the flinty path. At length, by easy stages, they came in view of an Indian settlement, when MARIA's long unbent features relaxed into a half smile, and turning to HENRY, "Here, my brother!" said she, "I shall find some of my own sex, to whom simple Nature, no doubt, has taught humanity; this is the first precept she inculcates in the female mind, and this they generally retain through life, in spite of every evil propensity." As she uttered this elogium in favour of the fair, the tawny villagers, perceiving their approach, rushed promiscuously from their huts with an execrable din, and fell upon the weary captives with clubs and a shower of stones, accompanying their strokes with the most virulent language; among the rest an old deformed squaw, with the rage of a Tisiphone,[12] flew to MARIA, aiming a pine-knot at her head, and would certainly have given the wretched mourner her quietus had she not been opposed by the savage that guarded Mrs. KITTLE; he at first mildly expostulated with his passionate country woman; but finding the old hag frantic, and insatiable of blood, he twisted the pine-knot from her hand and whirled it away to some distance, then seizing her arm roughly and tripping up her heels, he laid her prostrate, leaving her to howl and yell at leisure, which she performed without a prompter.—MARIA was all in a tremor, and hastily followed her deliverer, not caring to risk another encounter with the exasperated virago. By this time the range and tumult of the savages subsiding, the new-comers were admitted into a large wigwam, in the center of which blazed a fire. After they were seated, several young Indians entered with baskets of green maize in the ear, which, having roasted before the fire, they distributed among the company.

Mrs. KITTLE and her brother complaining of the bruises they met with at their reception, an old Indian seemed to attend with great concern; then leaving the place, in a little time returned with a bundle of aromatic herbs under his arm, the juice of which he expressed by rubbing them between two stones with flat surfaces; this he gave them to drink, applying the leaves externally. They instantly found relief from the medical quality of this extraordinary plant, and composing themselves to sleep, expected a good night's repose; but they were mistaken, for their entertainers growing intoxicated with spirituous liquors, which operating differently, it produced a most complicated noise of yelling, talking, singing, and quarrelling: this was a charm more powerful than the wand of Hermes[13] to drive away sleep: but grown familiar with the sorrow and disappointment, MARIA regarded this as a trifle, and when HENRY expressed his concern for her, smiling, she replied, "We must arm ourselves with patience, my brother! we can combat with fate in no other manner."

It were endless to recapitulate minutely every distress that attended the prisoners in their tedious journey; let it suffice, that having passed through uncommon misery, and imminent danger, they arrived at *Montreal*.—Here the savages were joined by several scalping parties of their tribe, and having previously fresh painted themselves, appeared in hideous pomp, and performed a kind of triumphal entry. The throng of people that came out to meet them, threw MARIA in the most painful sensations of embarrassment; but as the clamours and insults of the populace increased, a freezing torpor succeeded, and bedewed her limbs with a cold sweat—strange chimeras danced before her sight—the actings of her soul were suspended—she seemed to move mechanically, nor recollected herself till she found she was seated in the Governor's hall, surrounded by an impertinent, inquisitive circle of people, who were inquiring into the cause of her disorder, without attempting anything towards her relief. Discovering her situation, she blushingly withdrew to a dark corner from the public gaze, and could not help sighing to herself, "Alas! but a very few days ago I was hailed as the happiest of women—my fond husband anticipated all my desires—my children smiled round me with filial delight—my very servants paid me the homage due to an angel!—O my God! what a sudden, what a deplorable transition! I am fallen below contempt!" As she thus moralized on her situation, an English woman (whom humanity more than curiosity had drawn to the place) approached MARIA, and observing her tears and deep dejection, took hold of her hand, and endeavoured to smile; but the soft impulses of nature were too strong for the efforts of the dissimulation—her features instantly saddened again, and she burst into tears, exclaiming, (with a hesitating voice,) "Poor, forlorn creature! where are thy friends! perhaps the dying moments of thy fond parent, or husband, have been cruelly embittered with the sight of thy captivity! perhaps now thy helpless orphan is mourning for the breast which gave him nourishment! or thy plaintive little ones are wondering at the long absence of their miserable mother!"— "Oh! no more! no more!" interrupted MARIA; "your pity is severer than savage cruelty—I could stand the shock of fortune with some degree of firmness, but your sympathy opens afresh the wounds of my soul! my losses are beyond your conjecture—I have no parent, no sportive children, and, I believe, no husband, to mourn and wish for me!" These words were succeeded by an affecting silence on both sides: meanwhile the Indians testified their impatience to be admitted to the Governor by frequent shouts; at length his Excellency appeared, and having held a long conference with the savages, they retired with his Secretary, and our prisoners saw them no more.

After their exit the Governor turning round to MARIA and HENRY, demanded who they were? Mrs. KITTLE's perplexity prevented her reply; but HENRY in a most respectful manner, gave him a succinct account of their misfortunes. The Governor perceiving him sensible and communicative, interrogated him farther, but he modestly declined giving away political intelligence. Observing that MARIA suffered greatly in this interview, he soon concluded it, after having presented several pieces of calicoes and stuffs to them, desiring they would accept what they had occasion for. Mrs. KITTLE immediately singled out a piece of black calimanco with tears of gratitude to her benefactor; who, smiling, observed she might chuse a gayer colour, as he hoped her distresses were now over. MARIA shook her head in a token of dissent, but could make no reply. He then dismissed them, with a small guard, who was directed to provide them with decent lodgings.

HENRY was accommodated at a baker's, while his sister, to her no small satisfaction, found herself placed at the English woman's who, on her arrival, had expressed so much good nature. She had scarcely entered, when Mrs. D——, presenting her with a cordial, led her to a couch, insisting on her reposing there a little, "For," says she, "your waste of spirits requires it."

This tenderness, which MARIA had long been a stranger to, relaxed every fibre of her heart; she again melted into tears; but it was a gush of grateful acknowledgement, that called a modest blush of pleasure and perplexity on Mrs. D——'s cheek. Being left alone, she soon fell in a profound sleep; and her friend having prepared a comfortable repast, in less than an hour awakened her, with an invitation to dinner— "And how do you find yourself, my sister?" said she instinctively, seizing MARIA's hand and compressing it between hers; "may we hope that you will assist us in conquering your dejection?"—MARIA smiled benignly through a crystal atmosphere of tears, and kissing the hand of her friend, arose. Having dined, and being now equipped in decent apparel, MARIA became the admiration and esteem of the whole family. The tempest of her soul subsided in a solemn calm; and though she did not regain her vivacity, she became agreeably conversable.

In a few days, however, she felt the symptoms of an approaching fever. She was alarmed at this, and intimating to Mrs. D——

her fears of becoming troublesome, "Do not be concerned," returned that kind creature, "my God did not plant humanity in my breath to remain there an inactive principle." MARIA felt her oppression relieved by this generous sentiment; and indeed found her friendship did not consist in profession, as she incessantly tended her during her illness with inexpressible delicacy and solicitude. When she was again on the recovery, Mrs. D—— one day ordered a small trunk covered with Morocco leather to be brought before her, and opening it, produced several sets of fine linen, with some elegant stuffs and other necessaries.— "See," said she, "what the benevolence of *Montreal* has done for you. The ladies that beg your acceptance of these things, intend likewise to enhance the favour, by waiting on you this afternoon."—"Ah!" interrupted MARIA, "I want them not; this one plain habit is enough to answer the purpose of dress for me. Shut the chest, my dear Mrs. D——, and keep them as a small compensation for the immense trouble I have been to you."—"If this is your real sentiment," replied her friend, (shutting the chest, and presenting her the key,) "return your gifts to the donors; and since you will reward me for my little offices of friendship, only love me, and believe me disinterested and I shall be overpaid."—"I see I have wronged your generosity," answered MARIA. "Pardon me, my sister, I will offend no more—I did not think you mercenary—but—but—I meant only to disengage my heart of a little of its burden."—As this tender contest was painful to both parties, Mrs. D—— rising abruptly, pretended some business, promising to return again directly.

In the afternoon MARIA received her visitants in a neat little parlour. She was dressed in a plain suit of mourning, and wore a small muslin cap, from which her hair fell in artless curls on her fine neck: her face was pale, though not emaciated, and her eyes streamed a soft languor over her countenance, more bewitching than the sprightliest glances of vivacity. As they entered she arose, and advancing, modestly received their civilities, while Mrs. D—— handed them to chairs: but hearing a well-known voice, she hastily lifted up her eyes, and screamed out in an accent of surprise, "Good Heaven! may I credit my senses? My dear Mrs. BRATT, my kind neighbour, is it really you that I see?" Here she found herself clasped in her friend's arms, who after a long subsiding sigh, broke into tears. The tumult of passion at length abating—"Could I have guessed, my MARIA," said she, "that you was here, my visit should not have been deferred a moment after your arrival; but I have mourned a sister in affliction, (permit me to present her to you,) and while our hearts were wrung with each other's distress, alas! we inquired after no foreign calamity." Being all seated, "I dare not," resumed MARIA, "ask after your family; I am afraid you only have escaped to tell me of them."—"Not so, my sister," cried Mrs. BRATT; "but if you can bear the recollection of your misfortunes, do oblige me with the recital." The ladies joined in their intreaty, and Mrs. KITTLE complied in a graceful manner.

After some time spent in tears, and pleasing melancholy, tea was brought in; and towards sun-set Mrs. D—— invited the company to walk in the garden, which being very small, consisted only of a parterre, at the farther end of which stood an arbour covered with a grape-vine. Here being seated, after some chat on indifferent subjects, MARIA desired Mrs. BRATT, (if agreeable to the company) to acquaint her with the circumstances of her capture. They all bowed approbation; and after some hesitation Mrs. BRATT began:—

"My heart, ladies, shall ever retain a sense of the happiness I enjoyed in the society of Mrs. KITTLE and several other amiable persons in the vicinage of *Schochticook*, where I resided. She in particular cheered my lonely hours of widowhood, and omitted nothing that she thought might conduce to my serenity. I had two sons; she recommended the education of them to my leisure hours. I accepted of her advice, and found a suspension of my sorrows in the execution of my duty. They soon improved beyond my capacity of teaching. RICHARD, my eldest, was passionately fond of books, which he studied with intense application. This naturally attached him to a sedentary life, and he became the constant instructive companion of my evening hours. My youngest son, CHARLES, was more volatile, yet not less agreeable; his person was charming, his wit sprightly, and his address elegant. They often importuned me, at the commencement of this war, to withdraw to *Albany*; but, as I apprehended no danger, (the British troops being stationed above us, quite from *Saratoga* to the Lake) I ridiculed their fears.

One evening, as my sons were come in from reaping, and I was busied in preparing them a dish of tea, we were surprised by a discharge of musketry near us. We all three ran to the door, and beheld a party of Indians not twenty paces from us. Struck with astonishment, we had no power to move; and the savages again firing that instant, my CHARLES dropped down dead beside me. Good God! what were my emotions! But language would fail, should I attempt to describe them. My surviving son then turning to me, with a countenance expressive of the deepest horror, urged me to fly. "Let us be gone this instant," said he; "a moment determines our fate. O my mother! you are already lost." But despair had swallowed up my fears; I fell shrieking on the body of my child, and rending away my hair, endeavoured to recall him to life with unavailing laments. RICHARD, in the meanwhile, had quitted me, and the moment after I beheld him mounted on horseback, and stretching away to the city. The Indians fired a volley at him, but missed, and I flatter myself that he arrived safe. And now, not all my prayers and tears could prevent the wretches from scalping my precious child. But when they rent me away from him, and dragged me from the house, my grief and rage burst forth like a hurricane. I execrated their whole race, and called for eternal vengeance to crush them to atoms. After awhile I grew ashamed of my impetuosity: the tears began again to flow silently on my cheek; and, as I walked through the forest between two Indians, my soul grew suddenly sick and groaned in me; a darkness, more substantial than Egyptian night, fell upon it, and my existence became an insupportable burden to me. I looked up to Heaven with a hopeless kind of awe, but I murmured no more at the dispensations of my God; and in this frame of sullen resignation I passed the rest of my journey, which being nearly familiar to Mrs. KITTLE's, I shall avoid the repetition of. And now permit me (said she, turning to the French ladies) to acknowledge your extreme goodness to me. I was a stranger, sick and naked, and you took me in. You indeed have proved the good Samaritan to me, pouring oil and wine in my wounds."—"Hush, hush! (cried Madame DE

ROCHE,) you estimate our services at too high a rate. I see you are no connoisseur in minds; there is a great deal of honest hospitality in the world, though you have met with so little."

"I now reject, (interrupted Mrs. BRATT,) all prejudices of education. From my infancy have I been taught that the French were a cruel perfidious enemy, but I have found them quite the reverse."

Madame DE R. willing to change the subject, accosted the other stranger,—"Dear Mrs. WILLIS, shall we not be interested likewise in your misfortunes?"—"Ah! do, (added Mademoiselle V.) my heart is now sweetly tuned to melancholy. I love to indulge these divine sensibilities, which your affecting histories are so capable of inspiring."—MARIA then took hold of Mrs. WILLIS's hand, and pressed her to oblige them.—Mrs. WILLIS bowed, she dropt a few tears; but assuming a composed look, she began:—

"I am the daughter of a poor clergyman, who being confined to his chamber by sickness, for several years, amused himself by educating me. At his death, finding myself friendless, and without money, I accepted the hand of a young man who had taken a leased farm in Pennsylvania. He was very agreeable, and extravagantly fond of me. We lived happily for many years in a kind of frugal affluence. When the savages began to commit outrages on the frontier settlements, our neighbours, intimidated at their rapid approaches, erected a small fort, surrounded by a high palisade. Into this the more timorous drove their cattle at night; and one evening, as we were at supper, my husband (being ordered on guard) insisted that I should accompany him with the children (for I had two lovely girls, one turned of thirteen years, and another of six months.) My SOPHIA assented to the proposal with joy. 'Mamma, (said she,) what a merry woman the Captain's wife is; she will divert us the whole evening, and she is very fond of your company: come, I will take our little CHARLOTTE on my arm, and papa will carry the lantern.' I acceded with a nod; and already the dear charmer had handed me my hat and gloves, when somebody thundered at the door. We were silent as death, and instantly after plainly could distinguish the voices of savages conferring together. Chilled as I was with fear, I flew to the cradle, and catching my infant, ran up into a loft. SOPHIA followed me all trembling, and panting for breath cast herself in my bosom. Hearing the Indians enter, I looked through a crevice in the floor, and saw them, with menacing looks, seat themselves round the table, and now and then address themselves to Mr. WILLIS, who, all pale and astonished, neither understood nor had power to answer them. I observed they took a great pleasure in terrifying him, by flourishing their knives, and gashing the table with their hatchets. Alas! this sight shot icicles to my soul; and, to increase my distress, my SOPHIA's little heart beat against my breast, with redoubled strokes at every word they uttered.

"Having finished their repast in a gluttinous manner, they laid a fire-brand in each corner of the chamber, and then departed, driving poor Mr. WILLIS before them. The smoke soon incommoded us; but we dreaded our barbarous enemy more than the fire. At length, however, the flames beginning to invade our retreat, trembling and apprehensive, we ventured down stairs; the whole house now glowed like a furnace; the flames rolled towards the stairs, which we hastily descended; but just as I sat my foot on the threshold of the door, a piece of timber, nearly consumed through, gave way, and fell on my left arm, which supported my infant, miserably fracturing the bone. I instantly caught up my fallen lamb, and hastened to overtake my SOPHIA. There was a large hollow tree contiguous to our house, with an aperture just large enough to admit so small a woman as I am. Here we had often laughingly proposed to hide our children, in case of a visit from the olive coloured natives. In this we took shelter; and being seated some time, my soul seemed to awake as it were from a vision of horror: I lifted up my eyes, and beheld the cottage that lately circumscribed all my worldly wealth and delight, melting away before the devouring fire. I dropt a tear as our apostate first parents did when thrust out from *Eden*.

"The world lay all before them, where to chuse their place of rest, and Providence their guide. Ah, Eve! thought I, hadst thou been like me, solitary, maimed and unprotected, thy situation had been deplorable indeed. Then pressing my babe to my heart, 'How quiet art thou, my angel,' (said I) 'sure—sure, Heaven has stilled thy little plaints in mercy to us.'— 'Ah!' (sobbed SOPHIA,) 'now I am comforted again that I hear my dear mamma's voice. I was afraid grief would have forever deprived me of that happiness.'

And here she kissed my babe and me with vehemence. When her transports were moderated, 'How cold my sister is,' (said she,) 'do wrap her up warmer, mamma; poor thing, she is not used to such uncomfortable lodging.'

"The pain of my arm now called for all my fortitude and attention; but I forbade to mention this afflicting circumstance to my daughter.

"The cheerful swallow now began to usher in the dawn with melody; we timidly prepared to quit our hiding place; and turning round to the light, I cast an anxious eye of love on my innocent, wondering that she slept so long. But oh! horror and misery! I beheld her a pale, stiff corpse in my arms; (suffer me to weep, ladies at the cruel recollection.) It seems the piece of wood that disabled me, had also crushed my CHARLOTTE's tender skull, and no wonder my hapless babe was quiet. I could no longer sustain my sorrowful burden, but falling prostrate, almost insensible at the dreadful discovery, uttered nothing but groans. SOPHIA's little heart was too susceptible for so moving a scene. Distracted between her concern for me, and her grief for the loss of her dear sister, she cast herself beside me, and with the softest voice of sorrow, bewailed the fate of her beloved CHARLOTTE—her sweet companion—her innocent, laughing play-fellow. At length we rose, and SOPHIA, clasping all that remained of my cherub in her arms, 'Ah!' (said she,) 'I did engage to carry you, my sister, but little did I expect in this distressing manner.' When we came in sight of the fort, though I endeavoured to spirit up my grieved child, yet I found my springs of action begin to move heavily, my heart fluttered, and I suddenly fainted away. SOPHIA, concluding I was dead, uttered so piercing a cry, that the centinel looking up, immediately called to those in the fort to assist us. When I recovered, I found myself in a bed encircled by my kind neighbours, who divided their expressions of love and condolement between me and my child. I remained in the fort after this; but, ladies, you may think, that bereft as I was of so kind a husband and endearing child, I soon found myself solitary and destitute. I wept incessantly; and hearing nothing from my dear WILLIS, I at length resolved to traverse the wilds of *Canada* in pursuit of him. When I communicated this to my friends, they all strongly opposed it; but finding me inflexible, they furnished me with some money and necessaries, and obtained a permission from the Governor to let me go under protection of a flag that was on the way. Hearing likewise that a cartel was drawn for an exchange of prisoners, I sat out, flushed with hope, and with indefatigable industry and painful solicitude, arrived at *Montreal*, worn to a skeleton (as you see ladies) with fatigue.

"I omitted not to inquire of every officer, the names of prisoners who had been brought in. At length I understood that Mr. WILLIS had perished in jail, on his first arrival, of a dysentery.— Here my expectations terminated in despair. I had no money to return with, and indeed but for my SOPHIA no inclination—the whole world seemed dark and cheerless to me as the fabled region of *Cimmeria*,[14] and I was nigh perishing for very want, when Mrs. BRATT, hearing of my distress, sought my acquaintance: she kindly participated my sorrows, and too—too generously shared her purse and bed with me. This, ladies, is the story of a broken-hearted woman; nor should I have intruded it in any other but the house of mourning."

Here she concluded, while the ladies severally embracing her, expressed their acknowledgements for the painful task she had complied with to oblige their curiosity.—"Would to Heaven!" said Madame DE R. "that the brutal nations were extinct, for never—never can the united humanity of *France* and *Britain* compensate for the horrid cruelties of their savage allies."

They were soon after summoned to an elegant collation; and having spent the best part of the night together, the guests retired to their respective houses.

During two years, in which the French ladies continued their bounty and friendship to Mrs. KITTLE, she never could gain the least intelligence of her husband. Her letters, after wandering through several provinces, would often return to her hands unopened. Despairing at length of ever seeing him, "Ah!" she would say to Mrs. D——, "my poor husband has undoubtedly perished, perhaps in his fruitless search after me, and I am left to be a long—long burden on your goodness, a very unprofitable dependant."

In her friend's absence she would descend into the kitchen, and submit to the most menial offices; nor could the servants prevent her; however, they apprised Mrs. D—— of it, who seized an opportunity of detecting her at her labour. Being baffled in her humble attempt by the gentle reproaches of her indulgent patroness, she sat down on the step of the door, and began to weep. "I believe, good Mrs. D——," said she, "were you a hard taskmaster, that exacted from these useless hands the most slavish business, I could acquit myself with cheerfulness: my heart is like ice, that brightens and grows firmer by tempests, but cannot stand the warm rays of a kind sun." Mrs. D—— was beginning to answer, when hearing a tumult in the street, they both hasted to the door, and MARIA, casting her eyes carelessly over the crowd, in an instant recognized the features of her long-lamented husband, who sprang towards her with an undescribable and involuntary rapture: but the tide of joy and surprise was too strong for the delicacy of her frame: she gave a faint exclamation, and stretching out her arms to receive him, dropped senseless at his feet. The succession of his ideas was too rapid to admit describing. He caught her up, and bearing her in the hall, laid his precious burden on a settee, kneeling beside her in a speechless agony of delight and concern. Meanwhile the spectators found themselves wonderfully affected—the tender contagion ran from bosom to bosom—they wept aloud; and the house of joy seemed to be the house of lamentation. At length MARIA opened her eyes and burst into a violent fit of tears—Mr. KITTLE, with answering emotions, silently accompanying her; then clasping his arms endearingly round her, "It is enough, my love," said he, "we have had our night of affliction, and surely this blessed meeting is a presage of a long day of future happiness; let me kiss off those tears, and shew by your smiles that I am indeed welcome." MARIA then bending fondly forward to his bosom, replied, sighing, "Alas! how can your beggared wife give you a proper reception? she cannot restore your prattling babes to your arms—she comes alone! Alas! her presence will only serve to remind you of the treasures—the filial delights you have lost!"—"God forbid," answered he, "that I should repine at the loss of my smaller comforts, when so capital a blessing as my beloved MARIA is so wonderfully restored to me." Here he was in civility obliged to rise and receive the compliments of Mrs.

BRATT, Mrs. WILLIS, and Madame DE R——, who hearing of his arrival, entered just then, half breathless with impatience and joy. The company increased; an elegant dinner was prepared: in short, the day was devoted to pleasure; and never was satisfaction more general—festivity glowed on every face, and complacency dimpled every cheek.

After tea MARIA withdrew in the garden, to give her beloved an account of what had befallen her during their separation. The eloquence of sorrow is irresistible. Mr. KITTLE wept, he groaned, while all impassioned (with long interruptions of grief in her voice) she stammered through her doleful history; and yet she felt a great satisfaction in pouring her complaints into a bosom whose feelings were in unison with her's—they wept—they smiled—they mourned, and rejoiced alternately, with an abrupt transition from one passion to another.

Mr. KITTLE, in return, informed her, that having thrown himself into the army, in hopes of ending a being that grew insupportable under the reflection of past happiness, he tempted death in every action wherein he was engaged, and being disappointed, gave himself up to the blackest melancholy. "This gloomy scene," he observed, "would soon have been closed by some act of desperation; but one evening, sitting pensive in his tent, and attentively running over the circumstances of his misfortunes, a thought darted on his mind that possibly his brother HENRY might be alive." This was the first time the idea of any one of his family's surviving the general murder had presented itself to him, and he caught at the flattering suggestion as a drowning wretch would at a plank. "Surely, surely," said he, "my brother lives—it is some divine emanation lights up the thought in my soul—it carries conviction with it: I will go after him—it shall be the comfort and employment of my life to find out this dear brother—this last and only treasure." Persuaded of the reality of his fancy, he communicated his design to a few of his military friends; but they only laughed at his extravagance, and strongly dissuaded him from so wild an undertaking. Being discouraged, he desisted; but shortly after, hearing that a company of prisoners (who were enfranchised) were returning to *Quebec*, he got permission to accompany them. After a very fatiguing journey he arrived at *Montreal*, and was immediately introduced to the General Officer, who patiently heard his story, and treated him with great clemency. Having obtained leave to remain a few days in town, he respectfully withdrew, and turning down a street he inquired of a man who was walking before him, where lodgings were to be let? The stranger turned about, civilly taking off his hat, when Mr. KITTLE, staring back, grew as pale as ashes—"Oh, my God!" cried he, panting, "oh! HENRY, is it you! is it indeed you! No, it cannot be." Here he was ready to fall; but HENRY, with little less agitation, supported him; and a tavern being at hand, he led him in. The master of the hotel brought in wine, and they drank off many glasses to congratulate so happy a meeting. When their transports were abated, HENRY ventured to tell him that his MARIA was living and well. This was a weight of joy too strong for his enfeebled powers—he flared wildly about. At length, recovering himself, "Take care, HENRY," said he, "this is too tender a point to trifle upon."—"My brother," replied HENRY, "be calm, let not your joy have a worse effect than your grief—they both came sudden, and it behoves a man and a christian to shew as much fortitude under the one as the other."—"Alas! I am prepared for some woeful deception," cried Mr. KITTLE; "but, HENRY, this suspense is cruel."—"By the eternal God!" rejoined his brother, "your MARIA, your wife, is in this town, and if you are composed enough, you shall immediately see her." Mr. KITTLE could not speak—he gave his hand to HENRY, and while (like the Apostles friends) he believed not for joy, he was conducted to her arms, and found his bliss wonderfully real.

MARGARETTA V.
BLEECKER FAUGERES
(1771–1801)

The daughter of Ann Eliza Bleecker (see page 1) and John James Bleecker, Margaretta Van Wyck Bleecker was born in Tomhanick, New York, on October 11, 1771. Her childhood was disrupted by the outbreak of the American Revolution, a controversial war in New York during its early years. The Bleeckers, supporters of the war, were sometimes ostracized by their neighbors for their support of the Revolution. Margaretta's mother died when she was only twelve, and Margaretta may have lived with relatives in New York City thereafter. She had far more radical political opinions than did her mother. On July 14, 1792, she married a French immigrant and physician, Peter Faugeres; they chose their wedding date to honor Bastille Day.[1] Strong supporters of the French Revolution, the Faugereses shared an ardent political belief in national and individual rights of independence. They had one daughter, Margaretta Mason Faugeres.

Though they seem to have had a companionable marriage, when Peter died of yellow fever in 1798 Margaretta Faugeres discovered that he had squandered all of her inherited fortune. To survive and to support her daughter, Faugeres became a teacher at an academy in New Brunswick, and later in Brooklyn. She died in Brooklyn on January 9, 1801.

Well-known in the New-York Magazine *as the poet "Ella," Faugeres actually wrote under several pseudonyms for that periodical, for the* American Museum, *and for Philadelphia's* The Weekly Magazine. *A poet, essayist, and dramatist, she published her work in periodicals throughout the 1790s. She published two works in book form:* The

Posthumous Works of Ann Eliza Bleecker . . . *(1793), which included selections of her own essays and poetry as well as a biographical narrative about her mother's life; and* Belasarius *(1793), a historical drama that captures her strong political views on human rights.*

THE HUDSON.

1793.

NILE's beauteous waves, and TIBER's swelling tide
  Have been recorded by the hand of Fame,
And various floods, which through Earth's channels glide,
  From some enraptur'd bard have gain'd a name;
E'en THAMES and WYE have been the Poet's theme,
  And to their charms hath many an harp been strung,
Whilst Oh! hoar GENIUS of old *Hudson*'s stream,
  Thy MIGHTY RIVER never hath been sung:
Say, shall a *Female* string her trembling lyre,
  And to thy praise devote th' advent'rous song?
Fir'd with the theme, her genius shall aspire,
  And the notes sweeten as they float along.
Where rough *Ontario*'s restless waters roar
  And hoarsely rave around the rocky shore;
Where their abode tremendous north-winds make,
  And reign the tyrants of the surging lake;
There, as the shell-crown'd genii of its caves
Toward proud LAWRENCE urg'd their noisy waves,
A *form majestic* from the flood arose;
A coral bandage sparkled o'er his brows,
A purple mantel o'er his limbs was spread,
And sportive breezes in his dark locks play'd:
Tow'rd the east shore his anxious eyes he cast,
And from his ruby lips these accents past:
'O favour'd land! indulgent Nature yield
'Her choicest sweets to deck thy boundless fields;
'Where in thy verdant glooms the fleet deer play,

'And the hale tenants of the desert stray,
'While the tall evergreens[2] that edge the dale
'In silent majesty nod to each gale:
'Thy riches shall no more remain unknown,
'Thy wide campaign do I pronounce my own;
'And while the strong arm'd genii of this lake
'Their tributary streams to LAWRENCE take,
'Back from its source *my current*[3] will I turn,
'And o'er thy meadows pour my copious urn.'
   He said, and waving high his dripping hand:
Bade his clear waters roll toward the land.
Glad they obey'd, and struggling to the shore,
Dash'd on its broken rocks with thund'ring roar:
The rocks in vain oppose their furious course;
From each repulse they rise with tenfold force;
And gath'ring all their angry pow'rs again,
Gush'd o'er the banks, and fled across the plain.
Soon as the waves had press'd the level mead,
Full many a pearly footed Naïad[4] fair,
With hasty steps, her limpid fountain led,
To swell the tide, and hail it welcome there:
Their busy hands collect a thousand flow'rs,
And scatter them along the grassy shores.
There, bending low, the *water-lillies* bloom,
And the blue *crocus* shed their moist perfume;
There the tall *velvet scarlet lark-spur* laves
Her pale green stem in the pellucid waves;
There nods the fragile *columbine*, so fair
And the mild dewy *wild-rose* scents the air;
While round the trunk of some majestic pine
The blushing *honeysuckle*'s branches twine:
There too *Pomona*'s[5] richest gifts are found,
Her golden *melons* press the fruitful ground;
The glossy crimson *plumbs* there swell their rinds,
And purple *grapes* dance to autumnal winds;
While all beneath the *mandrake*'s fragrant shade
The *strawberry*'s delicious sweets are laid.

Now by a thousand bubbling streams supplied,
More deep and still the peaceful waters glide,
And slowly wandering through the wide campaign,
Pass the big billows of the grand CHAMPLAIN:
There, when *Britannia* wag'd *unrighteous war*,
    A *fortress*[6] rear'd her ramparts o'er the tide;
Till brave MONTGOMERY[7] brought his hosts from far,
    And *conquering*, crush'd the scornful Briton's pride.
The openings of the forests green, disclose
    TICONDEROGA (long since known to fame:)
There fiercely rushing on th' unwary foes,
    The gallant ALLEN[8] gain'd himself a name.
Hence flows our stream, meand'ring near the shore
Of the smooth lake[9] renown'd for waters pure,
Which gently wanders o'er a *marble bed*,[10]
Cool'd by projecting rocks, eternal shade.
Amid those airy clifts (stupendous height!)
    The howling natives of the desert dwell:
There, fearful *Echo* all the live long night
    Repeats the *panther*'s petrifying yell.

FORT-EDWARD.

But wherefore river creep thy waves so slow?
    Or why so mournfully pursue their course,
As though thou here had'st known some scene of woe,
    Whose horrors fain would fright thee to thy source?
Alas! alas! the doleful cause is known;
    'Twas here M'CREA,[11] guided by savage bands,
    Fell, (oh sad suff'rer!) by their murderous hands,
And *this flood* heard her last expiring groan!
This flood, which should have borne the nuptial throng,
    Found her warm blood deep tincturing its streams!

These woods, which should have heard her bridal song,
   Wildly responded all her hopeless screams!
CRUEL in MERCY, BARBAROUS *Burgoyne!*
   Ah, see an *aged sire*, with silver hairs,
(*Whose goodness* trusted much, *too much to thine*,
   Bathing his *mangled daughter* with his tears!
Hear a distracted *lover*'s frightful voice!
   See, as he bends to kiss the clotted gore
Senseless he sinks! but Death hath clos'd *thine eyes*,[12]
   And Mem'ry weeps, but will *reproach no more*.
   In *Edward*'s fortress, here a grand retreat
The Britons plann'd, but ere it was compleat
New Albion[13] vet'rans, with undaunted force,
Stood like a barrier and oppos'd their course.
Here broader swells the tide, and strong oar
Is heard to dash the waves: the shady shore
Sounds with the peasant's strokes, and the *tall wood*
The hand of *Commerce* bears along the flood;
Unnumber'd herds of *cattle* graze the plain,
And in the valley waves the *yellow grain*;
The *green maize* rustles on the mountain's brow,
And the thick *orchard*'s blossoms blush below:
For the luxuriance of the cultur'd soil
Amply rewards the hard rustic's toil.

Now the fair *Hudson*'s widening waters tend
Where SARATOGA's ancient forests bend,
Where GATES,[14] the *warlike* GATES, Columbia's boast,
Vanquish'd the proud *Burgoyne*'s astonish'd host!
Victorious chief! while here thou glad'st our eyes,
For thee, from the full heart a pray'r must rise;
Of the poor *orphan* all his friends remov'd,
And the sad *widow* reft of all she lov'd:
These, *while thou liv'st*, shall bless the hero who
Rescued *Columbia* from a cruel foe,
A *parent* to the *orphan'd child* restor'd,

And blest the *widow* with her *much lov'd lord*,
Reveng'd the cause of many a soldier slain,
And fixt on British arms a lasting stain!
And when the hand of Death thine eyes shall close,
And chanting angels guard thy soft repose,
Then will they, grateful, o'er thy cold tomb mourn,
And, weeping, hang a garland on thine urn.

Through many a 'blooming wild,' and woodland green,
    The *Hudson*'s sleeping waters winding stray;
Now 'mongst the hills its silvery waves are seen,
    And now through arching willows steal away:
Then bursting on th' enamour'd sight once more,
    Gladden some happy peasant's rude retreat;
And passing *youthful* TROY's *commericial* shore,
    With the hoarse MOHAWK's roaring surges meet.
Oh, beauteous MOHAWK! 'wilder'd with thy charms,
    The chilliest heart sinks into rapt'rous glows;
While the stern warrior, *us'd to loud alarms*,
    Starts at the thunderings of thy dread COHOES.[15]
Now more majestic rolls the ample tide,
    Tall waving elms its clovery borders shade,
And many a stately dome, in ancient pride,
    And hoary grandeur, there exalts its head.
There trace the marks of *Culture*'s sunburnt hand,
    The honied *buck-wheat*'s[16] clustering blossoms view,
Dripping rich odours, mark the *beard grain* bland,
    The loaded *orchard*, and the *flax field blue*.
ALBANIA's[17] gothic spires now greet the eye;
    Time's hand hath wip'd their burnish'd tints away,
And the rich fanes which sparkled to the sky,
    'Reft of their splendours, mourn in cheerless grey.
There many an ancient structure tottering stands;
    Round the damp chambers mouldy vapours creep,
And feathery-footed *Silence* folds her hands,
    While the pale genii of the mansion sleep.
Yet thither *Trade*'s full freighted vessels come;
    Thither the shepherds mercantile resort:

There *Architecture late* hath rais'd her dome,
  And *Agriculture*'s products fill her port.
The grassy hill, the quivering poplar grove,
  The copse of hazle, and the tufted bank,
The long green valley, where the white stocks rove,
  The jutting rock, o'erhung with ivy dank;
The tall pines waving on the mountain's brow,
  Whose lofty spires catch day's last lingering beam;
  The bending willow weeping o'er the stream,
The brook's soft gurglings, and the garden's glow:
These meet the wandering trav'ller's ardent gaze;
From shore to shore enraptur'd Fancy strays;
Each parting scene his anxious eyes pursue,
Till HUDSON's city rises to his view:
There, on the borders of the river rise
The *azure mountains* tow'ring to the skies,
Whose cloudy bluffs, and spiral steeps sublime,
Brave the rude gusts, and mock the strokes of Time.
High on the healing *firr tree*'s topmost bough
  The solitary *heron* builds her nest;
  There in security her offspring rest,
Regardless of the storms that rave below.
Wakeful remembrance, on thine ember'd plain
  Will pause ESOPUS,[18] and indulge a tear;
  Will bid again the scenes of woe appear;
Will bid the mouldering mansion blaze again.
She calls to mind when Britain's lawless bands
  Wag'd impious war with consecrated fanes;
Streach'd against HEAV'N their sanguinary hands,
  While *fear*, nor *awe*, their barbarous will restrains.
O HUDSON! HUDSON! from thy frighted shore
  Thou saw'st the bursting flame mount to the sky;
Thou heard'st the burning buildings' fearful roar;
  Thou heard'st the mournful shrieks of Agony.
See, from his couch defenceless *Sickness* driv'n!
  See bending *Age*, exhausted, creep along!
Weeping, they turn their hopeless eyes to heav'n,
  And piteous wailings murmur from their tongue.

Here a distracted *widow* wrings her hands,
   While griefs too keen forbid her tears to flow:
There all aghast a wretched *parent* stands,
   Viewing his beggarded babes in *speechless woe!*
Why did thy hand, O *desolating War!*
   Thy bloody banners o'er our land unfurl?
Why did thy cruel *hirelings* come from far,
   Murder and fire o'er every plain to hurl?
So as they glutted their dark souls with death,
   Be their attendants shame, remorse and pain:
While each sack'd village on th' ensanguin'd heath
   Shall from its smoking ashes rise again.

Low sunk between the Alleganian hills,
   For many a league the sullen waters glide,
   And the deep murmur of the crouded tide,
With pleasing awe the wond'ring *voy'ger* fills.
On the green summit of yon lofty clift
   A peaceful runnel gurgles clear and slow,
Then down the craggy steep side dashing swift,
   Tremendous falls in the white surge below.
Here spreads a clovery lawn its verdure far,
   Around it mountains vast their forests rear.
And long ere Day hath left his burnish'd car
   The dews of Night have shed their odours there.
There hangs a louring rock across the deep;
   Hoarse roar the waves its broken base around;
Through its dark caverns noisy whirlwinds sweep,
   While *Horror* startles at the fearful sound.
The shivering *sails* that cut the fluttering breeze,
   Glide through these winding rocks with airy sweep:
Beneath the cooling glooms of waving trees,
   And sloping pastures speck'd with fleecy sheep.

WEST-POINT.

Dash ye broad waves, and proudly heave and swell;
　　Rouse aged *Neptune* from his amber cave,
　　And bid the nymphs the pebbly strand who lave,
Round this grand bulwark sound their coral shell:
For, nightly bending o'er these streams,
Base TREASON plotted murderous schemes;
Then stealing soft to ARNOLD's[19] bed,
Her visions vague around him shed;
And while dark vapours dim'd his eyes
She bade these forms illusive rise:
First ANDRE[20] came; his youthful air
　　Allur'd the falling chieftain's eyes;
But when the glittering bribes appear,
　　A thousand strange ideas rise:
He saw Britannia's marshall'd hosts,
Countless, advance toward his posts;
Honour he saw, and *Wealth*, and *Fame*,
With every good that wish can frame,
Attend their train; he long'd to stretch
Beyond his *virtuous brethren*'s reach;
His heart *polluted*, vainly sigh'd
To *bound* and *swell* in TITLED pride.
Now fair COLUMBIA's armies come—
His hand hath seal'd their mournful doom;
And in an unrelenting hour
He yields them up to Albion's power:
Then *Murder* bloats with horrid pride!
A thousand fall on every side!
And coward *Cruelty*'s base bands
Dip in warm gore their barb'rous hands;
Then the broad-sword displays its force,
　　Drench'd to the *very hilt* in blood!
While the *brave warrior*, and the *frantic horse*
　　Wallow together in the purple flood!

Then rose a NAME and lo! From far
  He hears the hum of chariot wheels;
   '*Divinity*' within him feels,
And thunders forth, THE SOVEREIGN LORD OF WAR.
His anxious eyes he strain'd for more;
  But fickle *Fancy* dropt the scene;
  TRUTH's radiant rays around him pour,
  And shew'd the wretch 'twas all a *dream!*

Fierce bursting from between the sturdy hills,
More high the wealthy river's bosom swells;
Their circles broader now the waves expand,
Howl to the winds, and lash the answering strand;
Then rolling slow, they kiss the flinty mound,
For valiant WAYNE's[21] victorious acts renown'd;
'Twas there *Bellona*[22] rear'd her standard high,
  And bellowing engines pour'd forth storms of fire;
  While smoky columns slow to heav'n aspire,
Obscure the sun, and hide the glowing sky:
Ranks rush'd on ranks, and the bright blade
Its path through many a bosom made,
While furious men regardless tread
Upon the dying, and the dead!
O what a piteous scene of woes!
The blood in bubbling currents flows;
The fiends of battle shriek aloud,
Destruction hurls his shafts abroad,
And all the rocky caverns round
With sullen groans of *Death* resound!
But valor swell'd in FLEURY's[23] breast;
He sigh'd to give his vet'rans rest;
And listless of the deadly aim
With which Britannia's volleys came,
He rush'd among the awe-struck croud,
and bore away their banner proud.[24]
  For *this brave deed*, hath raptur'd Fame

Twin'd many a chaplet round his brow;
     And long as lasts COLUMBIA's name
The fragrant blossoms fair shall blow;
And when the hand of *Death*, so cold,
Shall wrap him in the valley's mold,
A modest stone shall mark the place;
     And there Affection's hand shall 'grave,
     "Here FLEURY lies, the warrior brave!"
And all the simple line who trace,
Shall heave a sigh or drop a tear,
And bless the soldier mouldering there!
     Soon as the ridgy mountains leave the eye,
Tall mural rocks²⁵ shoot proud into the air;
     In shapes fantastic lift their turrets high,
Fit for the *shadowy forms* who revel there:
     The hardy PINES that on their steep sides grow,
(Whose *naked roots* from chink to chink extend;
Whose boughs aspiring, tow'rd the dense clouds tend,)
     Appear like *shrubs* to the strain'd eyes below.
The wandering *goat* adventures to the brink,
     And peeps across the fretted edge with care;
Then from the awful precipice she shrinks,
     As though relentless *Ruin* hover'd there.
Yet there, when Night hath bid the world be mute,
     The sleepless *sailor* often clambers high,
And from some shadowy nook his sonorous flute
     Sends mournful accents to the neighbouring sky:
And while the flood reflects the broad moon bright,
     Conceal'd the budding *laurel*'s sweets among,
     There the sad *lover* pours his pensive song,
Filling with mellow sounds the ear of Night.
     But now the advancing sight admires
     The rising fanes and glittering spires
     Of EBORACIA's stately tow'rs,
     Which catch the Morning's splendid beam,
     And shining o'er the frothy stream,
Gild with refracted light the long extended shores.

Alas! how late the rude foe revel'd there,
(Their engines bellow mournful o'er the main,
And every street gleams with the dismal glare,)
Murder, and *Want*, and *Sickness* in their train:
Beneath the burning torch of *War* consum'd,
Her walls in smoking ruins lay scatter'd round;
While horrid fires her HOLY DOMES illum'd,
Whose blazing spires fell thundering to the ground,
Gilding the gloomy bosom of old Night.
    Then from the deadly prison's walls arise,
    Of *Hunger* fierce, the agonizing cries,
Filling the listening soul with wild affright!
But now the "crimson toils" of War are o'er,
Her dreadful clamourings meet the ear no more;
The grassy pastures, lately dy'd with blood,
Now on their bosoms hold some dimpling flood;
And the raz'd buildings, whose high polish'd stones
Sunk disregarded 'mongst half mouldering bones,
From their own ashes, *phoenix like*, arise,
And grandly lift their turrets tow'rd the skies:
The busy bands of *Commerce* croud her ports;
    Full in her harbours swells the snowy sail,
The springing breeze, the dancing streamer courts,
    And the deep vessel bows before the gale;
While from fair *Nassau*'s isle,[26] or *Jersey*'s shore,
The lab'ring *peasant* turns his heavy oar;
His broad boat laden with inviting fruits,
Delicious wild fowl, with salubrious roots,
And tasteful pulse; or else he draws the car,
    Fill'd with the tenants of the briny *sea*,
Or sedgy *creek*, or wood-edg'd *river* fair,
    And hies him to this busy mart with glee:
Where from the early dawn, a hardy throng
Spread various works the loaded shores along;
Sound the harsh grating saw, or hammer loud,
Or blow the roaring furnace, sable brow'd
Or ply the heavy hulks, propt up in air,
From smoking cauldrons, with ebullient tar,

Or guide the groaning wheels, and straining steed,
To where the sons of *Trade* their wealth unlade.
   PRIDE OF COLUMBIA! EBORACIA fair!
What happy region will with *thee* compare
For Nature's bounties fam'd? Where swells the shore
With *soil* so *fertile*, and with AIR SO PURE?
Two mighty rivers[27] round thee roll their streams,
   From the green bosom of the vasty sea,
Wooing the winds so cool, with *Sol*'s fierce beams
   Would singe the verdure of the thirsty *lea*.
O may the braying *trumpet*'s shrill tongu'd roar
Be heard among thine echoing wilds no more,
Nor purple blood thy lilied vallies stain,
Nor sounds of death affright the restless main,
Nor panting *steeds* neigh to the *clarion*'s blast,
   Mocking the vengeful sword, and glittering spear;
   Nor wounded *warriors* 'midst the hurtle drear,
Trampled beneath their courses, sigh their last;
But may thy virtuous sons unrivall'd stand,
The boast of *Science* and their native land,
Led by the hand of Truth, may they attain
The height for which have thousands sigh'd in vain;
Nor may a wish *ambitious* ever rise,
Save this, to be more *virtuous* and more *wise*;
And by no despot's iron laws confin'd,
Enjoying the vast freedom of the mind;
But while they throng the domes of *Liberty*,
   May they her sacred precepts ne'er profane;
Nor while they boast themselves 'the virtuous *free*'
   One *slave* beneath the cruel yoke retain.
May their fair daughters Wisdom's laws obey,
   Each *thought ungentle* from their breasts repel;
And skill'd in pious lore, to all display
   'Tis not in *beauty* they *alone* excel.
And may the GREAT SUPREME, when showering down,
   In rich profusion, all the joys of Peace,
Thine offspring for his favourite people own,
   And hearts bestow the donor's hand to bless:

Then shall thy 'habitants indeed be blest;
   Regions far distant shall revere thy name,
And nations long of every good possest,
   Stile *thee* UNEQUALL'D in the Scroll of Fame.
And tough, O RIVER! whose majestic stream
   Hath rous'd a *feeble hand* to sweep the lyre,
     Thy charms some loftier poet shall inspire,
  And *Clio*'s[28] self shall patronize the theme:
To hail thee shall admiring realms agree,
   Sing to thy praise, and bless our happy lot;
    And DANUBE's roaring flood shall be forgot,
And NILE and TIBER, when they speak of THEE!

ON SEEING A PRINT,
EXHIBITING THE
RUINS OF THE BASTILLE.

1792.

At each return of the auspicious day
  Which laid this mighty fabric in the dust,
  Let joy inspire each patriotic breast
To bless and venerate its August ray;
Let *Gallia*'s[1] sons attune the harp of joy,
And teach the trump its boldest notes t' employ;
  Let clarions shrill the deed declare,
  And blow their son'rous notes afar;
Let music rise from ev'ry plain,
  Each vine-clad mount or daisied dell,
And let *AEolus*[2] float the strain
  Across old Ocean's ample swell.

Ah! see the *Bastille*'s iron walls thrown down,
  That bulwark strong of *Tyranny*;
See her proud turrets smoke along the ground,
  Crush'd by the giant arm of *Liberty!*
Her gloomy *tow'rs*—her *vaults* impure,
  Which once could boast eternal night;
Her *dungeons* deep—her *dens* obscure,
  Are urg'd unwilling to the light.

Oft in these dreary cells, the *captive*'s moan
  Broke the dead silence of the midnight watch

When *Memory*, pointing to the days long gone,
   To wasting sorrows woke the feeling wretch.

Here everlasting Darkness spread
   Her veil o'er scenes of misery,
Where *Sickness* heav'd an anguish'd head,
   And roll'd a hopeless eye.
Here drown'd in tears, pale *Agony*
Spread her clasp'd hands toward the sky,
While all convuls'd, *extreme Despair*
   Swallow'd the earth in speechless rage,
   Or phrenzied gnaw'd his *iron cage*,
Tore off his flesh, and rent his hair.
   Such were thy glories, O Bastille!
   Such the rich blessings of *despotic pow'r*,
Whose horrid *daemon* quaff'd his fill,
   Daily of bitter tears and human gore:
But now 'tis o'er—thy long, long reign is o'er,
Thy thunders fright the trembling hosts no more;
Thy shafts are spent—thy sons no more engage
   To add new triumphs to thy train,
   To bind new victims to thy chain;
   For thy most valiant sons are slain
By the fierce strokes of kindled patriot rage.
Roll'd in the dust, behold thine honours lie,
The sport—the scorn of each exploring eye.

Hail gallant Gauls![3] heroic people hail!
Who spurn the ills that Virtue's sons assail,
Whose hearts benevolent, with ardour bound
The hard-got blessing to diffuse around:
Oh! be your struggles blest, and may you see
Your labours rivall'd by posterity;
'Till the small *flame* (which first was seen to rise,
'Midst threat'ning blasts, beneath *Columbian*[4] skies,
Which, as it taught its splendours to expand,

Arose indignant from Oppression's hand,
And blaz'd effulgent o'er the mighty plain)
Luring your heroes o'er the stormy main,
'Till this small flame, fed by their nurturing hand,
Not only canopies your native land,
But far extending its prolific rays,
Envelopes neighbouring empires in the blaze.
And thou, FAYETTE![5] whom distant lands deplore,
As no *self-banish'd* from thy native shore;
Tho' *zeal mistaken*, may a shadow throw
Athwart the laurels which adorn thy brow;
Yet shall they bloom—for in thy generous breast
No soul like *Coriolanus*[6] is confess'd:
To *Gallia* still thy warmest wishes tend,
And tho' an *injured exile*, still a friend!
When grateful nations tell thine acts to *Fame*,
America shall urge her oldest claim,
Point to the *worthies* whom her sons revere,
And place FAYETTE with those she holds most dear.

JULY THE FOURTEENTH.

1793.

Hark! hark how the clamours of war
   Thro' *Gallia*'s wide regions resound;
Bellona has mounted her car,
   And scatters her terrors around:
Captivity bursts off her chains,
   Her shoutings are heard on the heath,
Her vet'rans are crouding the plains,
   Resolv'd upon *Freedom* or *Death*.

But see! from her battlements high,
   Plum'd *Vict'ry* undaunted alight;
Her standard she waves in the sky,
   And urges her sons to the fight.
Their swords all indignant they clash,
   They rush round the *Bastille*'s strong walls.
Ah! heard you that horrible crash?
   The *tow'r* of proud *Tyranny* falls!

The minions of despotism fly,
   Pursu'd by destruction and wrath,
Fear wings their sad flight, and their *cry*
   Disturbs the deep slumber of *Death*.
Haste, haste, *man's disgrace* disappear,
   Vile wretches, of nature the blot,
And wherever your hamlets you rear,
   May *shame* and *distress* be your lot.

But *Gallia*, all hail! may thy chiefs
   A temple to *Liberty* raise;
And there may their feuds and their griefs
   Be lost in its altar's bright blaze.
And when they remember *this day*,
   Bedeck'd with the *laurel* and *vine*,
May anguish and care flee away,
   And their voices in anthems combine.

And *then* may the warblings of songs
   Be heard from *Columbia*'s green vales,
While Echo the wild notes prolongs,
   And whispers them soft to the gales.
And oh! let the zephyrs so fleet,
   Bear the sweet swelling tones o'er the main,
And *there*, let them fondly repeat
   In the ear of each *Frenchman* the strain.

JUDITH SARGENT MURRAY
(1751–1820)

Born in Gloucester, Massachusetts, on May 1, 1751, Judith Sargent was the eldest child of Judith Saunders and Winthrop Sargent. Both of her parents came from families who had prospered in the New England maritime industry. Largely self-educated, Judith became one of the most public of women intellectuals in eighteenth-century America.

On October 3, 1769, she married John Stevens, who, like her father, was a Gloucester sea captain and merchant. Theirs was a childless and strained marriage; in 1786, to escape creditors, John fled to the West Indies, where he died on March 8. Judith's struggle to rectify her financial affairs as a widow left her with an indelible sense of the need for women's financial security. Her second marriage was, unlike her first, one of love and companionship. She married John Murray on October 6, 1788. She had first met him in 1774, when he came to America to introduce a new religion to the country—Universalism, which Judith and her family embraced. The Murrays had two children: George, who was stillborn in 1789, and Julia Maria, born on August 22, 1791. A talented and prolific writer for nearly twenty years, Murray died on July 6, 1820, in Mississippi, where she had gone to live with her daughter for the last two years of her life.

Judith Sargent Murray's interest in women's equality began as early as 1779 when she wrote her now famous essay "On the Equality of the Sexes"; the essay was not published until 1790, and the published version included a defense of Eve, who was the most common religious symbol of the belief that women must maintain a subordinate position. Mur-

ray was a prolific essayist, a poet and dramatist, and an extraordinary letter writer (nearly 2,500 of her letters are extant). She had published essays and poetry in U.S. periodicals as early as 1784, but in 1790 she began her most sustained literary endeavors, writing under the pen name of "Constantia" for the Massachusetts Magazine. She was the first American woman to write a column for a magazine, and, in fact, she wrote two columns: "The Repository" contained essays that allowed her to explore religious issues, but it was the second column, "The Gleaner," that gained her fame. "The Gleaner" essays demonstrated her satirical wit as well as her abilities for political and cultural critique. The one hundred essays in this column were published in book form as The Gleaner in 1798, including the four-essay commentary "Observations on Female Abilities." Using women's historical contributions to Western culture, Murray expounds on one of her favorite subjects: women's rights to—and abilities for—equal opportunities in intellectual and cultural pursuits.

OBSERVATIONS ON FEMALE ABILITIES[1]

Part I.

Amid the blaze of this auspicious day,
When science points the broad refulgent way,
Her iron sceptre prejudice resigns,
And sov'reign reason all resplendent shines.

1798.

The reader is requested to consider the four succeeding numbers as supplementary to an Essay, which made its appearance, some years since, in a periodical publication of a miscellaneous nature. The particular paper to which I advert, was entitled, *The Equality of the Sexes*,[2] and, however well I may think of that composition, as I do not conceive that the subject is exhausted, I have thought proper, treading in the same path, to set about collecting a few hints, which may serve as additional, illustrative, or ornamental.

And, first, by way of exordium, I take leave to congratulate my fair country-women, on the happy revolution which the few past years has made in their favour; that in these infant republics, where, within my remembrance, the use of the needle was the principal attainment which was thought *necessary* for a woman, the lovely proficient is now permitted to appropriate a moiety of her time to studies of a more elevated and elevating nature. Female academies are every where establishing, and right pleasant is the appellation to my ear.

Yes, in this younger world, "the Rights of Women"[3] begin to be understood; we seem, at length, determined to do justice to THE SEX; and, improving on the opinions of a Wollstonecraft, we are ready to contend for the *quantity*, as well as *quality*, of mind. The younger part of the female world have now an inestimable prize put into their hands; and it depends on the rising generation to re-fute a sentiment, which, still retaining its advocates, grounds its arguments on the incompatibility of the present enlarged plan of female education, with those necessary occupations, that must ever be considered as proper to the department and comprised in the duties of a judiciously instructed and elegant woman; and, if our daughters will combine their efforts, converts to the new regulations will every day multiply among us. To argue against facts, is indeed contending with both wind and tide; and, borne down by accumulating examples, conviction of the utility of the present plans will pervade the public mind, and not a dissenting voice will be heard.

I may be accused of enthusiasm; but such is my confidence in THE SEX, that I expect to see our young women forming a new era in female history. They will oppose themselves to every trivial and unworthy monopolizer of time; and it will be apparent, that the adorning of their persons is not with them a *primary* object. They will know how to appreciate personal advantages; and, considering them as bestowed by Nature, or Nature's God, they will hold them in due estimation: Yet, conscious that they confer no *instrinsic* excellence on the *temporary* possessor, their admeasurement of *real virtue* will be entirely divested of all those *prepossessing ideas*, which originate in a beautiful exterior. The noble expansion conferred by a liberal education will teach them *humility;* for it will give them a glance of those vast tracts of knowledge which they can never explore, until they are accommodated with far other powers than those at present assigned them; and they will contemplate their removal to a higher order of beings, as a desirable event.

Mild benignity, with all the modest virtues, and every sexual grace—these they will carefully cultivate; for they will have *learned,* that in no character they can so effectually charm, as in that in which nature designed them the *pre-eminence.* They will accustom themselves to reflection; they will investigate accurately, and reason will point their conclusions: Yet they will not be assuming; the characteristic trait will still remain; and retiring sweetness will insure them that consideration and respect, which they do not presume to demand. Thinking justly will not only enlarge their minds, and refine their ideas; but it will correct their dispositions, humanize their feelings, and present them the *friends of their species. The beauteous bosom will no more become a lurking-place for invidious and rancorous passions*; but the mild temperature of the soul will be evinced by the benign and equal tenour of their lives. Their manners will be unembarrassed; and, studious to shun even the *semblance of pedantry*, they will be careful to give to their most systematic arguments and deductions, an unaffected and natural appearance. They will rather *question* than *assert*; and they will make their communications on a supposition, that the point in discussion has rather *escaped the memory* of those with whom they converse, *than that it was never imprinted there*.

It is true, that every faculty of their minds will be occasionally engrossed by the most momentous concerns; but as often as *necessity* or *propriety* shall render it incumbent on them, they will *cheerfully* accommodate themselves to the more *humble duties* which their situation imposes. When their sphere of action is enlarged, when they become wives and mothers, they will fill with honour the parts allotted them. Acquainted, theoretically, with the nature of their species, and experimentally with themselves, they will not expect to meet, in wedlock, with those faultless beings, who so frequently issue, armed at all points, from the teeming brain of the novelist. They will learn properly to estimate; they will look, with pity's softest eye, on the natural frailties of those whom they elect partners for life; and they will regard their virtues with that sweet complacency, which is ever an attendant on a predilection founded on love, and happily combining esteem. As mothers, they will assume with alacrity their arduous employment, and they will cheerfully bend to its various departments. They will be primarily solicitous to fulfil, in *every instance*, whatever can *justly* be denominated *duty*; and those intervals, which have heretofore been devoted to frivolity, will be appropriated to pursuits, calculated to inform, enlarge, and sublime the soul—to contemplations, which will ameliorate the heart, unfold and illumine the understanding, and gradually render the human being an eligible candidate for the society of angels.

Such, I predict, will be the daughters of Columbia; and my gladdened spirit rejoices in the prospect. A sensible and informed woman—companionable and serious—possessing also a facility of

temper, and united to a congenial mind—blest with competency—
and rearing to maturity a promising family of children—Surely,
the wide globe cannot produce a scene more truly interesting. See!
the virtues are embodied—the domestic duties appear in their
place, and they are fulfilled—morality is systematized by religion,
and sublimed by devotion—every movement is the offspring of elegance, and their manners have received the highest polish. A recip-
rocation of good offices, and a mutual desire to please, uniformly
distinguishes the individuals of this enchanting society—their conversation, refined and elevated, partakes the fire of genius, while it
is pointed by information; and they are ambitious of selecting subjects, which, by throwing around humanity, *in its connexion*, additional lustre, may implant a new motive for gratitude, and teach
them to anticipate the rich fruition of that immortality which they
boast. Such is the family of reason—of reason, cultivated and
adorned by literature.

The idea of the incapability of women, is, we conceive, in this
enlightened age, totally *inadmissable*; and we have concluded,
that establishing the *expediency* of admitting them to share the
blessings of equality, will remove every obstacle to their advancement. In proportion as nations have progressed in the arts of civilization, the value of THE SEX hath been understood, their rank in
the scale of being ascertained, and their consequence in society acknowledged. But if prejudice still fortifies itself in the bosom of
any; if it yet enlisteth its votaries against the said despot and its
followers, we produce, instead of arguments, *a number of well
attested facts*, which the student of female annals hath carefully
compiled.

Women, circumscribed in their education within very narrow
limits, and constantly depressed by their occupations, have, nevertheless, tinged the cheek of manhood with a guilty suffusion, for a
pusillanimous capitulation with the enemies of their country.
Quitting the loom and the distaff, they have beheld, with indignation, their husbands and sons flee in battle: With clasped hands,
and determined resolution, they have placed themselves in their
paths, obstructing their passage, and insisting, with heroic firmness, on their immediate return to death or conquest! They have
anxiously examined the dead bodies of their slaughtered sons; and

if the fatal wounds were received in front, thus evincing that they have bravely faced the foe, the fond recollection of their valour has become a source of consolation, and they have sung a *requiem* to their sorrows! Women, in the heat of action, have mounted the rampart with undaunted courage, arrested the progress of the foe, and bravely rescued their besieged dwellings! They have successfully opposed themselves to tyranny and the galling yoke of oppression! Assembling in crowds, they have armed themselves for the combat—they have mingled amid the battling ranks—they have fought heroically—and their well-timed and well-concerted measures have emancipated their country! They have hazarded the stroke of death in its most frightful form; and they have submitted to bonds and imprisonment, for the redemption of their captive husbands!

The character of the Spartan women[4] is marked with uncommon firmness. At the shrine of patriotism they immolated Nature. Undaunted bravery and unimpeached honour, was, in their estimation, far beyond affection. The name of Citizen possessed, for them, greater charms than that of Mother; and so highly did they prize the warrior's meed, that they are said to have shed tears of joy over the bleeding bodies of their wounded sons!

When Europe and Asia were infested by armed multitudes, who, emigrating for purposes of devastation and settlement, perpetrated the most ferocious acts, among all those various tribes of unprincipled invaders, *no discriminating line seems to have marked the sexes*; wives submitted to similar hardships with their husbands; equally they braved the impending danger; and their efforts and their sufferings were the same: Nor can their habits of endurance and patient fortitude admit a rational doubt.

The women of Hungary have rendered themselves astonishingly conspicuous in their wars against the Ottoman Empire[5]—But proofs abound; and numerous actions might be produced to evince, that courage is by no means *exclusively* a masculine virtue. Women have frequently displayed an intrepidity, not to be surpassed by men—neither is their bravery the impulse of the moment. They not only, when trained by education, and inured by subsequent habit, rise superior to the fears of earth; but, with unimpassioned and sedate composure, *they can endure life*—they can struggle with the fatigues and inconveniences—they can fulfil the duties, and they can support the irremediable calamities of war. They have achieved the most surprising adventures; indulgencies have been extended to them on the well-fought field; and they have expired with the weapons of death in their hands! Actuated by devotional zeal, and stimulated by the sublime expectation of an opening heaven, and a glorious immortality, they have rushed into the flames, have ascended the scaffold, have suffered the dismemberment of their bodies, have submitted to the tortures of dislocation, and to the most excruciating racks, in defence of truth! nor has the voice of murmuring or complaint escaped their lips!

Women have publickly harangued on religion—they have presented themselves as disputants—they have boldly supported their tenets—they have been raised to the chair of philosophy, and of law—they have written fluently in Greek, and have read with great facility the Hebrew language. Youth and beauty, adorned with every feminine grace, and possessing eminently the powers of rhetoric, have pathetically conjured the mitred fathers and the Christian monarchs to arm themselves for the utter extirpation of the enemies of their holy religion.

In the days of knight-errantry, females, elevated by the importance with which they were invested, discriminated unerringly between the virtues and the vices, studiously cultivating the one, and endeavouring to exterminate the other; and their attainments *equalled the heroism of their admirers*; their bosoms glowed with sentiments as sublime as those they originated; generosity marked their elections; the impassioned feelings, the burst of tenderness, were invariably blended with honour; and every expression, every movement, was descriptive of the general enthusiasm. Pride, heroism, extravagant attachments; these were common to both sexes. Great enterprises, bold adventures, incredible bravery—in every thing the women partook the colour of the times; and their taste and their judgment were exactly conformed. Thus the sexes are congenial; they are copyists of each other; and their opinions and their habits are elevated or degraded, animated or depressed, by precisely the same circumstances.

The Northern nations have generally been in the habit of

venerating the Female Sex. Constantly employed in bending the bow, in exploring the haunts of those animals, who were the victims of their pleasures and their passions, or of urging against their species the missive shafts of death, they nevertheless banished their ferocity, and assumed the mildest manners, when associating with their mothers, their sisters, their mistresses, or their wives. In their ample forests, their athletic frames and sinewy arms were nerved for battle, while the smiles of some lovely woman were the meed of valour; and the hero who aspired to approbation of the beautiful arbitress of his fate, authorized his wishes, and established his pretensions, by eminent virtue, and a long series of unbroken attentions.

A persuasion, that the common Father of the universe manifests himself more readily to females than to males, has, at one period or another, obtained, more or less, in every division of the globe. The Germans, the Britons, and the Scandinavians—from these the supposition received an easy credence. The Grecian women delivered oracles—the Romans venerated the Sibyls[6]—among the people of God, the Jewish women prophesied—the predictions of the Egyptian matron were much respected—and we are assured, that the most barbarous nations referred to their females, whatever they fancied beyond the reach of human efforts: And hence we find women in possession of the mysteries of incantation. Writers assert, that several nations have ascribed to women the gift of prescience, conceiving that they possessed qualities approximating to divinity; and the ferocious German, embosomed in his native woods, renders a kind of devotional reverence to the Female Sex.

Such is the character of those periods, when women were invested with *undue elevation*; and the reverse presents THE SEX in a state of humiliation, altogether as unwarrantable. The females among the savages of our country, are represented as submitting to the most melancholy and distressing oppression; slaves to the ferocious passions and irregular appetites of those tyrannical usurpers, who brutally and cruelly outrage their feelings. They encounter for their support, incredible hardships and toils, the women on the banks of Oronoko, urged by compassion, not unfrequently smother the female infant in the hour of its birth; and she who hath attained sufficient fortitude to perform this *maternal* act, esteems herself entitled to additional respect. Commodore Byron,[7] in his account of the inhabitants of South-America, informs us, that the men exercise a most despotic authority over their wives, whom they consider in the same view they do any other part of their property, and dispose of them accordingly: Even their common treatment of them is cruel; for, although the toil and hazard of procuring food lies entirely on the women, yet they are not suffered to touch any part of it, till their imperious masters are satisfied, and then he assigns them their portion, which is generally very scanty, and such as he has not an appetite for, himself.

Thus have THE SEX continued the sport of contingencies; unnaturally subjected to extremes; alternately in the mount of exaltation, and in the valley of unmerited degradation. Is it wonderful, then, that they evince so little stability of character? Rather, is it not astonishing, that their attainments are so numerous, and so considerable? Turning over the annals of different ages, we have selected a number of names, which we purpose, in our next Essay, to cite, as vouchers of THE SEX's merit; nor can we doubt, that their united suffrages will, on a candid investigation, effectually establish the female right to that *equality with their brethren, which, it is conceived, is assigned them in the Order of Nature.*

Part II.

The historic page with many a proof abounds,
And fame's loud trump THE SEX's worth resounds;
The patriot's zeal, the laurell'd warrior's claim,
The scepter'd virtues, wisdom's sacred name,
Creative poesy, the ethic page,
Design'd to form and meliorate the age,
With heroism, with perseverance fraught,
By honour, truth, and constancy enwrought,
And those blest deeds which elevate the mind,
With female genius these are all combin'd:
Recording story hands their virtues down,
And mellowing time awards their fair renown.

Plutarch,[8] in one of his invaluable compositions, speaking of men and women, thus expresses himself—"The talents and the virtues are modified by the circumstances and the persons, but the foundation is the same." This celebrated and truly respectable biographer has yielded every thing that we wish; and the testimony of so nice a distinguisher must be considered as a very powerful auxiliary.

It is not our purpose to analyze the properties of mind; we are inclined to think, that accurately to discriminate, or draw the intellectual line, is beyond the power of the best informed metaphysician within the purlieus of humanity. Besides, as we write for the *many*, and as it is notorious that a number of *well attested facts* have abundantly more weight with *the multitude*, than the finest spun systems which ever issued from the archives of theory, we shall proceed to summon our witnesses, arranging their testimonies with as much order, as the cursory turning over a number of volumes, to which a deficiency in memory necessitates us to apply, will permit; and here, (lest the patience of our readers should reluct at the idea of the motley circle, to which they may apprehend they are to be introduced) we take leave to inform them, that we shall be careful to abridge, as much as possible, the copious depositions which may present.

Many centuries have revolved, since the era when writers of eminence, giving a catalogue of celebrated women, have made the number to amount to eight hundred and forty-five: From these, and succeeding attestators, we shall select a few, not perhaps the most striking, but such as occur the most readily. Our object is to prove, by examples, that the minds of women are *naturally* as susceptible of every improvement, as those of men. In the course of our examination, an obvious conclusion will, we conceive, force itself on every attentive and ingenuous reader. If the triumphs and attainments of THE SEX, under the various oppressions with which they have struggled, have been thus splendid, how would they have been augmented, had not ignorant or interested men, after clipping their wings, contrived to erect around them almost insurmountable barriers? Descartes[9] expatiated on the philosophical abilities of THE SEX; and, if their supporting themselves with astonishing equanimity under the complicated oppressions to which they are not unfrequently subjected, may be called the practice of any branch of philosophy, the experience of every tyrant will evince their proficiency therein. But the highly respectable and truly honourable court, is, we presume, convened; the jury are empanneled, and we proceed to the examination of the witnesses, leaving the pleadings to those silent suggestions and inferences, which, we are assured, will voluntarily enlist themselves as advocates in every ingenuous bosom. The pending cause, as we have before observed, involves the establishment of the female intellect, or maintaining the justice and propriety of considering women, as far as relates to their understanding, in *every respect*, equal to men. Our evidences tend to prove them—

First, Alike capable of enduring hardships.
Secondly, Equally ingenious, and fruitful in resources.
Thirdly, Their fortitude and heroism cannot be surpassed.
Fourthly, They are equally brave.
Fifthly, They are as patriotic.
Sixthly, As influential.
Seventhly, As energetic, and as eloquent.
Eighthly, As faithful, and as persevering in their
    attachments.
Ninthly, As capable of supporting, with honour, the toils of
    government. And
Tenthly, and *Lastly*, They are equally susceptible of every
    literary acquirement.

And, *First*, they are alike capable of enduring hardships. A proposition so self-evident, supercedes the necessity of either arguments or witnesses. On the women of Brittany, and the females among the savages of our own country, fatigues almost incredible are imposed. Imbecility seems to have changed sexes; and it is in these instances, *masculine weakness and feminine vigour*. THE SEX, enervated and sinking amid the luxuries and indulgencies of an Asiatic climate, are elsewhere hardy and courageous, and fully adequate to all those exertions requisite to the support of themselves and their supine oppressors; and these well authenticated facts, are, I conceive, alone sufficient to prove the *powerful and transforming effects of education, and subsequent habits*. But we need not take a voyage to Brittany, nor penetrate the haunts of savages, to prove that women are capable of suffering. They are the *enduring sex*; and, by the irreversible constitution of nature, they are subjected to agonies unknown to manhood; while I do not recollect that they are exempted from any of the calamities incident to humanity.

Secondly, They are *equally* ingenious, and fruitful in resources. Female ingenuity will not, we apprehend, be controverted; every day furnishes fresh proof of their invention, and their resources are a consequence. We select, however, a corroborating instance, which, from its salutary effect, seems to claim a preference.

A certain sovereign, of avaricious memory, was so fond of amassing treasure, that he arbitrarily compelled a very large proportion of his subjects to labour in the mines; but while his majesty's ingots were rapidly augmenting, the grounds remained uncultivated; famine advanced with hasty strides; and the dreary prospect every moment gathered darkness. No one possessed sufficient intrepidity to remonstrate—the despot's nod was fate— from his decrees there was no appeal—and the love of life, although its eligibles may be in a great measure diminished, is generally a paramount passion. In this emergency, the ingenuity of the queen suggested a resource that snatched the nation from the horrors of that *dearth* which had seemed so inevitable. She secretly employed an artist to produce an exact imitation of those luxuries, in which the king most delighted, a variety of fish and fowl—bread and fruits of the most delicious kind, made of pure gold, were expeditiously completed, and displayed in order on the *costly* board—the table was highly decorated—and, when every thing was complete, the king, (after having been purposely diverted from taking his customary refreshment) was ushered into the banqueting-room. His Majesty took a seat—for a moment, astonishment suspended even the clamours of hunger, and his mind was occupied by admiration of the imagination of the queen, and the deceptive abilities of the artist. The event was proportioned to the most sanguine expectations of the lady. The mines were suddenly dispeopled, and the earth again produced the necessary support.

Thirdly, Their fortitude and heroism cannot be surpassed. Listen to a woman of Sparta, reduced by melancholy casualties to a state of servitude—She was captured, and afterwards sold as a slave. The question was put by him on whom her very existence seemed to depend—"*What knowest thou?*" "*To be free,*" was her characteristic reply: But the unfeeling despot, uninfluenced by indubitable indications of a noble mind, proceeded to impose his ignominious commands; to which she dispassionately returned, "*you are unworthy of me;*" and instantly resigned herself to death. Fortitude and heroism was a conspicuous trait in, and gave uncommon dignity to, the character of the Roman ladies. Arria, the wife of Paetus,[10] a Roman of consular dignity, is an illustrious instance of that transcendent elevation, of which the female mind is susceptible. With persevering firmness, and a tenderness not to be exceeded, she continued unwearied in her endeavours to procure the life of her husband—long she cherished hope; but, when the pleasing vision fled, and the portending storm was bursting over their heads: In that tremendous moment, while the disappointed man, trembling on the verge of dissolution, had not the courage to point the deadly weapon—with that exquisite delicacy, true fortitude, and *faithfulness; of affection, which is so highly sexual, she first imprinted on her own bosom the characters of death*; and, animated by that sublime consciousness becoming a being more than half celestial, she then presented him the pointed daggar, with this consolatory assurance—"*Paetus, this gives me no pain.*"

But fortitude and heroism are not confined to the Greek and Roman ladies; we have pledged ourselves not to multiply examples unnecessarily, otherwise a crowd of witnesses presenting, we could with difficulty suppress their testimony. Yet we find it impossible so speedily to close this part of our examination; and from the multitude of examples in the Island of Great-Britain, we produce the Lady Jane Gray,[11] who seemed an exemplification of every virtue and every grace which has been attributed to the male or female character. The excellent understanding she received from Nature was opened and improved by uniform application. At sixteen, her judgment had attained a high degree of maturity. She was at that age an adept both in the Greek and Latin languages;

and she was able to declare that her Greek Plato was a more pleasing entertainment to her than all those enchanting pleasures usually so captivating to the unexperienced mind. Nurtured in the bosom of parental affection, and of tender friendship—happy in the distinguishing regards of her sovereign, and permitted the sublime enjoyment of intellectual pursuits, she had no ambition for the pageantry of royalty, and her advancement to the throne was an era, over which she dropped the melacholy tear. We are sensible that in adverting to these traits in a character, affectingly interesting, we do in fact anticipate other divisions of our subject; but, contemplating a mind thus richly furnished, it is difficult to consider separately, endowments so nicely blended, and reflecting on each other such unusual lustre.

The passage of the Lady Jane, from the throne to the scaffold, was very short—her imposed queenship continued only ten days; yet she seemed displeased at their duration, and she received, with *heroic fortitude*, the message of death. The lover and the husband, whose vows she had recently accepted, was also under sentence of death; and, on the morning assigned for their martyrdom, he solicited for a parting interview; with solemn firmness she refused his request—yet her resolution originated not in a deficiency of tenderness; but it was nerved by an apprehension that her sensibilities, thus stimulated, might surmount her fortitude. With modest resignation she pursued her way to the place of execution— the officers of death, bearing the body of her husband, while the headless trunk yet streamed with blood, met her on her passage— neither of them had completed their seventeenth year—she looked—she sighed—and then, reassuming her composed sedateness, desired her conductors to proceed—she mounted the scaffold with an accelerated step—she addressed the surrounding spectators—she committed the care of her person to her woman; and, with a countenance descriptive of serene dignity, bowed her head to the executioner. Thus perished a spotless victim of despotism and of bigotry in the bloom of youth and beauty, rich in innocence, and adorned with every literary accomplishment and sexual grace. Latest posterity will lament her fate, and many hearts will join to execrate the sanguinary measures which procured it. Under this head we produce but one more testimony.

Miss Anna Askew,[12] a young lady of great merit, and possessed also of a beautiful exterior, lived during the tyranny of Henry VIII of England; a despot, who seemed to conceive the female world created on purpose to administer to his pleasures, or to become the victims of his cruelty and implacability. Miss Askew was arraigned as a transgressor; her crime was the denial of the *real presence in the eucharist*; and for this atrocious offence, she was rigorously imprisoned, and subjected to a series of barbarities that would have disgraced even savage inhumanity. Yet, in a situation which involved trials, that in a succeeding reign proved too mighty for the *resolution even of the virtuous Cranmer*,[13] her heroism and fortitude continued unshaken. With unyielding firmness she vindicated the truth of her opinion, and her hourly orisons were offered up to her Father God. The chancellor, a bigoted Catholic, sternly questioned her relative to her abettors; but she nobly disdained to present an accusation, the consequences of which she so rigorously experienced: Her unbending integrity furnished the pretence, and she was, without further delay, put to the torture; but still her fortitude receded not; and her heroic silence evinced her abundantly superior to their unmanly cruelties. The enraged chancellor, in whose presence she suffered, transported with diabolic zeal, grasping with his own hands the cords, violently stretched the rack, and almost tore her body asunder; while yet unappalled, her fortitude forsook her not, and her triumph over her barbarous tormentors was complete.

Her death-warrrant was next made out, and she recieved the sentence which condemned her to the flames as an emancipation from every evil. All her joints dislocated by the rack, she was borne to the place of execution; and there, after being bound to the stake, was offered her life on condition of retracting her supposed error; but she consistently rejected an existence to be purchased only by the forfeiture of that consciousness of rectitude, which the virtuous so well know how to prize; and as the flames that were her passport to regions of blessedness, enkindled around her, a song of thanksgiving was on her lips, and her exultation evidently augmented.

Fourthly, They are equally brave. Bravery is not a quality which figures *gracefully* in the list of female virtues, nor are we anxious it should take rank in the catalogue—far from it; we should rather lament to see it become a characteristic trait. We would have women support themselves with consistent firmness under the various exigencies of life, but we would not arm them with the weapons of death: Yet, when contending for *equality of soil*, it may be necessary to prove the *capability* of the female mind, to rear to perfection whatever seeds may be adventitiously implanted therein. We therefore proceed to produce a witness or two on this part of the question; and, consulting our records, we assign the precedence, *all circumstances considered*, to a young woman of Lemnos, an island in the Archipelago.

This magnanimous female beheld the streaming wounds of her expiring father, in the fatal moment in which he was slaughtered on the field of battle; and, instead of yielding to those tender sensibilities originating in nature, and generally associated with valour—instead of lamenting his fate by sighs and tears, or the wordy exclamations of clamorous sorrow, she undauntedly seized that sword and shield now rendered useless to the venerable warrior, and, arming herself therewith, reanimated the dispirited soldiers, led them once more to the charge; bravely opposed the Turks, who, having forced a gate, were rapidly advancing; and gloriously avenged the death of her father, by driving them back to the shore, and compelling them to take refuge in their vessels.

Jane of Flanders[14] next presents: This lady, during the imprisonment of her husband, nobly supported the declining honours of her house: With her infant son in her arms, she met the assembling citizens, and pathetically deploring her misfortunes, she secured their exertions in her favour. She sustained with unyielding firmness the attacks of a vigilant and active foe. In the frequent sallies made by the garrison, she herself led on her warriors. At the head of three hundred horse, with her own hand she set fire to the tents and baggage of the besiegers, thus necessitating them to desist from the general assault which they were in the moment of commencing; and, although intercepted in her return to the citadel, she nevertheless fought her way through one quarter of the French camp, and rejoined her faithful friends in triumph!

Margaret of Anjou[15] is a decisive proof that courage is not *exclusively* the property of man—Brave, indefatigable, and persevering—fruitful in resources—supporting by her genius and her exertions a pusillanimous husband—repeatedly emancipating him from prison, and replacing him on a throne which he had lost by imbecility, and which he was unable to retain—and equal to every thing which depended on undaunted courage, she headed her armies in person; directed their arrangements; and proceeded from rank to rank, animating them by her undaunted intrepidity and judicious conduct; and, when borne down by misfortunes, and apparently destitute of every resource, suddenly she emerged, and, followed by numerous armies, again appeared in the field; nor did she submit to fate, until she had fought, as a general and a soldier, *twelve decisive battles*!!!

The French women—Charlotte Corde[16]—But our depositions unexpectedly multiplying a recollection of our engagement can alone suppress their evidence.

Part III.

> *'Tis joy to tread the splendid paths of fame,*
> *Where countless myriads mental homage claim;*
> *Time honour'd annals careful to explore,*
> *And mark the heights which intellect can soar.*

Fifthly, They are equally patriotic. We have, in some measure, forestalled this article. The Grecian women have produced their testimonies, and that preference which they demonstrably manifested to the character Citizen; estimating it beyond the endearing appellations, Wife and Mother, incontrovertibly establishes their sex's *capability* of experiencing with an ardour *not to be exceeded*, the patriotic glow; and yet it is true, that sexual occupations frequently humiliating, and generally far removed from whatever has a tendency to elevate the mind, may rationally be supposed to chill, in the female bosom, the fine fervours of the *amor patrie*.

Women are not usually exercised in those extensive contemplations which engage the legislator: They are not called on to arm in their country's cause; to appear in the well fought field, or to put their lives at hazard: But when they part with him in whom is centered their dearest hopes, who blends the characters lover, friend, husband and protector—when they resign to the hostile career the blooming youth whom from infancy they have watched with all a mother's tenderness, and whose rich maturity hath become the pride and consolation of their declining life—in those moments of anguish, their heroism and their fortitude are indisputably evinced. Nor is the patriotism of the chief arrayed for the battle; nor his, who devotes himself with all a statesman's integrity to the public weal, condemned to an ordeal more severe.

The *patriotism* of the Roman ladies, procured a senatorial decree that funeral orations should be pronounced from the rostrum in their praise: Repeatedly they saved their country. And the *patriotism* of the mother and wife of Coriolanus,[17] while it snatched Rome from impending ruin, devoted to the inevitable destruction the husband and the son: Hence towered the temple consecrated to feminine honour; and it must be confessed they had purchased this distinction at a very high price. The venerable Senate, too, again interposed; public thanks were decreed; and men were ordered, on all occasions, to yield precedence to women.

Sixthly, They are as influential. The ascendancy obtained by females, is so notorious, as to have become proverbial. Instances are multiplied, wherein women have bent to their purposes the strongest masculine understanding. Samson, the victim of female blandishments, is not a singular instance. The example cited under the last article, is in point. Coriolanus rejected with unbending severity supplicating friendship, garbed in senatorial robes; succeeding deputies plead in vain—the ministers of religion, cloathed in sacerdotal habits, joined in solemn procession—they crowded around the warrior, commissioned to advocate a sinking people's cause; still, however, he continued obdurate, inflexibly firm and steady to his plans. But Veturia and Volumnia, his wife and mother, attended by the most illustrious of the Roman ladies, appear—they shed torrents of tears—they embrace his knees—the hero is disarmed—his heart is melted—his resentment and his resolutions vanish together—and Rome is saved.

Seventhly, They are as energetic, and as eloquent. Women always decree with fervour: Did it depend on them, their movements would be decisive. Their expressions are often as strongly marked, as they are vehement; and both their plans and the execution thereof, are endowed with all the vigour that existing regulations will permit. Their eloquence is indisputable. Possessing a richness of fancy, their words are sufficiently copious; and education, when they are indulged with its aids, prescribes the proper rules. Aspasia, of Miletus,[18] it is well known, taught the immortal Socrates rhetoric and politics. And, when Rome groaned under the enormous cruelties of her second Triumvirate, the three barbarians by whom she was enslaved, and who had armed themselves for the destruction of her citizens, as if desirous of spreading every possible calamity, seized not only the lives, but the treasures of the people, and equally greedy of gold as of blood, after exhausting every other mode of plunder, turned their rapacious views on those respectable matrons, who had hitherto been exempted from pecuniary exactions; an exorbitant tax was levied on every individual female, and the consternation occasioned by this unheard of assumption, was proportioned to the distress of which it was productive.

In this extraordinary emergency, the oppressed females earnestly solicited the aid of those advocates who were appointed to plead the cause of the injured and defenceless; but the orators, fearful of incurring the displeasure of those who had usurped the power of life and death, refused to interfere; and no means of redress appearing, submission to an imposition acknowledged grievous, seemed inevitable: It was, however, reserved to the talents and exertions of Hortensia[19] to furnish the desired aid.

This lady inherited all the abilities of her father; and she presented herself a voluntary advocate for her sex. With modest intrepidity she opened, conducted, and closed the proceedings. Persuasion dwelt on her tongue: Her arguments, resulting from rectitude, were pointed by reason: And it will be conceived that her rhetorical powers must have been of the first rate, when it is remembered that *the countenances of the tyrants betrayed sudden and evident tokens of that remorse which was then first enkindled in their bosoms*; the hue of guilt pervaded their cheeks, and they hastily repealed the injurious decree. For the brow of Hortensia, fame prepared an immortal wreath: To the utmost gratitude of her contemporaries she was entitled: Her triumph was the triumph of virtue and of talents: She enkindled even in the callous breasts of assassins, the almost extinguished sparks of humanity; and she stands on the page of history, a pattern of dauntless courage, and an example of genuine eloquence.

Eighthly, They are as faithful and as persevering in their attachments. Here countless witnesses crowd on retention, and the greatest difficulty is in choosing judiciously. Repeatedly have I seen the faithfully attached female, firmly persevering in that affection which was first implanted in the soil of innocence, and fondly watching with tender anxiety every symptom of the diseased man: With patient assiduity she hath hung over the couch, and sought to mitigate the pangs of him, whose lentious conduct had brought ruin on herself and her unoffending children! Had circumstances been reversed, *divorce* would have succeeded—a hospital must have sheltered the helpless woman; and, had then she received from the man she had injured any trivial attention, the unmerited gratuity would have resounded through the circle of the connexions, been dwelt on with rapture, and echoed by every tongue. But when virtue is the basis; when acts of kindness cement the union, THE SEX in many instances have set no bound to that faithful attachment which their hearts have exultingly acknowledged. Filial duty—conjugal affection—persevering constancy—these receive in the female bosom the highest perfection of which they are, in the present state, susceptible.

The young Roman, supporting her imprisoned parent by the milk of her own chaste bosom, if unparalleled in history, would yet, in like situation, obtain many imitators; and the feelings of a daughter would prompt, for the relief of the authors of her being, the noblest exertions. The celebrated Mrs. Roper,[20] eldest daughter of Sir Thomas More, continued his affectionate solace during his imprisonment: With heart-affecting anguish she rushed through the guards to catch, from the illustrious martyr, a last embrace. Bending under a weight of calamity, she obtained permission to pay him sepulchral honours; and, regardless of the tyrant's power, she purchased the venerable head of the meritorious sufferer: Yet, too noble to permit the consequences to fall upon another, with dauntless courage she became her own accuser; and, loaded with fetters for two crimes, "for having watched the head of her father as a relique, and for having preserved his books and writings," appeared with unconcern before her judges—justified herself with that eloquence which virtue bestows on injured merit—commanding admiration and respect—and spent the remainder of her life in solitude, in sorrow, and in study.

But women, unable to support existence, when deprived of those with whom they have exchanged the nuptial vow, have mounted the funeral pile, and hastened to rejoin their deceased partners in other worlds. Portia,[21] the daughter of Cato Uticensis, and wife of Brutus, hearing of the death of her husband, disdained to live; and when debarred access to the usual weapons of destruction, made her exit by resolutely swallowing burning coals of fire! Julia,[22] the wife of Pompey, expired upon seeing his robe distained with the blood which she imagined had issued from his veins. Molfa Tarquinia,[23] rendered illustrious by genius and literature, of unblemished virtue, and possessing, also, a beautiful exterior, although one of the brightest ornaments of the Court of Ferrara,[24] and receiving from the people of Rome, that unprecedented honour, the freedom of their city, mourned, nevertheless, through a long life, until the hour of her dissolution, the husband of her youth. Artemisia, wife of Mausolus,[25] rendered herself illustrious, and obtained immortality, by her devotion to the memory of her husband. The Mausoleum, which she reared in honour of him, was considered as one of the seven wonders of the world; and it gave name to all those succeeding monuments, which were distinguished by extraordinary marks of magnificence. Artemisia expired, the victim of inconsolable regret and tender sorrow, before the Mausoleum was completed. Victoria Colonna,[26] Marchioness of Pescaira, ardently engaged in literary pursuits, while fame did ample justice to her productions; yet, separated by the stroke of death, in the morning of her days, from an illustrious and gallant husband, appropriated her remaining years to unceasing grief, lamenting, in her pathetic Essays, the long-lost hero. The celebrated Mrs. Rowe,[27] equally conspicuous for genius and virtue, continued faithful and persevering in her attachment to her deceased husband; nor could a length of years abate her regrets.

Ninthly, They are capable of supporting, with equal honour, the toils of government. Semiramis[28] appears to have associated all the virtues and vices which have received the masculine stamp—she extended her empire from Ethiopia to India, and subdued many nations—her buildings and gardens were also magnificent—and she governed, in many respects, judiciously. Artemisia, queen of Caria, and daughter of Lygdamis, possessing, during the minority of her son, sovereign authority, distinguished herself, both by her counsels and her personal valour. Amalasuntha[29] governed with the greatest justice, wisdom, and prudence. Julia Mammaea[30] educated her son, Alexander Severus,[31] implanting in his bosom the seeds of virtue, and adorning him with every princely accomplishment: He was worthy of the high rank to which he was raised, and disposed to become the father of his people: His mother presided in his councils; the era of their administration was tumultuous and hazardous, and its disastrous termination is one of the events which the student of history will not fail to deplore.

Zenobia[32] united genius and valour—she was dignified by the title of Augusta. After the demise of her husband, the supreme authority devolving upon her, she governed with rectitude, firmness, and intrepidity. She preserved the provinces in their allegiance, and added Egypt to her dominions. Moreover, when led into captivity, she knew how to *bring into subjection, her feelings; she endured misfortune with the heroism of a noble spirit, and found a solace for the loss of royalty, and the pageantry of a throne, in those rational pursuits, which felicitude and freedom from care uninterruptedly permit.* Longinus[33] was her preceptor and friend; and she was worthy of his tuition and preferable attachment. Elizabeth of England was endowed with energetic talents; her reign was glorious for the people over which she presided; she was undoubtedly a great politician, and governed with uniform vigour; she is characterized as possessing much penetration, and an understanding fruitful of resources; her foreign negociations were conducted with propriety and dignity; her mind was opened and polished by all the aids of an extensive education, and adversity was among her preceptors. Christina,[34] queen of Sweden, governed her subjects twenty-one years, with uniform wisdom and unimpeached prudence, when she magnanimously resigned her crown; thus giving a rare example of an elevation of intellect, which has not been surpassed.

Tenthly, and *Lastly,* They are equally susceptible of every literary acquirement. Corinna,[35] it is said, triumphed a fifth time over the immortal Pindar,[36] who had publickly challenged her to contend with him in the poetical line. Sappho,[37] the Lesbian poetess, was admired by the ancients—she produced many poems, and was addressed as the tenth Muse. Sulpicia,[38] a Roman lady, who lived under the reign of Dimitian,[39] was called the Roman Sappho. Hypatia,[40] beautiful, learned, and virtuous, the daughter of Theon, presided over the Platonic school at Alexandria, about the close of the fourth century; she was judged qualified to succeed her father in that distinguished and important office; her wisdom was held in universal esteem; and from her judgment no one thought proper to appeal: Persons cloathed in public authority, even the first magistrates, deliberated with her on the most urgent and important emergencies; this unavoidably drew around her succeeding circles of men; yet she maintained her intercourse with characters of various descriptions, without the shadow of an impeachment of her reputation, until basely traduced, in a *single instance,* by bigotted and interested calumniators. Cassandra,[41] a Venetian lady, attained an accurate skill in languages, and made great proficiency in the learning of her time; she composed with facility, both in numbers and in prose, in the language of Homer, Virgil, and Dante;[42] she was a proficient in the philosophy of her own and preceding ages; she rendered theology harmonious; she supported theses with brilliancy; she lectured publickly at Padua; she blended the fine arts with her serious studies; and the mild complacency of her manners constituted the completion of her character: She received homage from sovereign pontiffs, and sovereign princes; and she continued an ornament of her Sex, and of humanity, one hundred and two years.

The daughter of Sir Thomas More, Mrs. Roper, already cited under the eighth article, whose virtues were polished by literary attainments, corresponded in Latin with the celebrated Erasmus,[43] and successfully appropriated many years of her life to study: Her daughter inherited her erudition, and her amiable qualifications. The Seymours, sisters,[44] and nieces of a king, wrote elegantly in Latin. Isabella of Rosera,[45] in Spain, by her substantial arguments, natural deductions, and able rhetoric, greatly augmented the number of believing Jews; the great church of Barcelona was open for the exertion of her pulpitorial abilities; and she acquired much honour by her commentaries upon the learned Scotus.[46] France knew how to estimate the talents of the Dutchess of Retz; she pursued her studies amid the seducing pleasures of a court; and, although young and beautiful, spoke the ancient languages with propriety and elegance. Mary Stuart, queen of Scotland,[47] possessing all the advantages of exterior, and every sexual grace, assiduously cultivated her mind: Her learning was as remarkable as her beauty; she could, we are informed, write and speak six languages; her numbers enchanted the Gallic ear; and, at an early age, she pronounced before the French Court a Latin oration, calculated to convince her hearers, that literary pursuits are proper to the Female Sex. Beauty could not plead in vain; the lovely speaker exemplified, in her own character and attainments, the truth she inculcated; she was, herself, that happy combination, the practicability of which she laboured to impress; and conviction undoubtedly irradiated the minds of her audience.

In the thirteenth century, a young lady of Bologna, pursuing, with avidity, the study of the Latin language, and the legislative institutions of her country, was able, at the age of twenty-three, to deliver, in the great church of Bologna, a Latin oration, in praise of a deceased person, eminent for virtue; nor was she indebted for the admiration she received, to the indulgence granted to her youth, or Sex. At the age of twenty-six, she took the degree of a Doctor of Laws, and commenced her career in this line, by public ex-positions of the doctrines of Justinian: At the age of thirty, her extraordinary merit raised her to the chair, where she taught the law to an astonishing number of pupils, collected from various nations. She joined to her profound knowledge, sexual modesty, and every feminine accomplishment; yet her personal attractions were absorbed in the magnitude and splendor of her intellectual abilities; and the charms of her exterior only commanded attention when she ceased to speak. The fourteenth century produced, in the same city a like example; and the fifteenth continued, and acknowledged the pretensions of THE SEX, insomuch that a learned chair was appropriated to illustrious women.

Issotta Nogarolla[48] was also an ornament of the fifteenth century; and Sarochisa of Naples was deemed worthy of comparison with Tasso.[49] Modesta Pozzo's[50] defence of her Sex did her honour; she was, herself, an example of excellence. Gabrielle, daughter of a king, found leisure to devote to her pen and her literary pursuits contributed to her usefulness and her happiness. Mary de Gournai[51] rendered herself famous by her learning. Guyon,[52] by her writings and her sufferings, have evinced the justice of her title to immortality. Anna Maria Schuman[53] of Cologne, appears to have been mistress of all the useful and ornamental learning of the age which she adorned: She was born in 1607; her talents unfolded with extraordinary brilliancy: In the bud of her life at the age of six years, she cut, with her scissors, the most striking resemblances of every figure which was presented to her view, and they were finished with astonishing neatness. At ten, she was but three hours in learning to embroider. She studied music, painting, sculpture and engraving, and made an admirable proficiency in all those arts. The Hebrew, Greek and Latin languages were familiar to her; and she made some progress in the oriental tongues. She perfectly understood French, English and Italian, and expressed herself eloquently in all those languages; and she appropriated a portion of her time, to the acquirement of an extensive acquaintance with geography, astronomy, philosophy, and the other sciences: Yet she possessed so much feminine delicacy, and retiring modesty, that her talents and acquirements had been consigned to oblivion, if Vassius, and other amateurs of literature, had not ushered her, in opposition to her wishes upon the theatre of the world: But when she was once known, persons of erudition, of every description corresponded with her; and those in the most elevated stations, assiduously sought opportunities of seeing and conversing with her.

Mademoiselle Scudery,[54] stimulated by necessity, rendered herself eminent by her writings. Anna de Parthenay[55] possessed great virtues, great talent, and great learning; she read, with facility and pleasure, authors in the Greek and Latin languages; she was a rationale theologician; she was a perfect mistress of music; and was as remarkable for her vocal powers, as for her execution of the various instruments which she attempted. Catharine de Parthenay,[56] niece to Anna, married to Renatus de Rohan,[57] signalized herself by her attention to the education of her children; and her maternal cares were crowned with abundant success: Her eldest son was the illustrious Duke of Rohan,[58] who obtained immortal honour by his zeal and exertions in the Protestant cause; and she was also mother to Anna de Rohan, who was as illustrious for her genius and piety, as for her birth. She was mistress of the Hebrew language; her numbers were beautifully elegant; and she supported, with heroic firmness, the calamities consequent upon the siege of Rochelle.

Mademoiselle le Fevre,[59] celebrated in the literary world by the name of Madame Dacier, gave early testimonies of that fine genius which her father delighted to cultivate. Her edition of Callimachus was received with much applause. At the earnest request of the Duke of de Montansier, she published an edition of Florus, for the use of the dauphin; she exchanged letters with Christina, queen of Sweden; she devoted herself to the education of her son and daughter, whose progress were proportioned to the abilities of their interested preceptress: Greek and Latin were familiar to her; and she was often addressed in both those languages, by the literati of Europe. Her translation of the Iliad was much admired. She is said to have possessed great firmness, generosity, and equality of temper, and to have been remarkable for her piety. Maria de Sevigne[60] appropriated her hours to the instruction of her son and daughter; she enriched the world with eight volumes of letters, which will be read with pleasure by every critic in the French language. The character of Mary II. Queen of England,[61] and consort to William of Nassau, is transcendently amiable. She is delineated as a princess, endowed with uncommon powers of mind, and beauty of person. She is extensively acquainted with history, was attached to poetry, and possessed a good taste in compositions of this kind. She had a considerable knowledge in architecture and gardening; and her dignified condescension, and consistent piety, were truly admirable and praiseworthy—Every reader of history, and lover of virtue, will lament her early exit. The Countess of Pembroke[62] translated from the French, a dramatic piece; she gave a metrical edition of the Book of Psalms, and supported an exalted character

Anna Killigrew,[63] and Anna Wharton,[64] were eminent, both for poetry and painting; and their unblemished virtue, and exemplary piety, pointed and greatly enhanced the value of their other accomplishments. Catharine Phillips[65] was, from early life, a lover of the Muses; she translated Corneille's Tragedy of Pompey into English; and in this, as well as the poems which she published, she was successful. Lady Burleigh, Lady Bacon, Lady Russell, and Mrs. Killigrew, daughters of Sir Anthony Cook,[66] received from their father a masculine education; and their prodigious improvement was an ample compensation for his paternal indulgence: They were eminent for genius and virtue, and obtained an accurate knowledge of the Greek and Latin languages. The writings of the Dutchess of Newcastle[67] were voluminous; she is produced as the first lady who attempted what has since been termed polite literature. Lady Halket[68] was remarkable for her erudition; she was well skilled, both in physic and divinity. Lady Masham,[69] and Mary Astell,[70] reasoned accurately on the most abstract particulars in divinity, and in metaphysics. Lady Grace Gethin[71] was happy in natural genius and a cultivated understanding; she was a woman of erudition; and we are informed that, at the age of twenty, "*she treated of life and morals, with the discernment of Socrates, and the elegance of Xenophon*"[72]—Mr. Congreve[73] has done justice to her merit. Chudleigh, Winchelsea, Monk, Bovey, Stella, Montague[74]—these all possess their respective claims. Catharine Macauley[75] wielded successfully the historic pen; nor were her exertions confined to this line—But we have already multiplied our witnesses far beyond our original design; and it is proper that we apologize to our readers, for a transgression of that brevity which we had authorized them to expect.

Part IV.

> Nor are the modern Fair a step behind,
> In the transcendent energies of mind:
> Their worth conspicuous swells the ample roll,
> While emulous they reach the splendid goal.

We take leave to repeat, that we are not desirous to array THE SEX in martial habiliments; we do not wish to enlist our women as soldiers; and we request it may be remembered, that we only

contend for the *capability* of the female mind to become possessed of any attainment within the reach of *masculine exertion*.
We have produced our witnesses; their depositions have been
heard; the cause is before the public; we await their verdict; and,
as we entertain all possible veneration for the respectable jury, we
shall not dare to appeal from their decision.

But while we do homage to the women of other times, we feel
happy that nature is no less bountiful to the females of the present
day. We cannot, indeed, obtain a list of the names that have done
honour to their Sex, and to humanity, during the period now
under observation: The lustre of those minds, still enveloped in a
veil of mortality, is necessarily muffled and obscure; but the curtain will be thrown back, and posterity will contemplate, with admiration, their manifold perfections. Yet, in many instances, fame
has already lifted her immortalizing trump. Madame de Genlis[76]
has added new effulgence to the literary annals of France. This
lady unites, in an astonishing degree, both genius and application!
May her indefatigable exertions be crowned with the success they
so richly merit—May no illiberal prejudices obstruct the progress
of her multiplied productions; but, borne along the stream of
time, may they continue pleasurable vehicles of instruction, and
confer on their ingenious author that celebrity to which she is indisputably entitled. France may also justly place among her list of
illustrious personages, the luminous name of Roland. Madame
Roland[77] comprised, in her own energetic and capacious mind, all
those appropriate virtues, which are characterized as masculine
and feminine. She not only dignified THE SEX, but human nature
in the aggregate; and her memory will be held in veneration, wherever talents, literature, patriotism, and uniform heroism, are properly appreciated.

The British Isle is at this moment distinguished by a constella-
tion of the first magnitude. Barbauld, Seward, Cowley, Inchbald,
Burney, Smith, Radcliffe, Moore, Williams, Wollstonecraft,[78] &c.
&C.—these ladies, celebrated for brilliancy of genius and literary
attainments, have rendered yet more illustrious the English name.

Nor is America destitute of females, whose abilities and improvements give them an indisputable claim to immortality. It is a
fact, established beyond all controversy, that we are indebted for

the discovery of our country, to female enterprize, decision, and generosity. The great Columbus, after having in vain solicited the aid of Genoa, France, England, Portugal, and Spain—after having combated, for a period of eight years, with every objection that a want of knowledge could propose, found, at last, his only resource in the penetration and magnanimity of Isabella of Spain, who furnished the equipment, and raised the sums necessary to defray the expenses, on the sale of her own jewels; and while we conceive an action, so honourable to THE SEX, hath not been sufficiently applauded, we trust, that the equality of the female intellect to that of their brethren, who have so long usurped an unmanly and unfounded superiority, will never, in this younger world, be left without a witness. We cannot ascertain the number of ingenious women, who at present adorn our country. In the shade of solitude they perhaps cultivate their own minds, and superintend the education of their children. Our day, we know, is only dawning—but when we contemplate a Warren, a Philenia, an Antonia, a Euphelia,[79] &c. &c. we gratefully acknowledge, that genius and application, even in the female line, already gild, with effulgent radiance, our blest Aurora.

But women are calculated to shine in other characters than those adverted to, in the preceding Essays; and with proper attention to their education, and subsequent habits, they might easily attain that independence, for which a Wollstonecraft hath so energetically contended; the term, *helpless widow* might be rendered as unfrequent and inapplicable as that of *helpless widower*; and although we should undoubtedly continue to mourn the dissolution of wedded amity, yet we should derive consolation from the knowledge, that the infant train had still a remaining prop, and that a mother could assist as well as weep over her offspring.

That women have a talent—a talent which, duly cultivated, would confer that independence, which is demonstrably of incalculable utility, every attentive observer will confess. THE SEX should be taught to depend on their own efforts, for the procurement of an establishment in life. The chance of a matrimonial coadjutor, is no more than a probable contingency; and if they were early accustomed to regard this *uncertain* event with suitable *indifference*, they would make elections with that deliberation, which would be calculated to give a more rational prospect of tranquility. All this we have repeatedly asserted, and all this we do invariably believe. To neglect polishing a gem, or obstinately to refuse bringing into action a treasure in our possession when we might thus accumulate a handsome interest, is surely egregiously absurd and the height of folly. The *united efforts of male and female* might rescue many a family from destruction, which, notwithstanding the efforts of its *individual* head, is now involved in all the calamities attendant on a dissipated fortune and augmenting debts. It is not possible to educate children in a manner which will render them *too beneficial* to society; and the more we multiply aids to a family, the greater will be the security, that its individuals will not be thrown a burden on the public.

An instance of *female capability*, this moment occurs to memory. In the State of Massachusetts, in a small town, some miles from the metropolis, resides a woman, who hath made astonishing improvements in agriculture. Her mind in the early part of her life, was but penuriously cultivated, and she grew up almost wholly uneducated: But being suffered, during her childhood, to rove at large among her native fields, her limbs expanded, and she acquired a height of stature above the common size; her mind also became invigorated; and her understanding snatched sufficient information, to produce a consciousness of the injury she sustained in the want of those aids, which should have been furnished in the beginning of her years. She however applied herself diligently to remedy the evil, and soon made great proficiency in writing, and in arithmetic. She read every thing she could procure; but the impressions adventitiously made on her infant mind still obtained the ascendancy. A few rough acres constituted her patrimonial inheritance; these she has brought into a state of high cultivation; their productions are every year both useful and ornamental; she is mistress of agricolation, and is at once a botanist and a florist. The most approved authors in the English language, on these subjects, are in her hands, and she studies them with industry and success.

She has obtained such a considerable knowledge in the nature of soils, the precise manure which they require, and their particular adaptation to the various fruits of the earth, that she is become the oracle of all the farmers in her vicinity; and when laying out, or appropriating their grounds, they uniformly submit them to her inspection. Her gardens are the resort of all strangers who happen to visit her village; and she is particularly remarkable for a growth of trees, from which, gentlemen, solicitous to enrich their fruit-gardens, or ornament their parterres, are in the habit of supplying themselves; and those trees are, to their ingenious cultivator, a considerable income. Carefully attentive to her nursery, she knows when to transplant, and when to prune; and she perfectly understands the various methods of inoculating and ingrafting. In short, she is a complete *husbandwoman*; and she has, besides, acquired a vast stock of general knowledge, while her judgment has attained such a degree of maturity, as to justify the confidence of the villagers, who are accustomed to consult her on every perplexing emergency.

In the constant use of exercise, she is not corpulent; and she is extremely active, and wonderfully athletic. Instances, almost incredible, are produced of her strength. Indeed, it is not surprising that she is the idol and standing theme of the village, since, with all her uncommon qualifications, she combines a tenderness of disposition not to be exceeded. Her extensive acquaintance with herbs, contributes to render her a skillful and truly valuable nurse; and the world never produced a more affectionate, attentive, or faithful woman: Yet, while she feelingly sympathizes with every invalid, she is not herself subject to imaginary complaints; nor does she easily yield to real illness. She has lately been indisposed—and a life so valuable, when endangered, embodied a host of fears for its safety: With difficulty she was persuaded to lie down upon her bed; and the young woman who attended her, and to whom she had endeared herself by a thousand good offices, after softly closing the shutters and door of her apartment, privately summoned the aid of a physician; and when the medical gentleman made his appearance, she accompanied him to the apartment of her friend; but behold, the bird was flown! and when pursued, she was found at a distance from her habitation, directing some labourers, who were employed in her service, and who, she was fearful, were not sufficiently attentive to her previous instructions. The event proved she had acted judiciously; for, braced by the fresh air, her nerves new strung, assumed their usual tone, her sickness vanished, and her native vigour returned.

Although far advanced in years, without a matrimonial connexion, yet, constantly engaged in useful and interesting pursuits, she manifests not that peevishness and discontent, so frequently attendant on *old maids*; she realizes all that independence which is proper to humanity; and she knows how to set a just value on the blessings she enjoys.

From my treasury of facts, I produce a second instance, equally in point. I have seen letters, written by a lady, an inhabitant of St. Sebastian, (a Spanish emporium) that breathed the true spirit of commerce, and evinced the writer to possess all the integrity, punctuality and dispatch, which are such capital requisites in the mercantile career. This lady is at the head of a firm, of which herself and daughters make up the individuals—Her name is *Birmingham*. She is, I imagine, well known to the commercial part of the United States. She was left a widow in the infancy of her children, who were numerous; and she immediately adopted the most vigorous measures for their emolument. Being a woman of a magnanimous mind, she devoted her sons to the profession of arms; and they were expeditiously disposed of, in a way the best calculated to bring them acquainted with the art of war. Her daughters were educated for business; and, arriving at womanhood, they have long since established themselves into a capital trading-house, of which, as has been observed, their respectable mother is the head. She is, in the hours of business, invariably to be found in her compting-house; there she takes her morning repast; her daughters act as clerks, (and they are adepts in their office) regularly preparing the papers and letters, which pass in order under her inspection. She signs herself, in all accounts and letters, *Widow Birmingham*; and this is the address by which she is designated. I have conversed with one of our captains, who has often negociated with her the disposal of large and valuable cargoes. Her consignments, I am told, are to a great amount; and one of the principal merchants in the town of Boston asserts, that he receives from no house in Europe more satisfactory returns. Upright in their dealings, and unwearied in their application, these ladies possess a right to prosperity; and we trust that their circumstances are as easy, as their conduct is meritorious.

"Would you, good Mr. Gleaner,[80] station us in the compting-house?" No, my fair country-women, except circumstances unavoidably pointed the way. Again I say, I do but hold up to your view, the *capability* of your Sex; thus stimulating you to cultivate your talents, to endeavour to acquire general knowledge, and to aim at making yourselves so far acquainted with some particular branch of business, as that it may, if occasion requires, assist in establishing you above that kind of dependence, against which the freeborn mind so naturally revolts. Far be it from me, to wish to *unsex* you—I am desirous of preserving, by all means, those amiable traits that are considered as characteristic—I reverence the modesty and gentleness of your dispositions—I would not annihilate a single virtue; but I would assiduously augment the faithfulness and affection of your bosoms. An elegant panegyrist[81] of your Sex, hath assigned you the superiority in the feelings of the heart; and I cannot more emphatically conclude my subject, than in his beautifully pathetic language:

"The pleasures of women must arise from their virtues. It is by the cradle of their children, and in viewing the smiles of their daughters, or the sports of their sons, that mothers find their happiness. Where are the powerful emotions of nature? Where is the sentiment, at once sublime and pathetic, that carries every feeling to excess? Is it to be found in the frosty indifference, and the sour severity of some fathers? No—but in the warm and affectionate bosom of a *mother*. It is she, who, by an impulse as quick as involuntary, rushes into the flood to preserve a boy, whose imprudence had betrayed him into the waves—It is she, who, in the middle of a conflagration, throws herself across the flames to save a sleeping infant—It is she, who, with disheveled locks, pale and distracted, embraces with transport, the body of a dead child, pressing its cold lips to her's, as if she would reanimate, by her tears and her caresses, the insensible clay. These great expressions of nature—these heart-rending emotions, which fill us at once with wonder, compassion and terror, always have belonged, and always will belong, only to Women. They possess, in those moments, an inexpressible something, which carries them beyond themselves; and they seem to discover to us new souls, above the standard of humanity."

HANNAH ADAMS
(1755–1832)

A lifelong resident of Massachusetts, Hannah Adams was born in Medfield on October 2, 1755, the only child of Elizabeth Clark and Thomas Adams, Jr. Adams's mother died when she was ten; her father remarried shortly thereafter, and she eventually had four step-siblings. Though not a financially successful businessman, Thomas was an avid bibliophile. Adams attended school intermittently; largely, her education came through access to her father's considerable library and through boarders who served as her tutors. The study of theology was a lifelong endeavor, and all of her publications focused on religious themes.

Her first publication was An Alphabetical Compendium of the Various Sects (1784). The success of that book—published in several editions in Boston and London—led Adams to a recognition of writing as a possible career. A Summary History of New England (1799) was her second book. Though a regional history, the text reflects Adams's real interest: religious history. But it also captures her expansive knowledge of legal issues and political debates, issues in which she would soon find herself immersed. While preparing An Abridgement of the History of New England, for the Use of Young People (1805), Adams became embroiled in a controversy with two conservative Congregational ministers, Jedidiah Morse and Elijah Parish. Charges were made that Morse and Parish had plagiarized from Adams's 1799 history for their own textbook, which was published a year before Adams's Abridgement. The controversy reflected a sense of male privilege in the field of history writing, political

differences, and religious differences between the Congrega-
tionalists and Unitarians (Adams's alignment) at the turn of
the century. With copyright laws vaguely written at the time,
legal recourse was doubtful. But when Adams brought
charges against her competitors, it was determined that
Morse and Parish should refrain from publishing their book
and that they should compensate Adams for her financial
loss. It was a long and public battle, with Adams having to
bear considerable legal costs. Morse seemed incapable of ac-
cepting his defeat; in 1814 he published an Appeal to the
Public, *to which Adams responded with* A Narrative of
the Controversy between the Rev. Jedidiah Morse D.D., and
the Author *(1814). Public sympathy seemed to be in Adams's*
favor.

In spite of this complicated beginning, Adams continued
to support herself through writing and teaching. She pub-
lished several other religious histories and commentaries, in-
cluding A History of the Jews from the Destruction of
Jerusalem to the Nineteenth-Century *(1812) and* A Concise
Account of the London Society for Promoting Christianity
Amongst the Jews *(1816). Adams's memoir, written shortly*
before her death on December 15, 1832, in Brookline, was
published posthumously.

A SUMMARY HISTORY
OF NEW-ENGLAND

1799.

TO THE READER.

Many, especially in early life, may wish to peruse a sketch of American affairs, before they have time or ability to acquire more enlarged knowledge. Though the compiler of the ensuing work is impressed with the many difficulties attending it, yet she hopes the charge of arrogance will not be incurred, since her design is merely to encourage and gratify such a wish, by giving the outlines of the interesting history of New-England. In the prosecution of this work, she has with great care and assiduity, searched the ancient Histories of New-England. For more modern information, she has recurred to Belknap's[1] History of New-Hampshire, Trumball's[2] History of Connecticut, Ramsay's[3] History of the American Revolution, Gordon's[4] History of the American War, Minot's[5] History of the Insurrection, and his Continuation of Hutchinson; Williams' History of Vermont, Sullivan's[6] History of the District of Maine, and Morse's[7] Geography. In abridging the works of those excellent authors, she is sensible of her inability to do them justice, and has sometimes made use of their own words. The reader is always referred, for further information, to those ingenious performances; and the highest ambition of the compiler is, that her imperfect sketch may excite a more general attention to the large and valuable histories of the country. In giving a sketch of the American war, her ignorance of military terms has rendered it necessary to transcribe more literally from the words of the authors, than in the other parts of the history. But though a female cannot be supposed to be accurate in describing, and must shrink with horror in relating the calamities of war, yet she may be allowed to *feel a lively interest in the great cause, for which the sword was drawn in America*. The compiler is apprized of the numerous defects of the work, and sensible it will not bear the test of criticism. Her incapacity for executing it has been heightened by a long interval of ill health, which has precluded much of that studious application, which, in a work of this kind, is indispensably necessary. She hopes, therefore, that generous humanity will soften the asperity of censure, and that the public will view with candor the assiduous, though, perhaps, unsuccessful efforts of a female pen.

CHAPTER I.

Discovery of America by Columbus. Divisions in England after the reformation. Persecution under the reigns of Elizabeth and James. Mr. Robinson and his congregation remove to Holland. Part of his congregation embark for America. Their settlement at Plymouth, and the hardships they endured. They are joined by a small party. Treaty of alliance with the Indian princes. Death and character of Mr. Robinson. A number of the Leyden congregation arrive at Plymouth. The colony obtain a patent. Character, government and religion of the settlers.

The discovery of America is one of the most celebrated achievements in the annals of history. Christopher Columbus, the discoverer, was a native of the Republic of Genoa. He was born in 1447, and, at the age of fourteen, entered upon a seafaring life, in which profession he was eminently distinguished. After a long and fruitless application to several courts of Europe, his plan of exploring new regions obtained the approbation of Isabella, Queen of Castile. Through her patronage he set sail, 1492, with three small vessels, which contained one hundred and twenty seamen. The formidable difficulties, which attended his voyage to regions hitherto unexplored, were, at length, surmounted by his astonishing fortitude and perseverance. After discovering several of the West-India islands, he built a fort, and left a garrison of thirty-five men in Hispaniola, to maintain the Spanish pretensions in that country. He set out on his return to Spain in 1493, and arrived in March, with the joyful intelligence of a new world, excelling the kingdoms of Europe in gold and silver, and blest with a luxuriant soil.

The voyages of Columbus paved the way for other European adventurers, who were stimulated by ambition and avarice to make further discoveries; till, finally, the rich empires of Mexico and Peru were subdued by lawless invaders. The feeling heart bleeds in reviewing the history of South-America, and is filled with horror at the successful villainy of its intrepid conquerors.[8]

The history of North-America exhibits a very different scene. Many of the first settlers of this country were animated, by the desire of possessing religious liberty, to abandon their native land, where they enjoyed ease and affluence; and to struggle through a variety of hardships, in an uncultivated wilderness inhabited by savages.

The settlements of New-England, which are the particular object of the ensuing history, owe their rise to the religious disputes that attended the reformation in England.

When King Henry VIII. renounced the papal supremacy, he transferred to himself the spiritual power which had been exercised by the Bishops of Rome. He set up himself as supreme head of the English church, and commanded all his subjects to pay allegiance to him in his newly assumed character.

This claim was maintained by his son and successor Edward VI. in whose reign the reformation made great progress, and a service book was published by royal authority, as the standard of worship and discipline. His sister Mary, who succeeded him, restored the papal supremacy, and raised such a violent persecution against the reformers, that numbers of them fled into Germany and the Netherlands, where they departed from the uniformity established in England, and became divided in their sentiments and practice respecting religious worship.

At the accession of Elizabeth, they returned to their native country with sanguine hopes of reforming the church of England, according to the respective opinions which they had embraced in their exile. But they soon found that the Queen was fond of the establishment made in the reign of her brother Edward, and strongly prejudiced in favor of pomp and ceremony in religion. She asserted her supremacy in the most absolute terms, and erected an high commission court, with extensive jurisdiction in ecclesiastical affairs. In consequence of the rigorous measures which were pursued to enforce uniformity, a separation from the established church took place. Those who were desirous of a further reformation from the Romish superstitions, and of a more pure and perfect form of religion, were denominated Puritans.[9]

During the reign of Elizabeth, the Puritans, or Non-Conformists, as they were called, from their refusing to conform to the ceremonies of the church of England, were severely persecuted. Some were cast into prison, where a number perished; others were banished, and a few were put to death. Those Protestants who, during the bloody reign of Mary, suffered all the rigor of persecution, now encountered each other with the same cruel animosity. The manner of proceeding was indeed softened; banishment, fines and imprisonment were substituted for the unrelenting vengeance of the stake. But the principle was the same, and produced a similar effect. In both reigns the number of those who refused to conform to the established worship increased.[10]

The persecution of the Puritans was continued with great severity during the reign of James I. until, despairing of redress, they determined to seek an asylum in a foreign land, where they could enjoy the free exercise of their religious opinions.

At the period, when the persecution in this reign had arisen to its highest degree under Archbishop Bancroft, Mr. Robinson,[11] a dissenting clergyman in England, with part of his congregation, removed to Amsterdam, in Holland, and, with permission of the magistrates, settled at Leyden the subsequent year. There they formed a church, and enjoyed religious liberty. After twelve years residence in Holland, they meditated a removal to America, because they judged it unsafe to educate their children in a country, where the day devoted by Christians to religious rest, was treated, by too many of the inhabitants, as a day of levity and diversion. The other motives, which induced them to emigrate to America were, to preserve the morals of the youth; to prevent them from leaving their parents, and engaging in business unfriendly to religion, from want of employment at home; to avoid the inconvenience of incorporating with the Dutch; to lay a foundation for propagating the gospel in the remote parts of the world; and, by separating from all the existing establishments in Europe, to form the model of a pure church, free from the admixture of human additions; and a system of civil policy unfettered by the arbitrary institutions of the old world.[12]

As the new world appeared the proper theatre for the execution of their designs, after serious and repeated addresses to Heaven for direction, they resolved to cross the Atlantic. They applied to the Virginia company for permission to establish themselves in America within their limits, and petitioned King James to allow them liberty of conscience.

The Virginia company freely consented to give them a patent, with as ample privileges as were in their power to grant. But such was the prevailing bigotry of the age, that the solicitations of some of the most respectable characters in the kingdom could not prevail on the king and Bishops to allow the refugees liberty of conscience under the royal seal. His Majesty, however, at last gave private assurance, that they should live unmolested, provided they behaved peaceably, but persisted in refusing to tolerate them by public authority. The hope that the distance of their situation would secure them from the jurisdiction of ecclesiastical courts, induced them, notwithstanding, to put their plan in execution; and, after long attendance, much expence, and labor, they obtained a patent.[13]

Whilst preparations were making for the departure of the adventurers for New-England, a day was appointed for solemn prayer, on which occasion Mr. Robinson, in a discourse from the lst of Samuel, xxiii. 3-4, endeavoured to dispel their apprehensions, and inspire them with Christian fortitude. As it was not convenient for all to remove at first the majority, with their pastor, concluded to remain for the present in Leyden. Mr. John Brewster, assistant to Mr. Robinson, was chosen to perform ministerial offices to the first adventurers. Two ships were prepared, one of which was fitted out in Holland, the other hired in London. When the time of separation drew nigh, their pastor preached a farewell discourse from Ezra, viii. 21. A large concourse of friends from Leyden and Amsterdam accompanied the emigrants to the ship, which lay at Delft-Haven. The night was spent in fervent and affectionate prayers, and in that pathetic intercourse of soul, which the feeling heart can better conceive than describe. The affecting scene drew tears even from the eyes of strangers. When the period, in which the voyagers were about to depart, arrived, they all, with their beloved pastor, fell on their knees, and, with eyes, hands and hearts raised to heaven, fervently commended their adventuring brethren to the blessing of the Lord. Thus, after mutual embraces, accompanied with many tears, they bade a long, and to many of them a final adieu.[14]

On the 22d of July, they sailed for Southampton, where they met the ship from London, with the rest of the emigrants.

On the 5th of August, both vessels proceeded to sea, but returned twice into port, on account of defects in the one from Delft, which was dismissed.

An ardent desire of enjoying religious liberty finally overcame all difficulties. A company of an hundred and one persons betook themselves to the London ship, and sailed from Plymouth the 6th of September. After many delays, difficulties and dangers, they made Cape-Cod on the 9th of November, at break of day, and entered the harbor on the 10th.

It was their intention to settle at the mouth of the Hudson's River; but the Dutch, with the view of planting a colony in that place, bribed the pilot to conduct them to these northern coasts, and then, under various pretences, to discourage them from prosecuting their former plan.[15]

As they were not within the limits of their patent from the Virginia company, they saw the necessity of establishing a separate government for themselves. Accordingly, having offered their devout and ardent acknowledgments to God for their safe arrival, they formed themselves into a body politic, under the crown of England, whilst on board, for the purpose of establishing "just and equal laws, ordinances, acts, constitutions and offices." On the 10th of November the adventurers subscribed this contract,[16] thereby making it the basis of their government. They chose Mr. John Carver,[17] a gentleman of piety and approved abilities, to be their governor the first year; and the practice of a annual election continued unchanged during the existence of their government.[18]

The first object of the emigrants, after disembarkation, was to fix on a convenient place for settlement. In this attempt they were obliged to encounter numerous difficulties, and to suffer incredible hardships. Many of them were sick in consequence of the fatigues of a long voyage; their provisions were bad; the season was uncommonly cold; the Indians, though afterwards friendly, were now hostile, and the adventurers were unacquainted with the coast. These difficulties they surmounted and on the 31st of December were all safely landed at a place, which they called Plymouth, in grateful remembrance of the last town they left in their native country.[19]

The historians of New-England relate two remarkable events, which wonderfully facilitated the settlement of Plymouth and Massachusetts. The one was a war begun by the Tarrantenes, a nation who resided eastward of Penobscot.[20] These formidable people surprised the chief sachem at his head-quarters, and destroyed him with all his family; upon which all the other sachems, who were subordinate to him, contended among themselves for the sovereignty; and in these dissensions many of them, as well as their unhappy people, perished.[21] The other was a mortal and contagious distemper which prevailed among the Indians two or three years previously to the arrival of the English at Plymouth, and proved fatal to such numbers, that some tribes were almost extinct. The extent of this pestilence was between Penobscot in the east, and Narraganset[22] in the west. These two tribes escaped, while the intermediate people were wasted and destroyed.[23]

The prospects and situation of the Plymouth settlers were gloomy beyond expression. The whole company which landed consisted of but one hundred and one souls. They were three thousand miles from their native country, with a dreary winter in prospect, in an uncultivated wilderness, surrounded with hostile barbarians, and without any hope of human succour. Their only civilized neighbors were a French settlement at Port-Royal,[24] and an English settlement at Virginia; the nearest of which was five hundred miles distant, much too remote to afford a hope of relief in a time of danger or famine. To obtain a supply of provisions by cultivating the stubborn soil required an immensity of previous labor, and was, at best, a distant and uncertain dependence. They were denied the aid or favor of the court of England—without a patent—without a public promise of a peaceable enjoyment of their religious liberties. In this melancholy situation, forty-five of their number died before the opening of the next spring, of disorders occasioned by their tedious voyage, with insufficient accommodations, and their uncommon exertions and fatigues.[25]

The new colony supported these complicated hardships with heroic fortitude. To enjoy full liberty to worship God, according to the dictates of their consciences, was esteemed by them the greatest of blessings. And the religious fervor, which induced them to abandon their native country, fortified their minds, and enabled them to surmount every difficulty, which could prove their patience, or evince their firmness.

To their unspeakable satisfaction, their associates in England sent them a supply of necessaries, and a reinforcement of colonists the subsequent year.[26]

The prudent, friendly and upright conduct of the Plymouth settlers towards the natives secured their friendship and alliance. As early as March Massassoiet, one of the most powerful sagamores of the neighboring Indians, with sixty attendants, paid them a visit, and entered into a treaty of peace and amity. They reciprocally agreed, to avoid injuries, to punish offenders, to restore stolen goods, to afford mutual assistance in all justifiable wars, to promote peace among their neighbors, &c. Massassoiet,[27] and his successors, for fifty years inviolably observed this treaty. His example was followed by others. On the 13th of September nine sachems declared allegiance to King James. Massassoiet and many of his sub-sachems, who inhabited round the bays of Plymouth and Massachusetts, subscribed a writing, acknowledging subjection to the king of England.[28]

The Plymotheans early agreed, and purchased a right to the lands, which they cultivated from the Indian proprietors.[29]

For several years after their arrival the whole property of the colony was in common, from which every person was furnished with necessary articles. In the beginning of each year a certain quantity of land was selected for planting, and their proportion of labor was assigned to each one.[30]

At the close of the year 1624 the plantation consisted of one hundred and eighty persons. They had built a town consisting of thirty-two dwelling houses, erected a citadel for its defence and laid out farms for its support.[31]

The following year the new colony received the melancholy intelligence of the death of the Rev. Mr. Robinson, who died at Leyden in the month of March, in the fiftieth year of his age. The character of this excellent man, who was distinguished both by his natural abilities and an highly cultivated mind, was greatly dignified by the mild and amiable virtues of Christianity. He possessed a liberality of sentiment which was uncommon for the age, in which he lived.[32] He was revered and esteemed by the Dutch divines, venerated and beloved by his people; and the harmony which subsisted between them was perfect and uninterrupted. His death was greatly lamented by the people of Plymouth, who were flattering themselves with the pleasing hope of his speedy arrival in New-England. In the beginning of the year 1629, they chose Mr. Ralph Smith for their pastor. Previously to his ordination, Mr. Brewster, who had been ruling elder to the church at Leyden, performed all the ministerial offices among them, except administering the sacraments.

After the death of Mr. Robinson, another part of his congreation joined their brethren in America.

When the plantation amounted to about three hundred persons, they obtained a patent from the council of Plymouth. By this grant their lands were secured against all English claims.[33]

It is a distinguished trait in the settlements of New-England, that they were established from religious motives, by persons of piety and information.

The Plymotheans were a plain, industrious, conscientious and pious people. Though their piety was fervent, yet it was also rational, and disposed them to a strict observance of the moral and social duties. The leading characters among them were men of superior abilities and undaunted fortitude. The respectable names of Carver, Bradford,[34] Winslow,[35] Prince and others, are immortalized in the annals of New-England.

Respecting their civil principles, an ardent love of liberty, an unshaken attachment to the rights of men, with a desire to transmit them to their latest posterity, were the principles, which governed their conduct.[36]

They made the general laws of England their rule of government, and never established a distinct code for themselves. They added, however, such municipal laws as were, from time to time, found necessary to regulate new and emergent cases, which were unprovided for by the common and statute laws of England.

During the infancy of the colony, the whole body of male inhabitants were frequently assembled, to determine affairs both legislative and judicial. When their increase rendered this method impracticable, the governor and assistants were the supreme judiciary power, and sole in judging high offences. Crimes of less magnitude were cognizable before inferior courts and single magistrates; and in civil matters appeals could be made from inferior jurisdictions to the supreme. In the year 1639, they established a house of representatives, composed of deputies from the several towns.[37]

As the professed design of the settlement of the colony was the advancement of religion, their principal object was to form churches on what they supposed to be the gospel plan. Part of the Plymouth settlers had imbibed the opinions of the Brownists;[38] but the instructions of Mr. Robinson lessened their attachment to their former sentiments, and they embraced the congregational system, which was maintained by this pious and benevolent divine. They were of opinion, that no churches or church officers had any power to controul other churches or officers; and that all church members had equal rights and privileges. Their church officers were pastors, ruling elders and deacons. In doctrinal points they agreed with the articles of the church of England, which are strictly Calvinian.[39]

Agreeably to the prevailing prejudices of the age in which they lived, they asserted the necessity of uniformity in religious worship. Yet, however rigid the Plymotheans might have been at their first separation from the church of England, they never discovered so great a degree of intolerance as, at a subsequent period, was exhibited in the Massachusetts colony....[40]

CHAPTER XII.

Of the supposed witchcrafts in New-England. . . .

New-England from its first settlement never experienced such complicated difficulties as at the commencement of Sir William Phips'[41] government. The country was involved in the war with the eastern Indians,[42] which has been briefly mentioned in the preceding chapter. In the same period a new species of distress filled the minds of the people with gloom and horror, which in some respects appeared more replete with calamity, than even the devastations of war.

Previously to the tragic scene at Salem, about to be related, several persons, in different parts of New-England, had been executed for the supposed crime of witchcraft. Those, who think the whole to be an imposture, account for it by the prevailing credulity of the age; the strength of prejudice; the force of imagination, operating on minds not sufficiently enlightened by reason and philosophy, which all conspired to produce this fatal delusion.

In the year 1692, a daughter and niece of Mr. Parris,[43] minister of Salem, girls of ten or eleven years of age, and two other girls in the neighborhood, were seized with uncommon and unaccountable complaints. A consultation of physicians was called, one of whom was of opinion that they were bewitched. An Indian woman,[44] who was brought from New-Spain, and then resided with Mr. Parris, had recourse to some experiments, which she pretended were used in her own country, in order to discover the witch. The children, being informed of this circumstance, accused the Indian woman of pinching, pricking and tormenting them in various ways. She acknowledged that she had learnt how to discover a witch, but denied herself to be one. This first instance was the occasion of several private fasts at Mr. Parris' house, of several others, which were observed by the whole village, and of a general fast through the colony. The attention paid to the children, with the compassion expressed by their visitors, it is supposed, induced them, and allured others to continue their imposture.

Hence the number of complainants, who pretended to be seized with similar disorders, increased, and they accused certain persons of being the authors of their sufferings. From these small beginnings, the distemper spread through several parts of the province, till the prisons were scarcely capable of containing the number of the accused.[45]

The most effectual method to prevent an accusation was to become an accuser; hence the number of the afflicted continually augmented, and the number of the accused increased in the same proportion.

The accused in general persisted in asserting their innocence. Some, however, were induced to confess their guilt, being warmly importuned by their friends to embrace this expedient, as the only possible way to save their lives. The confession of witchcraft increased the number of the suspected; for associates were always pretended by the party confessing. These pretended associates were immediately sent for and examined. By these means, more than an hundred women, many of them of fair characters, and of the most respectable families in Salem, Beverly, Andover, Billerica and in other towns, were apprehended, examined and generally committed to prison.[46]

Though the number of prisoners had been augmenting, from February to June, yet none of them had as yet been brought to trial. Soon after the arrival of the charter, commissioners of *oyer* and *terminer* were appointed for this purpose. At the first trial, there was no colony, nor provincial law in force against witchcraft. The statute of James I. must therefore have been considered as in force, in the province, witchcraft not being an offence at common law. Before the adjournment of the general court, the old colony law, which makes witchcraft a capital offence, was received and adopted by the whole province.

In this distressing period, nineteen persons were executed, one prest to death, and eight more condemned; the whole number amounted to twenty-eight, of whom above a third part were members of some of the churches in New-England, and more than half sustained excellent characters. Among those who were executed, was Mr. Burroughs,[47] formerly minister at Salem, who left his people upon some difference in religious sentiments. All who suffered death asserted their innocence in the strongest terms. Yet this circumstance was insufficient to open the eyes of the people; and their fury augmented in proportion as the gloom of imagination increased.[48]

Instead of acting with that deliberate coolness and caution, which the importance of the affair demanded, and suspecting and cross examining the witnesses, by whose evidence the pretended witches were condemned; the authority made use of leading questions, which helped them to answers. Most of the examinations, though in the presence of one or more of the magistrates, were taken by Mr. Parris. The court allowed the witnesses to relate accidents, which had befallen them twenty or thirty years past, upon some difference with the accused.[49]

The affairs of Massachusetts were now in such a wretched situation, that no man was sure of his life and fortune for an hour. An universal consternation prevailed. Some charged themselves with witchcraft, in order to prevent accusation, and escape death; some abandoned the province, and others were preparing to follow their example.[50]

In this scene of perplexity and distress, those who were accused of witchcraft were generally of the lowest order in society. A number, however, of respectable women still remained in prison: at length the pretend sufferers had the audacity to accuse several persons of superior rank and character. The authority then began to be less credulous. The prisoners were liberated; those who had received sentence of death were reprieved, and afterwards pardoned. The whole country became by degrees sensible of their mistake; and the majority of the actors in this tragedy declared their repentance for their conduct.

Whilst a review of the conduct of the inhabitants of New-England in this distressing period induces us to accuse them of credulity and superstition, we ought to soften the asperity of our censure by remembering, that, supposing the whole to have been an imposture, they were led into this delusion by the opinion of the greatest civilians and divines in Europe. A similar opinion respecting witchcraft was at the same time prevalent in Great-Britain; the law, by which witches were condemned, was copied from the English statutes, and the practice of courts in New-England, was regulated by precedents established in the parent country. These statutes continued in force in England some time in the reign of George II. when it was enacted, "That no prosecution should in future be carried on against any person for conjuration, witchcraft, sorcery, or enchantment."[51]

No public notice was taken of the authors of this calamity; some of the supposed sufferers became profligate characters; others passed their days in obscurity and contempt. Mr. Parris, in whose house the pretended witchcraft began, felt the effects of popular resentment. Though he made a public and private penitent acknowledgment of his error, his congregation insisted upon his dismission, declaring that they never would sit under the ministry of a man, who had been the instrument of such complicated distress. . . . [52]

CHAPTER XIV.

Of the attention paid to the promotion of learning in New-England. New buildings erected for the university of Cambridge. Yale college founded, and settled at New-Haven. The Connecticut churches are convened in a synod at Saybrook. The Episcopalian mode of worship is introduced into Connecticut. Of the different religious denominations in Rhode-Island. . . .

It may afford some relief to the mind, to take leave for the present of the distressing Indian wars, and turn the attention to a more pleasing subject.

The inhabitants of New-England, from their first settlement, were eminently distinguished by their attention to the promotion of learning, and neither their frequent contests with the natives, nor the other difficulties which they were obliged to encounter, could divert their attention from this important object.

The university of Cambridge was, at this period, in a flourishing situation. The Hon. William Stoughton,[53] lieutenant-governor of the province, erected a building for the accommodation of the students, which filled the space between Harvard and Massachusetts halls. It was called Stoughton hall, after his name, and served to perpetuate his memory.

In 1745, the widow and daughters of Samuel Holden, one of the directors of the bank of England, were at the expence of erecting Holden chapel, which commemorates their pious liberality.[54]

"In no part of the world," says Dr. Morse, "is the education of all ranks of people more attended to than in Connecticut. From the first settlement of this colony, schools have been established by law in every town and parish in it, for instructing all the children in reading, writing and arithmetic. The law also directs that a grammar school should be kept in every county town."[55]

In 1654, Mr. Davenport[56] brought forward the institution of a college, to which the town of New-Haven made a donation of four or five hundred pounds sterling, by governor Hopkins,[57] the general assembly erected the colony school into a college, for teaching the learned languages and sciences. Mr. Davenport took the care of this school for several years; till the trustees, with the magistrates and ministers, established the Rev. Mr. Peck, according to act of the assembly. This gentleman met with such a variety of discouragements, that the college was broken up in 1664, and terminated in a public grammar school, which continues to this day.[58]

In the beginning of the present century, ten of the principal divines in Connecticut were nominated and agreed upon, by a general consent both of the ministers and the people, to stand as trustees, or undertakers, to found, erect and govern a college. The ministers, soon after their nomination, met in New-Haven, accepted the charge and established the institution. The subsequent year [1701], they obtained a charter from the general assembly of Connecticut, and a grant of money for the encouragement of this infant seminary.

Soon after the reception of the charter, the trustees met, and established certain rules for the regulation of the seminary; and from their own number chose the Rev. Mr. Pierson, minister of Killingworth, to the office of instructing and governing the collegiate school, under the title and character of Rector. They fixed on Saybrook, as the most convenient place, at present, for the college; and here the first commencement was holden, on the 13th of September, 1702.

Several attempts were made to effect the removal of Rector Pierson to Saybrook, but without success; the smallness of the collegiate finances, and the opposition of his own congregation to the measure, prevented its execution. Although, therefore, the commencement was holden at Saybrook, the students, during Rector Pierson's administration, resided at Killingworth.

The college continued at Saybrook about seven years, without any remarkable alteration or occurrence. In 1716, the people subscribed large sums for the erection of a college edifice, where it would best accommodate them. The trustees, soon after, voted to remove the college from Saybrook, to New-Haven; and accordingly, for the first time, held commencement there on the 11th of September, 1717.[59]

The trustees, having received a number of valuable donations, were now enabled to finish a large and commodious edifice, which they had raised in October the preceding year; and which, within a year after, was fit for the reception of the students. At a splendid commencement, the 12th of September, 1713, in the presence of governor Saltonstall, and a large and respectable assembly, the trustees, in commemoration of governor Yale's[60] great generosity (who had made large presents of books, and other valuable articles to the seminary) called the edifice after his name, Yale college.[61]

For a few years the infant college contained, on an average, but twelve or fifteen scholars. At the period of its removal to New-Haven, the number had increased to about thirty. In the year 1727, it contained fifty or sixty; and in the year 1740, about ninety students.[62]

In 1745, an act was passed by the legislature of Connecticut, "for the more full and complete establishment of Yale college; and for enlarging its powers and privileges." By this act, the rector and trustees were incorporated, by the name of "The President and Fellows of Yale College, in New-Haven;" and they still retain the appellation.[63]

In 1750, by means of a lottery, and a liberal grant from the legislature, the corporation was enabled to erect another edifice, for the accommodation of the students. In grateful acknowledgment of the generosity of the government, the president and fellows, at the commencement in 1752, ordered that the new college be named Connecticut hall.[64]

The inhabitants of Connecticut paid great attention to the religious, as well as to the literary state of their colony. In the year 1708, a synod was convened at Saybrook, composed of the ministers and delegates from the churches of the four counties of Hartford, New-Haven, Fairfield and New-London, together with two or more messengers from a convention of the churches of each of the four counties. This synod drew up the form of church government and discipline, which is known by the name of the Saybrook platform; this was presented to the general court, passed into a law of the colony, and became the established constitution of the churches of Connecticut.[65]

Dr. Trumbull observes, "That though the council were unanimous in passing the platform of discipline, yet they were not all of one opinion. Some were for high consociational government, and in their sentiments, nearly Presbyterian; others were much more moderate, and rather verging on Independency; but they exercised great Christian condescension towards each other."[66]

During the term of about seventy years from the settlement of Connecticut, the congregational was the only mode of worship in the colony. But the society for propagating the gospel in foreign parts, in 1704, fixed the Rev. Mr. Muirson as a missionary at Rye. Some of the people at Stratford, who had been educated in the Episcopalian worship, made an earnest application to Mr. Muirson to visit at Stratford, and preach and baptize among them. About the year 1706, upon their invitation, he came to Stratford, accompanied with Colonel Heathcote,[67] a gentleman zealously engaged in promoting the Episcopal church. The ministers and people in that, and the adjacent towns, were alarmed at his arrival, and used their exertions to prevent their neighbors and families from attending his preaching. However, the novelty of the affair, and other circumstances, brought together a considerable assembly; and Mr. Muirson baptized five and twenty persons, principally adults. This was the first step towards introducing the church worship into this colony. In April, 1707, he made another visit to Stratford. He also preached at this time in Fairfield, and in both towns baptized a number of children and adult persons.

Both the magistrates and clergymen opposed the introduction of Episcopacy, and advised the people not to attend the preaching of the church missionaries. The oppostion only increased the zeal of the churchmen. Mr. Muirson, after this, made several journies to Connecticut, till the year 1722, when Mr. Pigot was appointed missionary at Stratford. The Episcopalians at first in that place consisted of about fifteen families, among whom were a few husbandmen, but much the greater number were tradesmen, who had been born in England, and came and settled in that town. Some of their neighbors joined them, so that Mr. Pigot had twenty communicants, and about an hundred and fifty hearers. In 1723, Christ Church, in Stratford, was founded, and the Rev. Mr. Johnson,[68] afterwards Dr. Johnson, was appointed to succeed Mr. Pigot.[69]

Rhode-Island, from its first settlement, was distinguished by liberality of sentiment; and by the variety of religious denominations, which found an asylum in that colony.

In 1671, a number of the members of Mr. Clark's[70] church, who had embraced the opinions of the seventh day Baptists, separated from their brethren, and erected a church under the pastoral care of Mr. William Hifcex.[71]

In 1700, the Friends, or Quakers, meeting-house was built at Newport. Their yearly meeting, till governor Coddington's[72] death, was held in his house, and he died a member of that body, in 1688.

In 1720, there was a congregational church gathered at Newport, and the Rev. Nathaniel Clap was ordained its pastor. Out of this church another was formed in 1728. The worship of God, according to the rites of the church of England, was instituted here in 1706, by the society for propagating the gospel in foreign parts. And in 1738, there were seven worshipping assemblies in this town, and a large society of Quakers at Portsmouth, at the other end of the island. . . . [73]

MERCY OTIS WARREN
(1728–1814)

Certainly the grande dame of the American Revolutionary cause, Mercy Otis was born in West Barnstable, Massachusetts, on September 25, 1728. She was the third of Mary Allyne and James Otis's thirteen children. James was a successful merchant and farmer, and he was a leading figure in opposing the governing policies of the British leaders of Massachusetts, such as Thomas Hutchinson, Esq.,[1] in the pre-Revolutionary years. Mercy's brother, James, pushed opposition to British rule even further, becoming one of the most outspoken opponents in the years leading into the Revolutionary era. On November 14, 1754, Mercy Otis married James Warren, who, like her father, was a notable merchant, farmer, and Whig. Thus Mercy Otis Warren was raised as a child and lived as an adult in the midst of revolutionary ideals.

A poet, dramatist, prolific letter writer, and historian, Warren helped shape the literary record of the American Revolution. In satiric dramas such as The Group (1775), Warren attacked British tyranny. Unlike Murray, though, Warren never had her dramas actually performed on the stage; they were published in both newspapers and pamphlets. The Group concludes with a woman's monologue, indicating Warren's interest in women speaking out on behalf of the American cause. In 1790, much of her later work was collected in Poems, Dramatic and Miscellaneous. But it was the publication in 1805 of Warren's three-volume History of the Rise, Progress and Termination of the American Revolution that marked her most sustained literary effort.

Influenced by her family members and by friends such as John Adams,[2] *as well as by her acquaintance with the British feminist and historian Catharine Macaulay, the* History *is an articulate rendering of her Republican, anti-Federalist political views. Unlike histories that look to the ancient past, accounts of the American Revolution in this period were of recent and lived history. Warren's text captures the urgency and commitment of one who was involved in the machinations of war, of developing a new nation, and of the fears inherent in the fragility of a project of such magnitude. Hers is not simply a hagiography of Revolutionary leaders, but rather a political assessment of the Revolution and of the corruption that can emerge in moments of national crisis.*

Political differences that led to criticism of her work by leaders such as John Adams, who felt his contributions to the war and the new nation were not sufficiently acknowledged by Warren, led her to assert shortly before she died, "History is not the Province of Ladies." But Warren's History . . . *of* the American Revolution *is today recognized as one of the major contributions to historical writings of the eighteenth century, and her body of work as a whole illustrates the importance of women's historical narratives. Having lived most of her life in Plymouth, Massachusetts, Warren died there on October 19, 1814.*

HISTORY OF THE RISE, PROGRESS AND TERMINATION OF THE AMERICAN REVOLUTION

1805.

CHAPTER I.

Introductory Observations

History, the deposite of crimes, and the record of everything disgraceful or honorary to mankind, requires a just knowledge of character, to investigate the sources of action; a clear comprehension, to review the combination of causes; and precision of language, to detail the events that have produced the most remarkable revolutions.

To analyze the secret springs that have effected the progressive changes in society; to trace the origin of the various modes of government, the consequent improvements in science, in morality or the national tincture that marks the manners of the people under despotic or more liberal forms, is a bold and adventurous work.

The study of the human character opens at once a beautiful and a deformed picture of the soul. We there find a noble principle implanted in the nature of man, that pants for distinction. This principle operates in every bosom, and when kept under the control of reason, and the influence of humanity, it produces the most benevolent effects. But when the checks of conscience are thrown aside, or the moral sense weakened by the sudden acquisition of wealth or power, humanity is obscured, and if a favorable coincidence of circumstances permits, this love of distinction often exhibits the most mortifying instances of profligacy, tyranny, and the wanton exercise of arbitrary sway. Thus when we look over the theatre of human action, scrutinize the windings of the heart, and survey the transactions of man from the earliest to the present period, it must be acknowledged that ambition and avarice are the leading springs which generally actuate the restless mind. From these primary sources of corruption have arisen all the rapine and confusion, the depredation and ruin, that have spread distress over the face of the earth from the days of Nimrod[3] to Cesar, and from Cesar to an arbitrary prince of the house of Brunswick.[4]

The indulgence of these turbulent passions has depopulated cities, laid waste the finest territories, and turned the beauty and harmony of the lower created into an aceldama.[5] Yet candor must bear honorable testimony to many signal instances of disinterested merit among the children of men; thus it is not possible to pronounce decidedly on the character of the politician or the statesman till the winding up of the drama. To evince the truth of this remark, it is needless to adduce the innumerable instances of deception both in ancient and modern story. It is enough to observe, that the specious Augustus[6] established himself in empire by the appearance of justice, clemency, and moderation, while the savage Nero[7] shamelessly weltered in the blood of the citizens; but the sole object of each was to become the sovereign of life and property, and to govern the Roman world with a despotic hand.

Time may unlock the cabinets of princes, unfold the secret negociations of statesmen, and hand down the immoral characters of dignified worth, or the blackened traits of finished villainy in exaggerated colours. But truth is most likely to be exhibited by the general sense of contemporaries, when the feelings of the heart can be expressed without suffering itself to be disguised by the prejudices of the man. Yet it is not easy to convey to posterity a just idea of the embarrassed situation of the western world, previous to the rupture with Britain; the dismemberment of the empire, and the loss of the most industrious, flourishing, and perhaps virtuous colonies, ever planted by the hand of man.

The progress of the American Revolution has been so rapid, and such the alteration of manners, the blending of characters, and the new train of ideas that almost universally prevail, that the principles which animated to the noblest exertions have been nearly annihilated. Many who first stepped forth in vindication of the rights of human nature are forgotten, and the causes which involved the thirteen colonies in confusion and blood are scarcely known, amidst the rage of accumulation and the taste for expensive pleasures that have since prevailed; a taste that has abolished that mediocrity which once satisfied, and that contentment which long smiled in every countenance. Luxury, the companion of young acquired wealth, is usually the consequence of opposition to, or close connexion with, opulent commercial states. Thus the hurry of spirits, that ever attends the eager pursuit of fortune and a passion for splendid enjoyment, leads to forgetfulness; and thus the inhabitants of America cease to look back with due gratitude and respect on the fortitude and virtue of their ancestors, who through difficulties almost insurmountable, planted them in a happy soil. But the historian and the philosopher will ever venerate the memory of those pious and independent gentlemen, who, after suffering innumerable impositions, restrictions, and penalties, less for political than theological opinions, left England, not as adventurers for wealth or fame, but for the quiet enjoyment of religion and liberty. . . .

CHAPTER IV.

The Character of Mr. Hutchinson, Etc. (1769)

It is ever painful to a candid mind to exhibit the deformed features of its own species; yet truth requires a just portrait of the public delinquent, though he may possess such a share of private virtue as would lead us to esteem the man in his domestic character while we detest his political, and execrate his public transactions.

The barriers of the British constitution broken over, and the ministry encouraged by their sovereign, to pursue the iniquitous system against the colonies to the most alarming extremities, they probably judged it a prudent expedient, in order to curb the refractory spirit of the Massachusetts, perhaps bolder in sentiment and earlier in opposition than some of the other colonies, to appoint a man to preside over them who had renounced the *quondam* ideas of public virtue, and sacrificed all principle of that nature on the altar of ambition.

Soon after the recall of Mr. Bernard,[8] Thomas Hutchinson,

Esq., a native of Boston, was appointed to the government of Massachusetts. All who yet remember his pernicious administration and the fatal consequences that ensued, agree, that few ages have produced a more fit instrument for the purposes of a corrupt court. He was dark, intriguing, insinuating, haughty, and ambitious, while the extreme of avarice marked each feature of his character. His abilities were little elevated above the line of mediocrity; yet by dint of industry, exact temperance, and indefatigable labor, he became master of the accomplishments necessary to acquire popular fame. Though bred a merchant, he had looked into the origin and principles of the British constitution, and made himself acquainted with the several forms of government established in the colonies; he had acquired some knowledge of the *common law* of England, diligently studied the intricacies of *Machiavellian* policy,[9] and never failed to recommend the Italian master as a model to his adherents. Raised and distinguished by every honor the people could bestow, he supported for several years the reputation of integrity, and generally decided with equity in his judicial capacity; and by the appearance of a tenacious regard to the religious institutions of his country, he courted the public *eclat* with the most profound dissimulation, while he engaged the affections of the lower classes by an amiable civility and condescension, without departing from a certain gravity of deportment mistaken by the vulgar for *sanctity*.

The inhabitants of Massachusetts were the lineal descendants of the *puritans*, who had struggled in England for liberty as early as the reign of Edward the sixth;[10] and though obscured in the subsequent bloody persecutions, even Mr. Hume[11] has acknowledged that to them England is indebted for the liberty she enjoys. Attached to the religious forms of their ancestors, equally disgusted with the hierarchy of the church of England, and prejudiced by the severities their fathers had experienced before their emigration, they had, both by education and principle, been always led to consider the religious as well as the political characters of those they deputed to the highest trust. Thus a profession of their own religious mode of worship, and sometimes a tincture of superstition, was with many a higher recommendation than brilliant talents. This accounts in some measure for the unlimited confidence long placed in the specious accomplishments of Mr. Hutchinson, whose character was not thoroughly investigated until some time after governor Bernard left the province.

But it was known at St. James's, that in proportion as Mr. Hutchinson gained the confidence of the administration, he lost the esteem of the best of his countrymen; for this reason, his advancement to the chair of government was for a time postponed or concealed, lest the people should consider themselves insulted by such an appointment, and become too suddenly irritated. Appearances had for several years been strong against him, though it was not then fully known that he had seized the opportunity to undermine the happiness of the people, while he had their fullest confidence, and to barter the liberties of his country by the most shameless duplicity. This was soon after displayed beyond all contradiction, by the recovery of sundry letters to administration under his signature.

Mr. Hutchinson was one of the first in America who felt the full weight of popular resentment. His furniture was destroyed, and his house levelled to the ground, in the tumults occasioned by the news of the stamp-act. Ample compensation was indeed afterwards made him for the loss of property, but the strong prejudices against his political character were never eradicated.

All pretences to moderation on the part of the British government now laid aside, the full appointment of Mr. Hutchinson to the government of the Massachusetts was publickly announced at the close of the year one thousand seven hundred and sixty-nine. On his promotion the new governor uniformly observed a more high-handed and haughty tone than his predecessor. He immediately, by an explicit declaration, avowed his independence on the people, and informed the legislature that his majesty had made ample provision for his support without their aid or suffrages. The vigilant guardians of the rights of the people directly called upon him to relinquish the unconstitutional stipend, and to accept the free grants of the general assembly for his subsistence, as usually practised. He replied that an acceptance of this offer would be a breach of his instructions from the king. This was his constant apology for every arbitrary step.

Secure of the favor of his sovereign, and now regardless of the popularity he had formerly courted with such avidity, he decidedly rejected the idea of responsibility to, or dependence on, the people. With equal inflexibility he disregarded all arguments used for the removal of the troops from the capital, and permission to the council and house of representatives to return to the usual seat of government. He silently heard their solicitations for this purpose, and as if with a design to pour contempt on their supplications and complaints, he within a few days after withdrew a garrison, in the pay of the province, from a strong fortress in the harbour of Boston; placed two regiments of the king's troops in their stead, and delivered the keys of the castle to colonel Dalrymple,[12] who then commanded the king's troops through the province.

These steps, which seemed to bid defiance to complaint, created new fears in the minds of the people. It required the utmost vigilance to quiet the murmurs and prevent the fatal consequences apprehended from the ebullitions of popular resentment. But cool, deliberate and persevering, the two houses continued to resolve, remonstrate, and protest, against the infractions on their charter, and every dangerous innovation on their rights and privileges. Indeed the intrepid and spirited conduct of those, who stood forth undaunted at this early crisis of hazard, will dignify their names so long as the public records shall remain to witness their patriotic firmness.

Many circumstances rendered it evident that the ministerial party wished a spirit of opposition to the designs of the court might break out into violence, even at the expense of blood. This they thought would in some degree have sanctioned a measure suggested by one of the faction in America devoted to the arbitrary system, "That some method must be devised, to take off the original *incendiaries* whose writings instilled the poison of sedition through the vehicle of the Boston Gazette."[13]

Had this advice been followed, and a few gentlemen of integrity and ability, who had spirit sufficient to make an effort in favor of their country in each colony, have been seized at the same moment, and immolated early in the contest on the bloody altar of power, perhaps Great Britain might have held the continent in subjection a few years longer.

That they had measures of this nature in contemplation there is not a doubt. Several instances of a less atrocious nature confirmed this opinion, and the turpitude of design which at this period actuated the court party was clearly evinced by the attempted assassination of the celebrated Mr. Otis,[14] justly deemed the first martyr to American freedom; and truth will enroll his name among the most distinguished patriots who have expired on the "blood-stained theatre of human action."

This gentleman, whose birth and education was equal to any in the province, possessed an easy fortune, independent principles, a comprehensive genius, strong mind, retentive memory, and great penetration. To these endowments may be added that extensive professional knowledge, which at once forms the character of the complete civilian and the able statesman.

In his public speeches, the sire of eloquence, the acumen of argument, and the lively sallies of wit, at once warmed the bosom of the stoic and commanded the admiration of his enemies. To his probity and generosity in the public walks were added the charms of affability and improving converse in private life. His humanity was conspicuous, his sincerity acknowledged, his integrity unimpeached, his honor unblemished, and his patriotism marked with the disinterestedness of the Spartan. Yet he was susceptible of quick feelings and warm passions, which in the ebullitions of zeal for the interest of his country sometimes betrayed him into unguarded epithets that gave his foes an advantage, without benefit to the cause that lay nearest his heart.

He had been affronted by the partizans of the crown, vilified in the public papers, and treated (after his resignation of office)[15] in a manner too gross for a man of his spirit to pass over with impunity. Fearless of consequences, he had always given the world his opinions both in his writings and his conversation and had recently published some severe strictures on the conduct of the commissioners of the customs and others of the ministerial party, and bidding defiance to resentment, he supported his allegations by the signature of his name.

A few days after this publication appeared, Mr. Otis with only one gentleman in company was suddenly assaulted in a public room, by a band of ruffians armed with swords and bludgeons.

They were headed by John Robinson, one of the commissioners of the customs. The lights were immediately extinguished, and Mr. Otis covered with wounds was left for dead, while the assassins made their way through the crowd which began to assemble; and before their crime was discovered, fortunately for themselves, they escaped soon enough to take refuge on board one of the king's ships which then lay in the harbor.

In a state of nature, the savage may throw his poisoned arrow at the man, whose soul exhibits a transcript of benevolence that upbraids his own ferocity, and may boast his blood-thirsty deed among the hordes of the forest without disgrace; but in a high stage of civilization, where humanity is cherished, and politeness is become a science, for the dark assassin then to level his blow at superior merit, and screen himself in the arms of power, reflects an odium on the government that permits it, and puts human nature to the blush.

The party had a complete triumph in this guilty deed; for though the wounds did not prove mortal, the consequences were tenfold worse than death. The future usefulness of this distinguished *friend* of his country was destroyed, reason was shaken from its throne, genius obscured, and the great man in ruins lived several years for his friends to weep over, and his country to lament the deprivation of talents admirably adapted to promote the highest interests of society. . . .

CHAPTER IX.

Declaration of Independence, etc. (1776)

The commissioners who had been announced as the messengers of peace, were now hourly expected; but the dubious aspect of their mission, and the equivocal character in which they were about to appear, was far from lulling to inattention the guardians of the cause of America. Their errand was ostensibly, to restore peace to the colonies; but many circumstances combined to evince that the design was in reality, to furnish new pretexts for the prosecution of the war, with redoubled vigor. Thus was the continental congress fully convinced of the impropriety of longer holding themselves in suspense, but delusory hopes, or the uncertain termination of their expectations or their fears. They were sensible the step they were about to take, would either set their country on the pinnacle of human glory, or plunge it in the abject state into which turbulent and conquered colonies have been generally reduced. Yet they wisely judged, that this was a proper period to break the shackles, and renounce all political union with the parent state, by a free and bold declaration of the independence of the American States. This measure had been contemplated by some gentlemen in the several colonies, some months before it took place. They had communicated their sentiments to the individual members of congress, but that body had been apprehensive, that the people at large were not prepared to unite in a step so replete with important consequences. But the moment of decision had now arrived, when both the congress and the inhabitants of the colonies advanced too far to recede.

Richard Henry Lee, Esq.,[16] a delegate from the state of Virginia, a gentleman of distinguished abilities, uniform patriotism, and unshaken firmness and integrity, was the first who dared explicitly to propose, that this decided measure, on which hung such mighty consequences, should no longer be delayed. This public and unequivocal proposal, from a man of his virtue and shining qualities, appeared to spread a kind of sudden dismay. A silent astonishment for a few minutes seemed to pervade the whole assembly: this was soon succeeded by a long debate, and a considerable division of sentiment on the important question.

After the short silence just observed, the measure proposed by Mr. Lee was advocated with peculiar zeal by John Adams, Esq., of the Massachusetts Bay. He rose with a face of intrepidity and the voice of energy, and invoked the god of eloquence, to enable him to do justice to the cause of his country, and to enforce this important step in such a manner, as might silence all opposition, and convince every one of the necessity of an immediate declaration of independence of the United States of America.

Mr. John Dickinson,[17] of Pennsylvania, took the lead in opposition to the boldness and danger of this decided measure. He had drawn the petition to the king forwarded by Mr. Penn,[18] and though no man was more strenuous in support of the rights of the colonies, he had always been averse to a separation from Britain, and shuddered at the idea of an avowed revolt of the American colonies. He arose on this occasion with no less solemnity than Mr. Adams had recently done, and with equal pathos of expression, and more brilliance of epithet, he invoked the Great Governor of the Universe, to animate him with powers of language sufficient to exhibit a view of the dread consequences to both countries, that such a hasty dismemberment of the empire might produce. He descanted largely on the happy effects that might probably ensue from more patient and conciliatory dispositions, and urged at least a temporary suspension of a step, that could never be revoked. He declared that it was his opinion, that even policy forbade the precipitation of this measure, and that humanity more strongly dictated, that they ought to wait longer the success of petitions and negociations, before they formally renounced their allegiance to the king of Great Britain, broke off all connexion with England, plunged alone into an unequal way, and rushed without allies into the unforeseen and inevitable dangers that attended it.

The consequences of such a solemn act of separation were indeed of serious and extensive magnitude. The energy of brilliant talents and great strength of argument, were displayed by both parties on this weighty occasion. The reasons urging the necessity of decision, and the indubitable danger of delay, were clear and cogent; the objections, plausible, humane, and important: but after a fair discussion of the question, an accurate statement of the reasons for adopting the measure, and a candid scrutiny of the objections against it, grounded either on policy or humanity, a large majority of the members of congress appeared in favor of an immediate renunciation of allegiance to the crown, or any future subjugation to the king of Great Britain.

A declaration of the independence of America, and the sovereignty of the United States, was drawn by the ingenious and philosophic pen of Thomas Jefferson, Esq., a delegate from the state of Virginia. The delegates from twelve of the American States, agreed almost unanimously to this declaration; the language, the principles, and the spirit of which were equally honorable to themselves and their country. It was signed by John Hancock, then president of congress, on the fourth of July, one thousand seven hundred and seventy-six.

The allegiance of thirteen states at once withdrawn by a solemn declaration, from a government towards which they had looked with the highest veneration; whose authority they had acknowledged, whose laws they had obeyed, whose protection they had claimed for more than a century and a half—was a consideration of solemnity, a bold resolution, an experiment of hazard: especially when the infancy of the colonies as a nation, without wealth, resources, or allies, was contrasted with the strength, riches, and power of Great Britain. The timid trembled at the ideas of final separation; the disciples of passive obedience were shocked by a reflection of a breach of faith to their ancient sovereign; and the enemies to the general freedom of mankind, were incensed to madness, or involved in despair. But these classes bore a small proportion to those who resented the rejection of their petitions, and coolly surveyed the impending dangers, that threatened themselves and their children, which rendered it clear to their apprehension, that this step was necessary to their political salvation. They considered themselves no longer bound by any moral tie, to render fealty to a sovereign thus disposed to encroach on their civil freedom, which they could now secure only by a social compact among themselves, and which they determined to maintain, or perish in the attempt.

By the declaration of independence, dreaded by the foes, and for a time, doubtfully viewed by many of the friends of America, everything stood on a new and more respectable footing, both with regard to the operations of war, or negociations with foreign powers. Americans could now no more be considered as rebels, in their proposals for treaties of peace and conciliation with Britain; they were a distinct people, who claimed the rights, the usages, the faith, and the respect of nations, uncontrolled by any foreign power. The colonies thus irretrievably lost to Great Britain, a new face appeared on all affairs, both at home and abroad.

America had been little known among the kingdoms of Europe; she was considered only as an appendage to the power of Britain: the principles of her sons were in some respects dissimilar, and their manners not yet wrought up to the standard of refinement reigning in ancient courts: her statesmen in general were acquainted with the intrigues necessary for negociation, and the *finesse* usually hackneyed in and about the cabinets of princes. She now appeared in their eyes, a new theatre, pregnant with events that might be interesting to the civil and political institutions of nations, that had never before paid much attention to the growth, population, and importance of an immense territory beyond the Atlantic.

The United States had their ambassadors to create, or to transplant from the bar of the compting-house. Their generals were many of them the yeomanry or the tradesmen of the country; their subordinate officers had been of equal rank and fortune, and the army to be governed was composed of many of the old associates of the principal officers, and were equally tenacious of personal liberty. The *regalia* of power, orders of nobility, and the splendor of courts, had been by them viewed only at a distance. The discipline of armies was entirely new; the difficulty of connecting many distinct states to act as it were by one will, the expenses of government in new exigencies, and the waste of war had not yet been accurately calculated by their politicians and statesmen. But their senators, their representatives, and their magistrates, were generally sagacious and vigilant, upright and firm; their officers were brave, their troops in spirits, and with a full confidence in their commander in chief: hope was exhilarated by the retreat from Boston, and the repeated successes of their arms at the southward; while new dignity was added to office, and stronger motives for illustrious action, by the rank America had now taken among the nations. Thus, by the declaration of independence they had new ground to tread; the scene of action was changed, genius was called forth from every quarter of the continent, and the public expectation enhanced by the general favorable appearance in all their military operations. . . .

CHAPTER XIII.

. . . Expedition into the Indian Territories (1778)

. . . A counterpart to the conduct of the more refined, though little more humanized commanders of the predatory parties in the middle and northern colonies, was exhibited in the southern borders, by their savage allies of the wilderness.

This was dreadfully realized by the inhabitants of Wyoming, a young settlement on the eastern branch of the Susquehanna. The population of this once happy spot had been remarkably rapid, and when the fury of civil discord first appeared among them, it contained eight townships of five miles square each. They were situated in a mild climate, in a country fertile, and beautifully displaying a picturesque appearance of that kind of primitive simplicity, only enjoyed before the mind of man is contaminated by ambition or gold. But party rage had spread its baneful influence to the remotest corners of America, and political animosities had at this period poisoned the peace, even of the most distant villages, where simplicity, friendship, and industry had reigned, until the fell fiend which prompts to civil war, made its frightful appearance, attended by all the horrors imagination can paint.

The inhabitants of this favored spot, perhaps more zealous than discreet, had so far participated the feelings of all America, as voluntarily to raise and send forward one thousand men, to join the continental army. This step disclosed the embers of opposition that had hitherto lain concealed, in the bosoms of a number of long disaffected to the American, and warmly attached to the royal cause. A rancorous spirit immediately burst from the latent spark, which divided families, and separated the tenderest connexions. Animosities soon arose to such a height, that some of the most active members of this flourishing and happy society, abandoned their plantations, forsook their friends, and joined and instigated the neighbouring savages to molest the settlements, and assisted in the perpetration of the most unheard of cruelties.

Several outrages had been committed by small parties, and many threatening appearances had so far alarmed the inhabitants, that most of them had repaired to some fortresses early erected for their defence against the native savages. Yet there was no apprehension of a general massacre and extermination, till the beginning of July, one thousand seven hundred and seventy-eight, when an army of near two thousand men, made its appearance on the Susquehanna, and landed on their borders. This body was composed of the motley materials of Indians, tories, half-blooded Englishmen, and British renegades, headed by one Butler,[19] who had nothing human about him, except a rough, external figure of a man.

All the inhabitants of those weak, defenceless settlements capable of bearing arms, embodied, and put themselves under the direction of a person of the same name, a near relation of the commander of the savages. This man, either through fear, weakness, or misplaced confidence, listened to the offers of treaty from his more artful kinsman, and suffered himself with four hundred men, to be drawn from fort Kingston by a delusive flag, that alternately advanced and retired, as if apprehensive of danger. Caught by the snare, he was completely surrounded before he had any suspicion of deception, and his whole party cut off, notwithstanding they fought with a spirit becoming their desperate situation.

The victor immediately pushed on, invested the garrison thus indiscreetly left, and demanded a surrender. The demand was accompanied by the horrid display of a great number of scalps, just torn from the heads, and yet warm with the blood, of their nearest friends and relations. In this situation of wretchedness, embittered by impotent resentment, colonel Donnison,[20] on whom the command had devolved, finding resistance impracticable, went out himself with a flag, to ask the terms of surrender. To this humiliating question, the infamous Butler replied, with all the *sang-froid* of the savage, and the laconism of an ancient Greek, *"the hatchet."*

The unfortunate Donnison returned in despair; yet he bravely defended the fort until most of his men had fallen by his side, when the barbarians without, shut up this and a neighbouring garrison, where a number of women and children had repaired for safety, and setting fire to both, they enjoyed the infernal pleasure of seeing them perish promiscuously, in the flames lighted by their bloody hands.[21]

After this catastrophe, the most shocking devastation was spread through the townships. Whilst some were employed in burning the houses, setting fire to the corn-fields, and rooting out every trait of improvement, others were cruelly and wantonly imbruing their hands in the blood of their parents, their brothers, and every near connexion, who had unfortunately held different political opinions. But a particular detail of the transactions of savages, stimulated by the agents of more refined and polished nations, with passions whetted by revenge, without principle to check its operation, is too painful to the writer, and too disgraceful to human nature to dwell on. Nor is it less painful to the impartial historian, to relate the barbarous, though by them deemed necessary, vengeance, soon after taken by the Americans.

The conflagration spread over the beautiful country of the Illinois, by a colonel Clark[22] of Virginia, equally awakes compassion, and was a counterbalance for the sufferings of the miserable Wyomings. It is true the Illinois, and other distant warlike tribes, were at the instigation of governor Hamilton,[23] the British commander at Detroit, generally assisting in the measures perpetrated under Butler and Brandt,[24] nearer the frontiers; and perhaps the law of retaliation may, in some measure, justify the depredations of Clark.

This intrepid ranger left Virginia in the course of this summer, with a few adventurers hardy as himself, and traversed a country of eleven or twelve hundred miles in extent; and surmounting all the hardships that imagination can paint, through a wilderness inhabited only by strolling hunters from among the savages, and the wild beasts that prowled before them, through hunger, fatigue, and sufferings innumerable, they reached the upper Mississippi. The Indian inhabitants, who had there long enjoyed a happy climate, and the fruits of a fertile soil, under a high degree of cultivation, fearless of danger from their distance from civilized neighbours, were surprised by Clark and his party; their crops were destroyed; their settlements broken up; their villages burnt, the principal of which was Kaskaskias. This town contained near three hundred houses; and had it not been surprised at midnight by these desperate invaders, bold, outrageous, and near starving in the wilderness, the natives might successfully have defended their lives and their plantations; but not a man escaped seasonably to alarm the neighbouring tribes.

A British officer, one *Rocheblave*, who acted as governor, and paymaster for American scalps, was taken and sent to Virginia, with many written proofs of the cruel policy of inciting the fury of savages against the American settlements. From Quebec, Detroit, Michilimackinac, &c., these orders every where appeared under the signature of the chief magistrates, acting in the name of the British king. Some of their principal warriors were made prisoners; the remainder who escaped the sword, had only to fly farther through a trackless wilderness, if possible to procure some new lodgement, beyond the reach of civilized pursuers.

Nor did the Cherokees, the Muskingums, the Mohawks, and many other savage tribes, feel less severely than the Illinois, the resentment of the Americans, for their attachment to the British nation, and their cruelties practised on the borders of the Atlantic states.

An expedition entrusted to the conduct of general Sullivan, against the Six Nations, who had generally been better disposed toward Americans than most of the savage tribes, was replete with circumstances that must wound the feelings of the compassionate heart; while the lovers of cultivation and improvement among all mankind, will be touched by a retaliation, bordering, to say the least, on savage fury. The sudden and unexpected destruction of a part of the human species, enjoying domestic quiet in the simplicity of nature, awakes the feelings of the first: the second must be disturbed in his philosophical pursuits of cultivation and improvement, when he contemplates fire and sword destroying all in their way, and houses too well built to be the workmanship of men in a state of rude nature, the prey of conflagration, enkindled by the hands of the cultivators of the arts and sciences.[25]

The rooting up of gardens, orchards, corn-fields, and fruit trees, which by their variety and growth, discovered that the industrious hand of cultivation had been long employed to bring them to perfection, cannot be justified; more especially where there is a mind capable of looking forward to their utility, and back to the time and labor it has cost to bring them to maturity. But general Sullivan, according to his own account in his letters to the commander in chief, to congress, to his friends and others, spared no vestige of improvement, and appeared little less proud of this war upon nature, than he was of his conquest of the savages.[26]

The difficulties, dangers, and fatigues of the march, required courage, firmness, and perseverance. Hunger and famine assailed them before they reached the fertile borders of the pleasant and well settled Indian towns; yet general Sullivan and his party finished the expedition in as short a time as could be expected, and to all public appearance, met the approbation of congress and of the commander in chief.

Yet there were some things in the demeanor of general Sullivan, that disgusted some of his officers, and raised a censure on his conduct that made him unhappy, and led him to resign in his military command. His health was indeed broken, which he imputed to the fatigues encountered on his hazardous march. Yet he lived many years after this period, and was advanced to the highest stations in the civil administration of the state of New Hampshire, and died with the reputation of a brave and active officer, both in military and civil life.

General Sullivan had acquitted himself during his military command with valor and reputation, in many instances. During the ravages of the British on the Jersey shore, in the latter part of the summer of one thousand seven hundred and seventy-seven, he had gained much honor by an expedition to Staten Island, concerted by himself. This he undertook without any orders from the commander in chief; and for this a court of inquiry was appointed to examine into his conduct. His reasons for such a step, without permission or command, were thought justifiable. He brought off a great number of prisoners, officers, soldiers, and tories, who had frequently made incursions on the borders of the Jersies, and harassed, plundered, and murdered the inhabitants in their sudden depredations. It appeared that general Sullivan had conducted this business with great prudence and success: he was, by the court of inquiry, acquitted with honor and applause, for planning and executing to great advantage, a design from which so much benefit had resulted.

It may be thought by some, an apology sufficient for the invasion of Clark and Sullivan, of Pickens, Van Schaick,[27] and others, that the hostile dispositions of the aboriginals had always led them to imbrue their hands in the blood of the borderers. The warriors of the distant tribes, either instigated by their own ferocity and resentment, or the influence of Europeans inimical to the United States, were ever ready to molest the young settlements. Jealous of their encroachments, the natives viewed them with such an hostile eye, that no treaties were binding: when a favorable opportunity presented, they always attacked the whites, perhaps from the same impulse that in human nature prompts all mankind, whether civilized or savage, to resist the invaders of his territory.

Indeed their condition and their sufferings, from the first emigration of the Europeans, their corruptions in consequence thereof, their wars, and their extirpation from a vast tract of the American continent, must excite a solemn pause in the breast of the philosopher, while he surveys the wretchedness of savage life, and sighs over its misery. Yet he is not relieved when he contemplates the havoc among civilized nations, the changes in society, the prostration of principle, and the revolutions permitted by Providence in this speck of creation.

The rivers of blood through which mankind generally wade to empire and greatness, must draw out the tear of compassion; and every sympathetic bosom will commiserate the sufferings of the whole human race, either friends or foes, whether dying by the sword, sickness or remorse, under the splendid canopy reared by their own guilty hands. These with equal pity look into the wilderness; they see the naked hunter groaning out his fierce soul on his native turf, slain by the tomahawk of his own savage tribe, or wounded by some neighbouring hordes, that prowl through an existence little elevated above the brute. Both stages of society excite compassion, and both intimate to the rational mind, that this is but the road to a more improved, and exalted state of existence.

But the unhappy race of men hutted throughout the vast wilderness of America, were the original proprietors of the soil; and if they have not civilization they have valor; if they have not patriotism they have a predilection to country, and are tenacious of their hunting grounds. However the generous or humane mind may revolt at the idea, there appears a probability, that they will be hunted from the vast American continent, if not from off the face of the globe, by Europeans of various descriptions, aided by the interested Americans, who all consider valor in an Indian, only as a higher degree of ferocity.

Their strenuous efforts to retain the boundaries assigned them by nature and Providence, are viewed with contempt by those descriptions of persons, or rather as a sanction to their own rapacity, and a warrant from heaven to exterminate the hapless race. But "the rivers, the mountains, the deserts, the savages clad in armor, with other destroyers of men," as well as the voice of heaven, and their natural boundaries, forbid these encroachments on the naked forester, content with the produce of nature in his own grounds, and the game that plays in his own wild woods, which his ancestors have possessed from time immemorial.

The ideas of some Europeans as well as Americans, that the rude tribes of savages cannot be civilized by the kind and humane endeavours of their neighbours, is absurd and unfounded. What were once the ancestors of the most refined and polite modern nations, but rude, ignorant savages, inured to all the barbarous customs and operations, with regard to the whole human species. There is no difference in the moral or intellectual capacity of nations, but what arises from adventitious circumstances, that give some a more early and rapid improvement in civilization than others. This gradual rise from the rude states of nature to the highest pitch of refinement, may be traced by the historian, the philosopher, and the naturalist, sufficiently to obviate all objections against the strongest efforts, to instruct and civilize the swarms of men in the American wilds, whose only natural apparent distinction, is a copper-colored skin. When the present war ceases to rage, it is hoped that humanity will teach Americans of a fairer complexion, to use the most strenuous efforts to instruct them in arts, manufactures, morals, and religion, instead of aiming at their extermination.

It is true at this period, when war was raging through all the United States, few of the tribes of the wilderness appeared to be contented with their own native inheritance. They were every where stimulated by the British government to hostility, and most of the inhabitants of the wilderness seemed to be in array against their former colonies. This created a necessity in congress, to act offensively against the rude and barbarous nations. Defensive war against any nation, whether civilized or savage, is undoubtedly justifiable both in a moral and political view. But attempts to penetrate distant countries, and spread slaughter and bloodshed among innocent and unoffending tribes, too distant to awaken fears, and too simple and unsuspicious to expect approaching destruction from those they had never injured, has no warrant from Heaven.

Even in the present war, instances may be adduced of the effects of civilization, which often soften the most savage manners; one of which may be here recorded. A part of the Muskingum tribe had professed themselves Christians of the Moravian sect. They considered war of any kind as inconsistent both with the laws of religion and humanity. They refused to take any part with the numerous hostile tribes of savages, in the war against the Americans. They observed with more rationality and consideration than is generally discovered in more civilized nations, "that the great Spirit did not make men to destroy, but to assist and comfort each other."

They persisted in this placid demeanor, until some of their savage neighbours were so enraged, that they forcibly removed them from their former settlement; and after committing great cruelties, and destroying a number of them, placed the remainder near the Sandusky. Their removal was in consequence of orders from the British commander at Detroit. They remained for some time in the enjoyment of their own simple habits; but some suspicions were afterwards infused among the settlers of the Monongahela, that their dispositions were not friendly to the Americans. It is painful to relate, that on this slight pretence, a number of Americans embodied themselves and marched to the Moravian town, where the principal men had repaired by permission, to reap the harvest they had left standing in the fields. The Americans followed them, and barbarously murdered the whole of this innocent and inoffensive band.

The whites at first decoyed them by a friendly appearance, which induced them to collect themselves together; when thus collected they, without resistance, suffered themselves to be bound and inhumanly butchered. They died professing their full expectation, that their troubles would soon be at an end. Thus they fell as martyrs to religion, by the hands of a people who had much longer professed themselves adherents to the principles of Christianity.

This instance of the treachery and cruelty of the whites, is one among many other proofs, of the truth of the observation made by a gentleman[28] afterwards,

> that the white savages were generally more savage than the copper colored; and that nine times out of ten, the settlers on the borders were the aggressors: that he had seen many of the natives who were prisoners at fort Washington; that they appeared to be possessed of much sensibility and gratitude: that he had discovered some singular instances of this among them, very honorable to the human character, before the advantages or the examples of civilized nations had reached their borders.

In short, no arguments are necessary to adduce the truth, or impress on the minds either of the philosopher or the politician, that it will be the indispensable duty of the American government, when quietly established by the restoration of peace, to endeavour to soften and civilize, instead of exterminating the rude nations of the interior. This will undoubtedly be attempted in some future period, when uncultivated reason may be assisted; when arts, agriculture, science, and true religion, may enlighten the dark corners which have been obscured by ignorance and ferocity, for countless ages. The embrowned, dusky wilderness, has exhibited multitudes of men, little distinguished from the fierce animals they hunted, except in their external form. Yet, in a few instances, the dignity of human nature has been discovered by traits of reason and humanity, which wanted only the advantages of education, to display genius and ability equal to any among the nations, that have hunted millions of those unhappy people out of existence, since the discovery of America by Europeans. But it is a pleasing anticipation, that the American revolution may be a means in the hands of Providence, of diffusing universal knowledge over a quarter of the globe, that for ages had been enveloped in darkness, ignorance, and barbarism.

CHAPTER XVII.

Distressed Situation of the Army, etc. (1780)

The year one thousand seven hundred and eighty, was a year of incident, expectation, and event; a period pregnant with future consequences, interesting in the highest degree to the political happiness of the nations, and perhaps ultimately to the civil institutions of a great part of mankind. We left England in the preceding chapter, in a very perturbed state, arising both from their own internal dissentions and the dread of foreign combinations, relative to their own island and its former dependencies.

At the same time, neither the pen of the historian, or the imagination of the poet, can fully describe the embarrassments suffered by congress, by the commander in chief, and by men of firmness and principle in the several legislative bodies, through this and the beginning of the next year. The scarcity of specie, the rapid depreciation of paper, which at once sunk the property and corrupted the morals of the people; which destroyed all confidence in public bodies, reduced the old army to the extremes of misery, and seemed to preclude all possibility of raising a new one, sufficient for all the departments; were evils, which neither the wisdom or vigilance of congress could remedy.

At such a crisis, more penetration and firmness, more judgment, impartiality, and moderation, were requisite in the commander in chief of the American armies, than usually fall within the compass of the genius or ability of man. In the neighbourhood of a potent army, general Washington had to guard with a very inadequate force, not only against the arms of his enemies, but the machinations of British emissaries, continually attempting to corrupt the fidelity both of his officers and his troops.

Perhaps no one but himself can describe the complicated sources of anxiety, that at this point pervaded the breast of the first military officer, whose honor, whose life, whose country hung suspended, not on a single point only, but on many events that quivered in the winds of fortune, chance, or the more certain determinations of men. Happy is it to reflect, that these are all under the destination of an unerring hand, that works in secret, ultimately to complete the beneficent designs of Providence.

Some extracts from his own pen, very naturally express the agitations of the mind of general Washington, in the preceding as well as the present year. In one of his letters to a friend[29] he observed,

> Our conflict is not likely to cease so soon as every good man would wish. The measure of iniquity is not yet filled; and unless we can return a little more to first principles, and act a little more upon patriotic ground, I do not know when it will—or—what may be the issue of the contest. Speculation—peculation—engrossing—forestalling—with all their concomitants, afford too many melancholy proofs of the decay of public virtue; and too glaring instances of its being the interest and desire of too many, who would wish to be thought friends, to continue the war. . . .

An extract of another letter from general Washington to the governor of Pennsylvania, dated August the twentieth, one thousand seven hundred and eighty, discovers the same anxiety for the fate of the contest, as the above. In this he said,

> To me it will appear miraculous if our affairs can maintain themselves much longer, in their present train. If either the temper or the resources of the country will not admit of an alteration, we may soon expect to be reduced to the humiliating condition, of seeing the cause of America held up in America by foreign arms. The discontents of the troops have been gradually nurtured to a dangerous extremity. Something satisfactory must be done, or the army must cease to exist at the end of the campaign; or it will exhibit an example of more virtue, fortitude, self-denial, and perseverance, than has perhaps ever been paralleled in the history of human enthusiasm.

While thus impressed with these apprehensions of the depreciation of public virtue, general Washington had to balance the parties, and to meliorate the distresses of the inhabitants, alternately ravaged by all descriptions of soldiers, in the vicinity of both armies. It was impossible for him to strike any capital blow, without money even for daily expenses, without a naval force sufficient to cover any exertions; his battalions incomplete, his army clamorous and discontented, and on the point of mutiny, from the deficiencies in their pay, and the immediate want of every necessary of life.

At the same time, the legislatures of the several states were in the utmost anxiety, to devise ways and means to supply the requisitions of congress, who had recently laid a tax of many millions on the states, in order to sink the enormous quantity of old paper money. The calls of an army, naked, hungry, and turbulent, even to the discovery of the symptoms of revolt, were indeed alarming. The pressing necessities of the army, and the critical exigencies of the times, crowded upon them in every department, and required the utmost wisdom, vigilance, and fortitude. . . .

The complicated difficulties already depictured, clearly prove, that such a spirit of avarice and peculation had crept into the public departments, and taken deep hold of the majority of the people, as Americans a few years before, were thought incapable of. The careful observer of human conduct will readily perceive, that a variety of concurring causes led to this sudden change of character. The opulent, who had been used to ease, independence, and generosity, were reduced, dispirited, and deprived of the ability of rendering pecuniary service to their country, by the unavoidable failure of public faith. Great part of the fortunes of the widow, the orphan, and the aged, were sunk in the public funds; so that the nominal income of a year, would scarcely supply the necessities of a day.

The depreciation of paper had been so rapid, that at this time, one hundred and twenty dollars of the paper currency was not an equivalent to one in silver or gold: while at the same time, a sudden accumulation of property by privateering, by speculation, by accident, or fraud, placed many in the lap of affluence, who were without a principle, education, or family. These, from a thoughtless ignorance, and the novelty of splendor total strangers, suddenly plunged into every kind of dissipation, and grafted the extravagancies and follies of foreigners, on their own passion for squandering what by them had been so easily acquired.

Thus avarice without frugality, and profusion without taste, were indulged, and soon banished the simplicity and elegance that had formerly reigned: instead of which, there was spread in America among the rising generation, a thirst for the accumulation of wealth, unknown to their ancestors. A class who had not had the advantages of the best education, and who had paid little attention to the principles of the revolution, took the lead in manners. Sanctioned by the breach of public faith, the private obligations of justice seemed to be little regarded, and the sacred idea of equity in private contracts was annihilated for a time, by the example of public deficiency.

The infantile state of government, the inexperience of its leaders, and the necessity of substituting a medium with only an imaginary value, brought an impeachment on congress, without voluntary deviations from probity, or willing breaches of faith. Perhaps nothing is more true, than an observation of a member of that body, that *"the necessity of affairs had often obliged them to depart from the purity of their first principles."* The complaint that the foundation was corrupt, was artfully diffused: however that might be, the streams were undoubtedly tainted, and contamination, with few exceptions, seemed to run through the whole body of people; and a declension of morals was equally rapid with the depreciation of their currency.

But a superintending Providence, that overrules the designs, and defeats of the projects of men, remarkably upheld the spirit of the Americans; and caused events that had for a time a very unfavorable aspect, to operate in favor of independence and peace, and to make a new nation of the recent emigrants from the old and proud empire of Britain. . . .

CHAPTER XXVIII.

Peace Proclaimed in America, etc. (1783)

The discordant sounds of war that had long grated the ears of the children of America, were now suspended, and the benign and heavenly voice of harmony soothed their wounded feelings, and they flattered themselves the dread summons to slaughter and death would not again resound on their shores. The independence of America acknowledged by the first powers in Europe, and even Great Britain willing to re-sheathe the sword on the same honorable terms for the United States, every prospect of tranquility appeared.

These were events for which the statemen had sighed in the arduous exertions of the cabinet; for which the hero had bared his breast, and the blood of the citizens had flowed in copious streams on the borders of the Atlantic, from the river St. Mary's to the St. Croix, on the eastern extreme of the American territory. Peace was proclaimed in the American army, by order of the commander in chief, on the nineteenth of April, one thousand seven hundred eighty-three. This was just EIGHT YEARS from the memorable day, when the first blood was drawn in the contest between the American colonies and the parent state, in the fields of *Concord* and *Lexington*.

The operation and consequences of the restoration of peace, were now the subject of contemplation. This opened objects of magnitude indeed, to a young republic, which had rapidly passed through the grades of youth and puberty, and was fast arriving to the age of maturity: a republic consisting of a number of confederated states, which by this time had received many as inhabitants, who were not originally from the stock of England. Some of them, indeed, were from more free governments, but others had fled from the slavery of despotic courts; from their numbers and abilities they had become respectable, and their opinions weighty in the political scale. From these and other circumstances it might be expected, that in time, the general enthusiasm for a republican system of government in America, might languish, and new theories be adopted, or old ones modified under different names and terms, until the darling system of the inhabitants of the United States, might be lost or forgotten in a growing rabiosity for monarchy.

Symptoms of this nature, already began to appear in the language of some interested and ambitious men, who endeavoured to confound ideas, and darken opinion, by asserting that *republicanism* was an indefinite term. In social circles they frequently insinuated, that no precise meaning could be affixed to a word, by which the people were often deceived and led to pursue a shadow instead of an object of any real stability. This was indeed, more the language of art than principle, and seemed to augur the decline of public virtue in a free state.

It required the utmost vigilance to guard against, and counteract designs thus secretly covered. It was not unexpected by the judicious observers of human conduct, that many contingencies might arise, to defeat or to render fruitless the efforts that had been made on the practicability of erecting and maintaining a pure, unadulterated republican government.

Time must unfold the futility of such an expectation, or establish the system on a basis, that will lead mankind to rejoice in the success of an experiment that has been too often tried in vain. Those who have been nurtured in the dark regions of despotism, who have witnessed the sale of the peasantry with the glebe they have cultivated from infancy, and who have seen the sire and the son, transferred with the stables and the cattle, from master to master, cannot realize the success of a theory that has a tendency to exalt the species, and elevate the lower grades of mankind to a condition nearer to an equality with adventitious superiority. It is not wonderful, that a people of this description and education, should be incredulous of the utility of more free modes of government. They are naturally tenacious of old customs, habits, and their own fortuitous advantages; they are unable to form an idea of general freedom among mankind, without distinction of ranks that elevate one class of men to the summit of pride and insolence, and sink another to the lowest grade of servility and debasement.

But Americans born under no feudal tenure, nurtured in the bosom of mediocrity, educated in the schools of freedom; who have never been used to look up to any lord of the soil, as having a right by prescription, habit, or hereditary claim, to the property of their flocks, their herds, and their pastures, may easily have been supposed to have grown to maturity with very different ideas, and with a disposition to defend their allodial inheritance to the last moment of their lives. . . .

CHAPTER XXX.

A Survey of the Situation of America on the Conclusion of War, etc. (1783)

We have seen the banners of Albion displayed, and the pendants of her proud navy waving over the waters of the western world, and threatening terror, servitude, or desolation, to resisting millions. We have seen through the tragic tale of war, all political connexion with Great Britain broken off, the authority of the parent state renounced, and the independence of the American states sealed by the definitive treaty. The mind now willingly draws a veil over the unpleasing part of the drama, and indulges the imagination in future prospects of peace and felicity; when the soldier shall retreat from the field, lay by the sword, and resume the implements of husbandry—the mechanic return to his former occupation, and the merchant rejoice in the prosperous view of commerce; when trade shall not be restricted by the unjust or partial regulations of foreigners; and when the ports of America shall be thrown open to all the world, and an intercourse kept free, to reap the advantages of commerce extended to all nations.

The young government of this newly established nation had, by the recent articles of peace, a claim to a jurisdiction over a vast territory, reaching from the St. Mary's on the south, to the river St. Croix, the extreme boundary of the east, containing a line of postroads of eighteen hundred miles, exclusive of the northern and western wilds, but partially settled, and whose limits have not yet been explored. Not the Lycian league, nor any of the combinations of the Grecian states, encircled such an extent of territory; nor does modern history furnish any example of confederacy of equal magnitude and respectability with that of the United States of America.

We look back with astonishment when we reflect, that it was only in the beginning of the seventeenth century, that the first Europeans landed in Virginia, and that nearly at the same time, a few wandering strangers coasted about the unknown bay of Massachusetts, until they found a footing in Plymouth. Only a century and an half had elapsed, before their numbers and their strength accumulated, until they bade defiance to foreign oppression, and stood ready to meet the power of Britain, with courage and magnanimity scarcely paralleled by the progeny of nation, who had been used to every degree of subordination and obedience.

The most vivid imagination cannot realize the contrast, when it surveys the vast surface of America now enrobed with fruitful fields, and the rich herbage of the pastures, which had been so recently covered with a thick mattress of woods; when it beholds the cultivated vista, the orchards and the beautiful gardens which have arisen within the limits of the Atlantic states, where the deep embrowned, melancholy forest, had from time immemorial sheltered only the wandering savage; where the sweet notes of the feathered race, that follow the track of cultivation, had never chanted their melodious songs: the wild waste had been a haunt only for the hoarse birds of prey, and the prowling quadrupeds that filled the forest.

In a country like America, including a vast variety of soil and climate, producing every thing necessary for convenience and pleasure, every man might be lord of his own acquistion. It was a country where the standard of freedom had recently been erected, to allure the liberal minded to her shores, and to receive and to protect the asylum from the chains of servitude to which they had been subjected in any part of the globe. Here it might rationally be expected, that beside the natural increase, the emigration to a land of such fair promise of the blessings of plenty, liberty, and peace, to which multitudes would probably resort, there would be exhibited in a few years, a population almost beyond the calculation of figures.

The extensive tract of territory above described, on the borders of the Atlantic, had, as we have seen, been divided into several distinct governments, under the control of the crown of Great Britain; these governments were now united in a strong confederacy, absolutely independent of all foreign domination: the several states retained their own legislative powers; they were proud of their individual independence, tenacious of their republican principles, and newly emancipated from the degrading ideas of foreign control, and the sceptred hand of monarchy. With all these distinguished privileges, deeply impressed with the ideas of internal happiness, we shall see they grew jealous of each other, and soon after the peace, even of the powers of the several governments erected by themselves: they were eager for the acquisition of wealth, and the possession of the new advantages dawning on their country, from their friendly connexions abroad, and their abundant resources at home.

At the same time that the wayward appearances began early to threaten their internal felicity, the inhabitants of America were in general sensible, that the freedom of the people, the virtue of society, and the stability of their commonwealth, could only be preserved by the strictest union; and that the independence of the United States must be secured by an undeviating adherence to the principles that produced the revolution.

These principles were grounded on the natural equality of man, their right of adopting their own modes of government, the dignity of the people, and that sovereignty which cannot be ceded either to representatives or to kings. But, as a certain writer has expressed it,

> powers may be delegated for particular purposes; but the omnipotence of society, if any where, is in itself. Princes, senates, or parliaments, are not proprietors or masters; they are subject to the people, who form and support that society, by an eternal law of nature, which has ever subjected a part to the whole.[30]

These were opinions congenial to the feelings, and were disseminated by the pens, of political writers; of Otis, Dickinson, Quincy,[31] and many others, who with pathos and energy had defended the liberties of America, previous to the commencement of hostilities.

On these principles, a due respect must ever be paid to the general will; to the right in the people to dispose of their own monies by a representative voice; and to liberty of conscience without religious tests: on these principles, frequent elections, and rotations of office, were generally thought necessary, without precluding the indispensable subordination and obedience due to rules of their own choice. From the principles, manners, habits, and education of the Americans, they expected from their rulers, economy in expenditure, (both public and private), simplicity of manners, pure morals, and undeviating probity. These they considered as the emanations of virtue, grounded on a sense of duty, and a veneration for the Supreme Governor of the universe, to whom the dictates of nature teach all mankind to pay homage, and whom they had been taught to worship according to revelation, and the divine precepts of the gospel. Their ancestors had rejected and fled from the impositions and restrictions of men, vested either with princely or priestly authority: they equally claimed the exercise of private judgment, and the rights of conscience, unfettered by religious establishments in favor of particular denominations.

They expected a simplication of law; clearly defined distinctions between executive, legislative, and judiciary powers: the right of trial by jury, and a sacred regard to personal liberty and the protection of private property, were opinions embraced by all who had any just ideas of government, law, equity, or morals.

These were the rights of men, the privileges of Englishmen, and the claim of Americans: these were the principles of the Saxon ancestry of the British empire, and of all the free nations of Europe, previous to the corrupt systems introduced by intriguing and ambitious individuals.

These were the opinions of Ludlow[32] and Sydney,[33] of Milton[34] and Harrington:[35] these were principles defended by the pen of the learned, enlightened, and renowned Locke;[36] and even judge Blackstone,[37] in his excellent commentaries on the laws of England, has observed, "that trial by jury and the liberties of the people went out together." Indeed, most of the learned and virtuous writers that have adorned the pages of literature from generation to generation, in an island celebrated for the erudite and comprehensive genius of its inhabitants, have enforced these rational and liberal opinions.

These were the principles which the ancestors of the inhabitants of the United States brought with them from the polished shores of Europe, to the dark wilds of America: these opinions were deeply infixed in the bosoms of their posterity, and nurtured with zeal, until necessity obligated them to announce the declaration of the independence of the United States. We have seen that the instrument which announced the final separation of the American colonies from Great Britain, was drawn by the elegant and energetic pen of Jefferson, with that correct judgment, precision, and dignity, which have ever marked his character.

The declaration of independence, which has done so much honor to the then existing congress, to the inhabitants of the United States, and to the genius and heart of the gentleman who drew it, in the belief, and under the awe, of the Divine Providence, ought to be frequently read by the rising youth of the American states, as a palladium of which they should never lose sight, so long as they wish to continue a free and independent people.

This celebrated paper, which will be admired in the annals of every historian, begins with an assertion, that all men are created equal, and endowed by their Creator with certain unalienable rights, which nature and nature's God entitle them to claim; and, after appealing to the Supreme Judge of the world for the rectitude of their intentions, it concludes in the name of the *good people* of the *colonies*, by their representatives assembled in congress, they publish and declare, that they are, and of right ought to be, Free and Independent States: in the *name* of the *people*, the fountain of all just authority, relying on the protection of Divine Providence, they mutually pledged themselves to maintain these rights, with their lives, fortunes, and honor.

These principles the *Sons of Columbia* had supported by argument, defended by the sword, and have now secured by negotiation, as far as the pledges of national faith and honor will bind society to a strict adherence to equity. This however is seldom longer than it appears to be the interest of nations, or designing individuals of influence and power. Virtue in the sublimest sense, operates only on the minds of a chosen few: in their breasts it will ever find its own reward.

In all ages, mankind are governed less by reason and justice, than by interest and passion: the caprice of a day, or impulse of a moment, will blow them about as with a whirlwind, and bear them down the current of folly, until awakened by their misery: by these they are often led to breaches of the most solemn engagements, the consequences of which may involve whole nations in wretchedness. It is devoutly to be hoped, that the conduct of

America will never stand upon record as a striking example of the truth of this observation. She has fought for her liberties; she has purchased them by the most costly sacrifices: we have seen her embark in the enterprise, with a spirit that gained her the applause of mankind. The United States have procured their own emancipation from foreign thraldom, by the sacrifice of their heroes and their friends: they are now ushered on to the temple of peace, who holds out her wand, and beckons them to make the wisest improvement of the advantages they had acquired, by their patience, perseverance, and valor. . . .

CHAPTER XXXI.

Supplementary Observations, etc. (1801)

The narration of the revolutionary war between Great Britain and her former colonies, brought down to its termination, leaves the mind at leisure for more geneal observations on the subsequent consequences, without confining it to time or place.

At the conclusion of the war between Great Britain and America, after the rejection of the claims of a potent foreign nation, the dissevering of old bands of governmental arrangement, and new ones were adopted, the proud feelings of personal independence warmed every bosom, and general ideas of civil and religious liberty were disseminated far and wide.

On the restoration of peace, the soldier had returned to the bosom of his family, and the artisan and the husbandman were stimulated to new improvements; genius was prompted to exertion, by the wide field opened by the revolution, and encouraged by the spirit of inquiry to climb the heights of literature, until it might stand conspicuous on the summit of fame.

Under such circumstances, every free mind should be tenacious of supporting the honor of a national character, and the dignity of independence. This claim must be supported by their own sobriety, economy, industry, and perseverance in every virtue. It must be nurtured by that firmness and principle that induced their ancestors to fly from the hostile arm of tyranny, and to explore and

begin a new nation in the forlorn and darksome bosom of a distant wilderness. The social compacts, the religion, the manners,
and the habits of wandering strangers, and their immediate successors, taught their sons the noble example of fortitude and love
of freedom, that has led them to resist the encroachments of kings
and nobles, and to dissipate the cloud that threatened to envelope
the mind in darkness, and spread the veil of ignorance over the
bright hemisphere that encircles the children of Columbia.

Indeed America was at this period possessed of a prize, replete
with advantages seldom thrown into the hand of any people. Divided by nature from three parts of the globe, which have groaned
under tyrants of various descriptions, from time immemorial, who
had slaughtered their millions to feed the ambition of princes, she
was possessed of an immense territory, the soil fertile and productive, her population increasing, her commerce unfettered, her resources ample. She was now uncontrolled by foreign laws; and her
domestic manufactures might be encouraged, without any fear of
check from abroad: and under the influence of a spirit of enterprise, very advantageous in a young country, she was looking
foward with expectations of extending her commerce to every
part of the globe.

Nothing seemed to be wanting to the United States but a contin-
uance of their union and virtue. It was their interest to cherish true,
genuine republican virtue, in politics; and in religion, a strict adherence to a sublime code of morals, which has never been equalled
by the sages of ancient time, nor can ever be abolished by the so-
phistical reasonings of modern philosophers. Possessed of this palladium, America might bid defiance both to foreign and domestic
intrigue, and stand on an eminence that would command the veneration of nations, and the respect of their monarchs: but a defal-
cation from these principles may leave the sapless vine of liberty to
droop, or to be rooted out by the hand that had been stretched out
to nourish it.

If, instead of the independent feelings of ancient republics,
whose prime object was the welfare and happiness of their country, we should see a dereliction of those principles, and the Americans ready to renounce their great advantages, by the imitation of
European systems in politics and manners, it would be a melan-

choly trait in the story of man: yet they, like other nations, may in time, by their servility to men in power, or by a chimerical pursuit of the golden fleece of the poets, become involved in a mist ascending from the pit of avarice. This may lead to peculation, to usurious contracts, to illegal and dishonest projects, and to every private vice, to support the factitious appearances of grandeur and wealth, which can never maintain the claim to that rich inheritance which they so bravely defended.

Thus it was but a short time after the restoration of peace, and the exhilarating view of the innumerable benefits obtained by the general acknowledgment among foreign nations of the independence of America, before the brightened prospect, which had recently shone with so much splendor, was beclouded by the face of general discontent. New difficulties arose, and embarrassments thickened, which called for the exercise of new energies, activity, and wisdom.

The sudden sinking of the value of land, and indeed of all other real property, immediately on the peace, involved the honest and industrious farmer in innumerable difficulties. The produce of a few acres had been far from sufficient for the support of a family, and at the same time to supply the necessary demands for the use of the army, when from the scarcity of provisions every article thereof bore an enhanced price, while their resources were exhausted, and their spirits wasted under an accumulated load of debt.

The general congress was yet without any compulsory powers, to enforce the liquidation of public demands; and the state legislatures totally at a loss how to devise any just and ready expedient for the relief of private debtors. It was thought necessary by some to advert again to a paper medium, and by others this was viewed with the utmost abhorrence: indeed the iniquitous consequences of a depreciating currency had been recently felt too severely, by all classes, to induce any to embrace a second time with cordiality such a dangerous expedient. Thus, from various circumstances, the state of both public and private affairs presented a very serious and alarming aspect.

The patriotic feelings of the yeomanry of the country, had prompted them to the utmost exertions for the public service.

Unwilling to withhold their quota of the tax of beef, blankets, and other necessaries indispensable for the soldiery, exposed to cold and hunger, many of them had been induced to contract debts which could not be easily liquidated, and which it was impossible to discharge by the products from the usual occupations of husbandry. While at the same time, the rage for privateering and traffic, by which some had suddenly grown rich, had induced others to look with indifference on the ideas of a more moderate accumulation of wealth. They sold their patrimonial inheritance for trifling considerations, in order to raise ready specie for adventure in some speculative project. This, with many other causes, reduced the price of land to so low a rate, that the most valuable farms, and the best accommodated situations, were depreciated to such a degree, that those who were obliged to alienate real property were bankrupted by the sales.

The state of trade, and the derangement of commerical affairs, were equally intricate and distressing at the close of the war. The natural eagerness of the mercnatile body to take every advantage that presented in that line, induced many, immediately on the peace, to send forward for large quantities of goods from England, France, and Holland, and wherever else they could gain a credit. Thus the markets loaded with every article of luxury, as well as necessaries, and the growing scarcity of specie united with the reduced circumstances of many who had formerly been wealthy, the enormous importations either lay upon hand, or obliged the possessor to sell without any advance, and in many instances much under the prime cost. In addition to these embarrassments on the mercantile interest, the whole country, from north to south, was filled with British factors, with their cargoes of goods directly from the manufacturers, who drew customers to their stores from all classes that were able to purchase. Every capital was crowded with British agents, sent over to collect debts contracted long before the war, who took advantage of the times, oppressed the debtor, and purchased the public securities from all persons whose necessities obliged them to sell, at the monstrous discount of seventeen shillings and six pence on the pound. At the same time, the continent swarmed with British emissaries, who sowed discord among the people, infused jealousies, and weakened their reliance on the public faith, and destroyed all confidence between man and man.

Nor did religion or morals appreciate amidst the confusion of a long war, which is ever unfavorable to virtue, and to all those generous principles which ennoble the human character, much more than ribbons, stars, and other playthings of a distempered imagination. These soon sink to the level of their own insignificance, and leave the sanguine admirer sickened by the chace of ideal felicity.

The wide field of more minute observation on these great and important subjects, shall at present be waved. Agriculture may be left to the philosophic theorist, who may speculate on the real value and product of the lands, in a country in such an improveable state as that of America; while the advance in the profits of the husbandman must be estimated by the ratio of future experiment. The statesman versed in the commerce and politics of Europe, and the commercial treaties which may be, or have already been formed, has a labyrinth to trace, and investigations to unfold, before every thing can be fixed on the principles of equity and reciprocity, that will give complete satisfaction to all nations. Religious discussions we leave to the observation of the theologian, who, however human nature may be vilified by some and exalted by others, traces the moral causes and effects that operate on the soul of man. The effects only are level to the common eye, which weeps that the result is more frequently productive of misery than felicity to his fellow beings.

Besides the circumstances already hinted, various other combinations caused a cloud of chagrin to sit on almost every brow, and a general uneasiness to pervade the bosoms of most of the inhabitants of America. This was discoverable on every occasion; they complained of the governments of their own instituting, and of congress, whose powers were too feeble for the redress of private wrongs, or the more public and general purposes of government. They murmured at the commutation which congress had agreed to, for the compensation of the army. They felt themselves under the pressure of burdens, for which they had not calculated; the pressure of debts and taxes beyond their ability to pay. These discontents artificially wrought up, by men who wished for more strong and splendid government, broke out into commotion in many parts of the country, and finally terminated in open insurrection in some of the states.

This general uneasy and refractory spirit had for some time shewn itself in the states of New Hampshire, Rhode Island, Connecticut, and some other portions of the union; but the Massachusetts seemed to be the seat of sedition. Bristol, Middlesex, and the western counties, Worcester, Hampshire, and Berkshire, were more particularly culpable. The people met in county conventions, drew up addresses to the general assembly, to which were annexed long lists of grievances, some of them real, others imaginary. They drew up many resolves, some of which were rational, others unjust, and most of them absurd in the extreme. They censured the conduct of the officers of government, called for a revision of the constitution, voted the senate and judicial courts to be grievances, and proceeded in a most daring and insolent manner to prevent the sitting of the courts of justice, in the several counties.

The ignorance[38] of this incendiary and turbulent set of people, might lead them to a justification of their own measures, from a recurrence to transactions in some degree similar in the early opposition to British government. They had neither the information, nor the sagacity to discern the different grounds of complaint. Nor could they make proper distinctions with regard to the oppressions complained of under the crown of Britain, and the temporary burdens they now felt, which are ever the concomitants and consequences of war. They knew that a successful opposition had been made to the authority of Britain, while they were under the dominion of the king of England; but they were too ignorant to distinguish between an opposition to regal despotism, and a resistance to a government recently established by themselves. . . .

Innumerable other instances might be adduced of the defeat of republicanism, in spite of the efforts of its most zealous friends: yet this is no proof that this system of government may not be more productive of happiness to mankind than that of monarchy or aristocracy. The United States of America have now a fair experiment of a republican system to make for themselves; they may perhaps be possessed of more materials that promise success than have ever fallen to the lot of any other nation. From the peculiar circumstances of the emigration of their ancestors, there is little reason to fear that a veil of darkness, tyranny, and barbarity will soon overspread the land to which they fled. These were a set of men very different in principles and manners from any that are to be found in the histories of colonization, where it may be observed, the first planters have been generally either men of enterprise for the acquisition of riches or fame, or convicted villains transported from more civilized societies. . . .

Great revolutions ever produce excesses and miseries at which humanity revolts. In America indeed, it must be acknowledged, that when the late convulsions are viewed with a retrospective eye, the scenes of barbarity were not so universal as have been usual in other countries that have been at once shaken by foreign and domestic war. Few histories have recorded examples of equal moderation and less violation of the feelings of humanity, where general revolt and revolution had pervaded such an extensive territory. The enthusiasm of opinion previous to the year one thousand seven hundred and seventy-five, bore down opposition like a torrent, and enkindled the flame which emancipated the United States. Yet, it was not stimulated by a fierce spirit of revenge, which, in similar circumstances, too frequently urges to cruelties which can never be licensed the principles of justice or freedom, and must ever be abhorrent to humanity and benevolence.

The United States may congratulate themselves on the success of a revolution which has done honor to the human character, by exhibiting a mildness of spirit amidst the ferocity of war, that prevented the shocking scenes of cruelty, butchery, and slaughter, which have too often stained the actions of men, when their original intentions were the result of pure motives and justifiable resistance. They have been hailed by distant nations in terms of respect and applause for the glorious and successful stand made by them in favor of the liberties of mankind. They have now to maintain their well-earned fame, by a strict adherence to the principles of the revolution, and the practice of every public, social and domestic virtue.

The enthusiastic zeal for freedom which had generally animated all classes throughout the United States, was retained, with few exceptions, to the conclusion of the war, without any considerable appearance of relaxation in any part of the union, until the sword was resheathed, and the conflict terminated by a general peace. After this indeed, though the spirit for freedom was not worn down, a party arose, actuated by different principles; new designs were discovered, which spread suspicions among the people, that the object of their exertions was endangered, from circumstances they had never calculated as probable to take place in their country, until some ages had elapsed. But notwithstanding the variety of exigencies, and the new opportunities which offered to interested individuals, for the aggrandizement of family, and the accumulation of wealth, no visible dereliction appeared, nor any diminution of that general partiality in favor of republicanism which had taken deep root in the minds of the inhabitants of the United States. These principles did not apparently languish, until some time after the adoption of the new constitution; exertions were then made to damp their ardor by holding up systems of government asserted by some to be better adapted to their happiness, and absolutely necessary for the strength and glory of the American states. The illusion was however discovered, and a constitutional ardency for general freedom revived among the people. The feelings of native freedom among the sons of America, and their own good sense taught them, that they did not need the appendages of royalty and baneful curse of a standing army to support it. They were convinced, that rational liberty might be maintained, their favorite system of republicanism might be revived, established, and supported, and the prosperity of their country heightened, at a less gorgeous expense than a resort to the usages of monarchic states, and the introducton of hereditary crowns and the proud claims of noble ancestry, which usually involve the mass of the people in poverty, corruption, degradation, and servility.

Under the benediction of Divine Providence America may yet long be protected from sanguine projects, and indigested measures, that have produced the evils felt or depictured among less fortunate nations, who have not laid the foundations of their governments on the firm basis of public virtue, of general freedom, and that degree of liberty most productive of the happiness of mankind in his social state. But from the accumulated blessings which are showered down on the United States, there is reason to indulge the benign hope, that America may long stand a favored nation, and be preserved from the horrors of war, instigated either by foreign combinations or domestic intrigue, which are equally to be deprecated.

Any attempt, either by secret fraud, or open violence, to shake the union, to subvert the constitution, or undermine the just principles, which wrought out the American revolution, cannot be too severely censured. It is true, there has been some agitation of spirits between existing parties; but doubtless the prudence of the inhabitants of the United States will suffer this to evaporate, as the cloud of the morning, and will guard against every point that might have the smallest tendency to break the union. If peace and unanimity are cherished, and equalization of liberty, and the equity and energy of law, maintained by harmony and justice, the present representative government may stand for ages a luminous monument of republican wisdom, virtue, and integrity. The principles of the revolution ought ever to be the pole-star of the statesman, respected by the rising generation; and the advantages bestowed by Providence should never be lost, by negligence, indiscretion, or guilt.

The people may again be reminded, that the elective franchise is in their own hands; that it ought not to be abused, either for personal gratifications, or the indulgence of partisan acrimony. This advantage should be improved, not only for the benefit of existing society, but with an eye to that fidelity which is due to posterity. This can only be done by electing such men to guide the national counsels, whose conscious probity enables them to stand like a Colossus, on the broad basis of independence, and by correct and equitable arrangements, endeavor to lighten the burdens of the people, strengthen their unanimity at home, command justice abroad, and cultivate peace with all nations, until an example may be left on record of the practicability of meliorating the condition of mankind.

The internal strength of America is respectable, and her borders are fenced by the barriers of nature. May the wisdom, vigour, and ability of her native sons, teach her to surmount every difficulty that may arise at home or abroad, without ever calling in the aid of *foreign* relations! She wants not the interference of any other nation, to give a model to her government, or secretly influence the administration by bribes, flatteries, or threats. The enterprising spirit of the people seems adapted to improve their advantages, and to rival in grandeur and fame those parts of creation which for ages have been meliorating and refining, until the period of decay seems to have arrived, that threatens the fall of some of the proudest nations. Humanity recoils at a view of the wretched state of vassalage, in which a great part of mankind is involved. Yet, America may sit tranquil, and only extend her compassion to the European world, which exhibits the shambles of despotism, where the purple of kings is stained by the blood of their subjects, butchered by thousands to glut the ambition of a weak individual, who frequently expires himself before the cup of his intoxication is full. The vesture of royalty is however still displayed, and weapons of war spread death over three fourths of the globe, without satiating the thirst that drinks up rivers of human gore, when the proud victor wipes the stained lip and covers the guilty visage with a smile at the incalculable carnage of his own species, by his mandates and his myrmidons.[39]

It will be the wisdom, and probably the future effort of the American government, forever to maintain with unshaken magnanimity, the present neutral position of the United States. The hand of nature has displayed its magnificence in this quarter of the globe, in the astonishing rivers, lakes, and mountains, replete with the richest minerals and the most useful materials for manufactures. At the same time, the indigenous produce of its fertile lands yields medicine, food, and clothing, and every thing needful for man in his present condition. America may with propriety be styled a land of promise; a happy climate, though remarkably variegated; fruitful and populous, independent and free, both necessity and pleasure invite the hand of the industrious to cherish and cultivate the prolific soil, which is ready to yield all that nature requires to satisfy the reasonable wishes of man, as well as to contribute to the wealth, pleasure, and luxury of the inhabitants. It is a portion of the globe that appears as a fair and fertile vineyard, which requires only the industrious care of the laborers to render it for a long time productive of the finest clusters in the full harvest of prosperity and freedom, instead of yielding thorns, thistles, and sour grapes, which must be the certain fruits of animosity, disunion, venality, or vice.

Though in her infantile state, the young republic of America exhibits the happiest prospects. Her extensive population, commerce, and wealth, the progress of agriculture, arts, sciences, and manufactures, have increased with a rapidity beyond example. Colleges and academies have been reared, multiplied, and endowed with the best advantages for public instruction, on the broad scale of liberality and truth. The effects of industry and enterprise appear in the numerous canals, turnpikes, elegant buildings, and well constructed bridges, over lengths and depths of water that open, and render the communication easy and agreeable, throughout a country almost without bounds. In short, arts and agriculture are pursued with avidity, civilization spreads, and science in full research is investigating all the sources of human knowledge.

Indeed the whole country wears a face of improvement, from the extreme point of the northern and western woods, through all the southern states, and to the vast Atlantic ocean, the eastern boundary of the United States. The wisdom and justice of the American governments, and the virtue of the inhabitants, may, if they are not deficient in the improvement of their own advantages, render the United States of America an enviable example to all the world, of peace, liberty, righteousness, and truth. The western wilds, which for ages have been little known, may arrive to that stage of improvement and perfection, beyond which the limits of human genius cannot reach, and this last civilized quarter of the globe may exhibit those striking traits of grandeur and magnificence, which the Divine Economist may have reserved to crown the closing scene, when the angel of his presence will stand upon the sea and upon the earth, lift up his hand to heaven, and swear by Him that liveth forever and ever, that there shall be time no longer.

SARAH POGSON
(1774–1870)

Little is known about Pogson's life until she was nearly fifty years old. She was born in Essex, England, on September 17, 1774, the daughter of Ann Wood and John Pogson. Her father had inherited a number of plantations in the West Indies and the family seemed to be prosperous. In 1793 she emigrated with her brother, the Rev. Milward Pogson, to Charleston, South Carolina. She lived in the United States for the remainder of her life. In 1823, Sarah married Peter Smith of New York; it was not a happy marriage, and the couple separated just three years later. Though they attempted several reconciliations, they never successfully reunited, and Sarah received an annual stipend from her husband. Though not extravagant, the annuity was sufficient support, and Pogson could focus on writing, most often to support a charitable cause that was of interest to her, such as the Ladies' Benevolent Society and the Protestant Episcopal Society.

Pogson published poetry, essays, and dramas, all of which reflected her interest in history and theology. The Female Enthusiast (1807) is her first known publication, and still ranks as her most accomplished work. Though Pogson takes some liberties in her account of Charlotte Corday's[1] murder of the radical French revolutionary leader Jean-Paul Marat,[2] the historical drama allows her to project her belief in the success of the American Revolution as opposed to the French cause. Whereas writers such as Margaretta V. Faugeres believed there was a continuum between the American and French Revolutions, Pogson uses the French historical backdrop to offer an alternative perspective, one that allows her to em-

phasize the importance of domestic peace for women. Pub-lished in The Monthly Register, *the play is not known to have been performed. Although Pogson was not known to support abolition or women's rights, she presents a vivid characterization of a woman who acts out of political and moral enthusiasm. Though Corday is depicted as nonheroic, she is given some of the most strident and articulate speeches of any female character in early U.S. literature.*

Most of Pogson's subsequent publications reflect her inter-est in Christianity, especially in comparison with other reli-gions. A drama, The Young Carolinians, or Americans in Algiers *(1818), was Pogson's next major publication, and, like many other of her dramas, its exotic location also allows her to present her nationalist ideologies through the enslave-ment of white Americans in a Middle Eastern location. Simi-lar settings occur in* The Power of Christianity, or Abdallah and Sabat *(1814), and* Zerah, the Believing Jew *(1837). A collection of Pogson's work,* Essays: Religious, Moral, Dra-matic and Poetical, *was published in 1818, and* Daughters of Eve, *a collection of thirteen poems, was published in 1826. A revised version of* The Power of Christianity *appeared in 1844 under the title* The Arabians; or, the Power of Chris-tianity. *Pogson died in Charleston on July 24, 1870.*

THE FEMALE ENTHUSIAST:

A TRAGEDY IN FIVE ACTS

1807.

CHARACTERS

CORDAY, *father of Charlotte and Henry*
DUVAL, *father of Estelle*
MARAT
CHABOT, *friend of Marat*
HENRY, *son of Corday*
BELCOUR, *Henry's friend*
DE VERNUEIL, *engaged to Charlotte*
LE BRUN, *formerly Henry's tutor, much attached to him*
OLD BERTRAND, *a blind cottager*
LITTLE BOYS, *Bertrand's grandchildren*
JAQUES, *Henry's servant*

CHARLOTTE CORDAY
ESTELLE
SUSETTE, *Bertrand's granddaughter*
ANNETTE, *Charlotte's maid*

OFFICERS, SOLDIERS, GUARDS, MOB

Scene: Sometimes at Caen; sometimes Paris.

ACT I

[*The garden of* CORDAY'S *house. Enter* JAQUES *in a soldier's undress uniform, a cockade in his hat, a small bird cage in his hand with a bird in it. Sun rises.*]

JAQUES:

>Where is Annette? She wakes not with the lark
>To meet me, and how many miles I've been
>To get this little bird for her. [*Looks at the bird.*]
>When I'm gone,
>Remind her of poor Jaques; but I think Annette
>Cannot forget me. She often tells me so,
>And then she says she hates this fine cockade! Strange,
>For 'tis my pride—and though I love her well,
>Can't consent to let another wear it;
>Cannot stay behind my brave young master,
>No—if he should lead me to the world's end,
>It never shall be said Jaques deserted,
>Ever, for the love of pretty Annette
>Or the dread certainty of a bullet.
>Where is she? Only one more morning left,
>And yet not here! She thinks I'm not returned;
>I'll go and place this songster at her window. [*Goes off.*]

[*Enter* CHARLOTTE. *She walks thoughtfully across the stage.*]

CHARLOTTE:

>Pure and refreshing is the morn'g air,
>And sweet the melody of birds. My voice
>Responds not now to the cheerful chorus;
>Its only breathing is a fond adieu
>To every dear and cherished object!
>Oh, could the happy time again return
>When blooming nature, all attractive, was
>"The world's first spring" to my delighted eyes.
>Abroad creation charmed. Its wondrous beauty
>Wrapped every sense; and while I gazed and thought,
>Adoring praise sprung from my soul to that
>Creative Power who placed me in a world
>So fair—so rich in all that could delight!
>Had any voice then sounded in my ear,
>That 'midst this scene of harmony divine,
>Vice poisoned bliss; wickedness was sanctioned;
>That cruel man destroyed without offense
>His fellow creature man, I should have turned

  Incredulous away, and to my home's
  Dear circle pointed. There simplicity
  Had imaged the true picture of mankind. [*Pauses.*]
 [*Re-enter* JAQUES, *takes off his hat.*]

JAQUES:
  My mistress rises with the sun's first beam,
  But she has bent too low o'er some sweet flower;
  I see a glistening dew drop on her cheek.

CHARLOTTE:
  Alas, Jaques, it is a *tear* of anguish.

JAQUES:
  Tears, my young lady? Oh, let those sorrow
  Who have some crime to mourn! Thy gentle heart
  Should rejoice in gladness, for it is kind,
  And ever feels for poor folks when they suffer.

CHARLOTTE:
  Too sensibly it feels for its own peace.

JAQUES:
  Ah, were the Chevalier de Vernueil here,
  Instead of Jaques, those tears had changed to smiles
  But duty called him hence, as now it does
  Him, who soon will prove as brave a soldier. [*Adjusts himself.*]
  Ah, ma'mselle, were the Chevalier Henry
  To see those tears, perhaps a soldier's eye,
  Which still is moistened by the dews of nature,
  Would glisten also. And maybe his kind breast
  Might grieve so much to see thee sad that he
  Would be too loath to go—though duty calls.
 [*Drum beats at a distance.*]
  Hark! I must to mine. [JAQUES *bows hastily and goes off.*]

CHARLOTTE:
  Had duty never called De Vernueil hence,
  Here had I stayed in peaceful ignorance—
  That duty which led me first to ask of wars,
  And governments and other scenes than those
  Enfolding sweet domestic harmony.
  Then to a wider field my views were opened.

Simplicity retired, but my heart throbbed
With keenest sensibility—alive
To virtue and humanity. Doth it not
Loathe a foe to either—mourn that on earth
Such foes exist, to wound mankind's repose?
Repose? If that were all! But oppression
Stalks abroad, and stains even the peaceful
Paths of life with blood! Merciless ferocity
Sways, with an uncontrolled dominion!
A monster spreads destruction! And while he
Desolates, calls out aloud, "Tis liberty"!
Why do his black deeds remain unpunished?
Is there not one avenging hand to strike?
[*Enter* ESTELLE.]

ESTELLE:

Charlotte! Why this trembling agitation?
Oh, tell me, what alarms? What hast thou seen,
Or heard, or thought to fix an impression
So very strong on that dear countenance?

CHARLOTTE:

Oh, my Estelle! Do not ask.
[*Puts her hand to her heart.*] Here swells . . . what
Even the disclosing tongue of friendship must conceal.
A foreign sentiment is here—
Nor can the power of language speak its force!

ESTELLE: [*Looks at her and pauses.*]

What dost thou mean?
Give to my heart whatever dwells in thine.

CHARLOTTE:

Has thou not always shared my joys and griefs?
When childhood's sports amused our infant fancies,
And since, in riper years, my thoughts and hopes
Have to thy ear, Estelle, been all unfolded,
And must thou ask my confidence in vain?
Oh, do not press me now! Some other time. [*Falls on her neck.*]

ESTELLE:

Be it then some other time, my Charlotte.

    Oh, could I see thy cheerful looks return!
    Why this deep dejection? De Vernueil lives,
    And fair renown approves his gallant name.
    Let then the youthful bosom's transport hope
    Again resume its power! De Vernueil
    Will return in safety to his Charlotte.
    Oh, then, once more let smiles adorn thy face;
    In them thy venerable father lives.
    Soon, on thy tenderness a double claim
    Will spring, for Henry must, alas, be gone.

CHARLOTTE:
    The chord of harmony is broke forever.
    Since the blest spirit of my mother fled
    To join the blissful choristers of heaven,
    Peace fled with her—and discord sprang in France.
    Ah, Estelle, where are our transient pleasures?
    Too pure to last, they all departed with her.
    Changed is the face of all things in our country.
    One universal overthrow of peace—
    Proved from the glittering palace to the cot;
    The hamlet totters, and the palace falls.
    The private bosom from the public chaos
    Convulsive rends, while dearest ties are torn.
    Thus, my loved father loses, gem by gem,
    Of all his heart's possessions. Henry goes,
    And I—Ah! Like a vision of the night,
    Bless his glad eyes a little space, and vanish!

ESTELLE:
    Charlotte, art thou ill?
  [*Enter* ANNETTE *with a basket on her arm.*]

ANNETTE:
    Madam, I've prepared
    Everything ordered for the cottage—

CHARLOTTE:
    Come, let us walk. Old Bertrand's children will
    Enjoy this treat, and their pleased looks disperse
    The heaviness that weighs my spirits down. [*They exit.*]
  [*Enter* HENRY.]

HENRY:

> The time draws near when I must quit these scenes—
> These native scenes, this dear and happy home—
> To 'Join the standard of bright liberty'—
> High-sounding word, filling each warm breast
> With sacred ardor's animating power.
> Each eye, each tongue must speak in its defense;
> Each arm extend to scatter wide its foes.
> Yet, would I serve it in another field
> Than that of carnage. But I will obey
> The wishes of the tenderest father—
> May he not stand in need of my support!
> My Charlotte's gentle assiduities,
> With tenfold kindness, will supply my place.
> But, oh, she droops! That sweet vivacity,
> Delighting all, gives place to deepest gloom.
> In vain the ray of cheerfulness would pierce
> This cloud of care—its beams, alas, too faint!
> Not e'en the sympathy of those she loves
> Dispels the secret gathering of thought.
> Even Estelle's friendship's unavailing!
> Estelle's friendship? Rich—rich possession
> Balm for all anguish—oh, transporting thought!
> Is not that friendship mine? Yet more—her love!
> How shall I go? How tear myself away?
> My truant thoughts would wander to these scenes;
> Glory have but half a willing votary.

[*Enter* BELCOUR.]

BELCOUR:

> Thy meditation's serious, Henry.
> One might suppose thou had'st just cheated
> Thy reverend confessor, keeping back
> Some great and grievous sin, which now torments
> For being left without companions.
> Thine is the first sad countenance I've met.
> Where is the *warrior's* animated glow?
> *How many* gallant youths in pride of heart
> Would wear thy envied crest with ecstasy!

For shame! Fire at the mention of tomorrow,
When thou wilt head these candidates for fame—
These youthful patriots lead to victory!
Could friendship envy—by all that's sacred,
I should envy thee such early honors.

HENRY:

Could those, my friend, who at this moment wish
My lot was theirs—if any such there are—
Of my heart's feelings take a real view,
I think, indeed, they would reject the change;
For, oh, my Belcour, I am not happy!

BELCOUR:

And why not happy, Henry? What has chilled
Thy glowing ardor and eye-speaking joy?
Sure thou'rt not a school boy, whining to stay
A little longer by thy father's side,
When all thy comrades burn to try the field?

HENRY:

They no doubt consider me devoted
To the pursuit of arms and fair renown.
They know not that the bias of my mind
Fondly inclines to sweet domestic life,
But principle, love of true liberty,
And my torn country's welfare all prompt me
To every action that may evince
My zeal for each. Reproach would wound my breast
Worse than a thousand swords, if it could shrink
From any danger which the profession
My father has chosen for me can present.
Belcour, I could die to serve my country!
And, had my years permitted, would have been
Among the first brave repellers of its
Foreign enemies. My day is now come
To meet our foes, and my hope is glory!
Yet, were I left a choice, I should prefer
Glory of another kind—that renown
Not gained 'midst battles, blood, and victories!
Thou and I, Belcour, should have changed fortunes.

BELCOUR:

> So much—so plain—thou never said'st before;
> Yet what avails it now? The line is traced.
> The road to laureled honor courts thy step.
> And when we parted, fame was thy mistress.

HENRY:

> Ha! My bosom had not then unfolded
> All its interests to their full extent.
> But I will give thee its most secret thoughts.
> True, I could face a cannon undismayed;
> Yet I do not desire the dangerous honor,
> And would rather be the generous statesman
> Planning the happiness, prosperity,
> And peace of my countrymen than leading
> To battle—even like a Julius Caesar!
> Could I so far be dictator, as to
> Re-establish tranquility and heal
> The wounds of bleeding France—by foreign swords
> Less injured than by internal discord—
> Remove those vultures who devour our peace,
> Then should I, indeed, attain true glory.
> But enough. My destiny is fixed.

BELCOUR:

> That destiny will lead to fairest honors.
> Thy father's patriotic breast warms with
> The glowing hope of seeing thee a soldier
> Well approved. Thou wilt not disappoint him.

HENRY:

> Various circumstances now combine
> To break the feeble bond 'twixt me and arms.
> Charlotte droops. Some anguish preys upon her.
> My father marks it with concern, and though
> He longs to see me head my brave companions,
> Yet would postpone the day of separation.
> Oh, Belcour, they both may need my support
> When too far distant even to know it.

BELCOUR:

> Never, Henry, shall they want a friend.

A son—a brother—will thy Belcour be.
Let this suffice, and set thy mind at ease,
Secure in all that friendship has to offer.

HENRY:

Best of friends! How deep my obligation.

BELCOUR:

Name not obligation! Friends know it not.
To serve a friend is but to serve oneself.
Thy sister feels the absence of De Vernueil;
That intelligent countenance cannot
Conceal her bosom's fond anxiety.
But hope will again blossom on her cheek
And sparkle in her eye. De Vernueil will return,
And with him thy Charlotte's peace and happiness.

HENRY:

And when will mine, Belcour? Oh, I have sought
This moment, when all my situation
Should be unfolded to that kind bosom!
Say wilt thou, then, increase my debt, and with
Another kindness swell my gratitude?

BELCOUR:

Command me every way to serve thee.
Judge by thine own heart how willing mine is
To serve its friend. In turn I have somewhat
To communicate—so interesting,
So flattering to all my hopes of bliss
That thou wilt rejoice in my bright prospects.
But I am impatient. Speak, Henry,
Every wish, and be assured of my zeal.

HENRY:

May all thy prospects be crowned w'h possession;
That generous mind never have to exert
Its manly strength in bearing up against
Misfortune's storms, blighting disappointment,
Or the pang of being separated
From all it fondly dotes on. Oh, Estelle! [BELCOUR *starts.*]

[*Enter* CORDAY. *He advances, bows to* BELCOUR, *then puts
his hand upon* HENRY'S *shoulder affectionately.*]

CORDAY: Good morning, Belcour. Good morning, my son.
>I must interrupt ye for a while—
>Some business requires Henry's attention.

HENRY:
>For the present, adieu! I will return. [*Exit* CORDAY *and*
>HENRY. BELCOUR *stands in amazement, having scarcely
>noticed the salutation of* CORDAY. *He repeats the excla-
>mation of* HENRY.]

BELCOUR:
>"Oh, Estelle"! What, Henry dote on Estelle?
>It cannot, must not be. Henry, I dote—
>All! All but this, of fortune and of fame,
>I could yield to thee! But Estelle never!
>She is entwined with every thought and nerve,
>And I could as soon change the course of day's
>Refulgent orb as remove from my hopes
>Their brightest object—my adored Estelle!
>Why did I not to Henry long ago
>Declare my intentions? But there no blame
>Attaches to my silence, more than his.
>Alas! That hateful journey sealed my lips;
>Nor would I trust my pen. He was doubtless
>By the same cause restrained—our separation.
>And thus, while gaining trash to fill my purse,
>The nobler treasure of my heart is lost! [*Exits.*]

ACT II.

Scene One

A wood. [*Enter* CHARLOTTE *and* ANNETTE.]
CHARLOTTE:
>Annette, why were my orders disobeyed?

ANNETTE:
>My mistress knows I never disobey.
>Dumont promised to be here at this hour. [ANNETTE *goes
>towards the* road. CHARLOTTE *walks backwards and for-
>wards in expecting agitation.* ANNETTE *returns.*]

ANNETTE:

> The chaise is now in sight, ma'mselle.
> But I am a poor guard. The road is bad.
> Would it not be better could Jaques—or—

CHARLOTTE:

> This time, Annette, I mean to go alone.
> Return home, and remember the cottage;
> Inform Estelle. If Colin is not better,
> She will do all that's needful while I am gone.

ANNETTE:

> But, ma'mselle, is it safe to go alone?

CHARLOTTE:

> Why not, good girl? 'Tis but a little way.
> Dumont is careful, and the road now good.
> No clouds are threatening to obscure the day.
> Go, Annette. Give this letter to Estelle. [*Gives a letter.* AN-
> NETTE *takes it with great surprise.*]

ANNETTE:

> Strange fears alarm me. Why? I cannot tell.
> I don't know how to go. Why this letter?
> Oh, pardon my boldness; but, dear ma'mselle,
> Pray, oh, pray take me! I shall neither sleep,
> Nor eat, nor drink for very anxiousness.

CHARLOTTE:

> Let no anxiety disturb thee, Annette.
> Danger awaits me at a greater distance.
> Leave me, kind Annette. I wish to be alone.

ANNETTE:

> Indeed, indeed, I cannot. Oh, take me!

CHARLOTTE:

> Do not thus distress me by persisting
> To ask what I must refuse. Convince me
> Of real affection by obedience.
> Thou wilt laugh at these unnecessary fears.

ANNETTE.

> Ah! Some evil will surely come of this. [*She looks mourn-
> fully at her mistress, then at the letter, and goes off slowly.*]

CHARLOTTE: [*After she walks about once or twice*]

Strong are thy claims, O nature! Now do I
Feel them with an iron force grasp my heart—
Unlike their former tender pressures but
As if some cruel power was tearing from
My bosom *its vitality* while nature,
Unwilling to forego its long abode,
Struggles with rude, convulsing violence.
Let me, then, whisper that foul name: Marat,
And the last conflict end. The monster's name
Steals every thought, and female weakness flies.
With strength I'm armed, and mighty energy
To crush the murderer and defy the scaffold.
Let but the deed be done. For it, *I'll die.*
For it, I sacrifice—I quit—myself
And all the softness of a woman's name,
Leave a venerable, doting father!
But, ah! Might not the fangs of fierce Marat
Seize on his hoary locks? For who escapes?
May not my brother raise his arm in vain
To save his aged parent and himself?
And to the countless list of victims, add
Their precious lives? No! My hand shall save them.
The innocent again shall walk in safety.
Thousands shall bless the blow by which he falls.

[*Pauses.*] And when, again,
Fond parental arms with joy enfold me,
And love and friendship spring to meet my heart,
All—all my present feelings will be lost
In the tumultuous overflow of bliss.
But, ah! What keeps me longer here? I linger
Amidst these shades; to quit them seems as the soul
Forced from the clinging and reluctant body.
That bench, those trees are eloquent. De Vernueil,
My Estelle, Henry—there have we listened
To the pure converse of the purest minds. [*Thunder is heard.*]
Hark! I must no longer stay. Oh, farewell! [*Looks around.*]
On all the past, oblivion cast thy veil.

Let no fond recollections hold my thoughts
From vengeance and Marat. [*Exits.*]

Scene Two

[*In another part of the wood, a cottage. Before the door,*
SUSETTE *is sitting at work, with a* LITTLE BOY *resting his head
on her lap.*]

SUSETTE:
    Why do I wish to see Jaques here again?
    For he never looks at simple Susette.
    Oh! When I think he loves some blooming maid,
    I wish there was no other maid but me!
    And is he going, too, to fight and die,
    Like my poor father, on the bloody field?
    Why do men fight, and leave their peaceful homes,
    When they can laugh, and work, and play, and sing,
    And "make tomorrow happy as today"?
    Now all our village maidens sigh like me.

[JAQUES *and* ANNETTE *approach. He is supporting her tenderly.*]
    How kind he looks. Why do I tremble so?

ANNETTE:
    I feel quite faint.

JAQUES:
    Lean upon me, Annette.

SUSETTE:
    What has happened?

ANNETTE:
    Oh! My ankle is sprained.

SUSETTE:
    I have a remedy will soon give ease. [SUSETTE *takes the
child in her arms.* JAQUES *seats* ANNETTE *and supports
her.* SUSETTE *turns around at the door, looks at them, and
exits with the child.*]

JAQUES:
    I wish the accident had befallen me.

ANNETTE:

> Yes, Jaques, if it would keep thee from the war.
> I dread to think, tomorrow is the day
> When from his Annette her dear Jaques must go.
> The tears that come into my aching eyes
> Quite dim my sight. And now this new distress—
> My mistress gone. Oh, Jaques, where is she gone?

JAQUES:

> Thou art made up of very fearfulness.
> Where e'er thy gentle mistress is, she's safe.
> I think it strange she should have gone alone;
> But we are told that God protects the good.
> And, as for me, why, ever think of Jaques
> As a lad that seeks an halberd'—not death.
> So, though I would surely scorn to run away,
> I should not rush into the thickest battle.
> For Annette's sake, Jaques will try to live.
> I love thee, Annette, better than myself. [*As* JAQUES *speaks,* SUSETTE *enters and drops a bottle she held.*]

SUSETTE:

> Ah! How unlucky! It was all we had.

JAQUES:

> Why, my pretty Susette, one would suppose
> It was thy little heart that thou had'st broke.

SUSETTE: [*Turning away from* JAQUES.]

> Is it not best to come into the house
> And rest awhile upon my bed, Annette?

ANNETTE:

> Oh, no! I have a letter to deliver,
> And must now hasten home as speedily
> As my lame steps can bear me.

JAQUES:

> Adieu, Susette. [JAQUES *and* ANNETTE *exit slowly.*]

SUSETTE:

> And what's this that swells w'th'n my heart?
> I seem to hate Annette. Hate Annette?
> What, when I am taught to love my enemies,

Shall I towards my friends with anger burn,
Because my fate is not so blest as hers?
Yet, I cannot bear to think Jaques loves her.
Oh! I will seek our curate, and confess
This great offense, and pray to be forgiven. [*Exits.*]

Scene Three

[*An apartment in* CORDAY'S *house. Enter* ESTELLE.]

ESTELLE:
Charlotte's deep inquietude alarms me.
While anxious for her repose, I almost
Forget my own distress, till solitude
Awakens it. Alas, what mingled sighs
From such contending feelings rend my heart.
Oh, my Henry! How shall I tell thee all?

[*Enter* HENRY.]

HENRY:
Oh, tell me, dearest Estelle, that I am
As welcome to thy sight as thou to mine
Most precious. Let us prize each moment
Of happiness. Soon I must be absent
From the treasure of my soul, but like the
Veriest parsimonious miser, shall
Forever turn to it in anxious thought.

ESTELLE:
Happiness, Henry! Oh,'tis a meteor
A transient vision that eludes our grasp!
Even when we see it close within our reach,
It flits away and leaves us in pursuit.
Shall we, then, think to possess a reality
That exists not under Heaven?

HENRY:
Estelle!
Thy looks are chilling as indifference.
Thou did'st not meet me thus when last we met!
Then, as now, our approaching separation

Thou knewest, yet did'st look with other eyes.
Those lips spoke words of comfort—hope—and talked
Of happiness when Henry should return
And bring his laurels home, to change them for
A wreath of love entwining.

ESTELLE:

I have now no words of comfort; no hope to bid me
Smile, and think of thy return.

HENRY: [*Much agitated*]

In pity,
Estelle, explain. Art thou changed? My heart is
Pierced with doubt. Speak, am I not dear to thee?

ESTELLE:

Cruel question, so dear Henry, that next
To duty's claim, thyself—thy happiness—
Occupy my thoughts and hopes. Changed! Indifferent!
No, Henry, thy worth and generous affection
Will live, while I live, engraved on my heart
In lasting characters, through every change
And chance of this varying existence.
After this assurance, thou need'st not doubt
My faithful love. But an unlooked-for bar
To our future union interposes.
Even should all thy sanguine prospects
Of a quick return meet with full success,
Thy hope to move my father in our favor
Will be vain.

HENRY:

Say not so. He shall consent.

ESTELLE:

Hear me with composure, and be assured:

HENRY:

Heavens! This is torture! What will follow?

ESTELLE:

What sometimes thou hast anticipated.
My father designs to establish me.

HENRY:

Oh, stop! Thou wilt destroy me. Yet go on—

ESTELLE:

>If not more thyself, I dare not—will not.
>Remember what I have so often vowed.

HENRY:

>Oh! It shall be a shield, defending me
>From every wound thy father or the world
>Can inflict. To know I live in thy esteem—
>In thy affection—will make all evils light.

ESTELLE:

>My father put two letters in my hand:
>One of them sought that hand; the other spoke
>Immediate, unreserved compliance.
>In agitation, I returned them both,
>While in my looks he plainly read rejection.
>With faltering timidity, I asked
>If such an answer he indeed would send.
>"Why not?" he sternly said; what objection
>Could I in reason make to such a man
>Every way unexceptionable?
>Ah! Dear Henry! Belcour—

HENRY: [*In astonishment*]

>Belcour! Belcour!
>Then happiness is indeed a vision!
>Belcour my rival? Did that letter go?

ESTELLE:

>It did, for entreaties availed me not.
>My tears fell on his hand, but did not soften
>The inflexible purpose of his will.
>I threw myself in anguish at his feet—
>On the point to confess our attachment,
>When, alas, the strong remembrance of his
>Singular prejudice, so lately known—
>His strange, solemn vow never to consent
>To his daughter's marrying a soldier—
>Suspended the words upon my lips, and
>Clasping his hand, I could only breathe out,
>"Oh! Do not, my Father, make me wretched."
>But the letter went, and Belcour came.

HENRY: [*Walking about in great agitation.*]
    I dread thy father's obstinacy;
    'Tis implacable and violent.
    Estelle, thou hast never yet opposed it;
    But is he right, even as a parent,
    To force thee to accept of any man
    Repugnant to thy own free will and choice?
    But, oh how winning, how good is Belcour!
    May not his worth erase my humbler merit?

ESTELLE:
    My Henry's merit must secure my love.

HENRY:
    Ah! Had Belcour known of my attachment,
    And that it was returned—what had he done?

ESTELLE:
    Resigned my hand to his deserving friend.

HENRY:
    Sensible of thy father's prejudices,
    He would never have resigned thee, knowing
    A soldier's hand would be disdained by him.
    Estelle, I abhor disobedience, but
    I also despise narrow prejudice,
    And hoped, till now, thy father might have been
    Induced to overcome the force of his.
    But, ah! The hope is void; he never will.
    Such singularity is culpable,
    And, in some instances, to oppose it
    Cannot be deemed a breach of duty.
    Are we to be thrown into a state
    Inimical to our happiness?
    And with the rod of prejudice be scourged?
    Oh, no! Consent to be mine; let this hour
    Unite our destiny, beyond the power
    Of earthly authority to sever. [*Takes her hand.*]
    Near the cloister's walls, I left old Ronville;
    Let us hasten to him, for tomorrow
    I must leave thee. No, I will not leave thee
    Till thou art mine by every sacred tie.

ESTELLE:

    Henry, forbear; yet let me once more say
    The strongest earthly power shall not prevail
    To make me break my plighted faith to thee.
    I must not listen to thy fond request.
    I must not marry with a father's curse!
    Oh, leave me Henry, and employ thyself
    In noblest acts of valor. We are young.
    Go, convince my father that a soldier
    Is worthy of his daughter, and his love.

HENRY:

    A cruel prospect is painted for me,
    In the dark coloring of disappointment.
    Will then thy resolution support thee
    Against the firm command of a parent?
    Thou dost not love, Estelle. Such cold reasoning,
    Such acquiescence to future changes
    Ill accord with my feelings towards thee.
    I dare not trust to the uncertain future;
    But as thy will directs, so I must obey.
    And thy stern father, too, will be obeyed.
    This heart, that fondly sues, will cease to beat;
    This ardent eye shall never more meet thine!
    But Belcour's will; he, thy fond protector,
    Shall strew thy path with flowers. I strew but thorns,
    And thou art wise to choose the path without them.

  [*Waves his hand, appears to be going.*]

ESTELLE:

    Stay, too hasty young man. Stay, my Henry—

HENRY:

    Forgive, my sweet Estelle, oh, forgive me.
    Heaven knows, if I beheld one ray of hope,
    I would not urge thee against thy duty;
    But I am now, as certain thou wilt be
    Compelled to marry Belcour, as if I—

ESTELLE:

    Henry, hast thou no confidence in me?

Oh, persuade me not to do what will impose
Deep anguish, and indeed strew my path with thorns.

HENRY:

Cold prudence is thy only sentiment.
Farewell forever! [*As he is hurrying off, enter* ANNETTE.]
Why this intrusion?

ANNETTE:

Oh, sir! My mistress!

ESTELLE:

What of thy mistress?

ANNETTE:

Oh, ma'mselle, I've been every where to search.
At the cottage I thought to have found you.
But here's the letter; my mistress is gone—[*Gives the letter.*]
Whither I know not. [ESTELLE *reads, in great alarm.*]

HENRY:

Gone? What does this mean?

ESTELLE:

Henry, what will become of thy sister? [*Gives him the let-ter; he reads.*]
How long, good girl, since thy mistress went?

ANNETTE:

A great while, ma'mselle. I should have been
Here long ago but for an ugly accident;
But the pain I feel is nothing, to that
In my heart. Oh! Where is my mistress gone?

ESTELLE:

Go, Annette. Thy mistress will soon return. [ANNETTE *limps out.*]

HENRY:

This is wonderful! Charlotte, thou art lost.
Enthusiastic girl, these sentiments
Are worthy of a Roman, yet are vain.
Oh, could I save thee! But take the vengeance
Thy grieved spirit meditates—how grateful
To my soul. Life is now of no value,
But as a barrier 'twixt thee and death

For death awaits thy deed. But I will strive
To save her. Now I no longer persist
In my request, oh my adored Estelle.
I would not leave thee a mourning bride.
No, forget me, and obey thy father's will.
Soon I shall overtake my Charlotte,
And the sure weapon of destruction
Shall be guided by a stronger hand.
Oh, Estelle! Bid me a last adieu!
Bless me with one more kind look of love.

ESTELLE:

Ah, Henry, I am indeed overcome!
These circumstances weigh far heavier
Than all thy fond and pleading arguments.
I see thy rash design. Impetuous,
Thou wilt plunge thyself into destruction—
Not save thy sister. I—I will consent
To blend my life with thine this hour, Henry.
Then thou wilt endeavor to preserve it.

HENRY:

Thus only could'st thou save me and thy friend.
Hasten, my love. Oh, Estelle, let us fly!

[*As he is leading her off, enter* BELCOUR.]

BELCOUR:

Ha! Henry! Proceed not, sir! That lady—

HENRY: [*As he turns his head.*]

I have much to say; meet me at the hotel. [*Exit* HENRY *and* ES-
TELLE.]

BELCOUR:

Hold, Henry! [BELCOUR *rushes on after them. As he is going
out, enter* LE BRUN, *who gently takes his arm.* BELCOUR *turns
round angrily.*]

BELCOUR:

Villain, whence this insolence?
Did thy master bid thee watch me? Coward—

LE BRUN:

Pardon me sir, but what hath Henry done?
How long since in thine eye he looked a coward?

BELCOUR:

> Away! By heaven, he answers with his life
> For this base conduct. Estelle! Oh, Estelle! [BELCOUR
> *again endeavors to pass.* LE BRUN *interposes himself.*]

LE BRUN:

> While with passion wild, I must detain thee.
> Why should'st thou seek the life of such a friend?
> A duel was the first of my errors.
> Oh, spare thyself remorse and endless woe!

BELCOUR:

> Spare thy lectures, old man. Leave me, leave me.

LE BRUN:

> Never shalt thou pass to injure Henry.

BELCOUR:

> Not another moment dare to keep me. [BELCOUR *pushes*
> LE BRUN *from him and exits.*]

LE BRUN:

> Some demon seems to hover over France,
> Infusing rancor in the gentlest breasts.
> World of tribulation, I'm weary of thee.
> Thy storms destroy; thy calms are voids we fly from.
> Nothing satisfies the ever-restless soul:
> It boils, or stagnates in cold apathy.
> Few, few, blessed spirits taste the balmy sweets
> Of that supreme and only true delight
> Springing from a mind well regulated—
> Enjoying wisely, feeling sensibly,
> Yet commanding those tempestuous passions
> That whirl the blood in eddies of distraction. [*Exits.*]

ACT III

Scene One

[MARAT *discovered, sitting meanly dressed with his hat on, sur-*
rounded by motley crew. CHABOT *at his right hand.* MARAT
rises and comes forward.]

MARAT:

      Citizens! These difficulties shall cease,
      And the head of each base conspirator—
      Each foe to liberty and equality
      Shall roll beneath us, an abject football.
      My countrymen, enlightened sons of France:
      Ye—ye, who comprehend true freedom!
      Boldly trample on the groveling hearts
      Of those who still adhere to kings—and priests.
      Free as the air, and equal as its surface,
      Citizens! Patriots! Spill your bravest blood;
      Raise high the pile of slaughtered sycophants!
      Exterminate all those who dare presume
      To check this radiant dawn of liberty,
      Which soon shall blaze a full meridian sun
      Too bright for despots and their cringing slaves
      To look on! Dazzled by its brilliancy,
      Unable to behold the great, resplendent,
      Full-orbed, mighty, glorious, liberty,
      Their narrow hearts will sink within their breasts
      Ignobly chained to proud nobility—
      To treacherous crowns—and wily priestcraft!
      Not daring to complain—much less redress
      The most oppressive burdens—meanly they
      Drag on existence in debasing bonds—
      In bonds which ye great, deserving Frenchmen
      Have so gloriously burst asunder.
      By yourselves ye are emancipated.
      Live! Live to triumph in the enjoyment
      Of reason and its rights. Never suffer
      Those dear rights again to be invaded.
      Let no ambitious, traitorous, haughty despot
      Chain your minds or bodies more—but be free!
      Frenchmen! Countrymen! My brethren! Be free.
      Stain your swords with the purple tide flowing
      From dying conspirators. Let the foes
      Of our liberty bleed. They are vipers.
      Let not bread which should nourish true Frenchmen

Be wasted on them! No! Destroy—destroy!
Justice calls aloud, destroy! Well ye know
Whose blood to spill—and whose to spare—without
The tedious mockeries of courts and judges.
Judge for yourselves—and quickly execute.
[*Enter a* MAN *who whispers to* MARAT. MARAT *replies aloud.*]
MARAT:
Tell the person business detained me.
I received her note, and will speak with her. [*Exit* MAN.]
Citizens! A person waits, well informed
Of circumstances highly important.
Delay is ever dangerous, and now
It would be culpable; therefore, I go
To hear what I trust will aid our cause.
My whole ambition is to serve it
With all my powers of mind and body.
This arm will not spare one aristocrat.
This breast harbors eternal enmity
To each opposer of its sentiments—
The sentiments of pure republicanism—
While ardor in its cause gives force and tone
To all my energies—even to my steps.
I feel a demigod—[*Struts about.*] How ennobled
By the boundless confidence of such men— [*Points to them.*]
Fellow citizens! I live to serve you. [*Exit* MARAT.]
CHABOT: [*Advances.*]
We, to support the champion of freedom,
And unanimous in defense of him—
We swear to stand or fall with great Marat
The people's friend. [*Exit all.*]

Scene Two

[CHARLOTTE *discovered in an antechamber.*]
CHARLOTTE:
A few short moments, and his doom is fixed.
My heart that sickened if an insect died,
My bosom nursed in softest tenderness

Burn to destroy—feel a powerful impulse
Strengthening every nerve, compressing
Every thought to one keen point—revenge!
Enthusiastic fervor bears me on,
And gentler passions fly before its power!
No other hand will rise. No other eye
Will throw death's fiat on the subtle serpent.
No more shall guileless innocence be stung
By his envenomed tongue and thirst of blood;
Nor shall those brave men his savage sword condemns
Add to the mound of butchered victims.
Oh, no! No! No! He dies.

Scene Three

[*Back scene opens to discover* MARAT *in his chamber, dressed in a loose bathing gown and slippers. At the farthest end of the room stands his bath.*[3]]

[MARAT *comes forward.*]

MARAT:
    I have too long detained thee, young woman.
    Now let me have the promised information.

CHARLOTTE:
    Citizen, my errand is important.
    Thy civism leads thee to destroy whatever
    Is prejudicial to true liberty,
    And to the welfare of France. I am come
    To point out the *deadliest* foe to *both,*
    And a sure way to rid our country of him.

[*Gives a packet.* MARAT *prepares to open it.*]

    Here in this packet is full information
    Of a well-planned and deep conspiracy;
    But ere thou dost examine the contents,
    Suffer me to ask, what will be the fate
    Of those conspirators who fled to Normandy,
    And of such people as conceal the traitors—
    Adopting, too, their dangerous opinions,
    Which threaten ruin to the noble cause

Espoused by every true-born son of freedom?

MARAT:

Ha! Would'st thou, then, know what will be their fate?
I tell thee, girl, that they, and many more
Who think themselves secure—their heads quite safe,
Will feel the sharp axe of the guillotine.

[*He looks down on the packet to open it.*]

CHARLOTTE:

First—feel this sharper weapon! Die, monster!
[*Stabs him.* MARAT *falls.*] There is an end to thy destruc-
        tive course!
Thou *ignis fatuus*[4] that deceived the simple;
Murderer of prisoners—of priests defenseless—
Of helpless women—die! The innocent
Shall live. Now art thou death's prisoner.

MARAT:

In sin's lowest depths, alas, I perish!
Thy friends, young woman, are too well avenged.
How did'st thou find this courage? Oh, great God!
God? Ha! That sacred name should not proceed
From my polluted lips. I dare not pray;
My prayers would be but impious mockery.
The sighs of others never reached my ear;
Can those from my remorseless heart e'er reach
The mighty throne omnipotent? Oh! Oh! [*Groans loudly.*]

[CHABOT *enters. He starts, then rushes up to* MARAT, *whom he
supports.*]

MARAT: [*Faintly*].

Is it thou, Chabot? Ah! Could I but live—
But no, I die—I die. The light recedes.
My eyes are closing . . . open! Open them! [*In agony.*]
Oh, save me from that yawning gulf! Save me!
Oh! Save me! Save—[*Springs, convulsed, from the support
of* CHABOT, *and dies.* CHABOT *seizes the poignard, and
grasps the arm of* CHARLOTTE *fiercely. She looks compos-
edly at him.*]

CHABOT:

Girl! What hast thou done? Did madness seize thee?

Tremble for the consequence of this crime.
A public expiation waits the deed;
Or my hand should now destroy, with the same
Destructive weapon, so well directed.
What instigated thee to such an act? [*Lets her go, and
drops the poignard.*]

CHARLOTTE:
The cause of virtue. The world contained not,
In all its wide circumference, so black
A traitor to its peace and liberty
As base Marat. My soul is satisfied.
A woman's arm, when nerved in such a cause,
Is as the arm of the avenging angel.
Think not I am a foe to liberty!
My father is a real patriot;
My brother, at this moment, joins the friends,
Soldiers of liberty! Not assassins.
They should sink beside that fallen enemy
To all but anarchy and cruelty. [*Points to* MARAT.]
To know that, by his death, thousands are free
Fully repays the danger I incur!
Lead me to prison, if thy conscience bids
But if one spark of heavenly liberty—
Of generous love towards thy country—
Glows within that bosom, then wilt thou say
Depart in safety. But I see thy purpose.

CHABOT:
Yes, I'll bid thee depart— Ho! Assistance!
[*Enter several* MEN.] To prison with her—where this heroism
Will soon be humbled, and that beautiful head
Bend lower than it deigns to do at present.
Away with her! [*They exit.*]

Scene Four

[*An apartment in* DUVAL'S *house.* DUVAL *is seated, looking
over the contents of a pocketbook. Enter* ESTELLE. *He looks
at her.*]

DUVAL:

> Still this dejected look, my dear Estelle?
> I fear thy tender health will suffer, child.
> Remember, while we sympathize with others,
> Their sorrows must not leave too deep a trace,
> Must not be made entirely our own.
> But I will say no more; the subject wounds.

ESTELLE:

> Alas! It does—

DUVAL:

> And where we cannot heal,
> Discussion only gives a keener pang,
> 'Tis not all anguish that can be partaken,
> Yet, would thy father take thy every grief,
> And bid that mouth forever wear a smile. [*Embraces her.*]

ESTELLE:

> My kind—my dear Father!

DUVAL:

> Tell me, my child.
> Hast thou considered the request I made,
> With deep attention weighed the matter well?
> Thou know'st I cannot bear opposition,
> 'Twas wrong to set thy father's will at naught.
> Thou canst not disappoint his darling hope.

ESTELLE:

> Disappoint thy darling hope, my Father? [*In agitation.*]

DUVAL:

> That were impossible. It was surprise:
> Thou had'st not thought of leaving me, Estelle,
> But, alas, I am in the vale of years;
> Thy mother is no more—and heaven knows
> That thou, my child, wilt need the fostering care
> Of one whose love can ward off every ill.
> Single—exposed! What—what might be thy fate
> Amidst these desolating, factious times,
> Sparing nor age nor sex? Ah! When I'm gone,
> Virtue will be thy only legacy;
> And that, if unprotected, often falls

A victim to designing villainy;
Or, vainly struggling against the dark stream
Of poverty, is overwhelmed and sinks.

ESTELLE:
Oh, far, far distant be the mournful day
That deprives me of so dear a parent!
But, my Father, when it pleases Him who gives,
And who resumes, to take thy precious life,
Paint not the future in so deep a shade.
Virtuous Industry, my dearest sir,
Is always rewarded with competence.

DUVAL:
There *is* a land where such indeed's the case.
Not thine, my child. It is America.
There, in the conjugal or single state—
In affluence or pale-cheeked poverty—
Each female who respects herself is safe.
Each walks the path of life secure from insult,
As strongly guarded by a virtuous mind
As she who's in a gilded chariot borne,
Surrounded by an host of glittering arms,
But here, the mind adorned with every grace,
Compelled to stoop and share the body's toll,
In gloomy, isolated poverty,
Too often droops—or if it makes a stand,
Its tones are blunted by adversity,
And though it springs to pierce this earthly veil,
And catch a vision of its future state,
Where virtue will surely be rewarded
And patient merit there receive its prize;
Yet, in this life, acts an imperfect part,
Unlike the scene of wedded excellence.
Fulfilling woman's dear and sacred duties,
Scattering sweets to all within its influence,
It shines the brightest gem in nature's works.
Then, let this lovely part be thine, Estelle.
Oh, make thy own happiness—and Belcour's!

ESTELLE:

> Forgive me, sir, but Belcour's happiness
> Can never blend with mine. Oh, forgive me!
> Look not so sternly.

DUVAL:

> What, still reject him?
> Ungrateful girl! Know I will be obeyed.
> Some puppy, sure, hath pleased thy silly eye;
> Some gaudy, trifling soldier stole thy heart.

ESTELLE:

> Are there, then, no good men, or brave, or great
> Among our country's valiant defenders?
> From whence arose so strong a prejudice?

DUVAL:

> I would sooner follow thee to thy grave,
> Than ever see thee, child, a soldier's wife.
> Tinsel dolls, or savages—I hate them.
> Even the very best I ever knew,
> De Vernueil, I cannot entirely approve.

ESTELLE:

> Where is there a fault in his noble nature?

DUVAL:

> What, hath he not in his letters said
> That Beaurepere acted a great man's part
> By terminating his own existence
> When unable, at the siege of Verdun,
> To make his gallant defense successful?
> Soldiers used to be Christians; not so now.
> They cease to consider religious duties,
> And much I fear that even De Vernueil
> Would desert the post assigned him on earth,
> Braving the danger of offended heaven,
> Than endure disgrace before his fellow man,
> Or bear the slighter evils that assail.
> But, I hear Belcour. Be wise and happy.
> I have promised thy hand; refuse it not,
> Or my blessing is refused forever. [*Exit* DUVAL.]

[*Enter* BELCOUR.]

BELCOUR:

> Pardon, if I intrude. Think not, Estelle,
> Presumption brings me here. 'Tis sympathy.
> We feel alike the sorrows of our friends,
> With deep anxiety. Yet, let us hope.

ESTELLE:

> A succession of painful circumstances
> Depress me almost beyond the reach of hope.

BELCOUR:

> Estelle, I cannot bear to see thee thus.
> Oh, how willingly would I endure the
> Weight of anguish that now oppresses thee!

ESTELLE:

> If thou dost, indeed, feel for my distress,
> Then leave me, I beseech thee.

BELCOUR:

> First, hear me.
> With thy father's approbation I am come.
> Oh, give me but the most distant hope, Estelle,
> And I will sigh a thousand miles away,
> Till the blest hour when thou shall say return.

ESTELLE:

> Desist, for I can never bid thee hope.
> If thou dost love me, create my happiness.

BELCOUR:

> If I love thee? Oh, thou more precious far
> Than even love's most eloquent language
> Could portray, know that my fate hangs on thee,
> My all of happiness! Oh, blast not, then,
> Its blooming hopes forever! [*Kneels.*]

ESTELLE:

> Rise, Belcour.
> For an instant I will not deceive thee.
> No length of time can change my sentiments.

BELCOUR: [*Rises in anger.*]

> I am despised—because thou lov'st another. [*Turns away.*]

DUVAL:

    Ha! Ungrateful girl, thou shalt not treat him thus.

    Hence with this disobedience! Give thy hand. [*Forcibly takes her hand.*]

ESTELLE: [*Looks mournfully at her father.*]

    No, my Father. It cannot, cannot be.

BELCOUR:

    Estelle, never will I cause thy misery.

ESTELLE:

    I am ill. Oh, suffer me to withdraw! [DUVAL *lets her hand fall. She retires.*]

BELCOUR:

    Forbear all violence. To take an hand

    Without an heart would bring me wretchedness.

    Time in my favor may produce a change.

DUVAL:

    Time, sir? 'Tis time she should be dutiful;

    But this hated, monstrous revolution

    Seems to extend its baleful influence

    Even to the hearts of individuals,

    Making our children as disobedient

    To the natural government of parents

    As to the good old regime of France.

    But, I'll be obeyed. [*Exit* DUVAL.]

BELCOUR: [*Pauses.*]

    She shall not hate me;

    Sooner would I linger on the rack.

    But can I exist without Estelle?

    Oh, Henry, art thou indeed a rival?

    Was I but sure he met return of love,

    Could I, then, resign the sweet girl to him?

    Perhaps she treats him, too, with cold disdain—

    Disdain, which now destroys my peace. Ah! No,

    That interesting scene betrayed the truth.

    Yet, it might have been Charlotte's departure

    Was the sole subject of their conference,

    Which then I knew not. So Henry may love

With hopeless fervor, like myself, in vain.
No sparkling hope shot from his languid eye
When last we were together—yes, one look,
One glance, declared it, when he named Estelle.
Oh! That interruption—but it is past—
Would that I had gone instead of written.
Now, meet when we will—we meet enemies.

ACT IV

Scene One

[CORDAY'S *house.* CORDAY *appears. He is seated with folded arms. He rises suddenly.*]

CORDAY:

Thus shall I finish the career of life—
When, in the arms of children, age should rest
Safe from the world's alarms, encircled there!
What! Here alone? No portion left but tears,
Of all my fair possessions. My daughter—
Oh, sweetest, best of children—my delight!
And thou, my Henry, where—where are ye now?
Oh, Thou, that dwellest in yon realms above—
That dost behold affliction's downcast eye—
Pour into my soul, meek in resignation.
Bid me look up, then to Thy mandates bow.
Yet, let—oh, let Thy servant once embrace
The blessings Thou did'st give! But no. Never—
Never shall these streaming eyes again behold
Their joy—their overflowing joy—my children!
Ah! What can save my poor, deluded girl
But Thy protecting mercy? Oh, shield her!

[*Enter* DE VERNUEIL *in a horseman's uniform.* CORDAY *gazes at him.*]

DE VERNUEIL:

My friend, my Father!
[*Embraces* CORDAY.] Where is my Charlotte?

Where is Henry? He is not gone, I hope—
I bring dispatches from the army,
Making this my route to snatch the bliss
Of seeing those I love.

CORDAY:

[*Mournfully.*] Ah! De Vernueil!

DE VERNUEIL:

What mean these looks of anguish?

CORDAY:

My daughter!

DE VERNUEIL:

What—what! Is she dead? Oh, in mercy speak.
[*Takes hold of* CORDAY'*s hand with trembling agitation*]

CORDAY: [*Looking at him with pity and speaking fearfully.*]
Not yet. Oh, fly! Fly and save thy Charlotte!
[*Enter a* MOB. *They cry out, "A la lanterne! A la lanterne! He shall not live! Marat, the people's friend, is assassinated by Corday's daughter. Seize him—seize him."* DE VERNUEIL *snatches a sword from one of the mob, which he puts into* COR-DAY's *hand, then draws his own broadsword and places himself before* CORDAY.]

DE VERNUEIL:

My friend! Endeavor to defend thyself.

CORDAY:

Dear youth, my weak defense will not avail.

DE VERNUEIL:

And is it thus ye treat this good old man?
Behold the veteran's scars, your soldier,
Whose age these threatening arms should now defend!
[MOB *rushes on, exclaiming, "Marat! Vengeance!"*]

DE VERNUEIL:

Through my heart, your swords shall only pierce him.
[*After a struggle in which the* MOB *are kept off, one goes behind* CORDAY *and stabs him. He falls instantly.* DE VERNUEIL *turns around and kills the man.*]
[*Enter* BELCOUR, OFFICER, *and* SOLDIERS.]

OFFICER:

Disperse—disperse! Away. [SOLDIERS *drive the* MOB *off.*]

[DE VERNUEIL *kneels down, raising* CORDAY'S *head in his arms.*]

CORDAY:

De Vernueil, where art thou? Oh. De Vernueil!
Tell my beloved children we shall meet
Where cruelty shall wound no more. Farewell!
Ah! My children! [*Dies.*]

BELCOUR:

Alas, we come too late.
Dear De Vernueil, my heart bleeds with thine!
Why, oh, why was I not here to save?
Rise, rise my friend. Thou must not longer stay;
Thy life's in danger. Hasten far from here.

[DE VERNUEIL *still leans over the body. He gently rests the head down.*]

DE VERNUEIL:

Gone! Gone! Oh, that some pitying angel
Would pour the balm of life into these wounds!
What does this horror mean? [*Rises up in great agitation.*]

BELCOUR:

Here, De Vernueil,
It is impossible to explain. Go—
Estelle will unfold the dreadful story. [DE VERNUEIL *casts a lingering look at* CORDAY, *then around the apartment; clasps his hands; and exits.*]

Scene Two

[*A prison.* CHARLOTTE *discovered.*]

CHARLOTTE:

While the soul ranges through the boundless scope
Of never dying thought, and views at ease
Each object cherished by its mortal ties,
What are the body's bonds? Mere spider threads.
Yet when we long to clasp a father's hand;
To meet a brother's eye, a friend's caress;
To hear the accents of the voice we love—
How strains the eye, how bends the listening ear!

The arms extend—but, ah, extend in vain!
The visions fade, and the sick heart is void. [*Pauses.*]
In blest reality we yet shall meet!
Oh, may my tongue defend its noble cause,
Convincing, with triumphant energy,
That vice should be destroyed and virtue live—
That he has perished who was most its foe,
And justly fell a victim at its shrine.

[*Enter* CHABOT *and* SOLDIERS.]

CHABOT:
    Charlotte Corday! Thou art now summoned
    To appear and answer to the charge
    Of assassination.

CHARLOTTE:
    I am prepared
    To stand the charge, as one whose act was just,
    And for the welfare of my suffering country,
    Whose gratitude and justice will proclaim me
    A benefactor—not an assassin.

CHABOT:
    Thou art mistaken, mad enthusiast!
    France will condemn thee to the guillotine—

CHARLOTTE:
    If such my doom, France is the fettered slave
    Of factious, criminal, blood-thirsty men—
    And soon will fall beneath a *weight of crimes.*

CHABOT: Lead on! [CHARLOTTE *walks out with dignity.*
    CHABOT *follows.*]

Scene Three

[*The inside of the cottage.* BERTRAND *and his* GRANDCHIL-
DREN *discovered as* SUSETTE *is feeding the blind old man. Two
or three little* BOYS *play around them.*]

BERTRAND:
    Can it be, Susette, that our young lady
    Is gone from her father's house—none knows where?
    I listened all this morn to hear her voice,

And to feel her soft hand on my shoulder,
So kind—so gentle. Take my dinner, child;
I cannot swallow. [*Leans upon the little table.*]

SUSETTE:

Oh, do try, Papa.
She will no doubt return. [BERTRAND *shakes his head. The*
BOYS *look anxiously at the plate.*]

BERTRAND:

I cannot eat.
Give it to the children. But don't forget
Thyself, my Susette, and little—

[*Enter* DE VERNUEIL. *A little* BOY *older than the rest has hold
of his hand, appearing quite delighted. The children run up to
him.* SUSETTE *curtsies.*]

DE VERNUEIL:

Oh, this scene! Could I behold its ornament,
My Charlotte—the blessing of this family!
Old Bertrand, thy son knew me as I passed.
I spare one moment from my *precious* time
To ask, how fares it with thee, good old man?

BERTRAND:

Ill, young gentleman—nor shall I be well
Till the voice we love again shall greet us.

DE VERNUEIL:

Heaven bless me with "its silver tones" again.
Farewell! Farewell! [DE VERNUEIL *puts a purse on the
table and exits.*]

[*Enter* ANNETTE *at the opposite door.*]

ANNETTE:

The poor old gentleman!
[ANNETTE *rests her arm on the table, discovers the purse.*]
What is this, Susette? 'Tis an heavy purse!

BERTRAND:

A purse, Annette? Generous De Vernueil!
Just like our lovely mistress—good and kind.

ANNETTE:

Alas, Bertrand, 'tis said she'll ne'er return!

My sweet mistress is accused of murder!
Ah, 'tis a sad story.

BERTRAND:

Of murder, girl?
She is a very lamb, and could not kill
The gnat that stung her tender, lily hand.

ANNETTE:

My dear—my kind old master, too, is gone,
Killed by ruffians who were deaf to pity!
Nor could De Vernueil save the good old man. [*Loud tumult is heard.*]

SUSETTE:

Hark! Where is that noise? 'Tis coming near us.
[*Looks.*] Annette—Annette. Look at those angry men.

BERTRAND:

Be calm, my children.
They seek De Vernueil,
But he is gone, and we have naught to fear.
Should they ask us questions, my little boys,
Deny not that De Vernueil has been here;
For to take refuge in a lie is base.
But ye all have courage to be silent.

[*Enter a* MOB, *the same ruffians who killed* CORDAY.]

MAN:

Where is De Vernueil?

BERTRAND:

Friends! He is not here.

[*A* MAN *goes up to* BERTRAND *and seizes him roughly by the arm.*]

MAN:

'Tis false! He is hid within the cottage.

BERTRAND:

I tell no falsehood. De Vernueil is not here.

LITTLE BOY:

Rude man, let go Papa. You will hurt him.

MAN:

Yes I will, if he don't now give up

The young villain who murdered my brother.
Tell me, old man, where is that De Vernueil?
Speak, or thou shalt quickly be made to tell.
[*Shakes his arm roughly and holds a cutlass up in a menacing way.*]
[ANNETTE *and* SUSETTE *take hold of his upraised arm.*
SUSETTE *appears in the utmost terror.*]

ANNETTE:

Oh, believe me! De Vernueil is not here.
Search the cottage, but be not so cruel
As to hurt a defenseless, blind old man.

MAN:

Where is De Vernueil gone? For he was here.

ANNETTE:

We know not.

LITTLE BOY:

And if we did, would not tell!

MAN:

Ali! Is it so? Take a lesson for that. [*Cuts the* BOY *down, who falls. The other* CHILDREN *scream out.* SUSETTE *falls into the arms of* ANNETTE.] Tell where he's gone, or all shall have the same.

BERTRAND: [*In great agitation.*]

What has the man done?
Oh, speak, Annette! Susette!
Children, tell me. I cannot, cannot *see*—[*Clasps his hands in agony and rises.*]

MAN:

Given an example of what is due
To insolence and to obstinacy.
Now let us have the truth from some of ye.

[SUSETTE *kneels at the feet of the* MAN, *and grasps his knee.*]

SUSETTE:

De Vernueil was here for a little while,
But mounted his horse and rode full speed away.
Oh, spare—spare my grandpapa, our only friend—
But if we must all die, take my life first. [*Points to her bosom and looks in his face.*]

MAN:

> Well . . . stand aside. Let us search the cottage. [*As* MOB
> *enters the inner room,* ONE *of the men steals the purse
> from the table.*]

Scene Four

[HENRY'S *lodgings at Paris.* JAQUES *walking backwards and
forwards.*]

JAQUES:

> And is this Paris, that I longed to see?
> Oh, that we were a thousand leagues away!
> Better to front the furious cannon ball,
> Than here be waiting for the guillotine.
> I am sick enough of what is called the world,
> If shedding blood is all I am to view.
> Ah, Annette, if we ever meet again,
> I think I'll rather dig for daily bread,
> Than labor on the road to fame or wealth
> Through blood, or knavery to make me great—[*Walks
> about impatiently.*]
> Fear, at last, has seized upon my heart;
> Yet 'tis not for myself. That I do feel
> These terrors that unman my firmest thoughts—
> 'Tis for thee, my hapless mistress, and thou
> For whom I'd freely give my worthless life:
> The kindest master heaven ever made.
> Why does he stay? Alas! Perhaps he's dragged
> By some fierce bloodhound, and condemned to die!
> The good Le Brun—ah! He will perish too,
> While on a fruitless errand I have been.
> Oh! I will know their fate, or die myself,
> Should I not find them here when I return,
> Or meet them near that horrid prison's wall. [*Exits.*]

[*Enter* HENRY *and* LE BRUN.]

HENRY:

> Jaques not arrived?
> But all will not do, Le Brun. And she is lost

Irrevocably. Oh that I could devise
Some happy plan for her escape! Oh, help
Point out a way to save this dear sister.

LE BRUN:

Would a father do more to save his child?
But, ah, how impotent are our attempts
Against the strong, ungovernable rage
Of deluded, revengeful multitudes—
Against the sanguinary friends of Marat!
[*Tumult heard. "Ca ira! Ca ira!" sung loudly.*]
Heaven! Shall these horrors go unpunished?

HENRY:

My blood scarcely circulates.
Oh my Charlotte, are heralds of thy doom!
A span but separates thee from that hour
When these savages will proclaim thy death.
Le Brun, I cannot wait an instant here.
My sister's execution shall not glut
Their brutal animosity. I will die,
Or rescue her from ignominy—
Hark! Some new bloody deed is celebrating.
Heaven! Shall these horrors go unpunished?

LE BRUN:

I follow thee, Henry,
Jaques sure will join us at the appointed place,
When he finds we do not meet him here. [*They exit.*]

Scene Five

[*An apartment in* DUVAL'S *house.*]

ESTELLE:

Sorrow pursues me. 'Tis vain I fly
To hope's deceptive, treacherous promises.
They will deceive me—not restore my friends.
Ah! Could I serve them, this terrible suspense—
This torturing distress—would be relieved;
But I can only think, and fear, and think,
Till every sense with terror's palsied.

My Charlotte! My companion! Where art thou?
Oh, if false justice should demand thy life,
De Vernueil will defend it with his own!
And thou, my Henry, thou wilt not spare thine. [*Pauses.*]
But if they save thee—where is thy father?
Gone! Gone forever to the silent grave.
His fond arms will never more enfold thee.
Thine eyes, so full of sweet intelligence,
Will never dwell on that revered face,
To mark the movements of the noblest soul. [*Pauses again.*]
And is it possible such energy
Strung the meek fibers of my Charlotte's mind
To such a cord as mine could not have borne?
My spirit never could have soared so high.
Virtue I love, and hate its opposite;
But I leave to heaven's avenging hand
To punish, as its sovereign will directs—
A public scourge or individual foe.
[*Enter* BELCOUR.]

BELCOUR:
Still a prisoner to this apartment?

ESTELLE:
Liberty, to me, is not desirable.
Had I permission to go where I pleased,
This room would still retain its prisoner.
When real sorrow doth afflict the heart,
It will naturally seek solitude.

BELCOUR:
Sorrow is relieved when participated.
Let me, then, bear away thy every grief,
So double anguish shall consume me quite.
But far hence be every selfish thought,
Till brighter prospects for thy friends arise!

ESTELLE:
And are they not thy friends also, Belcour?
[BELCOUR *looks earnestly at her. She appears confused.*]

BELCOUR:
These unconscious looks are daggers to my heart.

Henry's not unfortunate—not hopeless.
Estelle, dost thou not love Henry Corday?

[BELCOUR *turns away his head, as if afraid to hear the reply.*]

ESTELLE:

I will never deceive thee. I do love—

BELCOUR:

Ha! Beware, I cannot bear to hear it.
What would I not give to obtain that love?
The world's wide range would be a paltry step;
Its farthest verge my willing feet should find
To serve thee—blessed pilgrimage to me
If, when I returned, thy welcome smile,
Thy dear loved hand the rich, too rich reward.
And must I never hope again?

ESTELLE:

Never!

BELCOUR:

I must. It is my sole existence.
I cannot part with hope! No, Estelle!
No, never—till thou art another's.

ESTELLE:

Not . . . if my happiness required it?
Oh, let me prove the generosity
Which once declared that thou would'st sacrifice
Thy heart's best interest to secure my peace!

BELCOUR:

Name the sacrifice. Behold me ready.
Oh, bid me say—do—think—live or expire—
And, though it would be torture to resign thee,
Bid me again despair! I will say adieu! [*Looks anxiously at*
ESTELLE.]

ESTELLE:

Ah! Wilt thou, then, receive my confidence?
And, though I create a pang in that heart
Where I would ever fix content and peace,
Yet there is an act of duty which I owe
Both to myself and thee. It is to impart
A secret most important—

BELCOUR:

> Oh, proceed—

ESTELLE:

> I am married—

BELCOUR:

> Married! Married, Estelle?

ESTELLE:

> Heaven knows I am the wife of Henry.
> Soften that angry look. He is thy friend!

BELCOUR:

> Thou'rt not married. I dare not believe it.

ESTELLE:

> Would I impose a falsehood on thee?
> Good Belcour, be our friend—our brother.

BELCOUR:

> Thy friend? Thy brother?

ESTELLE:

> Alas! Our Henry,
> Too, too soon he may be taken from us.
> How critical his present situation!
> If his father was not spared even here—
> So distant from the fatal scenes at Paris—
> How very poor the hope of his escape
> From the fury of Marat's associates.
> Oh, could'st thou behold the upraised arm
> Preparing cruel execution—
> The blow impending, that would bear away
> A precious friend forever from thy sight—
> No, no, Belcour, thy nature is more kind.
> Thou could'st not endure the heart-rending scene,
> Much less thine own arm raise against the youth,
> Who was—who is thy friend! [BELCOUR stands as if motionless for a time.

[At length, he approaches ESTELLE and respectfully takes her hand.]

BELCOUR:

> And still shall be.
> Great was the effort, but 'tis conqueror now.

Surely thou wilt forgive, and Henry too.
I could not bear to see him lead thee off.
Then, the mean supposition that Le Brun
Was stationed there to watch me stung my soul;
And mad with rage, revenge, jealousy,
I sunk the prey of stormy passions.
But no more. All my endeavors shall be
To promote thy happiness. Allow me
Still to visit here, till by slow degrees
Thy father is weaned from his present plans.
Oh, farewell! [*Exit* BELCOUR.]

ESTELLE:

Heaven give thee full reward! [*Curtain falls.*]

ACT V

Scene One

[*A prison darkened.* CHARLOTTE *is seated in a melancholy attitude. Enter* HENRY *disguised in an old surtout and slouched hat. A* GUARD *attends him with a small lantern.*]

HENRY:

Retire for a moment. [*Takes the lantern.*]

GUARD:

Remember, sir, My life's the forfeit of discovery. [GUARD *retires.*]

CHARLOTTE: [*Rises.*]

Ha! What light is that? Say, who approaches?

HENRY: [*Puts the lantern on the table.*]

My sister! My Charlotte, 'tis thy brother. [*He goes up to embrace her, but she withdraws, fearfully looking around.*]

CHARLOTTE:

My kind brother! Too generous Henry! Stay not here.
Leave me—leave me, or that life
That valued life—in my misfortune dies.
Oh! Fly from danger, thou best of brothers.

HENRY:

> Ah! Could I, then, leave thee here to perish
> After obtaining, through peril and disguise,
> This ardently desired meeting? No,
> One way remains by which thou shalt escape.

CHARLOTTE:

> Escape, Henry? Ah, thou canst not save me.

HENRY:

> Oh, that the wretch had died by other means,
> Some other heart had felt the zeal of thine,
> Still had'st thou been our tender father's joy!
> The darling comfort of his closing days;
> His prop while duty called me from his side,
> From that domestic scene of tranquil ease
> Which each revolving sun gilded anew.

[CHARLOTTE *lays her hand on his arm.*]

> And did this hand perform so rough a deed?
> When for that deed, the sentence was pronounced—
> The fatal sentence which decreed thy death—
> Oh, when I beheld thy sudden paleness,
> Then the swift blood remount into thy cheek,
> Saw the fixing of all eyes upon thee,
> While, through a blush, thy lips spoke words of gold,
> And patriotism must have gained its meed
> But for the bloody villain who presided,
> I could have rushed through the gazing crowd,
> With meaning tenderness clasped thee to my breast!
> And then—then as now—have died to save thee! [*He embraces her. She falls upon his neck, but suddenly raises her head and speaks solemnly.*]

CHARLOTTE:

> Those hours of delight we both have tasted
> Can never be renewed again to me,
> But I would not step back into the scene
> To let that scourge of France remain unpunished.
> I waited, looked in vain to see some arm
> Hold forth the glittering sword of vengeance,
> And from the face of earth exterminate

Its pestilence, Marat. No sword appeared.
The people bled; not ceased the copious stream.
My heart bled for them, while its keen feelings,
Bursting the bands which mark the female course,
Called on revenge and dared to act the Roman!
Think not I fear death! No, on the scaffold
I'll expiate what now is called a crime—

HENRY:
Name not the scaffold! Oh, why would'st thou die?

CHARLOTTE:
'Tis but the body's death; my fame shall live,
And to my memory a tomb arise
On which all France will read and venerate
The act for which it now ordains my death.
For now, as when my steps shall mount the scaffold,
I feel the strong conviction that I bleed
For the benefit of my poor country;
And should the demon of carnage present
Another fiend as murderous as Marat,
May he soon share that horrid monster's fate,
And the true patriot who dares cut him off
Find in his country's gratitude reward.
Delusion now blinds the rude multitude,
And the worst enemy is called a friend,
While their best friends must meet a traitor's doom.

HENRY:
Never—If thou wilt be guided by me—

CHARLOTTE:
No effort now, my Henry, can save me.
I yield myself a victim to the times.
Draw me not back with hope's delusive hand;
For I have banished every living thought.
Yet, once more I'll think of those loved objects,
Which I shall never more on earth behold!
Bear my last adieu to our dear parent,
My Henry—what a dying child would say.
Speak for thy sister to her suffering father.

Embrace Estelle, and to my loved De Vernueil,
Oh, be a soothing guardian angel!
Watch over him, and save him from himself.
Thou know'st his passions have no medium,
For in their whelming stream his reason sinks,
When no kind voice sustains their rapid force.
And now, farewell! I conjure thee, go—
Or thou art lost with me forever!

HENRY:

'Tis thou must go. Oh, my sister, hear me:
We both may live. Hasten—take this disguise,
And in it, thou may'st instantly escape.
When discovered, I shall be liberated,
As not the guilty person, and unknown.

CHARLOTTE:

Such cannot be thy real expectation.
No, my beloved brother, our enemies
Would, with tenfold rage, seize on thy life
When disappointed of their *idol's* victim.

HENRY:

But thou shalt be preserved. [*Unbuttons his surtout as if to take it off, when a note drops from his bosom.*] Ha! what is this?

[*Picks up the note.*] Oh, may it bring some cheering ray of hope!

Just as I followed my conductor here,
Jaques gave this note with trembling eagerness,
And in my haste I thrust it in my bosom.

[*Opens it, stoops to the lamp and reads.*]

"In a state of mind not to be described, I arrived in Paris a few minutes ago,

and had the good fortune to meet Jaques. I am hurrying on to deliver my

dispatches, then obtain my adored Charlotte's release, or die. My influence

is considerable, and hope supports me. . . . Alas, I have to write what I

could not utter, a terrible calamity! Oh, that I could soften
   its horrors.
Summon your fortitude. Your father, Henry, fell a victim
   to some furious
partisans of Marat, and—" [HENRY *drops the note.* CHAR-
   LOTTE *leans in dumb despair against the wall.*]
Gracious Heaven! He is killed!

CHARLOTTE: [*In a tone of agony.*]
   My father killed?
   [*She faints in* HENRY'*s arms.*]

HENRY:
   Wretched Charlotte.
   [CHARLOTTE *revives. She puts her hands to her head.*]

CHARLOTTE:
   Was it some horrid dream?
   Henry, did'st thou say our father was killed?
   And I, who would have led for him, the cause?
   Where is he? Oh, say not dead, my brother!
   [GUARD *rushes in.*]

GUARD:
   Unfortunate young man, thou'st stayed too long.
   The messenger of death now approaches.
   We both are lost—
   [*Enter* CHABOT *with* OFFICER *and* GUARDS.]

CHABOT: [*To the* GUARD.]
   Villain! Who is that man?

CHARLOTTE:
   That man's my lover, yet innocent—
   Admitted here by him, whose kind compassion
   Could not resist the pleading voice of anguish;
   Could not refuse his wretched fellow creatures
   A mournful meeting and a last adieu!
   This soldier was not bribed. He is a Christian!

HENRY:
   Noble Charlotte, I will save his life. Hear! [HENRY *takes
   hold of* CHABOT'*s arm, who repulses him and speaks to
   the* GUARD.]

CHABOT:

>A guard *once* a traitor offends no more.
>We must have faithful servants. Take thy reward. [*Stabs the* GUARD, *who falls.*]

>[CHARLOTTE *turns away in horror.*]

>Young man, away! But that this woman's deeds
>Bespeak a soul above mean falsehood's art,
>I should suppose that thou wert her accomplice.
>She says thou'rt innocent, and I believe her.
>Hence!
>Soldiers, now conduct the prisoner!

HENRY:

>Oh, stop! I kneel! In mercy, let me speak. [*Kneels and takes hold of* CHABOT's *arm.*]

CHARLOTTE:

>Henry! Obey my last request. Oh, leave me.
>Remember what claims demand thy safe return.
>Henry, dear Henry, remember Estelle!

HENRY: [*Rises and clasps his hands.*]

>This—this is too much for me to endure.

CHABOT:

>I can no longer wait. [*Drums beat outside the prison, and tumult heard: they cry, "To the guillotine! To the guillotine!"*]

HENRY:

>Oh, my sister! [HENRY *holds* CHARLOTTE *to his bosom.*]

CHABOT:

>Sister?

CHARLOTTE:

>Sister of his *heart!* Beloved youth,
>A last farewell! But we shall meet above. [*She looks up.*]

CHABOT:

>Proceed! [CHARLOTTE *turns and looks at* HENRY *with tenderness. Drums beat louder. Cry heard.— "To the guillotine! To the guillotine!" They go off, and* HENRY, *with horror in his countenance, follows.*]

Scene Two

[HENRY's *lodgings. Enter* DE VERNUEIL. *He takes off his helmet and passes his hand over his forehead.*]

DE VERNUEIL:

Tired nature can no longer support me.
Each nerve is tortured by this harassed mind.
While the blood rushes through my burning veins,
Distracting terror maddens all my thoughts!
But I will see thee once again, my love,
Even if I perish with ten thousand wounds.
Ah! If my interest falls, and she is lost!
Wait! Must I wait? And if in vain? Hark! Hark!
The execution—heavens, what a word— [*With horror.*]
Cannot take place until tomorrow.
There is hope. One day—one day remains.

[*Enter* LE BRUN *and* HENRY, *followed by two* MEN *bearing* CHARLOTTE's *coffin.* HENRY *still disguised;* JAQUES *assisting.*]

HENRY:

Rest your burden. I need no further service.
Jaques, guard the door. Ah, De Vernueil! De Vernueil. [*Exit* JAQUES *and* MEN. DE VERNUEIL, *not knowing what or whom approached, had retired to the end of the room, standing from the first entrance of the coffin, with his hands clasped, from which his helmet drops. He advances, strikes his bosom, again in a frantic manner clasps his hands, and in agony speaks.*]

DE VERNUEIL:

Why do I breathe? My Charlotte, art thou there?
Where thou dost repose, there will De Vernueil.
Barbarians, have ye then murdered her?
Oh, false, vile treachery that deceived me!
But her soul thou could'st not murder! Oh, stay,
Angelic spirit! Rest on thy radiant wing,
And I will join thy flight to realms of perfect bliss. [*Draws a pocket-pistol, and before* HENRY *can prevent, shoots himself and falls.* HENRY *catches his arm as it drops—*]

HENRY:

Oh, De Vernueil, spare—

[HENRY *stoops to recover him.*] Too late! He is dead.

Wretched sight! Le Brun, support me. I sink.

Where's fortitude? Alas, it is not here. [*Strikes his breast.*]

I sink amidst this crush of happiness. [*Leans on* LE BRUN's *shoulder, then rises and stands in a desponding attitude.*]

LE BRUN:

Dear boy, look up! There is a firm support.

Misfortunes prove our pious trust in Him

Who doth direct events, nor will afflict

Dependent man beyond his power to bear.

Exert thyself to rise above this storm,

To stem the torrent of affliction's stream.

So shall the mercy of approving heaven

Calm all thy sorrows and restore thy peace.

[HENRY *still looks down, wrapped in gloom.*]

Ah! Henry, thou dost not hear thy friend.

Wilt thou quite destroy thy old Le Brun? [*Takes his hand.*]

Hast thou lost Estelle? Think how she suffers.

Wilt thou not live for her? Oh, quit this house—

[HENRY *starts, then looks wildly at the coffin and* DE VERNUEIL.]

HENRY:

I cannot go

Till I have seen these loved remains entombed,

Beyond the power of further injury.

LE BRUN:

Thy Estelle also must not be entombed!

Leave to my care the last sad office here.

Quit Paris. Thou art beset with dangers,

Already hast by miracle escaped.

Here we are ill secured. I dread each sound.

I charge thee, go.

HENRY:

No, no, I must remain.

Order Jaques to procure what is needful.

Le Brun, indulge me; do this one kind act.
Here will I watch and weep. [*Seats himself.*]

LE BRUN:
May heaven guard thee! [*Exits.*]

Scene Three

[DUVAL'S *house. Enter* BELCOUR.]

BELCOUR:
Of all the passions in our nature wove,
Love is the ligature that binds the whole.
Ambition bows, casts off his crested helm
Dissolves his iron sword in beauty's tears;
And the loud trumpet calls in vain to arms,
While the young hero is a slave to love!
In vain the statesman views the height of power—
Its portal open—and the wreath of fame;
His eager step no longer climbs the ascent,
For love's allurements draw him to the vale.
And does not honor—mighty honor—tremble,
Even to the base of holy virtue's seat,
When tyrant love opposes all his wiles
To wrest a generous impulse from the heart!
Still in my breast this passion's unsubdued,
Breaks the weak bond that reason has imposed,
While hopes arise which almost overwhelm
Virtue and honor, friendship, and my peace.
Away! Away! Her Henry will return.
Vile, selfish, despicable thoughts—away!

[*Enter* ESTELLE *at one door. As she approaches* BELCOUR, LE
BRUN *enters at the opposite.* ESTELLE *rushes up to him and
grasps his hand, unable to speak.*]

BELCOUR:
Alone, Le Brun? [*In agitation.*]

LE BRUN:
Alas! I am alone.

ESTELLE:
And Henry! Henry Corday! Where is he?

LE BRUN: [*With compassion.*]
>   In defense of his sister's loved remains
>   The gallant youth was killed. Our aid was vain.
[*Enter* DUVAL.]

ESTELLE:
>   Henry! My husband! [*Falls on* LE BRUN, *who supports her.*]

DUVAL:
>   Henry! Thy husband?
[*Enter* HENRY *in his own dress, followed by* JAQUES *and* AN-
NETTE. HENRY *takes* ESTELLE *in his arms.*]

HENRY:
>   Do I again enfold thee, my Estelle? [*She revives.*]

ESTELLE:
>   My Henry! [*They kneel at* DUVAL'*s feet.*]

HENRY:
>   Forgive!

DUVAL:
>   Oh, never! Never!
>   Thou hast stolen my child. Hence from my sight!

BELCOUR:
>   Dear sir, pardon!

DUVAL:
>   Not while I live, Belcour. [*Exit* DUVAL.]
[HENRY *and* ESTELLE *rise. She looks after her father in evident
distress, follows him almost to the door, then turns towards*
HENRY, *who embraces her.*]

LE BRUN:
>   Glad amazement makes me think I dream!
>   What, is my Henry here? Alive! Unhurt?
>   I saw thee fall. I sought thee long, dear boy,
>   Convinced at last the blow that felled thee down
>   Was fatal. But he lives! My Henry lives! [*Embraces* HENRY.]

HENRY:
>   Stunned by a ruffian's savage blow, I fell.
>   They thought me dead and left me on the ground.
>   To him, [*Points to* JAQUES.] my faithful Jaques, I owe my
>   life.

For, soon as the murderous riot ceased,
He bore me to a place of safety,
From whence I flew to seek my all of peace,
The only balms to heal my wounded soul—
Love and true friendship! My friend! My Belcour!
Am I in thy heart? [*Goes up affectionately to* BELCOUR—]

BELCOUR:

Live ever in it! [*They embrace.*]

HENRY:

But we must part, and cross the Atlantic wave—
Seek that repose we cannot here possess.
Ah, my Estelle! France and thy father frown—

JAQUES: [*Takes* ANNETTE's *hand.*]

But let them frown or smile. Jaques and Annette
Will not leave their generous benefactors.

HENRY:

Come then, ye faithful servants. Good Le Brun,
I cannot leave thee. Come where quiet reigns.
Under the protection of America,
Domestic ease securely reposes.
There, we may yet enjoy tranquility;
And, 'midst the sons of true-born liberty,
Taste the pure blessings that from freedom flow.
Thy father, my Estelle, shall yet relent.
Belcour will charm each angry thought away,
And in our peaceful cot, he'll bless our union.

Finis

SARAH PIERCE
(1767–1852)

Sarah Pierce was born on June 26, 1767, the youngest child of Mary Paterson and John Pierce of Litchfield, Connecticut, where Sarah would live her entire life. Given a formal education in New York City, Pierce was twenty-five when she founded Litchfield Female Academy in 1792; the school became one of the most important female academies in early America, surviving until 1827. Pierce's students were training not only in reading, writing, and arithmetic, but also in geography, history, and science. Many of Pierce's students went on to become educators, and some—including Catharine Beecher[1] and Harriet Beecher Stowe[2]—also became authors in their own right. Pierce directed the Litchfield Female Academy until 1825, when she appointed her nephew John Pierce Brace as principal. Although she no longer undertook the arduous daily running of the school, she continued to teach her favorite subject, history. When Brace left the school eight years later, Pierce returned as head of the Academy, teaching for another ten years. She died in Litchfield on January 19, 1852. Few women of the era had as significant an impact on female education as did Sarah Pierce.

Sketches of Universal History *was a three-volume compendium intended for use in schools, including her own. At the end of volumes 1 and 2, subscribers' names are listed; they are all female, the list probably largely made up of former and current students. The second volume includes chapter breaks, unlike the first, suggesting that Pierce continued to adapt her sense of how best to present history to students as she wrote and published* Sketches *between 1811 and 1817. It is an important document because it demonstrates the pedagogical means Pierce used to make history of interest and memorable to her female students. Unfortunately, today there is only one copy of* Sketches *still extant, and it is in fragile condition, with pages missing from the second volume. The third volume, published by a different publisher than the first two volumes, ends rather abruptly with Theban history. There is no concluding commentary on the significance of history or other remarks that one might expect, considering the style of* Sketches; *Pierce may have intended more volumes, but they were never produced. Unlike many of her contemporaries, who focused on Puritan or Revolutionary history, Pierce was interested in ancient history—biblical and Greek—and its potential for moral as well as historical training.*

SKETCHES OF UNIVERSAL HISTORY

COMPILED FROM SEVERAL AUTHORS.

For the Use of Schools.

1811–1817

PREFACE

Having from long experience found that children and youth imbibe ideas most easily, when placed in the form of question and answer, and not finding any historical work of that kind, of sufficient length to interest the mind, I have compiled these Sketches for the use of Schools, endeavouring to intermix moral with historical instruction, and to obviate those objections which arise in the minds of youth against the justice of God, when they read the wars of the Israelites.—I have attempted also to give them a general notion of the government of God, and of the truth of the Scripture, by a partial account of the fulfillment of prophecy. I am sensible that all this has been done by many able writers; but as their works are too expensive to put into the hands of children, and of greater magnitude than they have time or patience to study, I have compiled this abridgement for their benefit. This history may also be useful in private families, which are not able to purchase the larger works from which it is selected.

UNIVERSAL HISTORY.

QUES. What account can you give of the creation of the world?

ANS. God created the visible world in six days. A chaotic mass seems first to have been instantaneously created out of nothing, and then gradually reduced to order and beauty.

Q. How do we know the world was thus formed?

A. By faith we understand that the worlds are framed by the word of God, so that things which were seen, were not made of things which do appear, Heb. xi.iii. Reason is capable of approving, appropriating, and applying the information conveyed to us by the word of God; but not of anticipating it. The Scriptures, in harmony with reason, tell us, that God is from everlasting to everlasting; and that all else had a beginning: but of that eternity past, that vast abyss which involves all our reflections in confusion, nothing is mentioned to gratify idle curiosity.

Q. How was man created?

A. From the dust of the earth; "God said, let us make man in our own image." The language here used is that of consultation—by which it appears that the three persons in the sacred Trinity concurred in counsel and operation, in the creation of man, as afterwards in his recovery from the fall.

Q. In what sense was man created in the image of God?

A. It could not have been with respect to his body; for God is a spirit, which no bodily shape can in any respect resemble: it must, therefore, have been in the rational soul; and though as a creature his knowledge was limited, yet, in a degree, his mind, will and affections, resembled his Creator.

Q. What did God do on the seventh day?

A. He rested from all his works, and commanded Adam to keep that day holy, that is, to consecrate it to religious worship; as this, even in Paradise, would be conducive to his happiness and God's glory.

Q. What covenant did God enter into with Adam?

A. He covenanted to give him everlasting life, on condition of his perfect obedience, giving him command over every living creature, to which he gave names, and of whose properties, and nature, he seems to have had a much better knowledge than the most sagacious observers since the fall have acquired.

Q. What had Adam given him for food?

A. Every tree of the garden of Eden, except the tree of knowledge or good and evil. That one tree was left as a test of his obedience.

Q. Did Adam continue faithful?

A. No—The devil, under the shape of a serpent, tempted Eve, our mother, and she took of the forbidden fruit, and persuaded Adam to join with her in the repast.

Q. What art did Satan make use of to seduce our first mother?

A. He operated on her ambition and vanity, persuading her that the reason God had forbidden them to eat of that tree was, to keep them in a subordinate state, and that if they eat thereof, they would be as gods, knowing good and evil. Eve, like many of her foolish daughters, believed Satan instead of God; and found by sad experience, that to know good and evil, was good lost, and evil entailed upon herself and her posterity. Satan in his artful address, takes no notice of the numerous gifts of God, but only of this one limitation. Of what arguments Eve made use to seduce Adam we are not informed; though St. Paul insinuates, that he was not deceived in the same manner and degree as his wife: yet he partook of the fruit, forfeited his own right to heaven, and brought death to all his descendants. The divine image was defaced, and the image of Satan stamped on Adam and all his race.

Q. Are all mankind doomed to endless misery, by Adam's transgression?

A. God entered into a new covenant of grace, promising that by the seed of the woman, (which is Christ) as many of the children of men as should believe, and turn from the evil of their ways, should be saved.

Q. What became of Adam and Eve after the fall?

A. They were driven out of the garden of Eden, and the ground was cursed for Adam's sake. Instead of the delicious fruits of Paradise, he had to subsist by his own labour on the herbs of the field. The animals also became subject to death. Thus sin, not only introduced sorrow to man in his own person, but the additional weight of woe in seeing all creation suffer with him.

Q. What children had Adam?

A. Scripture gives us the names of only three: Cain the eldest, who was a wicked man, and slew his brother; Abel, who was a good man, and beloved of God, which excited the envy of Cain, and tempted him to murder his brother. Thus Adam saw the dreadful depravity of our nature acted out in the person of his eldest son.

Q. What is it supposed were Eve's ideas when Cain was born?

A. It is supposed that Eve considered him as the promised seed. How soothing to the maternal heart must have been such a possession. The name she gave him signifies possessed; and perhaps her partiality nurtured those seeds of pride and envy which produced the fatal event just related. At Abel's birth no such high expectations seem to have been entertained. The name of Abel signifies vanity.

Q. What became of Cain?

A. He was driven out from the presence of God, and dwelt in the land of Nod. The earth received a new curse for his crime. It refused to yield its strength to a murderer's hand. Pursued by his fears, he fled from the face of man.

Q. Of whom could Cain be afraid, now Abel was dead?

A. It is believed that Adam had many more children beside, Cain and Abel. The number might have been at the time of Abel's murder, (which happened in the year 129) increased by a moderate calculation, to several hundred. Cain, it appears from the narration, decoyed his brother into solitude under the mask of friendship. What added to the malignity of the act was, that Abel was a good man, and *his brother*.

Q. Was man's first disobedience a slight evil?

A. No; it introduced the most desperate wickedness into the world: Yet death, at whatever time, or in whatever shape it arrives, is a messenger of joy to a good man. Happy Abel! thy dust is mingled with its native earth, but thy spirit is flown to the God who gave it.

Q. What were the feelings of Cain after he had accomplished his bloody purpose, when the envied, hated virtues of his brother, no longer reproached him. No eyes saw him commit the murder—Was he not then at rest?

A. Yes, the eye of Cain saw him, the eye of God saw him: hence the whole earth became all eye to behold, all tongue to accuse him; and, flee where he might, a guilty conscience still pursued him, with the cry of murder.

Q. What does this teach us?

A. This horrid transaction teaches us to stifle the first emotions of envy and wrath, for malice in the heart is the embryo of actual murder. It also teaches us, that the believer's happiness is not in this world. In Cain we see the father of all those murderous tyrants, falsely called heroes, who have to this day filled the earth with blood.

Q. Does history relate any thing more of Cain and his descendants?

A. Cain seems immediately to have left the ordinances of God, and the society of his worshippers: this might have been in consequence of the curse denounced upon him. But continuing impenitent, he probably soon after flung off all appearance of religion, which of course introduced idolatry into his family. Cain probably had many children before this event; for we read of his building a city soon after, which must have been peopled by his descendants. The city was named after his son Enoch: thus Cain attempted to get to himself a name by worldly grandeur, as he had forfeited the praise of virtue.

Q. Who was Lamech?

A. A descendant from Cain, who deviated from the original institution of marriage, by taking two wives. He seems by his own account, to have been a murderer also; and by comparing his case with that of Cain, to have encouraged himself by the patience of God in sparing Cain, to expect impunity in sin and to defy the vengeance of his adversaries.

Q. What other son of Adam is mentioned in history?

A. Seth, who was given in the room of Abel; and in his days men began to call on, or by the name of the Lord; that is, in a public manner to protest against the wickedness of the world, and to separate from the society of idolaters.

Q. What progress did the arts and sciences make in the first age of the world?

A. The descendants of Cain appear to have made the first attempts to acquire those arts which are still the delight of worldly men. They invented musical instruments, the harp and organ; they wrought in brass and iron, and probably adorned their houses and persons with that costly furniture, and those decorations which constitute the "pride of life, and the lust of the eyes." While the children of Seth, more simple in their lives, were more eminently endowed with the spirit of wisdom and understanding. Thus we find Enoch, the seventh from Adam, so eminent for his piety, that he was introduced into the immediate presence of God, without undergoing the change of death. . . .

Q. How great was the degeneracy of Sodom?

A. The unparalleled wickedness of that city is most forcibly described in the simple narration in Scripture, and is an example of speaking practise too shameful to be mentioned in language. It shews also to what a pitch of wickedness sinners arrive, when laws are not enforced, and government is corrupt, and should make us thankful that our government was formed under the direction of men, who had the fear of God before their eyes; and that we still have a remnant of righteous among us, or ere this we should have been like unto Sodom and Gomorrah. And at the day of judgment, when God shall bring to light the hidden things of darkness, and manifest the secrets of all hearts, and when the wicked shall suffer the vengeance of eternal fire, we shall see the justice of their condemnation, as we now see that of the abominable cities of Sodom.

Q. What did the angels do when they arrived at Sodom?

A. They commanded Lot to collect all his family, and flee from Sodom, for the Lord would destroy it: but out of Lot's connections, only his wife, and his two unmarried daughters obeyed his summons; so little reverence had they for his word; and even these would have lingered till too late, had not the angels laid hold of their hands, and, as it were, forced them to a place of safety: and out of this small number, one was lost. Lot's wife, in unbelief, and love to Sodom, and its riches, regretting what was left behind, and proposing to return, looked back, contrary to God's express command, and was instantly struck dead, and petrified, and thus remained to after ages a visible monument of divine displeasure.

Q. What do we learn from this portion of history?

A. We see in it, a striking illustration of the benevolence of divine sovereignty. Neither Lot or any of his family, would have escaped from Sodom, had not God in mercy forced them from the city; yet the favour shewn to Lot's family was no injustice to his sons in-law, and the rest of his household, who refused to hear his voice, and flee for safety. It also shews the necessity of a redeemer and intercessor, for guilty man. Lot was saved as a righteous man; yet his deliverance was owing to Abraham's prayers, rather than his own goodness.

Q. How was Abraham made acquainted with the destruction of Sodom?

A. The morning after Sodom was destroyed, Abraham rose early, probably to enquire after the success of his prayers, and to renew them: but the awful scene he witnessed, effectually precluded further intercession, for Sodom and the other cities. Dreadful change! He beheld that beautiful plain, which had allured the eyes of Lot, in one eventful day, converted into a vast smoking furnace; cities and their inhabitants swallowed up in one deluge of fire.

Q. What appearance does the country now present?

A. The whole plain where those cities stood is converted into a lake, called the Salt, or Dead Sea; which exhibits an appearance in many respects extraordinary, and dissimlar to all other seas or lakes.

Q. What account can you give of Sarah's death?

A. She died at Hebron in the land of Canaan, at the age of 127, B.C. 1860. She is the only woman whose entire age is recorded in Scripture; and her history proves, that life though lengthened to an hundred years, is still vanity and vexation of spirit. That beauty which conjugal affection had doated on, and which at the age of 89 was the admiration of princes, could not secure happiness to its possessor. Discontented because she had no child, she induced her husband to marry a second wife, contrary to the law of God; then tormented with jealousy, she committed an act of injustice and barbarity, which remains a lasting disgrace on her character; for although the promises of God were accomplished by the expulsion of Ishamel, from Abraham's family, this fact forms no excuse for Sarah's severity. The last 37 years of her life, she seems to have been tranquil and happy, enjoying the unabated affection of her beloved lord, and educating her only son Isaac, whose accomplishments and virtues, rendered him the favourite of God and man. But the time at length arrived when she must pay the debt of nature. Affecting change! now the eyes of Abraham cannot endure to look upon her, whom once he shuddered that another should see with pleasure; and he is as eager to bury her out of his sight, as he formerly was to retain her to himself. Let the lovely and admired think of this and be humble, remembering that the beauty of Sarah is now forgotten, while her jealousy and severity, and the other faults of her character, are placed fully before us. But notwithstanding her defects she was a partaker of Abraham's faith, and through the merits of her Saviour, is now enjoying the blessing of heaven.

Q. What is the first money transaction on record?

A. The purchase of a burying place for Sarah. Abraham bought the field of Ephron the Hittite, and the cave of Macpelah.

Q. What do we find to admire in this transaction?

A. The whole of this transaction is a beautiful picture of the simplicity of ancient manners, and exhibits a style of unaffected kindness and civility, which strikingly condemns the covetousness of the present day. Tender and affectionate, Abraham was desirous of honouring in death, the remains of what he prized in life. Generous and independent, he refused to pay respect to Sarah's memory, with that which cost him nothing. Civil and polite, he repaid the courtesy of his neighbours with affability and condescension. Scrupulously just and honest, he would give nothing less than the full price for what was frankly offered him as a gift. . . .

VOL. II, CH. XII.

The History of Judah, Israel, and Greece, from the Death of Jehoshaphat, to the Reign of Amaziah.

Q. What was the state of Judah at this time?

A. The face of affairs was greatly changed at Jerusalem. [B.C. 898.][3] Jehoram, the son of the pious Jehoshaphat, had succeeded his father. Athaliah, the daughter of Ahab and Jezebel, brought impiety along with her into the kingdom of Judah. Jehoram, instigated by her councils, forsook the service of God, and obliged the people to worship in high places. He slew all his brethren, and several of the magistrates who were obnoxious to him, either on account of their popularity, or piety. Yet the Lord would not destroy him and his house, on account of the convenant made with David; yet he punished him with great severity.

Q. What was the punishment he received?

A. The Edomites revolted from under his government, and became an independent nation. He raised other powerful enemies, who came against Jerusalem, and slew all his sons except the youngest, who was secreted. After this, God smote him with a loathsome and painful disease, of which he died. These events had been predicted to him in a letter, written either by Elijah before his translation, or by Elisha, which made the punishment more conspicuous.

Q. Who succeeded him?

A. His son Abaziah, who was the only remaining of all his children.

Q. How did Abaziah reign?

A. Very badly; he was ruled entirely by his mother. The only act recorded of him, is a war in which he engaged with Jehoram, king of Israel, to recover Ramoth Gilead from Hazael, king of Syria. They succeeded in taking the city, but Jehoram received a dangerous wound in the attack, and was obliged to leave the city to the care of Jehu, one of his captains, and retired to Jezreel to be healed. Abaziah accompanied him.

Q. What commission did Elisha receive at this time?

A. He was commanded to anoint Jehu, king over Israel. He accordingly sent a young prophet privately to Ramoth to anoint Jehu, and gave him instructions to execute divine vengeance on Ahab's ungodly family.

Q. Did Jehu execute his commission immediately?

A. Jehu, having received this important message, acquainted his companions with his unexpected elevation, rode with all speed to Jezreel, and slew Jehoram at the vineyard for which Naboth had lost his life. The king of Judah was also involved in Jehoram's fate. Jezebel was thrown from a window in the palace, and trodden under foot by the horsemen, and afterward devoured by dogs. Jehu also wrote letters to the governors of Samaria, who had seventy of Ahab's descendants under their protection, desiring them to choose one of the number for their king, and prepare to defend him by their arms.

Q. Did these governors elect a king?

A. No: they determined to sacrifice Ahab's descendants rather than incur Jehu's resentment. Jehu, finding them fit instruments for his vengeance, commanded them to send all the heads of the young princes to him, in baskets, the next morning. On receiving the horrid present, he appeared at the gate of Jezreel, to remind the people of God's denunciation against the house of Ahab, and to justify his conduct. . . .

Q. Did Jehu restore the true worship of Jehovah?

A. No; he permitted the Israelites to worship the golden calves which had been set up in Bethel and Dan, by Jeroboam: for this God punished him severely by the hands of the Syrians, who, under Hazael, committed those barbarities predicted by Elisha. Jehu reigned twenty-eight years. [B.C. 856.] But his actions were of so little importance, they are not recorded. We may suppose that the miseries of Israel were very great during his reign, and that he was personally punished for his hypocrisy; notwithstanding, his posterity, to the fourth generation, were continued on the throne, in recompence of his fidelity in destroying the wicked house of Ahab, and the worship of Baal.

Q. Who took possession of the throne of Judah upon the death of Abaziah?

A. Athaliah, his mother, slew all the descendants of the house of David, even her own grand-children, except one who was saved from her revengeful ambition. Joash, the youngest son of Abaziah, was stolen by his aunt Jehosheba; she carried him to her husband Jehoiada, who was the high priest. Johoiada concealed the young prince in the temple six years, during which time Athaliah reigned over the king of Judah, and, like a genuine daughter of Jezebel, established the worship of Baal at Jerusalem.

Q. Did the people submit peaceably to her government?

A. They were so degenerate they made no resistance, till Jehoiada informed the elders of Judah their lawful sovereign was alive, and taking them into the temple, presented him to them. Joash was immediately proclaimed king with universal shouts of joy, and Athaliah slain. [B.C. 878.]

Q. Will you give me an account of the state of Greece?

A. The Greeks had began to cultivate the fine arts. Hesiod, and after him Homer, had written those beautiful poems which, even to this day, are admired. In them we may behold the primitive manners of ancient nations. About this time Lycurgus gave those famous laws to Sparta, which are still the admiration of the world.

Q. Who was Lycurgus?

A. He was the son of Eumenes, king of Sparta, who was killed in an insurrection. After the death of his eldest brother he ascended the throne; but his brother's widow gave birth to a son, whom Lycurgus proclaimed king.

Q. Could not Lycurgus have retained the power himself?

A. Yes; he might have done it, for his brother's widow informed him, if he would marry her, she would destroy her offspring before it saw the light. Lycurgus detested the treachery, and by his artful conduct preserved the child. This disinterested action secured him the hearts of the nation, and prepared the way for the establishment of his laws.

Q. What was the situation of Sparta at this period?

A. For about nine hundred years, two princes of the race of Heraclidae, jointly occupied the throne. This divided royalty, was a source of perpetual dissensions, and tore in pieces a kingdom which was unprovided with wholesome laws. Lycurgus lamented the misery of his country. He visited foreign nations to learn their customs and laws, and having collected what he thought most beneficial to his country, he, partly by force, and partly by persuasion, induced the Spartans to adopt them.

Q. What were the most considerable of Lycurgus' laws?

A. Without banishing royalty, he created a mixed government, where three powers mutually balanced each other. He left little to the kings except the command of the armies, and the respect which was attached to the throne. He established a senate, consisting of twenty-eight members, beside the two kings, to counterbalance the influence of the princes and the people; so that royal authority might not degenerate into tyranny, nor popular liberty into rebellion.

Q. What was the particular duty of the senate?

A. To examine and propose the business of the state, which the people had a right to approve or reject, and, of course, were masters of the legislative power. The senators were chosen for life, and therefore did not stand in awe of the multitude.

Q. What were the Ephod?

A. A council chosen by the people annually; it consisted of five members, they had power to displace, imprison, or even put to death, any of the senators. Their formidable authority extended even to their kings, whom they might arrest and suspend from their office, till an oracle gave orders for their being replaced. This council was established about 130 years after Lycurgus.

Q. How was property distributed?

A. To banish both poverty and riches, two fatal sources of corruption, all property was held in common. The lands were equally divided. Instead of gold and silver money, Lycurgus substituted iron, which was excessively unwieldly, and could be of no value out of Sparta. He prohibited all the arts which contributed to pleasure and luxury, ordering the floors of their houses to be made only with a hatchet, and the doors with a saw. In short, he made riches, and all the arts of polished life contemptible; but found means, in the midst of general poverty, to prevent any individiual from being in real want.

Q. What was the use of these severe restrictions[?]

A. They banished covetousness, fraud, injustice, voluptuousness, and effeminacy from the country, and rendered Lacedemonia like one family. The citizens eat together at public tables, and subsisted on the coarsest fare. Here the aged instructed the young, who were particularly taught silence, submission to their superiors, to speak the truth, and to keep a secret inviolable.

Q. Was this the only education the Spartan youth received?

A. No; the children, who were born with a robust constitution, were committed to nurses chosen by the magistrates, and every thing that could render them hardy and fearless, was attended to with care. At the age of seven, they were given up to public masters, formed into classes, where they were all taught to discharge the same duties. They were accustomed to bear pain and fatigue, and to distinguish themselves by military arts, or robust exercise. Those who particularly distinguished themselves, commanded the rest, but always in presence of the elders, who were constantly attentive to reprove and correct them. No action was looked up as indifferent; even their amusements were exercises of virtue and courage.

To habituate them early to the stratagems of war, they were taught to steal from the public tables, but if they were so inexpert as to be discovered in the act, they were severely chastised. The Spartan manners jutified this practice, otherwise it must have been a folly, or a dangerous vice.

Q. The robust children were publicly educated; what became of the infirm?

A. They were exposed to death, that they might have none but firm or healthy citizens. This practice was both barbarous and impolitic, weakly children often making the careful members of society.

Q. What other instances of cruelty were the Spartans guilty of?

A. In order to accustom their children to endure pain, they scourged them, sometimes even to death, at the altar of Diana, without their even daring to utter a complaint; mothers looking on unmoved. The Spartan women prided themselves on receiving, with transport, the news of their sons dying nobly in the field of battle. They also treated their helots, or slaves, with great rigour, making them drunk to inspire their children with horror of the vice. If any helot distinguished himself in the field, or was admired for his size or mien, they put him to death as an enemy of the state. These barbarities cannot be imputed to Lycurgus. They began after pride and jealousy had corrupted the Spartan virtue.

Q. How were women educated?

A. They were taught the manly exercizes, but modesty and decorum were unknown at Sparta. In the first ages of their history, they are represented as inspiring the young men with love of heroic deeds; but in the last ages of the republic, the Spartan women degenerated, and were considered a disgrace to the Grecian name[.] . . .

Q. How should we estimate Spartan laws, and Spartan virtue?

A. We are not to consider them as a perfect model. Spartan austerity, carried to excess, presents to our view some objects shocking to humanity. It stifled pity and the natural affections, those valuable sentiments which are the sweetest bond of social life. Had they tempered their severe virtues with gentleness, modesty and humanity, they would have been entitled to higher encomiums. Their contempt of riches, their love of glory, and of their country; their obedience to the laws, and their heroic courage, have ranked them above all other heathen nations. They had, in general, that greatness of soul which made Pedaretus rejoice when he was rejected from being one of the council of three hundred, and say, "*he was happy that Sparta had found three hundred citizens better than himself.*" . . .

HANNAH MATHER CROCKER
(1752–1829)

The daughter of Hannah Hutchinson and Samuel Mather, Hannah was born in Boston, Massachusetts, on June 27, 1752, and became a member of the distinguished Mather family of colonial renown. Little is known of her early life, but in 1779, she married Joseph Crocker, a captain in the Continental Army during the American Revolution. Hannah gave birth to ten children; she raised the children to adulthood before beginning her career as a writer.

She published two books prior to Observations on the Real Rights of Women: A Series of Letters on Free Masonry *(1815), and* The School of Reform, or Seaman's Safe Pilot to the Cape of Good Hope *(1816). But it is* Observations, *published in 1818, that has remained her most notable, if under-examined, text. As Constance Post, the only scholar to have produced significant critical work on Crocker, has noted, the text is constructed in three major sections: the first part examines the religious roots of women's rights; the second part is a history of notable women from earliest times to Crocker's era; and the third part is a defense of women's rights based on Christianity, the Enlightenment's emphasis on reason, and the rights of citizens in a democracy.*

Observations was Crocker's last publication, though a number of essays, sermons, a play, poetry, and a memoir are among her unpublished papers. Crocker died on July 11, 1829, in Roxbury, Massachusetts.

OBSERVATIONS ON THE REAL RIGHTS OF WOMEN

A Series of Letters on Free Masonry

1818.

INTRODUCTION.

This little work is not written with a design of promoting any altercation or dispute respecting superiority or inferiority, of the sexes; but the aim will be to prove, in a pleasant manner, and, we hope, to even demonstrate; that though there are appropriate duties peculiar to each sex, yet the wise Author of nature has endowed the female mind with equal powers and faculties, and given them the same right of judging and acting for themselves, as he gave to the male sex; although it is plain, from scripture account, that the woman was the first in the transgression, she justly forfeited her original right of equality for a certain space of time, and a heavy and humiliating sentence was past upon her, that her sorrow should be multiplied, and that under the Jewish dispensation, the man should rule over her; and she was under the yoke of bondage, till the birth of our blessed Saviour, which, according to the promise given, was the seed of the woman, that should bruise the serpent's head.

We shall consider woman restored to her original right and dignity at the commencement of the christian dispensation, although there must be allowed some moral and physical distinction of the sexes agreeably to the order of nature, and the organization of the human frame, still the sentiment must predominate, that the powers of mind are equal in the sexes. We shall produce examples, both from sacred and profane history, of the great abilities and exertion of many females, when called into action, either on political or religious account. For the interest of their country, or in the cause of humanity, we shall strictly adhere to the principle and the impropriety of females ever trespassing on masculine ground: as it is morally incorrect, and physically improper.

We shall therefore state in a plain manner the beauty and order that must arise, from each sex performing their appropriate duties with mutual fidelity and harmony; a plan or theory, or a christian system will be drawn, by which means the mutual happiness of the sexes, may be promoted; and the rights, liberties, and independence of a brave and free people shall continue secure to them, by the mutual virtues and integrity of the sexes; the plan must be reduced to practice, by mutual agreement, and the mantle of charity be drawn over every little imperfection, that peace and harmony may prevail.

May the same mantle be extended to the following pages by the candid reader.

CHAP. I.—

Of the Creation and Fall of our First Parents.

The foundation stone of the present work must be laid in the first creation of the human race. When the great Jehovah had created the earth, and all things therein, he created man; male and female created he them, in his own image, so far as he endowed him with intellectual powers and faculties, and gave him an immortal and rational soul, and powers of mind capable of reasoning on the nature of things. And the Lord God said, it is not good for man to be alone; I will make him an help meet, for him; And the Lord God caused a deep sleep to fall upon Adam, and he slept and he took one of his ribs, and closed up the flesh instead thereof. And the rib, which the Lord God had taken from man, made he a woman: and brought her unto the man, and Adam said, this is now bone of my bone, and flesh of my flesh: she shall be called woman, because she was taken out of man; as she partakes of my original nature, she shall therefore partake of my name; therefore shall a man leave his father and his mother, and shall cleave unto his wife, and they shall be one flesh: See Gen. ii. 24.

It seems, says an able commentator,[1] to have been the Creator's design to have inculcated the lesson of perfect love and union, by forming the woman out of the man's body, and from a part of it so near the heart, as well as to make woman of a more refined and delicate nature, by thus causing the original clay to pass, as it were, twice through his refining hand. Now it is consistent to say, if they are become one flesh, there should be but one and the same spirit operating equally upon them both, for their mutual happiness. Adam, having given her a name, and placed himself as her guardian, became in some measure responsible for her conduct, as the rightful protector of her innocence. It should be recollected, as a small palliative for Eve, that the command, respecting the tree of knowledge and forbidden fruit, was before the woman was made: see Gen. ii. 16 and 17. And the Lord God commanded the man, saying, of every tree of the garden thou mayest freely eat; but of the tree of knowledge, of good and evil thou shalt not eat, for in the day thou eatest thereof, thou shalt surely die. She must therefore have received her information from Adam, if she knew of any command; as she probably had heard of it, by her answer to the serpent. Perhaps Adam communicated it to her as the injunction of their Maker, but possibly with such mildness and indifference, that she was not fully impressed with the importance of the command.

It seems, that, in an unfortunate hour, these then pure and happy beings, were separated. Oh, fatal hour! Oh, inconsiderate Adam! How couldst thou leave the friend of thy affection to wander in the garden, unaided by the support and strength of thy arm, and the pleasure of thy conversation? Didst thou for one moment feel the supreme dignity and full consequence of being placed lord of the lower creation? Didst thou walk forth to survey the animals created for thy use, and subjected to thy dominion? No, no; we say pride had not then polluted the human heart. Thou wast not then puffed up with the idea of knowing good and evil; but thou might have had tenderness enough for thy 'rib, that was taken from thy side,' to have kept near enough to her to protect her innocence from the wiles of the tempter. Nothing can justify Eve's imprudence in parlaying with the serpent at all; and she is condemnable for holding any converse, or supposing knowledge was ever desirable, that must be obtained in any clandestine or dishonorable manner. No one can approve of the asperity of Adam's answer to his Maker, when called on to answer how he knew that he was naked. He answered evidently with a very indignant air: The woman thou gavest to be with me, gave me of the fruit of the tree, and I did eat. It does not appear, from his own account, that Adam withstood the temptation with more fortitude than Eve did; for she presented the fruit, and he received it without hesitation; but it is plain she did not yield immediately, though the most subtle agent of the devil told her that her eyes should be opened, and that she should be like a god. When indeed she saw that the tree was good for food, and that it was pleasant to the eyes, and a tree to be desired to make one wise, she took of the fruit thereof, and did eat. It appears her desire was to obtain knowledge, which might be laudable, though her reason was indeed deceived.

And reason is quickly deceived, says the eloquent Saurin, when the senses have been seduced. It was already yielding to the temptation, to hearken so long to the tempter.

By the joint transgression of our first parents, sin, misery and death were introduced into this present world: They appear equally culpable; yet God, who is ever wise and just in his dealings, passed the most severe sentence on the woman, as she was told her sorrows should be multiplied. And a still harder fate attended her. She was reduced, from a state of honorable equality, to the mortifying state of subjection: Thy desire shall be to thy husband, and he shall rule over thee. Heaven never intended she should be ruled with a rod of iron; but drawn by the cords of the man, in the bonds of love. It is however evident, Adam was placed over her as her lord and master, for a certain period, and by the express will of his maker, and was taught to appreciate his own judgment, as every creature was brought to him to give them names; and whatsoever names he gave them, they were called: And he gave his rib the name of woman, and displayed some judgment in the reason given for calling her woman: For she is bone of my bone, and flesh of my flesh, and therefore she shall be my equal. She shall have equal right to think, reason, and act for herself, with my advice corroborating. He should therefore have resisted the temptation with manly fortitude, and, not only by precept, but by example, strengthened her resolution to resist the evil spirit: but he fell a prey to his own credulity, and sunk his posterity in depravity.

However strange their conduct may appear to the human understanding, we fully believe, in the great scale of divine providence, it was perfectly just they should be left to commit sin and folly, to convince the human race of their insufficiency, when left to act for themselves; and, from their example, shew to their posterity, the propriety of placing their dependence on Him, who alone is able to keep us from falling.

There is a very beautiful description of our primeval parent's first interview, in Miss Akin's epistles on women. We give the extract in her own style:

> See where the world's new master roams along,
> Vainly intelligent, and idly strong;
> Marks his long listless steps and turpid air,
> His brow of densest gloom, and fix'd infantile stare.
> No mother's voice has touch'd that slumb'ring ear,
> Nor glist'ning eye beguiled him with a tear.
> Love nurs'd not him with sweet endearing wiles,
> Nor woman taught the sympathy of smiles.
> Ah! hapless world, that such a wretch obeys,
> Ah! joyless Adam, though a world he sways.
> But see they meet, they gaze, the new born pair,
> Mark now the youth, and now the wond'ring fair.
> Sure a new soul that moping idiot warms,
> Dilates his statue, and his mein informs.
> A bright crimson tints his gloomy cheeks,
> His broad eye kindles, and his glances speaks.

From this description, there appears to commence a sympathy of nature, or mutual affection, inherent in nature, which perhaps might operate on Adam's sensibility, and cause him insensibly to partake of the forbidden fruit that proved their fatal fall, and her deepest humiliation; as she is placed under subjection to the man: And the command was put into full force under the old Jewish dispensation, as they bought and sold their wives and daughters, and made trafficks of them as they did their cattle. But, blessed be

God, the bonds are dissolved, the snare is broken, and woman has escaped by the blessing of the gospel.

CHAP. II.—

Woman is Restored to Her Original Rights of Equality Under the Christian Dispensation.

Here, indeed, is the love of God manifested to the disobedient children of men. Though by the fall of our first parents misery and death was the consequence; yet the promise is made good to man, that the seed of the woman should bruise the serpent's head, and that in her seed, all mankind should be restored to peace and happiness. And at the appointed time Jehovah was pleased to overshadow the espoused wife of Joseph: and there was more than a common presence of the divine eradicator attending at his birth. The wise men or astrologers of the east, had calculated a new star that would appear about that time, and it forboded some great event to take place. Agreeably to the calculations, at the very time they were gazing for the stranger, behold it did appear agreeable to their expectation, and by the bright and effulgent light of this new and till now unknown star, the wise men of the east were directed till the star reflected on the menial place of the birth of our Saviour. And here was the degraded woman found; exalted to the highest honour of embracing in her maternal arms the Son of God himself in human nature. What an interesting scene it must have been to the wise men that had been looking for some great event to take place! What a scene it must have been to the man of sensibility! The amiable, the devout Mary, apparently degraded, is now exalted to the highest honour among men; and life and immortality are brought to light, by the divine influence of the gospel, under the dispensation of grace. She, who was condemned to servitude, is now, by the blessing of the dispensation, restored to her original privileges: As the woman was first in the transgression, and, in some measure, the cause of their fall, she is now, by divine goodness, made the instrument of bringing life and future happiness to mankind. . . .

CHAP. III—

Of the Strength of Mind, and Writings of Many Illustrious Females, Both in Sacred and Profane History.

From Dr. Hunter's Sacred Biography, which places females in a very desirable point of light, the following character of Deborah is extracted:

He says, And whither are our eyes turned or directed at this time? To behold the Saviour of a sinking country, behold the residue of the spirit is on the head of a woman: The sacred flame of public spirit smothered and dead in every manly breast, yet glows in a female's bosom; and the tribunal of justice, deserted by masculine virtue and ability, is honourably and usefully filled by feminine sensibility, discernment, honest and zeal.

Deborah was a prophetess, the wife of Lepidoth, she judged Israel at that time. She was a wife and mother in Israel; and such a wife is a crown to her husband, and the pride and glory of her children; but her capacious soul, embraced more than her own family; she aimed at the happiness of thousands; she sweetly blended public, with private virtue. It is not unreasonable to suppose, the discreet and wise management of her own household first procured her the notice and esteem of the public; and the prudent deportment of the matron past by an easy transition to the sanctity of a prophetess, and the gravity of a judge. Certain it is that the reputation which is not established on the basis of personal goodness, is like a house built on the sand, which must soon sink and fall. Hitherto we have seen only holy men of God speaking as they were moved by the Holy Spirit. But the great Jehovah is no respecter of persons or sex: The secrets of the Lord are with them that fear him, and he sheweth unto them his holy covenant. The simple dignity of her unadorned and unassuming state is beautifully represented.

She dwelt under the palm tree of Deborah, between Ramah and Bethel, in mount Ephraim, and the children of Israel came up to her for judgment. Behold a female mind exalted, above the pageantry and pride of external appearance, not deriving consequence from the splendour of her attire, the charms of her person, or the number of her retinue: but from the affability of her manners, the purity of her character, and sacredness of her office; the impartiality of her conduct, the importance of her public services; not wandering from place to place, panting after little empty applause, but sought unto of all Israel, from the eminency and extensive ability of her talents and virtue.

Her canopy of state was the palm tree, her rule of living God, her motive the inspiration of the Almighty, her aim and end the glory of God, and the good of his people, her reward, the testimony of a good conscience and the respect of a grateful nation, the admiration of future generations, and the smiles of approving heaven. In her, united poetry and musical skill, fervent devotion, heroic, intrepidity, and prophetic inspiration.

A combination how rare! how instructive! how respectable! To her life is affixed an historical note, short indeed, but highly interesting and important. And the land had rest forty years. This is the noblest eulogium of Deborah, and the most honourable display of her talents and virtues. If there are feelings worthy of envy, they are those of this exalted woman. How lasting and extensive is the influence of real worth! There is one way by which every person may be the saviour of his country, that is, by cultivating the private virtues.

I now proceed to illustrate the female character, its amiableness, usefulness, and importance, in persons and scenes of a very different complexion; in the less glaring, but not less instructive history of Ruth the moabitess, and Naomi her mother. Let us wait her appearance in silent expectation, and muse on what is past.

She had a soul capacious and capable of fond respect for departed worth and living virtue: She had magnanimity to sacrifice every thing the heart held dear to decency, friendship, and religion. In Ruth we have this higher principle likewise beautifully exemplified, rational, modest, and unaffected piety.

We proceed to unfold from sacred history, the character and conduct of Hannah. Every thing, of any importance for us to know respecting Hannah, is what related to her son Samuel, and to that, accordingly, the scripture account is confined. She is the fourth, as far as we can recollect, recorded in the same similar case; and she is not the least respectable.

The manner in which Elkanah and Hannah lived together was exemplary and instructive. They have one common interest, they have one darling object of affection, they express one and the same wish, in terms of mutual kindness and endearment. Hannah's song of praise, possesses all the majesty, grace, and beauty of ancient oriental poetry. It is one of the happiest effusions of an excellent female heart, labouring under a grateful sense of the highest obligation.

From the sacred records in the New Testament, we find many females celebrated for virtue, religion and true holiness; and some were admitted to the highest dignity and honour, in attending on, and having the friendship and blessing of their Lord and Saviour Jesus Christ.

Russel says, The courage of the christian women was founded on the noblest principles and motives, and animated by the glorious hopes of immortality. Those to whom the church assign's the compound title of saint and orator, recommended to admiration the christian women.

But he who speaks of them with most zeal, is St. Jerome, who, born with a soul of fire, spent twenty-four years in writing, combating and conquering himself. The manners of this saint were probably more severe than his thoughts. He had a number of illustrious women at Rome, among his disciplines. But, though surrounded with beauty, he escaped weakness without slander, and flying the world, the women, and himself, he retired to Palestine, where all which he had quitted pursued him, and still tormented him, under the penitential sackcloth, and in the midst of solitary deserts, reechos in his ears the tumults of Rome.

Such was St. Jerome, the most eloquent panegyrist of the christian women, of the fourth century. That warm and pious writer, though harsh and austere, softens his style in a thousand instances, to praise, the Marcelas, the Paulas, and many other Roman women, who, at the capital had embraced christianity, and studied in Rome the language of the Hebrews, to read the books of Moses.

When the Roman empire, like some venerable column, was pushed from its basis, and broken in pieces by the myriads of the north, christianity passed from the conquered to the conqueror by the zeal of the women, who at the same time, diffused the gospel, and softened the manners of the savages. It has been observed in every age, that christian women have been more anxious to make proselytes, than men have been. However just this observation may have been, or from what motive they were actuated, the world has been obligated to them for their ardour. It was woman, who, making the charms of their sex subservient to religion, raised to thrones by their beauty, drew over their husbands to their opinion, and spread christianity over the greatest part of Europe. It was by their means that France, Germany, Bavaria, Hungary, Lithuania, Poland, and Russia, and for some time, that Persia, received the gospel. By the same influence Lombardy renounced the opinion of Arius;[2] women were then desirous of attaining every species of learning, and some have succeeded in every age of the world. In former ages what has since been called society, was not then known. Luxury and the want of occupation had not introduced the fashion of sitting five or six hours at the glass to invent fashions. Some use was then made of time, and hence the languages and sciences were acquired by females. If the women of those ages were ambitious of arraying themselves in the knowledge of men, the men were at all times ready with their panegyricks to return the compliment.

It was the sequel of the general spirit that carried gallantry into letters, as it had introduced it into arms. Greece was governed by eloquent men, and the influence courtezans had held in public affairs was by the influence of the celebrated courtezans held over the orators. There was not one, but they had some influence over; even the thundering, the inflexible Demothenes,[3] so terrible to tyrants, was subjected to their sway. Of that great master of eloquence, it has been said, what he had been a whole year in erecting, a woman overturned in one day.

The illustrious Zenomia,[4] though not of Roman extraction, presents herself to view, as a widow who reigned in great glory for some time. The celebrated Longinus was her preceptor and secretary. Not being able to brook the Roman tyranny, she declared war against the emperor Aurelian,[5] who took her prisoner and led her in triumph to Rome, and butchered her principal nobility, and among others the excellent Longinus, who taught her to write as well as to conquer. She was afterwards unfortunate with dignity, and she consoled herself for the loss of a throne with the sweets of solitude and the joys of reason.

Jane of Flanders is highly celebrated by Rapin[6] and other historians. When John was taken prisoner and sent to Paris, which misfortune must certainly have ruined his party, had not his interest been supported by the extraordinary abilities of his wife, Jane of Flanders, a lady who seems to possess all the excellent qualities of both sexes. Bold, daring, and intrepid, she fought like a hero in the field; shrewd, sensible and sagacious, she spoke like a politician in the council; and endowed with the most amiable manners, and winning address, she was able to draw the minds of her subjects by the force of her eloquence, and mould them to her pleasure. She happened to be at Rennes[7] when she received the news of her husband's captivity. But that disaster instead of depressing, raised her native courage and fortitude. She assembled the citizens, and holding her infant son in her arms, recommended him to their care and protection, in the most pathetic terms, as the male heir of their ancient dukes, who had governed them with lenity and indulgence, and to whom they had ever professed their zealous attachment. She declared herself willing to run all hazards with them in so just a cause. She pointed out to them the resources that yet remained in the alliances with England, earnestly beseeching them to make one vigorous effort against the usurper, who being forced on them by the intrigues of France, would, as a mark of gratitude, sacrifice the liberties of Britanny to his protector. The people, moved by the affecting appearance of the princes, vowed to live and die with her in defence of the rights of her family.

There has been many eminent and distinguished writers in almost every age of the world. In 1643, a piece appeared at Paris, under this title, The Generous Woman; who shews her sex are more noble, more patriotic, more brave, more learned, more virtuous and economical than men. In 1665, another lady published at Paris, a book entitled The Illustrious Dames, where, by good and strong reasoning it is fairly proved that women surpass the men. In 1673, a performance appeared, entitled, The Equality of the Sexes, shewing the importance of divesting ourselves of prejudices. These discourses were philosophical and moral. Madam De

Gournay wrote upon her sex; but being more modest, she confined herself and pretensions, and was contented with equality.

Mary Shurman, born at Calona, is extolled for extraordinary capacity in learning. She was a painter, musician, engraver, sculptor, philosopher, and geometrician, and understood nine different languages.

Elizabeth, queen of England, is noticed by some historians, for the great strength of mind she discovered in her youth. Mr. Ascham,[8] her tutor, in a letter to his friend Sturminus, says, I am reading Greek with the princess. The orations she understood at first; not only the meaning of the orator, but the whole force of the language, and the whole system of the laws, customs, and manners of the Athenians. Some historians say, the reign of Elizabeth was justly esteemed as one of the most shining periods of English history; and for purity of manners, vigour of mind, vigour of character, and personal address, it is perhaps unequalled. The magnificent entertainments which that illustrious princess so frequently gave her court, and at which she generally appeared in person, with a most engaging familiarity, rubbed off the ancient reserve of nobility, and increased the taste of society, and even of gallantry.

Some historians assert that the reign of queen Anne was the summer, of which William was only the spring. Every thing was ripe and nothing was corrupted. It was a short, but glorious period of heroism, and national capacity, of taste and science, learning and genius, gallantry without licentiousness, and politeness without effeminacy.

Lady Jane Gray is described by Dr. Fuller,[9] as possessing the innocency of childhood, the beauty of youth, the solidity of maturity, and the gravity of age.

In the character of Sir Thomas More are found blended the perfections of the male sex, as neither his religion, or learning, blunted or soured his temper, or his taste for society. His love, affections, and ideas of the female character would do honour to any gentleman of the present day. In an elegant latin piece to a friend on the choice of a wife, he writes, May you meet with a woman not stupidly silent, nor always prattling nonsense. May she be learned, if possible, or at least capable of being made so. A

learned and accomplished woman will be always drawing sentiments out of the best authors. She will be herself in all the vicissi-
tudes of fortune, neither blown up by prosperity, or broken down
by adversity. She will be your friend at all times. You will spend
your time in her company with delight. You will be always finding
out new beauties in her mind. She will keep your soul in continual
serenity, agreeably to these delicate sentiments. It is virtue, learning, and religion, which constitute the real felicity of the connu-
bial relation.

From history we shall furnish a few more instances of exalted
characters that have shone as bright luminaries, in different ages,
for virtue, learning, religion, and for filial and maternal affection.

Cornelia,[10] the illustrious mother of the Gracchi, after the death
of her husband, who left her twelve children, applied herself to
the care of her family, with a wisdom and prudence, that acquired
her universal esteem; only three lived to maturity, one daughter
named Semphronia,[11] who was married to the second Scipio
Africanus;[12] two sons, Tiberius and Caius,[13] whom she brought
up with so much care, that, though they were generally acknowledged to have been born, with natural talents and happy dispositions, it was judged that they were still more indebted to
education, than nature. The answer she gave a Campanian lady
concerning them, is very famous, and includes in it great instructions for ladies and mothers. That lady who was very rich, and
still fonder of pomp and shew, after having displayed in a visit to
her, her diamonds, pearls, riches, and jewels, earnestly desired
Cornelia to let her see her jewels also. Cornelia turned the conversation to another subject, to wait the return of her sons, who were
gone to the public school. When they returned and entered their
mother's apartment, she said to the Campanian lady, pointing to
them with her hand, these are my jewels and the only ornaments I
admire. And such ornaments are the strength and support of society, and add a brighter lustre to the fair, than all the jewels in the
east.

Valerius Maximus[14] relates a singular fact of a woman of illustrious birth, who had been condemned to be strangled. The
Roman praetor delivered her to the triumvir, who caused her to
be carried to prison in order to her being put to death. The gaoler

who was ordered to execute her, was struck with compassion, and could not resolve to kill her; he chose therefore to let her die of hunger, besides which he suffered her daughter to see her in the prison, taking care however that she brought nothing for her to eat. As this continued many days, he was surprised that the prisoner lived so long without eating and suspecting the daughter, upon watching her, he discovered that she nourished her mother with her own milk. Amazed at so pious, and at the same time so ingenious an invention, he told the fact to the triumvir, and the triumvir to the praetor, who believed the thing merited relating in the assembly of the people. The criminal was pardoned. A decree was passed that the mother and daughter should be supported for the rest of their lives at the expense of the public, and that a temple sacred to piety should be erected near the prison.

The same author gives a similar instance of filial piety, in a young woman named Xantippe,[15] to her aged father Cimonus, who was also condemned to die, and in prison, and which is universally known by the name of the Roman charity. Both these instances appear so extraordinary and uncommon to that people, that they could only account for them, by supposing, that the love of children was the first law of nature.—*Plin. Hist.* 1, 7, 36.

Lady Burleigh is noticed in English history as an amiable example of beneficence. She was wife of the famous Lord Burleigh, lord high treasurer of England, and privy counselor to queen Elizabeth.

Madam Maintenon, Madam de Severns and Madam Chapon,[16] rank high in history, as letter-writers, in their day. Miss Wollstonecraft mentions some ladies with energy. Of Mrs. Chapon she says, I only mention her letters, as they are wrote with such good sense and unaffected humility, and contain so many useful observations, that I notice them to pay the worthy writer a tribute of respect. The word respect, reminds me of Mrs. Macaulay, a woman undoubtedly of the greatest abilities this country ever produced, and yet this woman has been suffered to die without sufficient respect having been paid to her memory; posterity will be more just, and remember Catharine Macaulay was an example of intellectual acquirements, supposed to be incompatible with the weakness of her sex. In the style of her writing, indeed no sex appears, for it is like the sense it conveys, strong and clear. Her judgment is the profound mature fruit of thinking; she writes with sober energy.

Mary Wollstonecraft was a woman of great energy and a very independent mind; her Rights of Women are replete with fine sentiments, though we do not coincide with her opinion respecting the total independence of the female sex.[17] We must be allowed to say, her theory is unfit for practice, though some of her sentiments and distinctions would do honour to the pen, even of a man. Her distinction between modesty and humility is certainly very ingenious. She says, modesty, sacred offspring of sensibility and reason, true delicacy of mind, may I unblamed presume to investigate thy nature, and trace to its covert the mild charms, that, mellowing each harsh feature of character, renders what would only inspire admiration, lovely.

Milton was not arrogant when his suggestion of judgment suffered that to escape, which proved a prophecy. Nor was General Washington, when he accepted the command of the American forces. The latter has always been characterised a modest man. Had he been merely modest, he would have probably shrunk back irresolute; and afraid to trust himself with the direction of an enterprize on which so much depended. A modest man is presumptuous; this is the observation many characters have led me to form. Jesus Christ himself was modest, Moses was humble, Peter was vain.—*Vol. II, p.* 314.

These questions are put to the higher class of ladies, who have been weak enough to consult old gypsies for the knowledge of future events. Do you believe that there is but one God, and that he is powerful, just, and good? Do you believe that all things were created by him, and that all things are dependent on him? Do you rely on his wisdom, so conspicuous in his works, and in your own frame; and are you convinced, that he has ordered all things that do not come under the cognizance of your senses, in the same perfect harmony, to fulfil his designs? Do you acknowledge that the power of looking into futurity and seeing things that are not as if they were, as an attribute of the Creator? And should he see fit, by an impression on the mind of his creatures, to impart any event hid in the shades of time, to whom would he reveal the secret by immediate inspiration? The opinion of ages will answer this question—To reverend old men, distinguished for eminent piety.

Impressed by their solemn, devotional parade, a Greek or Roman lady might be excusable to inquire of the oracle, when she was anxious to pry into futurity.—*Wollstonecraft's Observation.*

In this enlightened age, it seems almost impossible that any one, either in Europe or America, can be so infatuated as to encourage such a class of artful vagrants, who pretend to reveal future events. Be not deceived by their juggling tricks, but put your trust in the All-wise Disposer of the affairs of human life, and know that it is not in man that walketh to direct his steps, neither is it wise or prudent for any person to pry into the hidden mysteries of futurity, but trust in providence, that what we know not in this state, shall be revealed to us in another.

There are few females at the present day, that would wish to claim the Otaheite's strength, as represented by Capt. Wallis. He says, that Oberach, queen of Otheite,[18] lifted him over a marsh with as much ease, as he could a little child.

For strength of mind, and real virtue and dignity, we must now introduce queen Isabella, whose influence in the court of Spain determined them to support Columbus, in his voyage to America. Had it not been for her energy, the plan must have been frustrated, and perhaps the continent not discovered till this present time. She offered to pawn her jewels to defray the expenses, rather than the voyage should fail. The court were so impressed with the magnanimity of her conduct, that they resolved to support the case without the aid of her jewels.

It certainly is not beneath the dignity of the female character, to aid, assist or advise, when any thing of importance labours, either in church or state. They have a right to even pawn their jewels, or any other ornament, for the general good of the community.

CHAP. IV.—

The Female Character and Writings Are Equal in the Present Day to Any Former Period; and Some Miscellaneous Sentiments Respecting the Sex.

Madam de Staal, for strength of mind, true magnanmity, patriotism, and independence, as well as her literary talents and acquirements, shines unequalled. Her late work of the Influence of Literature on Society, would do honour to the able pen of a man. She can have no rival.

For poetic fancy and genius few have ever excelled Lucy Akin. Her Epistles on Women, and other poems, do honour to her pen. We give a further specimen of the general spirit of the author.

> Does history speak; drink in her loftiest tone
> And make Cornelia's virtues all thy own.
> Thus self endow'd, thus arm'd for every state,
> Improve, excel, surmount, subdue your fate;
> So shall enlighten'd man at length efface,
> That slavish stigma, sear'd on half the race;
> His rude forefather's shame, and pleas'd confess,
> Tis your's to elevate, tis your's to bless.
> Your interest, one with his, your hope the same,
> Fair peace on earth, in death undying fame,
> And bliss in words, beyond the species general aim,
> Rise shall he say, O woman, rise, be free,
> My life's associate, now partake with me.
> Rouse thy keen energies, expand thy soul,
> And see and feel, and comprehend the whole.
> My deepest thoughts intelligent divide;
> When right confirm me, and when erring guide;
> Soothe all my cares, in all my virtues blend,
> And be my sister, be at length my friend.

Epist. on Women.

Many other authors could be produced who have done honour to the female pen and character in their writings.

We must now say of the amiable Miss H. More,[19] "many daughters have done virtuously, but thou hast excelled them all." Her works from the smallest grade to the most important, are all calculated to improve the mind, and mend the heart.

American Character noticed.

America though as yet but young in the arts and sciences, will not long remain in the back ground, as she can now claim the birth-right of many respectable female writers, both in prose and verse.

The lovely Morton[20] may view with many in Europe for her sublime and poetic fancy. She, with many other respectable writers, who have not been sufficiently appreciated, still shine with the lustre of the aurora borealis in the northern hemisphere.

Among the most distinguished historians are seen a Warren, and an Adams, who have done honour to themselves, their country and sex, as faithful compilers of history. Mrs. Warren, in her History of the American Revolution (vol. I. page 4), observes, There are appropriate duties assigned to each sex, and surely it is the peculiar province of masculine strength, not only to repulse the bold invader of his country's rights, but in the nervous style of manly eloquence, describe the blood stained field, and relate the story of slaughtered armies.

In vol. II. page 30, she mentions Mrs. Ackland, who was a British officer's lady, as a pattern of female heroism and conjugal affection. She came with her husband to America, and shared with him all the hardships of the camp life; he was badly wounded and taken prisoner, and she by her fortitude supported him, as she lost not her resolution or usual spirits. The American commander, pleased with her firmness, gave orders that she should have every attenion paid to her rank, character, and sex.

There might now be recorded a number of American ladies, who left domestic peace and retirement, to share with the partners of their affections, all the trials and fatigue of a camp life; suffice it to notice two in particular, Mrs. Washington,[21] and Mrs. Jackson,[22] who with six little boys, left her rural retreat to accompany the Colonel to the field of battle. She partook with him in the fatigues and inconveniences of the camp life; he was soon commissioned as a general officer: Under her own guardian eye she had these sons trained and disciplined, till they were efficient to become respectable officers, which they all were in the American army.

Mrs. Washington shone a bright example of female excellence; she followed the foot paths of her beloved hero, by her firmness and christian fortitude; with affection she soothed every care of his long war-worn life. She has left a bright example, of every virtue that adorns the christian or female character. Mrs. Warren says, Having personally known her I can say, her whole deportment was blended with such a sweetness of manners, that she not only engaged the affection of her intimates, but of all who had the felicity of knowing her, and even strangers were captivated with her mild and affectionate address. To every child of sorrow and affliction, she lent a listening ear, and often extended the hand of meek charity, to alleviate the cruel anguish of poverty. She shone as the patriotic wife, the meek christian, and the truly upright in heart. She was like her Fabius,[23] modest, but not timid. She may with propriety be esteemed a model of female perfection, and highly worthy the imitation of the American fair. May her memory, with her virtues, be engraven on the tablet of every female's heart. She has erected a temple of virtue and fame, for the female standard.

By the mutual virtue, energy, and fortitude of the sexes, the freedom and independence of the United States were attained and secured. The same virtue, energy, and fortitude, must be called into continual exercise, as long as we continue a free, federal, independent nation. The culture and improvement of the female understanding will strengthen the mental faculties, and give vigour to their councils, which will give a weight to any argument used for their mutual defense and safety. No nation nor republic ever fell prey to despotism, till by indolence and dissipation, it neglected the arts and sciences, and the love of literature. They then

became effeminate and degraded; and by them the female character was degraded. As long as the german women were free and honoured by the men, it acted as a stimulous to their ambition. On
the value and integrity of both sexes their success and independence very much depended.

If we take a retrospect of the world, from the creation, it will
be found, that in every age where ignorance prevailed most,
women were most degraded. Before the christian era, and through
the dark ages, very little light was thrown upon their characters.
They were supposed to have the command of Pandora's[24] iron
box, which contained all the accumulated evils incident to human
nature. Some authors say, from the circumstance attending this
box, at that period, that age was called the iron age, and has been
known by that name ever since.

There are some excellent sentiments respecting women in a
small treatise, entitled The Friend of Women, by De Villamont, in
French, translated by Maurice. He says, every one speaks of
women according to the disposition of his heart; and the most vi-
cious men are most disposed to paint them in the most odious
colours. He says, whatever we meet with in the different opinions
of men with regard to women, the lively interest they regard them
with, is always the principal.

Every thing which this lovely half of the human race does, has a
right to interest us; we are born the friends of women, and not
their rivals, still less their tyrants. Let women then, who lead in
our first circles, condescend to cultivate their minds, and encourage useful reading; their merit will cause a swarm of thoughtless
beaux to disappear from their presence, and men of more merit
will form a circle about them, more worthy the name of good
company; in the new circle they will join on the score of friendship, without losing any thing in point of cheerfulness; merit is
not naturally gloomy; on the contrary, there is generally found
among polite people, who are well bred, a mild serenity far
preferable to bursts of stupid and ignorant merriment. Happily
for us, the day is past that condemned women, as well as the nobility, to rustic ignorance, though there has always been some
women found, who dared to think, and speak reasonably. . . .

ANNE NEWPORT ROYALL
(1769–1854)

Anne Newport Royall, a controversial figure in her life and her writings, brings an important perspective to early historical records by including accounts of the Southern and Mid-Atlantic states in her assessment of the United States. She was born near Baltimore on July 11, 1769, the daughter of Mary and William Newport. She had a disrupted childhood, due to the deaths of her father and stepfather. When she was eighteen, the family settled near Sweet Springs Mountain in Virginia; her mother worked as a housekeeper for Major William Royall, a farmer and veteran of the American Revolution. William allowed Anne access to his substantial library and began to direct her education. Ten years later and in spite of a nearly thirty-year difference in age, they were married, on November 18, 1794. Although it seems to have been a happy marriage, William died in 1812 from causes related to alcoholism; Anne inherited seven thousand acres of land, several slaves, and a substantial amount of livestock. She sold it all and moved to Charleston. She became an active businesswoman in the thriving city. However, her financial situation was precarious over the years, due to the flux of her investments and to lawsuits brought by one of William's nieces and her husband. The eventual success of their lawsuit for rights to William's estate left Anne Royall destitute. With little money, but with a talent for travel writing, Royall began her life as a writer. Some of her travel was supported by a benefit from her husband's friends in the Freemason movement and some by newspaper editors, and she became well-known in both circles. Between 1826 and 1831, she published five books based on her travels, and one novel (The Tennessean; a Novel, Founded on Facts, 1827). Royall's strong personality became as much a topic of the reviews of her books as did the content. She moved to Washington, D.C., during this time, and she became equally well known in political circles. Royall interviewed every president from John Quincy Adams to Franklin Pierce. But her resistance to the evangelical revival of the period, led by Presbyterians, resulted in her being brought to trial as a "common scold"; found guilty, she was not dunked in water as required, but fined ten dollars, which her supporters insisted on having the honor of paying.

In 1830, she started her own newspaper, Paul Pry, advertised as an independent investigative journal. She wrote, often scathingly, about political life in the capital, opposed government usurpation of Native American lands, and opposed slavery. Because of her outspoken criticism of politicians, some postmasters would not deliver the newspaper, and it did not supply enough income for Royall's support. She ended publication of Paul Pry in 1836, but two weeks later began another investigative newspaper, The Huntress, which was equally strong in its pursuit of government corruption and graft. She always reminded readers that the money lost to corruption could have been used for widows, children, or the impoverished. She edited The Huntress over the next eighteen years, until her death on October 1, 1854; she was buried in a pauper's grave.

Sketches of History, Life, and Manners in the United States (1826) is Anne Royall's first travel narrative, and her best. Traveling widely, she wrote of the natural features of each region, its history, the people's distinctive characters, and personal anecdotes, all of which made for educational and entertaining reading. Sketches sold quite well, opening the door for Royall's five years of publishing in travel and history.

SKETCHES OF HISTORY, LIFE, AND MANNERS, IN THE UNITED STATES

1826.

Lewisburg [Virginia].—Lewisburg takes its name from Gen. Andrew Lewis,[1] who commanded at the battle of the Point [Pleasant] already mentioned. On his way thither, he encamped upon the ground where Lewisburg now stands, which, at that time, was nothing more than a bleak savannah. In the following year, Col. John Stewart,[2] (now living) and Mr. George Matthews, of Augusta, Va. opened a store on this savannah; a fort was likewise built on it, to protect them from the Indians. I am now (1824) sitting on the site where this fort once stood: not the least vestige of it, however, remains. It is now the property of Mrs. Welsh, whose house and garden stand within the limits once occupied by this fort. From Mrs. W. who is now in her seventieth year, I collected these particulars. She is now sitting by me; and goes on to relate "That she was one of the earliest permanent settlers of Greenbriar, and lived within a mile of the fort just mentioned, which was called Fort Savannah. She was then the wife of a Mr. Arbuckle, who was in the famous battle of the Point and spent all his time in guarding the settlements. There was, besides Fort Savannah, another about eight miles northeast of it, called Donnally's Fort.

"The Indians, actuated by revenge, for the treatment they met with from Gen. Lewis and his men mediated the destruction of this second settlement of Greenbriar, and sat off accordingly in a large body, from their towns, with this design. At that time there was a party of men stationed at Point Pleasant," (where the battle was fought,) by government, with a view of guarding the settlement, and to watch the movements of the Indians. These men, by some means got intelligence of their march; but who would undertake the perilous task of going to apprise those unsuspecting People of their danger! The Indians were several days on their march before they were informed of it. It was an enterprise that required the utmost courage, trust, and dispatch: a counsel was held; silence, for a long time reigned in the terrified party. At length, two champions stepped forth; John Prior and Philip Hammond: We will go, said these brave and worthy men. No time was to be lost, they sat off that instant, travelled night and day, saw the Indians as they passed them; almost spent arrived, and out of breath, they arrived at the settlement the third day, a few hours before the Indians.

The inhabitants flew to Donnally's Fort, to the amount of three hundred souls. It was late in the evening before the they were all fairly in, principally women and children: there were but four men besides Col. Donnally, and a negro man belonging to him, and three or four guns in the fort. The negro's name was Dick Pointer, and Dick saved the fort!—On the same night the Indians drew near, old Dick (as he now is, for he is still living,) and the four men, were standing one hundred and fifty miles distant from the settlement, with vast mountains and rivers between guard. Col. Donnally's house made a part of the fort, the front of it forming a line with the same, the door of the house being the door of the fort. Near this door, Dick and his companions were stationed, and about midnight Dick spied, through a port-hole, something moving, but the night was so dark, and the object making no noise, it was long before he discovered it to be an Indian, creeping up to the door on all fours.

The negro pointed it out to his companions, and asked "if he might shoot;" "no," they replied, "not yet." In about twenty minutes after this, a large force was at the door, thundering it to pieces with tomahawks, stones and whatever weapon offered. The door being of the stoutest sort, resisted their efforts for some time; at length they forced one of the planks. Dick (who from every account, is as brave as Cesar,) had charged his musket well with old nails, pieces of iron, and buck shot; when the first plank dropped, he cried out to his master, "May I shoot now, sir?" "Not yet, Dick:" he stood ready with his gun cocked. The Indians, meanwhile, were busy, and the second plank began to tremble. "O master may I shoot now?" "Not yet," his master replied. The second plank fell; "Now Dick," said his master; he fired, killed three, and wounded several; the Indians ran into some rye, with which their fort was surrounded, leaving the dead bodies at the door. Shortly after this, or at least before day, they were attacked by a large party of men, under the command of Col. Samuel Lewis, who had during the while, been collecting and preparing for that purpose, and were totally routed by these men. Mrs. Welsh's husband, Arbuckle, was one of them. But had it not been for Dick Pointer's well-timed shot, every soul in the fort must have been massacred. I have had the relation from several persons, and from old Dick himself. The poor old creature wanders about very shabby: the country does allow him something, but his principal support is derived from donations by gentlemen, who visit this place and admire his character. He does not know how old he is, he thinks he was twenty-five at the attack of Donnally's Fort. His head is as white as wool, which contrasted with his black keen eye, gives him a singular appearance. His master, some years after the signal service he rendered his country, set him free.

But to return to Mrs. Welsh, the most extraordinary woman I ever saw; she has been, and is now possessed of much personal beauty. Although this female has spent her life in the western wilds of America, often running from the Indians and cooped up in forts among people as rude as the savages themselves, yet she is eminently qualified to adorn the most polished assembly. Her pleasing and courteous manners are unequalled, and every way bewitching; with a mind unimpaired, she possesses all the gaiety and sprightliness of youth; but her predominant trait is benevolence. God knows what she must have been when in youth, for she is irresistible now. She has a daughter living here, (Mrs. Reynolds,) in every respect her counterpart. How nature managed to combine so many virtues and charms in one family is a matter of great wonder. There are few people in whom we do not see something to admire; but on Mrs. R. nature has bestowed the choicest of her gifts; she has adorned her with a liberality that seldom marks her munificence to the sex. . . .

General Character.—The people of these counties are remarkable for moral and inoffensive manners: there does not exist a country, which embraces an equal extent, in which fewer crimes are committed. Murder is almost unknown but two instances of murder are recollected, and so of every other crime. They are very kind and hospitable to strangers, and of all people they are the least suspicious. Their females are very domestic, particularly the married ladies. The young ladies, however, are very affected—I mean the fashionable ones. Some of the old men, and a few of the young ones, (if I am not mistaken,) love to drink whiskey; this to be sure is a growing evil, and a very serious one.—The following anecdote may serve to illustrate the character of these people.— "Three gentlemen from East Virginia, travelling to the springs, missed their way and were lost in the mountains. The name of a mountain which neither had ever seen, made the hair rise on their heads; but to be lost on one was dreadful. After riding a few miles, they heard the sound of an axe. They therefore made up to the sound, and soon discovered the wood-cutter to be a white man, which they had expected to find black. They told him their business and their misfortune, and asked the favour of him to give the necessary directions for regaining the road. He looked at them for a minute, and laying down his axe, without speaking a word, beckoned them to follow him. His readiness in quitting his work without a stipulated reward, alarmed them very much, for now they are to be robbed undoubtedly—each one concluding that he could intend no other than to betray them. They thanked him, and said they would not trouble him so far—they would take directions. He insisted, and set off cheerfully: as was natural to expect, he walked before, which gave to their fears considerable relief, as they would have the better opportunity of defending themselves, in case of an attack from robbers, which they expected to see jump out of the bushes every moment. They were well armed, each having a brace of pistols, besides a dirk. They drew out their pistols, primed them afresh, examined the flints, and awaited their fate—when at length they found themselves safe in the road! But what was their astonishment, when, upon offering him a dollar, he refused it with disdain. Thus were these sons of courage put to the blush for their mean suspicion, by this generous mountaineer. This trait may be applied to the whole community: you could not offer them a greater insult than to attempt to reward them for any trifling service. These men related this anecdote to me, and added, that nothing surprised them more than his refusing their bounty; that had they offered fifty cents to one of their peasants, he would have received it with demonstrations of joy, and that he would have negotiated for his fee before he performed the service. Finally, they are people of moderate talents, but they set a great value upon those they have." . . .

Natural Curiosities.—In Greenbriar county, there is a natural bridge over a creek sixty feet wide; it is said to be from 130 to 200 feet perpendicular, which nearly equals height of the natural bridge in Rockbridge county: this bridge is about twenty miles northeast of Lewisburg. This information I received from Capt. John Williams. These counties abound with caves; the most remarkable of which, is the Singing cave, in Monroe. This cave is three miles in length; it runs under a mountain, and from it great quantities of salt-petre have been made. It is of unequal breadth. In the same county is what is called the Hanging-rock about six miles southwest of the road that leads those from Fincastle to the sweet springs, and about ten miles from the latter place. It is on the highest part of what is called Price's, or the middle mountain, and is considerable higher than it. From the top of the sweet spring mountain, from which it is nine miles distant, it looks like a huge house hanging from a precipice. I have been on this rock: it is amazingly large. It can really be ascended by fetching a circuit as you approach it, up the mountain, which is three miles in height from the valley below, over which it projects. The main body of the rock reclines in the bosom of the mountain, while it presents a perpendicular front, which projects to a wonderful extent clear of the mountains on the north side. When you are on the top of this rock, you have one of the grandest views in the United States, you can see to the distance of an hundred miles, in every direction: you can see the peak of Oater east, North Carolina south, with the naked eye. You see eight counties at one view, to say nothing of the endless mass of mountains of which the globe seems made. Over this vast expanse, farms are here and there distinguished, which appear in small spots no larger than a lettuce bed; these, and the streams that run near the ridges of the mountains, render the whole superlative grand. The rock itself

combines enough of the awful and sublime to gratify the most enthusiastic admirer of the works of nature. Particularly that part of
it which projects over the mountain. This is partly convex and
partly smooth; it may be about an hundred and fifty feet from the
top to the bottom, though it is hard to ascertain, from the nature
of its figure and situation. It commands, however, a view of the
valley beneath it. But no one has the courage to approach the edge
of this precipice. The Salt-pond on this same mountain, is not
only a great natural curiosity, but amongst the greatest phenom-
ena of nature. The mountain just mentioned keeps a southwest
course from the Hanging-rock, and enlarges as it proceeds until it
gains Montgomery county, Va., (adjoining Giles,) in which is the
Salt-pond. This pond is on the top of the highest part of the
mountain from which it takes the name of the "Salt-pond mountain." But what is singular, no bottom has, as yet, been discovered. It has been rising for several years: the last time I heard from
it, it was from three quarters to a mile in diameter: myriads of
trout and other fish live in it, and the margin used to be covered
with cranberries, but lately they are overflowed by the rising of
the water. Some think it will form a mighty river some day, when
it can be no longer confined within its present limits. Though no
visible stream issues from this pond, yet, a very bold stream
rushes out of the mountain about three miles distant from it,
which might lead one to believe that it had some communication
with this lake. It strikes me that the water has a brackish taste,
from which it probably took its name. Not far from the Hanging-
rock, near a creek, called Pott's creek, there is a place called the
Paint banks; I have seen these banks, they are a great curiosity.
The banks rise up directly from a bold stream, called the Paint-
banks run; and form a perpendicular of considerable height, and
the whole of it is a reddish colored earth, as red as deep burnt
bricks; from these banks, it is said, the Indians procured their
paint. On the opposite side of the same mountain, there is a creek,
called Sinking creek; it is large enough to turn a mill, and runs
very bold for several miles, when it suddenly sinks, and no more is
seen of it until within a few miles of New river, the main branch
of Kenhawa. In Monroe county, near to the former residence of
Maj. William Royall, the mountain, known by the name of

Sweet-spring mountain, presents another phenomenon. Part of it, with the trees still standing, has moved for the distance of several yards. These mountains abound in iron ore, and the most delicious honey, and game of every sort; while the vallies below afford the richest milk; wild turkies, and pheasants, (a most exquisite delicacy,) are numerous; and in the streams are caught multitudes of trout. No lime stone is found in these mountains; they are covered with a hard blackish colored stone, impregnated with iron. Fine springs abound throughout the whole country—very good mill-stones are found in Greenbriar county—salt is made in small quantities on Greenbriar river.

I had the unspeakable pleasure this morning of seeing for the first time a South American. He has just left us, on his way to the sulphur springs for his health; from thence he is to go on to the eastern states, and finally to Havana, where it appears he is a temporary resident. He observed that he had been for some time in the western states, with which he was much pleased. But our country, he said, was too cold for him; it had given him a violent cough. From his deportment he appeared to be a person of distinction. He is about the middling height, of very delicate make, and very handsome features. His colour was that of the offspring of a white and a mulatto. His hair and eyes were deep black; but his greatest personal beauty was his eye, which sparkled like diamonds, and of all men, he had the most suasive manners. His countenance wore a continual smile; he spoke the English language with great facility, and was very communicative. He called at Mrs. Hutchinson's, where I board, for the purpose of taking breakfast, and feeding his horse. Mrs. Hutchinson very politely apprised me of his arrival, and the moment he took his seat at the breakfast table, I took a seat opposite to him, with a view of enjoying his company, and conversation. He seemed to enter very readily into my motives, and gave me all the satisfaction our short interview afforded. After taking one cup of coffee, he asked the landlady for a glass of milk; she enquired whether "he would have sweet milk or sour," (common in this country,) "sweet milk, to be sure, madam," said he, "I like nothing that is sour, I like everything sweet, a sweet temper, a sweet voice, and sometimes even a sweet heart." He spoke in terms of the highest praise of our country, our people, and our government, but added "the climate was too cold for him:" he had some letters to write, and although it was August, he had a fire made in his room. I enquired of him "how he happened to acquire such a perfect knowledge of the English language," he replied "that he learned it at college, in Buenos Ayres," of which place he is a native. He made several judicious remarks on the English language, said it had no melody, and was of all languages the most difficult to acquire. He pronounced his native state "Boness Iris." I told him how we pronounced it; "ah," he replied, "and you spell cough c-o-u-g-h, why don't you spell it c-o-f-f." He was attended by one servant only, a free black man, whom he hired in Kentucky. When he finished his letters, he, and his servant, both got into the gig, (by which conveyance he travelled,) he took the reins himself, telling his horse to "come abeyout here, as de yankee say," and drove off. It was with infinite regret I saw him depart. His name is Marilla. . . .

Baltimore.—I just arrived in time enough in the evening to have a view of this (to me) great city. A host of wonders bursted upon me at once, the vast number, heighth and density of the houses, the massy public buildings, the Washington monument, the Baltimore monument, the great expanse of water, the quantity of shipping, the number of well dressed people in the streets, overwhelmed me with astonishment. I have not the least doubt but this remark may excite a smile, particularly in those who were never out of a populous town, but they must remember that till now I was never in one, and that those things which are a matter of so much indifference to them, are as gratifying to me, as our long, deep, smooth-flowing rivers, our endless prairies, our solemn forests, our wild mountains and deep caverns, our flowery plains, rude hamlets and fertile fields of beading corn, would be to them. It is natural for one to desire to see whatever is new or uncommon, and next to this, a description of them; but that person to whom they are new, will be more likely to point out their distinguished traits, than one who has spent his life amongst them. One who has spent his days in a great city, sees it without emotion, because it is familiar to him. I begin too late to discover, that I have fell very short, in describing the western states, from having always resided there.

Dropping this digression, however, I shall endeavor to convey my own impressions, as best calculated to give satisfaction to those who like myself, have always lived in the back country.

Had an awkward back woods country person, myself for instance, been taken up and dropped down in this world of houses, I should have been afraid to budge, lest those formidable cars and waggons might have settled the question with me for ever; and as for entering one of those splendid houses, it would be the last thing I should think of. I should have been afraid the lord of the mansion would look me out of existence. But I had been in Alexandria, I had been in Washington, and had, it is true, seen a few fashionable people, and some splendid houses in the western states, but not so many by half. If such be Baltimore, thought I, what must be Philadelphia and New-York? I put up at the same house where Gen. La Fayette lodged, and saw the room which the General occupied, just as he left it, the furniture had not been disturbed out of respect to him.

Baltimore lies on the north side of the Patapsco river, 18 miles from the Chesapeake. It stands upon an elevated situation, with a gentle descent to the harbour. The city is divided into the old town, and Fell's Point, by a creek called Jones's creek, (Called by the citizens the falls.) This creek strikes the harbour at a right angle, and divides the town into east and west. The east is Fell's Point, which projects some distance into the basin, and gives the city the form of a bow. Large ships come up to Fell's Point, whilst none but the smallest size come to the west part of the town. I had been told that Fell's Point was low and unhealthy; it is so represented by geographers; what was my astonishment to find it no ways inferior to the other part of the town, either for beauty or situation; if any thing, it is the most desirable part of the city. Elegant buildings, fine paved streets, and splendid churches distinguish Fell's Point. Its bridges at least, are thrown over the creek mentioned, and so close do the houses come to it, that the creek is hardly perceptible. It is walled up with stone on each side for a considerable distance above the mouth.

Baltimore is two miles in length, and of different widths. The streets are paved and lighted; the houses, though well built, do not look so handsome as those of Washington, because they are older, they have not that fresh appearance. The houses of Washington too, standing so far asunder, have not the same change of being tinged with smoke. . . .

Prison.—From the hospital I went to the prison, which is also in the suburbs of the city; it is likewise a large building of brick, several stories high, and has an extensive yard attached to it, enclosed by a wall of considerable height. At the opposite end of this wall stands the penitentiary, also a fine brick building. The prison is secured by a double gate, and huge bars of iron; the opening of which takes up no little time. I found thirty prisoners, including the debtors; which last are kept separate from the criminals. The apartments were not large, and several were confined in one room; all have the privilege of walking in the yard at certain hours of the day. They looked cheerful, and bore the appearance of kind treatment, though they were all destitute of bedding, except those that were able to furnish it themselves. The apartments are warmed by stoves. But my feelings were much shocked upon finding amongst the prisoners, six females confined for debt, and without even a blanket to repose on, or a seat of any description. I offered a few words of consolation to these unfortunate females, at which several of them burst into tears, and cast on me a look which I shall never forget, as I hastened abruptly from the scene! The keeper happened to say in the presence of the male prisoners, "that I was going to write their history;" one of them (a criminal) spoke out, laughing at the same time, that "he hoped I would say something clever about him." I was unable to get into the penitentiary, though I saw the prisoners at work from the walls; they were clean and neat in their dress, and looked well. The keepers both of the prison and penitentiary were men of much apparent humanity and mildness, as well as experience and education; such as ought always to be selected for such places; a brutal keeper, such as I have seen, has it too much in his power to exercise cruelty toward his fellow creatures; why it is the case is not material, but certain it is, give an ignorant man power over the liberty of his fellow men, and he will exercise it without mercy. Much credit is due to the constituted authorities of Maryland, whoever they may be, for giving such obvious proofs of humanity and attention toward their fellow men.

Colleges.—I met with a total defeat on the subject of the colleges: the president, or principals, were absent except in that restricted (as I was told,) to the education of priests. I found only a French priest, who could speak hardly a word of English, and withal appeared rather averse to giving me any information. He had on a woollen night-cap, and the rest of his dress accorded therewith. His face was wrinkled with age, or ill humor; and in short he looked more like something broke loose from bedlam than any thing else. Upon making my business known to him, he jabbered something which I could not understand, and wheeled to the right about, and marched off without more ceremony! But my misfortune did not end here; I entered the other part of the college, which was within a few steps, where the boys are taught, but found no person whatever. I went through such of the apartments as were open, and found them not in that condition we would expect: neither of these buildings are any thing to boast of. Baffled in my endeavours, I made one more attempt; seeing a number of boys engaged at play near the college, I walked towards them, and enquired for their teacher: they pointed to a man who was walking towards us, in a shabby great coat. When he drew near I apprised him of my business, but what was my astonishment to find him another foreigner! This last was an Irish-man, who spoke worse English if possible than the other, and the most uncouth being I ever saw. I turned from him in disgust; not however without condemning my countrymen, who could invest such men with the control of a matter of the first importance. I addressed several of the students (who were the youths just mentioned) with such questions as "what studies they pursued? how many classes? the number of professors?" but from them I received such replies as reflect little honor upon the institution. The Irish-man, who was standing by, was brought to blush at their behaviour, shook his head at them, and seemed no little concerned at their rudeness. The medical college is also called a university; it has six professors, and is said to be in a flourishing condition. Besides these three colleges, there are said to be many schools and academies. A great storm of wind and rain prevented my seeing the alms house.

Markets.— Nothing pleased me more than the markets—here I found ample scope for my curiosity; never had I before seen any thing equal to it, either for variety or abundance, and every thing much cheaper than I had expected—vegetables of all sorts, fruit, meat, and fish, both fresh and salt—in short, every thing that was to be eaten. Here an old woman sitting with a table spread with nice bread and butter, veal cutlet, sausages and coffee; there another, with a table bending under the weight of candy, sweet cakes, oranges and apples; another with choice-vegetables; another with fowls, as fat as corn could make them. These take their stations at each end of the market-houses, and form a perfect phalanx. The market-houses are in the streets, long and narrow.

Manners and Appearances.—The people of Baltimore are polite and affable in their manners, liberal, brave, and hospitable; they are active, enterprising, and attentive to business. The men, generally speaking, dress plain; but the ladies dress gay, and even fantastical.—Both sexes walk as though they were walking for wager; the streets are full from morning till night. The constant buzz of the multitude, with that of carts, waggons and coaches, nearly distracted me. Both men and women, in stature, are much like those already described, east of the mountains: the men are small, but well shaped, and both sexes are very sprightly. Their complexion is dark, with black eyes; their features are very delicate, but regular and handsome, with much expression of countenance. Baltimore is the third commercial city in the Union; it has several manufactories of glass, tin, and leather, and contains 62,738 inhabitants.

History.—Baltimore was located, in the year 1730, in the north side of Patapsco river, upon the land called Cole's harbour, or Todd's range: sixty acres were laid out into sixty lots by an act of the legislature. Major Thomas Tolly, Wm. Hamilton, Wm. Buckney, Dr. Geo. Walker, Richard Ghrist, Dr. Geo. Buchanan, and Wm. Hammond,[3] were appointed commissioners for carrying said act into execution. The history of Maryland is very imperfectly known; it was a mere accident that I happened to meet with the foregoing act, and a few other sketches of the history of Maryland. As we are fond of tracing things to their source, it may afford some gratification to add, with respect to Baltimore city, that at the time it was erected into a town, a man by the name of Fleming, (a tenant of Mr. Carrol,[4]) resided in a house (the only one in the place) called the Quarter, which stood on the north bank of Usher's run, near the house of Gen. Striker,[5] in Charles-street. All we know of Baltimore since, is, that it has advanced in wealth and commerce, at a career unparalleled by any other city, until within a few years back.

Maryland, it is well known, was settled by Lord Baltimore,[6] who was a Roman Catholic in religion. The Catholics being oppressed by the British government, a number of gentlemen of rank and distinction, with Lord Baltimore at their head, set sail from Cowes, in the Isle of Wight, and arrived in the Chesapeake, at Old Point Comfort, in Virginia, in 1634. He sailed up the Potomac, thirteen leagues, and came to an Indian town, called Potomack, from whence this river took its name.—The Indians received Lord Baltimore with great hospitality, and after some conversation with them, he asked the chief, "If he was willing to let him and his companions stay in the country?" to which the chief replied, "I do not bid you go, nor bid you stay; use your own discretion." The governor (as Lord Baltimore was now called,) not willing to hazard a settlement amongst these Indians, sailed back again, and proceeded up a smaller stream, where he found other Indians, called Yoamancos.[7] He landed here, and gave it the name of St. Mary's after having purchased the land of the natives. The first thing he did after landing, was to build a guard-house and a store house. This place is still known in Maryland by the name of St. Mary's. A singular anecdote is related of Lord Baltimore and these Indians. Shortly after the governor landed, a number of them came to visit him, and amongst others the king of Patuxent,[8] who had formerly been a prisoner of the English in Virginia. To please these people, the governor made an entertainment on board the ship, then at anchor. The king of Patuxent was placed at table between the governor of Maryland and the governor of Virginia (Sir John Harvey,[9] then on a visit to Lord Baltimore,) in a great state. All was mirth and glee, and mutual good humour over spread every countenance. But an incident happened which had like to have destroyed the pleasure of the feast:—A Patuxent Indian coming on board, while they were at dinner, and seeing his king thus seated, started back and refused to enter the cabin, supposing that his king was confined there as a captive, and would have leaped overboard, had not the king himself interposed, and satisfied him that he was in no danger. These Indians lived amicably with this colony: they went to hunt, every day, with the new comers, killing and fetching home deer and turkies. Meantime the colony cultivated the soil, planting corn on the land formerly cleared by the Indians, with such success that the next year or the year following, they exported 10,000 bushels, and the utmost harmony for many years subsisted between them and the Indians. The first assembly met in 1638, the governor taking the chair as speaker of the house; but it was long before the king of England could be brought to sanction any of their laws.

Having written some dramatic pieces while in Washington, I waited on Messrs. W. and W. proprietors of the theatre in this city, to whom I had a letter of introduction. The first of these (though I had claims of a sacred nature upon him, which it is needless to mention in this place,) received me with a snarling growl, not unlike that of a surly, ill-natured dog, when another of his species enters his tenement. Had I been a highways robber, monsieur could not have treated me with less ceremony; he brushed by me, as though he would have overset me, without uttering more than one short sentence, which as near as I could distinguish, was "that he wished to have no concern with me." I am fond of seeing human nature in all its variety, and taking everything into view, I must say, this was one new, as it was unexpected. I stood a few moments, thunderstruck as it were, and summoning my resolution I waited on the other W. He was as polite and affable, as the other was vulgar and abrupt. He received me with an air worthy of Chesterfield[10] himself, but when he understood that the piece I wished him to patronize was my own production, "oh," said he, "that is out of the question, we play no American pieces at all, you must excuse me nor give yourself further trouble." This last, I found was the chief of the band, and if he objected the matter was at an end. Thus those foreigners, (for I am told they are both Englishmen,) who are so generously patronized by us, and live on the fat of the land, refuse us their patronage in turn. No wonder the English cry down American works when they find their account in it. And here I cannot help lamenting the taste of my own country, which leads it to prefer foreign works. As in the persons alluded to, they are too contemptible to be brought into question, although they have the impudence to laugh at the credulity of the generous sons of Columbia, who save them from starving. Yet it would be pleasing to us, could we awaken a spirit of encouragement in favour of our own literature. We are sorry to find the American character, so praise-worthy in other respects, should fall short in one by which it is ultimately to rise or fall. It may be said of nations as of individuals as that man must be blind indeed, who would sacrifice his personal interests to the aggrandizement of another, so that nation must be blind to its interest which enriches another by means that impoverish itself. I would by no means exclude foreign literature, but I condemn that rage for it, which hurries us beyond reason, beyond interest, and beyond national pride. I have now a letter before me, from a noted bookseller in Philadelphia, wherein he says "that American works do not pay the expense of publishing, owing to the rage of the American people for foreign productions." Another says, "such flimsy stuff is unworthy of support." We might as well say that because a mechanic spoils a piece of cloth, or a shoemaker should make a flimsy pair of shoes, we will not encourage domestic manufacturers, we will revoke the tariff, and let them shift for themselves, we will rather encourage the manufactures of others than our own. We aspire to great actions, we pride ourselves upon being a great nation; will we then neglect the growing genius of our country, is it alone unworthy in our regard? It is labour in vain to contend for schools and colleges, for expensive establishments to educate our sons and daughters, when all the advantages derived from these would not keep them from the poorhouse! For if they were to write a book, they would find no purchaser, because the writer lived on this side of the Atlantic. Away with such policy. I shall only further observe, that all our efforts ought to go hand in hand, to the grand design of national excellence. Instead of that, we are in effect pulling down with one hand, what we put up with the other.

My visit to Baltimore being limited to ten days, I prepared to leave it for Philadelphia. I cannot, however, depart without one more remark, which forms a link in the long chain of human depravity; and proves, that as men become refined in the arts and sciences, they also become refined (if I may be allowed the expression,) in knavery. The circumstance alluded to, is a fraud committed against myself, in the purchase of a piece of silk, from one of the merchants. The clerk, either willingly or through mistake, kept back part of the silk. Discovering the default, I requested the silk or the money. He putting on a sarcastic grin, refused to do either; I applied for justice to the proprietor in the counting-room; but from him I received nothing but the most wanton, the most brutal insults! Being in haste to leave the city, and withal unwilling to swear to a man I never saw but once, I quit them so. Taking the whole into consideration, the insults, and the manner by which I obtained the money to make the purchase, viz. a donation from the ——— of Baltimore, I must say, the man who would be guilty of such an act, would rob the dead.

Respect and gratitude for the citizens of Baltimore, compel me to apologise to them for exposing the turpitude of those men, not meaning to say, but they would be as unwilling to screen such an action. "It is not one diamond which gives lustre to another, it is the rough stone compared with it which proves its genuine value;" so the conduct of these men serve to cast a bright lustre on that of their fellow citizens, whose memory will ever live in my heart.

On my way to Albany, I had an opportunity of seeing many Dutch families, for the first time: what are called Dutch where I came from, are from Germany, and form a distinct people from the Hollanders: they are as remarkable for sluttishness, as the Hollanders are for neatness. This I had heard, but now I had occular proof. Every utensil in their house, even the stoves shine like silver; their apparel and furniture correspond with these in neatness. These country Dutch are mild and simple in their manners, particularly the young females; these have a sweetness and innocence in their countenance which is peculiar. Both men and women are slow in their movements; the females are better shaped than the men; a broad face is common in both, and a middling complexion. When we arrived at Albany (at least in the neighbourhood,) we have the Hudson to cross, it being on the opposite side from N.Y. city. Some doubts were suggested as to the strength of the ice, and to be upon the safe side, the passengers got out of the

state, and walked over the river on the ice, leaving the Trojan and
I, to sink or swim together; being a man of unwieldy size, the
other passengers insisted very hard upon him to join them, lest his
weight might cause the stage to break through; but no entreaty
could prevail with cuffy, and finally he and the driver mutually
growled at each other, during the drive over the river.

Upon gaining the western shore of the Hudson, you are in Albany. A few paces brought us to Palmer's where a comfortable
stove, a good supper, and a kind landlady, added to the thoughts
of seeing one of the greatest men of the age, DeWitt Clinton,[11] together with the legislature, then sitting consoled me for the fatigue
and cold I underwent during my journey.

Albany.—Albany stands on the west side of the Hudson, 150
miles from New-York city. The compact part of the city lies on
two principal streets, viz. Market- and State-streets, which, in relation to Hudson river, takes the form of the capital letter T, reversed thus, (upside down T). The base is Market-street, near the
shore of the Hudson, and the perpendicular is State street. Market-street is handsome, and two miles in length; State-street is
quite short, and terminates at the capitol: it is, however, a beautiful street, as wide as any of the avenues in Washington.— These
streets are crossed by others at right angles, but the main body of
the town lies on these, and one which leads back from the capitol.
Market-street is on a level, and runs parallel with the Hudson, but
from this, the city rises up till it gains the top of a considerable
eminence, upon which stands the capitol, precisely at the end of
State-street. The capitol, from whatever point you view it, is strikingly handsome, being one of the finest edifices in the United
States. But the view *from* the capitol, for beauty of scenery, baffles
all description. You have the whole city, the Hudson, the grand
canal, the basin, the villages on the opposite shore, with the gently
swelling hills, peeping up behind them, the Catskill, and the distant mountains of Vermont, all under your eye at once! Between
Market-street and the river, there is another street running the
same way, called Dock-street; Pearl-street is also considerable, and
runs the same way above. Albany, though it does much business,
falls far behind New-York, in bustle and activity—not a fourth so

many people in the streets—it is handsomely built, mostly of brick, and covered with slate and tile. Many of the houses, either for size or beauty, are not inferior to any in New-York, take away the marble fronts. It is the seat of government for the state of New-York, and the principal officers of the government, with the governor, reside in Albany. Its public buildings are a capitol, a state-house, a prison, an alms-house and hospital, an arsenal, 2 theatres, a museum, an academy, a city powder-house, a chamber of commerce, a lancasterian school, a library, 4 banks, Knicker-bocker hall, a mechanics' hall, a Uranian hall, a post-office, and 2 market-houses: it also contains 12 places for public worship, viz. 3 Presbyterian, 1 Baptist, 1 Methodist, 1 Lutheran, 1 Apostolic, 1 Cameronian, 2 Dutch Calvinists, 1 Roman Catholic, 1 African. The capitol stands upon an elevation of 130 feet above the level of the Hudson; it is built of stone, and has a portico on the east front, facing the Hudson, of the Ionic style, tetrastile, adorned with stucco. The east front is 90 feet in length, the north front 115; the wall is 50 feet high; the whole is finished in a style of the first architecture; it cost $120,000. It has a large square of ground in front, which is nearly enclosed and planted with trees. The judiciary and the mayor of the city, as well as the legislature, hold their sittings in the capitol, the building being laid off into suitable halls, lobbies, and offices. The representative hall is a splendid apartment, yielding nothing to congress hall in the richness of the furniture and drapery; it is nearly the same, excepting only the size, marble columns, and the speaker's chair. Their clerks stand up at a superb desk, on the left of the speaker. The hall is heated by fire places, one on the right and the other on the left of the speaker, called north and south. When the speaker takes the chair, which he never does till after prayers, he cries with an audible voice, "the gentlemen of the north will please take their seats, those of the south will," &c.

I attended the debates toward the close of the session, and was much surprised at the facility and dispatch manifested in their proceedings, although worn out by their long session. I never saw finer looking men, as to appearance, stout, well made, and fine complexions; they appeared to be all nerve, some were far advanced in life, as their gray hairs bespoke; most of them, however,

were in the prime of manhood. But my attention was attracted
from them to the Hon. speaker, Clarkson Crolius, a most interesting man, modest, dignified, and manly; he strove to rally his broken spirits, exhausted by his long and arduous duties—serene and
unmoved amidst the tumult of an 130 members, (besides the officers of the house,) all in commotion and disorder, about to take
their seats, yet each unwilling to forego the liberty of the present
moment. Loath to interpose his prerogative, the speaker, in accents of the most winning sweetness, conjures them to be seated;
"Gentlemen, the day is far advanced and we have much to do,
take your seats, and let the house come to order." But his voice is
drowned by the mingled sound of doors, foot-steps, and the hum
of human voices. He strikes the desk with his mace and allures
them by looks of anxious solicitude to come to order.

The senate chamber is a small apartment, though very handsomely ornamented; here I found a very thin house, not more than
a dozen members present; they were men of mature age, differing
little, in other respects, from the representatives. I waited some
time in each house, to hear a specimen or their abilities, as speak-
ers, but was very sadly disappointed, their proceedings being confined to examining bills and matters no way intersecting. . . .

Manners and Appearances.—Albany embraces three distinct
classes of people. The first class comprises the executive officers of
the government, the supreme judges, the gentlemen of the bar, the
physicians, and a few of the reverend clergy, with the principal
merchants of the city. These constitute the first circle, take them
on what ground you will; amongst them are the Clintons, the Van
Rensselaers, the Taylors, the Lansings, the Spencers, the Wood-
worths, the Laceys, the Chesters, the Ludlows, and the celebrated
De Witt family,[12] with many others, whose talents may rank them
with the first men of any country. The second class comprises
shop-keepers, mechanics, clerks, &c. &c. This, the middle class,
constitute the religioso of the place, and are the people of moderate pretensions on the score of philosophy and learning. Between these and the better sort, the line of distinction is strongly
marked, the one, as remarkable for intelligence, affability, and liberality of sentiment, as the other is for bigotry, harsh and un-
courtly manners.—In those you find cheerfulness, hospitality, and

highly polished manners; in these a grim, cold, contracted deportment, in all they say or do. This is not the effect of religion, but
the want of it. The reign of bigotry, however, is short in Albany;
that attention which is bestowed on education, will, in a few
years, compel it to fly to some other region—it is a monster that
cannot endure the light. In all towns I have visited, I have not
found education in a more flourishing condition than in Albany.
Guess my astonishment at seeing little boys, and even little girls
with Euclid in their hands. The last and third class of citizens, are
mostly foreigners, who rank with blacks and sailors; having little
commerce with the respectable citizens.

The churches of Albany are very splendid indeed, particularly
the north Dutch; it is second to none I have seen in my travels; its
glittering domes are the greatest ornaments of the city. The south
Dutch is also a splendid building; the furniture is superb in all,
and the music is fine. Their clergy rank high in theology, being
men of the first literary attainment. Being no respecter of sect or
party, I went to hear them all, and was much disappointed at the
display of eloquence. Amongst their first preachers stands the Rev.
Dr. C., Rev. L. Lacey, and Ferris. Dr. C. is an orator of the first
class. But of all their clergy, I was most pleased with the Rev. Mr.
Lacey, of the Episcopal church; a man of the most captivating
manners; his modesty and christian meekness, incontestibly prove
his devotion to his divine master.

History.—In tracing the history of Albany to its origin, we discover the commencement of the state, as the first permanent settlement was effected at this place. Albany was settled by the
Hollanders, in 1614; they built a fort, a store-house, and a
church, the commencement of the present city. The name of the
commander was "Christiaens," which has been mentioned. It is
matter of much regret that the history of New-York is very imperfectly known, the original account being kept in Holland, in the
Dutch language; by the change of masters which took place, and
through the most unpardonable neglect on all hands, much of the
most interesting history of New-York is lost. In Mrs. Grant's[13] letters, I found a few particulars relating to Albany, and its primitive
inhabitants. She mentions this fort, as being at one time occupied
by an independent company, commanded by Captain Massy, the

father of Mrs. Lennox, the celebrated protégé of Doctor Johnson. She also makes mention of Colonel Philip Schuyler,[14] a most enlightened gentleman, who first settled what is called the Flats, where he displayed great power of mind in maintaining peace and harmony with the Indians. She likewise makes honourable mention of the principal families who settled this part of the state, many of whose descendants are still in possession of their ancient patrimony. Amongst these is the respectable family of the Van Rensselaers. They possessed, by patent, large tracts of land which they leased out to the poor; they were called patroons, which means landlord; they still go by that name. The present patroon of Albany is Gen. Stephen Van Rensselaer, one of the most worthy of the human race. But to return to Mrs. G.—"there was one wide street in Albany which run parallel with the river. The space between the street and the river was laid out into gardens. There was another street which run east and west, (now called State-street,) this street was still wider than the other. In the middle of this street stood all their public buildings. In the center of the town rose a steep hill; this last street passed over the hill and descended rapidly towards the river; at the bottom of this descent, stood the old low Dutch church. In the winter season the young people used to amuse themselves by sleighing (so they do now,) down this hill, the sleigh being pulled by themselves instead of horses. I have enjoyed much pleasure in standing near (continues Mrs. Grant,) and contemplating this patriarchal city; these primitive beings were dispersed in porches, grouped according to similarity of years and inclination; at one door young matrons, at another, the elders of the people; at a third, the youths and maidens, gaily chatting or singing together; while the children played around the trees, or waited by the cows (who wore little tingling bells,) for the chief ingredient of their supper, which they generally ate sitting on steps, in the open air." "In my time," (continues the same author,) "one of those vallies was inhabited by a Frenchman; his residence was called a hermitage. The Albanians respected him as something supernatural; they imagined that he had retired to that sequestered spot from having committed some deed in his life time; they considered him, however, in the light of an idolater, because he had an image of the Virgin Mary. There was always a governor, a few troops, and a small court in Albany."

Albany is in latitude 42 deg. 38 min. N., at the head of tide water. Besides the public buildings already noticed, it contains 2,000 houses and 17,000 inhabitants. It is governed by a Mayor, Recorder, and ten Aldermen. The streets are paved and lighted. It is the oldest city in the United States, next to Jamestown in Virginia.

Secretary Yates and Mr. Moulton are now engaged in writing a complete history of this state. From the ability and talents of these gentlemen, and their indefatigable researches we may expect the best compilation that has ever been published. Mr. Yates, the present Secretary of State of New-York, is said to be a gentleman of high literary attainments; and, from his appearance, I would suppose him justly entitled to the character. He is apparently about thirty years of age, middling stature, and fine figure; his manners very suasive, his countenance mild and pleasing. Mr. Moulton is also a gentleman of very interesting manners. But of all the gentlemen I met with in Albany, I was most pleased with Gen. Van Rensselaer, the present member of Congress, and Mr. Southwick, the poet. Of Gen. Van Rensselaer little may be said, his actions speak his praise wherever he is known, and even where he is not. He lives at the northern extremity of Market-street, quite out of the city. His house fronts the end of the street, and stands near the Hudson. It is the finest building in the vicinity; the ground, shrubberies, gardens, and walks attached to it are laid out in a style of taste and elegance worthy its generous owner. The ancestor of this great and good man owned twelve miles square adjoining Albany, granted to him by the states of Holland. He leased those lands out, "while water ran, or grass grew," exacting the tenth sheaf of grain the land produced. He reserved to himself a large demesne, which has descended to the present patroon, as the general is called. He is in every respect worthy his princely fortune; being one of those rare few who may truly be said to lay up treasure in heaven. Perhaps no man of the present age can equal him in acts of charity and benevolence. His house is the resort of the poor and the distressed, both strangers and citizens. His purse and his heart are alike open to all, he turns none empty away. When he is absent, which is a great part of the year, his strict orders to his steward are to relieve the poor. He has a great number of tenants, many of whom often fall short of their rent, and relate their inability to pay; when he has heard their story, he, like Henry the fourth of France, pulls out his purse and divides the contents with them. In short, he is the idol of the poor, and the admiration of all who know his worth. This amiable man is advanced in years. In his person he is tall, slender, and perfectly shaped, his eye a deep hazel, his countenance what his actions bespeak, the very milk of human kindness. Mr. Southwick though not possessed of a princely fortune, has a princely heart, and "though his portion is but scant, he gives it with good will." Mr. S. once a man of independence, has suffered shipwreck, and in the decline of life has to struggle with untoward fortune, encumbered with a numerous family. He is one of your warm hearted yankees, though long a resident of this place, the victim of too generous a heart. His misfortunes it is thought, drew from him that beautiful poem, "the pleasures of poverty." He is at present vending lottery tickets, in a passage scarcely wide enough to turn about in. He laughs at the incident, (speaking very fast,) and says he must be going to heaven; "I am in the straight and narrow way." He has nine (if not more) sons, the handsomest youths I ever saw, and he himself is the handsomest man I have seen in this state.

Amongst the great men of Albany, it will be expected, particularly by my western friends, that I am not to overlook one whose fame is held in veneration by them; I mean Governor Clinton. His Excellency DeWitt Clinton, the present governor of New-York, is about fifty years of age; he is six feet (at least) in height; robust, and a little inclined to corpulency; he is straight and well made; he walks erect with much ease and dignity; his complexion is fair, his face round and full, with a soft dark gray eye, his countenance mild and yielding; he regards you in silence, with a calm winning condescension, equally removed from servility and arrogance, while it inspires the beholder with admiration and respect. His whole deportment is dignified and commanding, with all the ease and grace of an accomplished gentleman. Like all men of sense, he uses few words. I had two interviews with him, during which I never saw him smile, nor did he speak half a dozen words; in short, the predominant traits in his countenance, are benignity, and modesty, lighted by genius. To a mind highly endowed by nature, he has added a rich store of practical and theoretical knowledge: in a few words, Governor Clinton is a man of great size, great soul, great mind, and a great heart. To him may be applied that line of Thomson;[15] "serene, yet warm; humane, yet firm his mind."—DeWitt Clinton, Jun., about twenty-five years of age, promises fair to rival his father, in those qualities which constitute a great man. Fame begins to whisper his growing merit, and predicts the natural result of genius, improved by education. He is tall, and comely in his person, fair complexion, his features regular and handsome, his visage thin, his countenance soft, though luminous and pleasing. In his manners he is still more fascinating than his father. The ancestors of this distinguished family, were originally of Ireland; we hear of them, from their first arrival down to this day, filling the first offices of their country. Besides Mr. S. I met with many yankees in Albany, whose generosity and benevolence overwhelms a stranger with obligation and delight. Amongst these, I cannot forego a remark on O. Kane, Esq. His magnificent mansion and pleasure-grounds may well be styled an earthly paradise. He lives at the southern extremity of the city, in a most superb building, which stands upon an eminence, with an extensive shrubbery in front, descending towards the Hudson. This shrubbery is enclosed by a parapet, and communicates with Market-street by an avenue leading from the front of the building. In the rear of the mansions are the gardens: the beauty and magnificence of the whole plan taken together, of this delightful spot, is only equalled by its generous and hospitable owner.

It was my design to enliven these sketches with anecdotes, and detached incidents of daily occurrence, such as the gossip of the day, &c. but the principal subjects have so increased upon my hands, that I find it impossible. I cannot, however, resist an anecdote of two countrymen at the theatre. They were in the same box with myself, and it appeared from their conversation, they had never witnessed a stage performance before. They were both well dressed, the one a young, the other a middle aged man. The young man assumed a knowledge of the world, and explained to his friend the meaning of the wonders before them. "What is all them there things for, that's upon the doors, or whatever they are, that looks like they are painted, but I suppose that's the play," replied the friend: "You'll see live people a playing, and running about like mad, and making love, and making speeches, and the most funnyest things that ever you saw; John Steward says it will make you split your sides with laughing." "What's all them people doing down there?" (pointing to the pit,) said the first, "O they're the players, you'll see um begin presently, (looking at his watch) it's most time." Thus the one continued to enquire, and the other to explain, until their patience became exhausted: the commencement of the play, being from some cause protracted nearly an hour beyond the time mentioned in their bills, they in a violent passion, at being cheated out of their money by a lazy set of fellows, that just made fun of them, were actually about to quit the box, when the bell rang, and I informed them the players were coming on the stage; at this moment the curtain flew up, and our fascinated strangers were amply compensated for the delay. It was amusing enough to hear them during the performance, "that's a tarnation pretty gall, isn't she," all aloud. When the actress (as was sometimes the case,) would seem to shrink back as though afraid, the young one would rise up and eagerly exclaim, (beckoning to her at the same time,) "come out, come out, let's look at you, don't be afraid." The house was in one continued roar: of all things, they disliked the clapping and the drop of the curtain.

EMMA WILLARD
(1787–1870)

Emma Hart was born February 23, 1787, in Berlin, Connecticut. She was the fifteenth of sixteen children in Lydia Hinsdale's and Samuel Hart's family. Her father encouraged her education, and in her late teens she taught at several female academies, including one in Middlebury, Vermont. On August 10, 1809, Emma married Dr. John Willard, who was twenty-eight years older than she, and turned to raising her stepchildren. Due to family financial problems and her own interests in female education, she opened a girls' school in their home in 1812. Following in the footsteps of Sarah Pierce, she insisted that girls should be educated in mathematics and other subjects, not just in the basics of reading, writing, and sewing. Her desire was to create a publicly endowed seminary for females; like its counterpart for males, it would have a board of leaders in the community to act as supervisors of the institution. With the encouragement of New York Governor DeWitt Clinton, she published her plan and sent copies to many prominent men throughout the country. The school, first begun in Waterford, New York, floundered in the beginning, largely because the New York legislature would not fund the project. But the Troy Common Council stepped forward, and the Troy Female Seminary opened its doors in 1821. The first class consisted of ninety girls, about a third from Troy and the rest from around the country. It became the premier educational institution for girls in the United States. Many of her students went on to illustrious careers of their own, including Elizabeth Cady Stanton.[1] Willard dedicated her life to advancing women's education;

in 1846 alone, she traveled nearly eight thousand miles, presenting workshops and lecturing on the subject.

Emma Willard was a leader in education for females in the early nineteenth century, but she was not a part of the women's rights movement. Though privately she seems to have believed that women were the intellectual equals of men, she never declared so publicly, fearing it would affect public support of her school. She was, however, very vocal about her prejudices against African Americans and Native Americans. She represents a not-unusual combination of abilities to advance certain causes—such as female education—while remaining quite conservative in other realms of reform movements that were emerging with great force in the early nineteenth century. Willard's husband died in 1825. On September 17, 1838, she was married for the second time, to Dr. Christopher Yates, but it was an unsuccessful union and the couple divorced in 1843. Emma Willard died in Troy, New York, on April 15, 1870.

When she determined that there were no history textbooks sufficiently rigorous for her students, she published History of the United States, or Republic of America *(1828). An ambitious project, the text is divided into ten "epocha," beginning with Columbus's voyage in 1492 and ending in 1826 with the deaths of John Adams and Thomas Jefferson. Willard is identified on the title page as "Principal of Troy Female Seminary."* History *is a prime example of how history textbooks can reflect an author's political beliefs, and Willard's ardent nationalism is evident throughout the text, as it was in all of her subsequent historical writings.* History *was produced in fifty-three reprintings between 1828 and 1873; it was published in abridged versions and translated into German and Spanish.*

HISTORY OF THE UNITED STATES, OR REPUBLIC OF AMERICA[2]

1828.

INTRODUCTION.

That the advantages of history are, at the present day, duly appreciated in our country, appears from its general introduction as a study into our schools. Important reasons may be given to show that every student or reader of history should commence with that of his own country; and further, that the history of the United States or Republic of America is a better study for youth, as regards the most essential objects of the study of history, than that of any other nation.

When the course of events is studied, for the purpose of gaining general information, the natural order of the thoughts must be regarded, if we expect that memory will treasure up the objects of attention. Each individual is to himself the centre of his own world; and the more intimately he connects his knowledge with himself, the better will it be remembered, and the more effectually can it be rendered in after life subservient to his purposes. Hence in geography he should begin with his own place, extending from thence to his country, and to the world. In history, the natural order, by which best to assist the memory, would be, to let the child begin with some of the leading events in his own history, and that of his family; connnecting them in chronology with some capital event in that of his country. For example, teach the young learner in what year of the world he was born, and what event of his country happened at or near the time. Pursuing this plane, perhaps you will say to him, your father was born in such a year, so much before or after the date of the American independence; such was the date of your mother's birth, and such the connecting event—such of the marriage of your parents, and of the birth or death of your brothers and sisters. Thus the record of the family Bible, with a few important national events, which the mother might easily connect and teach to her little children, should be the first foundation of their knowledge of history and chronology; and this well laid would be enduring as the mind. Something of this kind is incidentally, if not systematically done in every family. At the period of receiving school education, the pupil having learned the epochas of the history of his family, wants those of his country; and these will of necessity, connect her history with that of contemporary nations.

Another reason why the student should learn the history of his own country earlier and more minutely than that of any other is, that he may be presumed to know its geography better, and it is of more importance that he should accurately understand it. We shall read to the best advantage, the history of that country of which we have the best geographical knowledge. But the study of the history of the United States, pursued as is laid down in the system here presented to the public, must give to the student a minute knowledge of its geography in the various stages of its progression.

The attention of our youth to the interesting events of American history, in connexion with the geography of the country, will probably, in the result, contribute much to the improvement of our national literature, and consequently to the growth of wholesome national feeling. The imagination of man is to him the darling attribute of his nature. He *will* expatiate in the fields of poetry and romance, and draw from them the "beau ideal" of his heart. Unfortunately from a deficiency of native productions of this class, the American too often locates this imaged excellence within the old world, where the fair scenes of fancy are drawn. But let the present generation of our youth learn to connect the mental sublime of the story of our fathers with the natural grandeur of our scenery, and some among them will, in future life, be warmed to supply the deficiencies of our literature, by filling up the chasms of truth, with the glowing tracery of imagination.

These are reasons why our youth should be directed first to the study of our own history, keeping in view its connexion with our geography; but there are other reasons, why the study of American history is better not only for our own students, but for those of other countries, than that of any other nation, with which we are acquainted. History, it is said, is the school of politics. It is not, however, the mere knowledge of events, in which the student sees little connexion, which lays a foundation for his political knowledge. It is only when he is led to perceive how one state of things, operating on human passions, leads to another, that he is prepared when he comes into life, to look over the whole moving scene of the world—predict the changes which are to succeed— and should his be the hand of power, to put it forth to accelerate or stop the springs of change, as he finds their tendency to be good or evil. There is no species of events like those related of America for producing this effect; and the young politician of other countries might begin with this, as the most easily comprehensible subject in the whole field of history. Here effects may be traced to their causes. We behold in the first place a wilderness, inhabited by tribes of savage and independent men. Distant nations, on the mere plea, that they had found this wilderness, sent out their subjects to take it into their possession. At first unalarmed, and little valuing small portions of land, they did not resist and destroy, as they might have done, the incipient nation in its germ. But when the colonies spread and began to be powerful, the natives took the alarm, and, as might be expected, bloody wars ensued, whose object was extermination.

Again, from understanding the extent of the patents granted, the young student might, in the course of the history, be led to predict the wars which occurred on account of the first settlers of the country being under different European powers. The causes of these collisions are, upon our plan, addressed to the eye. The student sees upon his map the English stretching along the sea coast, and settling under grants, which run indefinitely west; and, at the same time, the French, extending along the St. Lawrence, having received, from their government, the right of jurisdiction over lands running indefinitely south; thus, large portions of country were claimed by both nations. We can see, that while the setlers should keep along the eastern and northern boundaries, every thing might go on peaceably; but let them increase, and extend themselves into the interior, and the same land being claimed by both powers, the contest, which follows, is the natural consequence. So it may also be seen that the same ground being, in many instances, granted, by the same government, to different patentees, jars and contentions would naturally arise.

The skilful politicians of the times preceding our struggle for freedom, did, from the state of affairs, and the temper of the times, foresee the war of the revolution before it occurred. So might the learner of our history, if he first obtained a clear understanding of the circumstances and feelings of the English and Americans, see that war was the event which must necessarily follow; and that a war with the mother country would produce a union of the colonies; since men ever unite, when pressed by common interest and common danger.

As it respects the most important advantage in the study of history, which is improvement in individual and national virtue, we come boldly forward to advocate a preference for the history of the American Republic. Here are no tales of hereditary power and splendour to inflame the imaginations of youth with desires for adventitious distinction. Here are no examples of profligate females, where the trappings of royalty or nobility give to vice an elegant costume; or, as with the celebrated Scot, where beauty and misfortune make sin commiserated, till it is half loved. Here are no demoralizing examples of bold and criminal ambition, which has "waded through blood to empire." The only desire of greatness which our children can draw from the history of their ancestors, is to be greatly good.

It is not in the formal lesson of virtue, that her principles are most deeply imbibed. It is in moments when her approach is not suspected, that she is fixing her healing empire in the heart of youth. When his indignation rises against the oppressor—when his heart glows with the admiration of suffering virtue—it is then that he resolves never to be an oppressor himself; and he half wishes to suffer, that he too may be virtuous. No country, ancient or modern, affords examples more fitted to raise these ennobling emotions than America, at the period of her revolution.

And may not these generous feelings of virtue arise, respecting nations as well as individuals; and may not the resolution which the youth makes, with regard to himself individually, be made with regard to his country, as far as his future influence may extend? Would the teacher excite these feelings in his pupil, let him put into his hands the history of the struggle of America for her independence. Though doubtless there existed great personal turpitude in individuals in America, and great personal virtue in those of England, yet, as nations, how great is the disparity in the characters exhibited. England, seeking to make her filial child slave, refuses to listen to her duteous pleadings, and applies the scourge. She deigns not to give even the privileges of civilized warfare, but sends forth the brand which lights the midnight fire over the heads of the sleeping family, and the tomahawk which cleaves the head of the infant in the presence of the mother. England also descends to base arts. She bribes, she flatters, she sows dissensions, she purchases treason, and she counterfeits money. In the conduct of France too, though gratitude rises in our hearts for her actual services, yet history compelled, though sometimes sorrowfully, to follow truth, must pronounce that in her conduct of a nation, there is nothing virtuous or generous. Unlike her La Fayette, it was in success, not in misfortune, that she declared for America; and if at length she combatted with her, it was not that she loved her, or honoured her cause; it was that she feared and hated her enemy. If America had not taken care of herself, bitter to her would have been the care which France would have taken of her. Her embrace of friendship would have been found the pressure of death. How interesting in her youthful simplicity, in her maiden purity, does America appear, contrasted with these old and wily nations. Who shall say, in reading the history of these transactions, that there is no such thing as national vice, or national virtue?

Will not acquaintance then with this tale, warm the young heart of the future statesman of America, to the detestation of national as of individual wickedness: and to the love of national as of personal virtue? He will say with exultation, my country was the most virtuous among the nations; this is her pride—not the extent of her dominion, nor the wealth of her revenue; this is the source of that greatness which it becomes her sons to preserve! and he will then resolve, that when manhood shall have placed him among her guardians, he will watch the purity of her character with jealous tenderness, and sooner part with existence than be made the instrument of her degradation!...

1692. Sir William Phipps arrived at Boston, May 14, 1692, bearing the new charter, and a commission, constituting him governor and captain general of Massachusetts. He was received with the most flattering tokens of distinction, and entered immediately upon the duties of his office.

Amidst the distresses under which the New England colonies laboured, from the war with the French and Indians, others of a different, though not less destructive nature, opened upon the people of Massachusetts, in 1692. This is the period of what is called the "Salem witchcraft." This delusion, with respect to the supposed intercourse with evil spirits, the first settlers brought with them from the mother country. Laws making witchcraft a capital crime, existed in England, and were early enacted in Massachusetts. The mania began in Springfield, in 1645, when some individuals were accused of witchcraft, but were at last acquitted. Some few years after, persons at Charlestown, Dorchester, and Cambridge, were accused, and actually executed for the supposed offence. But Salem was the devoted place where this weakness was converted into a phrensy. The belief of this fearful and mysterious evil, had prepossessed the public mind, when some young women, perhaps in part deluded by their own imaginations, complained of being strangely affected. Their complaints, attributed to this alarming cause, were reported, and doubtless magnified, until they became objects of universal attention, and those who experienced them, prime heroines in a gossiping and credulous neighbourhood. This, doubtless, encouraged others to set up for the same distinction. Witches, of course, increased with the number bewitched. At first, it was old women only, who were suspected of having leagued with the devil, to inflict upon the diseased, the various torments which they asserted that they felt; and which they often appeared to the spectators actually to feel. The magistrates, partaking of the general mania, pursued a course, which placed the accused in situations, where "they had need to be magicians not to be convicted of magic." They confronted them with those who accused them, and asked, Why do you afflict these children? If answered, I do not afflict them, they commanded them to look upon them; at which the children would fall into fits, and then declare they were thus troubled by the persons apprehended. On such evidence were these unfortunate persons condemned to execution.

Advantage was doubtless taken of this state of things, to gratify private resentment or rivalry. The accused were no longer old and poor women only, but witches were found of every age, in every rank and situation. More than a hundred women, many of them of fair characters and reputable families, were apprehended, examined, and generally committed to prison. Twenty suffered death. No person was safe; and the lives of the best were at the mercy of the most worthless of the community.

Society now saw its error, and was struck with remorse. The prison doors were opened, and all confined for witchcraft set free. Several of the jurors, and one of the judges, who had assisted at these trials, voluntarily made public confessions, and asked pardon of God and man; and a day of public penance and prayer was ordained to be observed by all, for their common sin.

Gov. Sloughter died in 1691; and in 1692, Col. Benjamin Fletcher arrived with the commission of governor. Gov. Fletcher was a good soldier, and having fortunately secured the friendship of Major Schuyler, he was, by his advice, enabled to conduct the Indian affairs of the colony, to the acceptance of the people. He was, however, avaricious, irascible, and a bigot to his own mode of faith, which was that of the church of England. Under pretence of introducing uniformity into the language and literature, as well as the religion of the colony, the inhabitants of which were a heterogeneous mixture of Dutch and English, he brought into the assembly, a bill for the settlement, throughout the province, of Episcopalian ministers, such as should be by himself selected. The assembly, after much debate, agreed that ministers should be settled in certain parishes, but left the choice to the people. This was very offensive to the governor, who, after an angry speech, dissolved the assembly. Episcopalian ministers were, however, settled in several parishes; and thus was introduced a religious order, which, at this day, forms so respectable a portion of the population of the state. Col. Fletcher was empowered to take command of the militia and garrison on Connecticut. That colony immediately despatched General Winthrop as an agent to remonstrate with the kind and council against this extraordinary power; Col. Fletcher, however, went to Hartford, in 1693, and, in his majesty's name, demanded the surrender of the militia to his command; but, after a resolute and spirited refusal on the part of Connecticut, the demand was withdrawn. . . .

1760. As early as 1760, the mutual jealousies between the colonies and the mother country appeared in Massachusetts, on the occasion of an attempt to enforce the act, by which duties were laid on foreign sugar and molasses, which, having been considered oppressive, had been evaded. The custom-house officers were directed, in case of supposing these articles to be concealed, to apply to the superior court of the colony for what were termed, "writs of assistance," which appear to have been a kind of general search warrant. Any petty custom-house officer, armed with one of these, might, on pretence of searching for these articles, invade, at his pleasure the family retirement of any gentleman in the province. Besides this apprehended grievance, the trade of the colonists would suffer severely from the rigid collection of these duties. The people of Boston, therefore, determined to oppose the granting of writs of assistance, and employed two of their most eminent lawyers, Oxenbridge Thatcher and James Otis, for this purpose. The latter of these gentlemen defended the cause of American rights with such impetuosity of eloquence, that one who heard him, John Adams, afterwards himself so highly distinguished, said, "Otis was a flame of fire!—Every man of an immense crowded audience, went away ready to take arms against writs of assistance. Then and there was the first scene of opposition to the arbitrary claims of Great Britain; then and there American Independence was born."

The court took time to deliberate on the question of granting the writ; and, after various delays, and an unsuccessful attempt to move the officers of the English government not to press the subject, the writs were, at length, under certain restrictions, granted; but such was their unpopularity, that they were little used. These circumstances are, however, material in history, as they show the spirit of the times. It will be recollected that this scene was acted, before the attempts of the British military in parliament, to introduce into America a regular system of taxation, to which, as has been remarked, the revolution has often been solely referred. . . .

1776. General Washington had continued the blockade of Boston during the winter of 1775–76, and at last resolved to bring the enemy to action, or to drive them from the town. On the night of the 4th of March, a detachment, under the command of General Thomas,[3] silently crossed the neck of land which separates Dorchester Heights from the town; and constructed, in a single night, a redoubt which gave them command of the heights, and menaced the British shipping with destruction. When the light of the morning discovered to General Howe the advantage the Americans had gained, he perceived, that no alternative remained for him, but to dislodge them, or evacuate the place. He immediately despatched a few regiments to attempt the former, but a violent tempest of wind and rain rendered their efforts ineffectual. The Americans had continued, with unremitting industry to strengthen their works, until they were now too secure to be easily forced. After the failure of this attempt, a council of war was held, in which it was resolved to evacuate the town. Preparations were immediately made for the embarkation of the troops; and, on the morning of the 17th, the whole British force, with such of the loyalists as chose to follow their fortunes, set sail for Halifax. As the rear of the British troops were embarking, Gen. Washington entered the town in triumph.

In the plans for the campaign of 1776, besides the relief of Quebec, and the recovery of Canada, two expeditions were resolved upon by southern colonies; and the command of which was given to Gen. Clinton[4] and Sir Peter Parker;[5] and the object of the other was to gain possession of New-York. The command of this was given to Admiral and Sir William Howe, who had succeeded Gen. Gage,[6] in the command of the British troops.

Arnold had continued the siege of Quebec, and had greatly annoyed the garrison; but he found himself oppressed with many difficulties. His army had suffered extremely from the inclemency of the season, the garrison of Montreal had been sent to reinforce him, he had, at this time, scarcely one thousand effective men. The reinforcements which had been ordered by Congress, to his relief, were slow in arriving; and when they reached Quebec, they were greatly reduced in numbers by disease. Added to this, the river was now clear of ice, and the British fleet was daily expected to arrive.

Gen. Thomas, who had been sent by congress, now succeeded Arnold in command. He was unwilling to raise the siege of Quebec, without making another effort to reduce the place. With the view of burning the vessels of the governor, he sent a fire-ship down the river, intending to take advantage of the disorder, which would ensue, to make an assault upon the town; but the garrison, perceiving his design, took measures to frustrate it; and the attempt failed. Having now nothing further to expect from a siege, and seeing his troops daily diminish, both in numbers and courage, Gen. Thomas resolved to abandon the enterprise. On the very day appointed for raising the siege, several British vessels came in sight of Quebec, bringing reinforcements to the garrison. These ships now had the command of the river, and prevented any communication between the different parts of the American camp. Gen. Thomas found it necessary to retreat with the greatest precipitation, leaving behind him the baggage, artillery, munitions, and whatever else might have retarded the march of the army. Many of the sick, together with all the military stores, fell into the hands of the enemy.

Had Gen. Carleton[7] vigorously pursued the Americans, they could not, probably, have effected their retreat; but he seemed only desirous of driving the besiegers from the neighbourhood. He treated with great kindness the sick, and other prisoners that fell into his hands. The Americans continued their retreat to the river Sorel, having marched the first forty-five miles without halting. Here they found a reinforcement of several regiments, under the command of Gen. Thompson,[8] waiting their arrival. Gen. Thomas was now seized with the small pox, of which he died; when the command devolved upon Gen. Sullivan.

Adverse fortune seemed, in every part of Canada, to follow the American arms. While the troops before Quebec were compelled to retreat by a superior force, a calamity, resulting from cowardice, was experienced by a body of the Americans, in another quarter. A garrison of 400 men, under the command of Col. Bedel,[9] was stationed at the Cears, about forty miles above Montreal, at the head of one of the rapids. Col. Bedel, having received information, that Captain Foster,[10] with about five hundred royalists and Indians, was descending the river, to attack the post, immediately proceeded to Montreal to obtain assistance, leaving the command with a subordinate officer. They invested the fort; and the American officer, intimidated by the threat of Captain Foster, that if any of the Indians were killed, a general massacre of the Americans would take place, surrendered the post, without resistance. A reinforcement, under the command of Maj. Sherburne, was ordered to march from Montreal. While on his way thither, ignorant of the surrender of the fort, Maj. Sherburne[11] was attacked by the Indians, to whom, after a spirited defence, he was obliged to surrender. The loss of the Americans at this place could not have been less than 500.

The British army in Canada was now augmented to 13,000 men; and although they were scattered along the banks of the St. Lawrence, yet the general place of rendezvous was at Three Rivers, a village about half way from Quebec to Montreal. The party stationed at this place, was under the command of Gen. Frazer;[12] another, under Gen. Nesbit, was near them, on board the transports; one greater than either, with generals Carleton, Burgoyne, Philips,[13] and the German baron, Reidesel,[14] was on its way from Quebec.

Gen. Sullivan detached Gen. Thompson from the river Sorel, with a considerable body of troops, to attack the enemy at Three Rivers. He dropped down the river by night, with the intention of surprising Gen. Frazer. The troops passed the ships, without discovery; but, arriving at the place an hour later than had been intended, they were discovered at their landing, and the enterprise was frustrated, with the loss of 200 men, who were made prisoners.

Gen. Sullivan was induced, by the unanimous opinion of his officers, to abandon the post at Sorel, after the British entered it. He was joined at St. John's by Gen. Arnold, who had crossed at

Longueil, just in time to save the garrison from falling into the hands of the enemy. Gen. Sullivan, at the Isle Aux Noix, received the orders of Gen. Schuyler to embark on the lakes for Crown Point; which post they reached in safety, June 15th, 1776. On the Sorel the pursuit stopped. The Americans had the command of the lakes, and the British general deemed it prudent to wrest it from them, before he advanced further. Thus ended the enterprise against Canada. It was a bold, though unsuccessful effort to annex that extensive province to the United Colonies. It had, however, in its commencement, been attended with success to Americans, and displayed the military character of the colonial officers in the most honourable point of view.

The British fleets, under Sir Peter Parker and Gen. Clinton, united at Cape Fear, and proceeded together to Charleston, where they arrived early in June. The fleet under Parker, brought the expected reinforcements, with Lord Cornwallis,[15] Gen. Vaughn,[16] and Col. Ethan Allen, who was now exchanged. This officer, with his fellow prisoners, had been confined in Pendennis castle, in Cornwall.

Fortunately, an official letter had been intercepted early in the year, announcing the departure of this armament from England, and its destination against the southern states. This gave the colonists an opportunity to be prepared for its reception. Sullivan's island, at the entrance of Charleston harbour, had been strengthened; and a fort had been constructed with the palmetto tree, which very much resembles the cork. On learning the near approach of the enemy, the militia of the country were summoned to defend the capital. The popularity of Gen. Lee,[17] the commander, soon collected a force of 5 or 6,000 men; and his high military reputation gave confidence to the citizens as well as soldiers. Under him were colonels Gadsden,[18] Moultrie,[19] and Thompson. Col. Gadsden commanded a regiment, stationed on the northern extremity of James' island; two regiments, under colonels Moultrie and Thompson, occupied the opposite extremities of Sullivan's island. The remainder of the troops were posted at various points. Gen. Clinton landed a number of his troops on Long Island, separated from Sullivan's Island, on the eastern side, by a small creek. The fort on Sullivan's island was garrisoned by about 400 men, commanded by Col. Moultrie. The attack on this fort commenced on the morning of the 28th of June. The ships opened their several broadsides upon it; and a detachment was landed on an adjoining island, and directed to pass over where the sea was fordable, and attack it in the rear. The discharge of artillery upon this little fort was incessant; but Moultrie and his brave Carolinians returned the fire with such skill and spirit, that many of the ships suffered severely; and the British, after persisting in their attack until dark, were repulsed and forced to abandon the enterprise. Their loss amounted to about 200; that of the Americans to ten killed and twenty-two wounded. The palmetto wood, in this instance, proved an effectual defence; as the enemy's balls did not penetrate, but sunk into it as into earth. The name of the fort was henceforth called, from its brave defender, Moultrie.

During this engagement, a singular circumstance occurred. After a dreadful volley from the British, the flag of the fort was no longer seen to wave; and the Americans were, every moment, expecting to see the British troops mount the parapets in triumph. But none appeared; and, after a few moments, the striped banner of America was once more unfurled to their view. The staff had been carried away by a shot, and the flag had fallen upon the outside of the works. A brave serjeant, by the name of Jasper, jumped over the wall, and, amidst a shower of bullets, fastened it in its place.

It had early occurred to Washington, that the central situation of New-York, with the numerous advantages attending the possession of that city, would render it an object of great importance to the British. Under this impression, before the enemy evacuated Boston, Gen. Lee had been detached from Cambridge, to put Long Island and New-York in a posture of defence. Soon after the evacuation of Boston, the commander-in-chief followed, and with the greater part of his army, fixed his head quarters in New-York.

A few days after the repulse at Charleston, the British fleet, with the troops on board, set sail for the vicinity of New-York, where the whole British force had been ordered to assemble.

On the 7th of June, Richard Henry Lee, of Virginia, made a motion in congress, for declaring the colonies FREE AND INDE-PENDENT STATES.

The most vigorous exertions had been made by the friends of independence, to prepare the minds of the people, to perceive the necessity and advantage of such a measure. Among the numerous writers on this momentous question, the most luminous and forcible was Thomas Paine.[20] His pamphlet entitled "Common Sense," was read and understood by all. While it demonstrated the necessity, the advantage, and the practicability of independence, it treated kingly government and hereditary succession, with ridicule and opprobrium. Two years before, the inhabitants of the colonies were the loyal subjects of the king of England, and wished not for independence, but for constitutional liberty. But the crown of England had, for their assertion of this right, declared them out of its protection; rejected their petitions; shackled their commerce; and finally employed foreign mercenaries to destroy them. Such were the excitements, which, being stirred up and directed by the master spirits of the times, had, in the space of two years, changed the tide of public feeling in America, and throughout her extensive regions, produced the general voice—"WE WILL BE FREE."

Satisfied by indubitable signs, that such was the resolution of the people, congress deliberately and solemnly decided to make, in a formal manner, this declaration to the world—"AMERICA *is, and of right ought to be*, A FREE AND INDEPENDENT NATION." ...

1777. Great preparations were now made by the English at Staten Island and New-York; but whether their object was to co-operate by the Hudson, with the Canadian army, or to conquer Philadelphia, was indeterminable.

On the night of July 10th, occurred the capture of General Prescott,[21] then in command on Rhode Island. Colonel Barton,[22] with forty country militia under his command, proceeded from Warwick, ten miles in their whale boats, landed between Newport and Bristol, marched a mile to Prescott's quarters, took the general from his bed, and conducted him with despatch to a place of safety on the main land.

Meantime great preparations were making for a descent upon the United States from Canada. The plan of dividing the states, by effecting a junction of the British army through lake Champlain and the Hudson, was, at the beginning of this year, looked to by the whole British nation, as the certain means of effecting the reduction of America. This plan had gained new favour in England, by the representations of General Burgoyne, an officer who had served under Carleton, and whose knowledge of American affairs was therefore undisputed. Burgoyne, by his importunities with the British ministry, obtained the object for which he had made a voyage to England. He was appointed to the command of all the troops in Canada, to the prejudice of Governor Carleton, and was furnished with an army and military stores. With these he arrived at Quebec in May. General Carleton exhibited an honourable example of moderation and patriotism, by seconding Burgoyne in his preparations, with great diligence and energy. To increase the army, he exerted, not only his authority as governor, but also his influence among his numerous friends and partizans. Though himself averse to employing the savages, yet such being the orders of the British government, he aided in bringing to the field even a greater number than could be employed.

Burgoyne's army was provided with a formidable train of artillery. The principal officers who were to accompany him, were General Philips, who had distinguished himself in the German wars, Brigadiers Frazer and Powel;[23] the Brunswick Major General Baron Reidesel, and Brigadier General Specht.[24] The army consisted of 7,173 British and German troops, besides several thousands of Canadians and Indians.

Burgoyne's plan of operation was, that Col. St. Leger[25] should proceed with a detachment by the St. Lawrence, Oswego, and fort Stanwix, to Albany. Burgoyne, proceeding by Champlain and the Hudson, was to meet St. Leger at Albany, and both join General Clinton at New-York.

His preparations completed, Burgoyne moved forward with his army, and made his first encampment on the western shore of lake Champlain, at the river Boquet. Here, in two instances, he betrayed that vanity which his biographers consider the characteristic weakness of his character. He made a speech to his Indian allies, in which, in terms of singular energy, and with an imposing manner, he endeavoured to persuade them to change their savage mode of warfare. He also published a proclamation, in which, by arguments, promises, and threats, (threats of savage extermination!), he seemed to expect that he should bring the republicans to the royal standard; as if words which he should speak, could change the natural character, and established manners of a nation: or those which he could write, could have power to subvert the purpose of men, whom all the previous measures of his government had failed to intimidate.

St. Leger had united with Sir John Johnson,[26] and having nearly 2,000 troops, including savages, they invested fort Stanwix, then commanded by Col. Gansevoort,[27] on the 3d of August. Gen. Herkimer,[28] having collected the militia, marched to the relief of Gansevoort; but he fell into and English ambuscade on the 6th of August, and was defeated and slain, with 400 of his troops. St. Leger, wishing to profit by his victory, pressed upon the fort. In this perilous moment, Col. Willet[29] and Lieut. Stockton[30] left the fort, fighting their way through the English camp, and, eluding the Indians, they arrived at German Flats, and proceeded to Albany, to alarm the country, and gain assistance.

Gen. Schuyler, on hearing the danger of the fort, despatched Arnold to its relief. On hearing of his approach, the Indians, having previously become dissatisfied, mutinied, and compelled St. Leger to return to Montreal. On the way, they committed such depredations on the British troops, as to leave the impression that they were no less dangerous as allies than as enemies.

To preserve a connected view of the expedition of St. Leger, we have gone nearly two months ahead of the operations of Burgoyne. On the 30th of June, that general advanced to Crown Point, from whence he proceeded to invest Ticonderoga, which was garrisoned by 3,000 men, under the command of Gen. St. Clair.[31] This was a place of great natural strength, and much expense and labour had been bestowed upon its fortifications; but up to this period, a circumstance respecting it seems to have been strangely overlooked. It is commanded by an eminence in its neighbourhood, called mount Defiance. The troops of Burgoyne got possession of this height on the 5th of July, and St. Clair, finding the post no longer tenable, evacuated it on the same night. The garrison, separated into two divisions, were to proceed through

Hubbardton to Skeenesborough. The first division, under St. Clair, left the fort in the night, two hours earlier than the second, under Colonel Francis.[32] The stores and baggage, placed on board 200 batteaux, and conveyed by five armed gallies, were to meet the army at Skeenesborough.

Gen. Frazer, with 850 of the British, pursued and attacked the division at Hubbardton, under Col. Francis, whose rear was commanded by Col. Warner.[33] The Americans made a brave resistance, during which 130 of the enemy were killed; but the British, in the heat of the action, receiving a reinforcement under Reidesel, the republicans were forced to give way. They fled in every direction, spreading through the the country the terror of the British arms. In this unfortunate action, the Americans lost in killed, wounded, and prisoners, nearly 1,000 men. Many of the wounded perished in the woods. Col. Francis was among the slain.

A part of the stores and armed galleys, which had been sent up the lake, fell into the hands of the British. St. Clair, on hearing of these disasters, did not pursue his intended route, but struck into the woods on his left. At Manchester, he was joined by the remnant of the vanquished division, conducted by Gen. Warner. After a distressing march, he reached the camp of Gen. Schuyler, at fort Edward. Warner remained in Manchester, with a detachment, which proved of great importance in the affair, which shortly after occurred at Bennington.

Burgoyne, meanwhile, took possession of Skeenesborough; and the American army, under Schuyler, retired from fort Edward to Saratoga, and, on the 13th of August, to the islands at the mouth of the Mohawk.

This period of the history was gloomy to America, and triumphant to England. When the news of Burgoyne's successes reached that country, the ministers were every where felicitated on the success of their plans; and rejoicings were made, as though their object was already attained. On the other hand, the Americans saw that the juncture was critical and alarming; but their spirit rose with the occasion, and their exertions increased with their danger.

Gen. Schuyler, before leaving the northern positions, obstructed the roads, by breaking the bridges, and, in the only passable defiles, by cutting immense trees on both sides of the way, to fall cross and lengthwise. These, with their branches interwoven, presented to the enemy an almost insurmountable barrier.

Congress was aware of the great merits and exertions of Gen. Schuyler; yet they found that the misfortunes of the army had, though undeservedly, made him unpopular; and, therefore, it was necessary to supersede him, in order to make way for a leader, who should inspire a confidence that would draw volunteers to the service. Accordingly, Gen. Gates[34] was appointed to the command, but did not arrive at the camp until the 21st of August. Lincoln[35] also was ordered to the north, as were Arnold and Morgan,[36] whose active spirits and brilliant achievements, it was hoped, would reanimate the dispirited troops. The celebrated patriot of Poland, Kosciusko,[37] was also in the army, as its chief engineer.

Burgoyne, having, with great expense of labour and time, opened a way for his army, from Skeenesborough to the Hudson, arrived at fort Edward, on the 30th of July. But being in a hostile country, he could obtain no provisions, but from Ticonderoga; and these he was compelled to transport by the way of lake George. Learning that there was a large depot of provisions at Bennington, he sent 500 men, under Lieut. Col. Baum,[38] a brave German officer, to seize them. Gen. Stark,[39] with a body of New Hampshire militia, was on his march to join Gen. Schuyler, when hearing of Baum's approach, he recruited his forces from the neighbouring militia, and with 1,600 men, met him four miles from Bennington. After a sharp conflict, Baum was killed, and his party defeated. The militia had dispersed, to seek for plunder, when a British reinforcement of 500 men, under Col. Breyman,[40] arrived. Fortunately for the Americans, the Green Mountain Boys, under Col. Warner,[41] appeared at the same time, and the British were again defeated, and compelled to retreat. Their loss in both engagements was six hundred, the greater part of whom were taken prisoners.[42] The republican loss was inconsiderable.

The victory at Bennington was important in its consequences, as it proved the turning of the tide of fortune which had heretofore set so strongly in favour of the British arms. It embarrased, weakened, and dispirited Burgoyne, while it revived the drooping hearts of the Americans, and gave the impulse of hope to their exertions. This was strengthened by an impulse of another kind, but operating in the same direction. A cry of vengeance for murder was raised against the British, on account of an atrocious act, committed by their Indian allies. Miss M'Crea, an interesting girl of fort Edward, was betrothed to Captain Jones, then in the army of Burgoyne, which had now approached near to that place. Impatient for his marriage, the lover sent a party of Indians, as the safest convoy he could procure for his bride, across the woods to the British camp; having secured, as he thought their fidelity, by promise of reward. Confiding love prevailed, in her mind, over her strong fears of these terrible guides; and the unfortunate girl left, by stealth, the kind shelter of her paternal roof. Meantime, her anxious lover, to make her safety more sure, sent out another party, with like promises. The two met; and the last demanded that the lady should be committed to them. Rather than give her up, and thus, as they supposed, lose their reward, the barbarians tied to a tree, their innocent and helpless victim, and shot her dead. Instead of his bride, the bridegroom received the bleeding tresses, which the murderers had cut from her dying head. The sight withered and blasted him; and, after lingering a few years, he died.

The complicated miseries of a battle crowd the picture, and confuse the mind, and thus often produce less sympathy than a single case of distress. In the present instance, every man could feel, what it would have been, or would be to him, to have his bride torn, as it were, from his arms, shrieking, and murdered in the hour of his love and expectation; and every pain was used to awaken these sympathies to their utmost extent, and turn them against the British commander, who had let loose such bloodhounds upon the land. There was a general rising in the northern region, and it seemed, as if every man, who could bear arms, was rushing to the camp of Gates, to avenge the death of the young M'Crea, no less than to deliver his country.

The army at the islands, having been thus reinforced, and now amounting to 5,000, Gates left that encampment, the 8th of September, and proceeding to Stillwater, occupied Behmus heights.

On the 12th, Burgoyne crossed the Hudson, and on the 14th,

encamped at Saratoga, about three miles distant from the American army. An obstinate and bloody battle occurred at Stillwater, on the 19th. At first it was partial, commencing with a skirmish between the advanced parties. Each side sent successive reinforcements to their own combatants, until nearly the whole were in action. The American combatants took advantage of a wood which lay between the two camps, and poured from it a fire too deadly to be withstood. The British lines broke; and the Americans, rushing from their coverts, pursued them to an eminence, where their flanks being supported, they rallied; charging in their turn, they drove the Americans into the woods, from which they again poured a deadly fire, and again the British fell back. At every charge, the British artillery fell into the hands of the Americans, who could neither carry it off, or turn it on the enemy. At length night came on, and to fight longer, would be to attack indiscriminately friends and foes. The Americans retired to their camp, having lost between 3 and 400 men; the loss of the British was 500. Both sides claimed the victory; but the advantage gained was clearly on the side of the Americans.

Skirmishes, frequent and animated, occurred between this and the 7th of October, when a general battle was fought at Saratoga. At this time, the right wing of Gen. Gates occupied the brow of the hill, near the river. This camp was in the form of the segment of a large circle, the convex side towards the enemy.

Gen. Burgoyne's left was on the river, his right extending at right angles to it, across the low grounds, almost two hundred yards, to a range of steep heights, occupied by his choicest troops.

The guard of his camp upon the high grounds, was given to Brigadiers Hamilton and Specht; that of the redoubts and plain, near the river, to Brigadier Gole. Burgoyne commanded in person the centre detachment of 1,500, and was seconded by Philips, Reidesel, and Frazer. His left flank, composed of grenadiers, was commanded by Maj. Ackland;[43] his right consisting of infantry, by the earl of Balcarras.[44]

The Americans, under Gen. Poor,[45] attacked the left flank and front of the British; and, at the same time, Col. Morgan attacked their right. The action became general. The efforts of the combatants were desperate. Burgoyne, and his officers, fought like men who were defending, at the last cast, their military reputation; Gates and his army, like those who were deciding whether their native land should be free, or become the prey of invaders. The invading army gave way, in the short space of fifty-two minutes. The defenders of the soil pursued them to their entrenchments, forced the guard, and killed Col. Breyman, its commander. Arnold, the tiger of the American army, whose track was marked by carnage, headed a small band, stormed their works, and followed them into their camp. But his horse was killed under him; he was himself wounded; and darkness was coming on. He retired; and thus was reserved to another day, the utter ruin of the British army.

The loss in killed and wounded, was great on both sides, but especially on the part of the British, of whom a considerable number were made prisoners. Gen. Frazer, whose character was as elevated as his rank, received a mortal wound.

The Americans had now an opening into the British camp. They rested on their arms the night after the battle, on the field which they had so bravely won; determined to pursue their victory with returning light. But Burgoyne, aware of the advantage which they had gained, effected, with admirable order, a change of his ground. The artillery, the camp, and its appurtenances, were all removed before morning, to the heights. The British army, in this position, had the river in its rear, and its two wings displayed along the hills upon its right bank. Gates was too wise to attack his enemy in this position, and expose to another risk, what now wanted nothing but vigilance to make certain. He now made arrangements to enclose his enemy, which Burgoyne perceiving, put his army in motion at nine o'clock at night, and removed to Saratoga, six miles up the river. He was obliged to abandon his hospital with 300 sick and wounded, to the humanity of the Americans.

Burgoyne now made efforts in various directions, to effect a retreat, but in every way he had been anticipated. He found himself in a hostile and foreign country, hemmed in by a foe, whose army constantly increasing, already amounted to four times his own wasting numbers. The boats, laden with his supplies, were taken, and his provisions were failing. He had early communicated with Sir Henry Clinton at New-York, and urged his co-operation.

More recently, when his fortune began to darken, he had en-treated him for speedy aid; stating, that, at the most, his army could not hold out beyond the 12th of October. The 12th arrived, without the expected succour. His army was in the utmost dis-tress, and Burgoyne capitulated on the seventeenth.

The army surrendered amounted to 5,752 men, which together with the troops lost before, by various disasters, made up the whole British loss to nine thousand two hundred and thirteen. There also fell into the hands of the Americans, thirty-five brass field pieces, and 5,000 muskets. It was stipulated, that the British should pile their arms at the word of command, given by their own officers, march out of their camp with the honours of war, and have free passage across the Atlantic; they, on their part, agreeing not to serve again in North America, during the war. They were treated with delicacy by the Americans. Their officers, especially their commander, received many kind attentions. The worthy Gen. Schuyler hospitably entertained Burgoyne, at his own house; although much of his private property, especially an elegant villa, had been destroyed by command of that officer.

On hearing of the defeat of Burgoyne, the British garrison at Ticonderoga, returned to Canada, and not a foe remained in the northern section of the Union. Thus ended an expedition from which the British had hoped, and the Americans had feared so much.

The effects of their success were highly propitious to the cause of the republicans. It weakened and discouraged the enemy, gave them a supply of artillery and stores, and, what was still more im-portant, raised them in their own estimation, and in that of for-eign nations. . . .

1816. In April, 1816, an act was passed by congress, to establish a national bank, with a capital of thirty-five millions of dollars.

In August, fort Appalachicola, which was occupied by runaway negroes and hostile Indians, was destroyed by a detachment of American troops. More than one hundred were killed, and the re-mainder were taken prisoners.

In September, General Jackson[46] held a treaty with the Chicka-saws, Choctaws, and Cherokees. He made purchases of their lands particularly favourable to the wishes and security of the frontier settlements. The tranquillity which was restored among the Indians themselves, contributed to favour the recommencement of the work of civilization, which, previous to the war, had made considerable progress.

In December, the Indiana territory was admitted into the union as a state.

As early as the year 1790, establishments for spinning cotton, and for manufacturing coarse cotton cloths, were attempted in the state of Rhode Island. They were at first on a small scale; but as the cloths found a ready market, the number and extent of these manufactories gradually increased. The embarrassments to which commerce was subjected some years previous to the war, had increased the demand for American goods, and led the people to reflect upon the importance of rendering themselves independent of the manufactures of foreign nations. During the war, large capitals were vested in manufacturing establishments, from which the capitalists realized a handsome profit. But at the close of the war, the English having made great improvements in manufacturing, and being able to sell their goods at a much lower rate than the American manufacturers could afford, the country was immediately filled by importations from England. The American manufacturers being in their infancy, could not resist the shock; and many large establishments failed. The manufacturers then petitioned government for protection, to enable them to withstand competition; and in consequence of this petition, the committee on commerce and manufactures, in 1816, recommended that an additional duty should be laid on imported goods. A new tariff was accordingly formed, by which the double imposts which had been laid during the war, were removed, and a small increase of duty was laid upon some fabrics, such as coarse cotton goods. The opposition to the tariff, from the commercial interest, and in some sections of the country, from the agricultural, was so great, that nothing effecutal was at that time done for the encouragement of manufactures; and the question of its expediency is still considered as of the first importance.

A society for colonizing the free blacks[47] of the United States, was first proposed in 1816, and was soon after formed. It was not under the direction of government, but was patronized by many of the first citizens in all parts of the union. The society purchased land in Africa, where they yearly removed considerable numbers of the free blacks from America. Their object was, by removing the free negroes, to diminish the black population of the United States; and by establishing a colony in Africa, to prevent the traffic in slaves which then existed. It would also give those owners of slaves who were desirous of liberating them, an opportunity of doing so, without exposing the country to the dangers apprehended from a numerous free black population.

Mr. Madison's[48] second term of office having expired, he followed the examples of his predecessors, and declined a re-election. James Monroe[49] was elected president, and Daniel D. Tompkins,[50] vice president; and, March 4th, 1817, they entered upon their official duties. During the summer of this year, Mr. Monroe visited all the northern and eastern states, and was received with every demonstration of affection and respect.

A treaty was, this year, concluded by commissioners appointed by the president of the United States, and the chiefs of the Wyandot, Delaware, Shawnese, Seneca, Ottoway, Chippewa, and Pottowattamie Indians, by which these tribes ceded to the United States all lands to which they had any title within the limits of Ohio. The Indians were, at their option, to remain on the ceded lands, subject to the laws of the United States.

The territory of Mississippi was, this year, admitted into the union of the states.

About this period, a band of adventurers, who pretended to act under the authority of the South American states, took possession of Amelia island, near the boundary of Georgia, with the avowed design of invading Florida. This island having been the subject of negotiation with the government of Spain, as in indemnity for losses by spoliations, or in exchange for lands of equal value beyond the Mississippi, the measure excited a sentiment of surprise and disapprobation; which was increased, when it was found that the island was made a channel for the illicit introduction of slaves from Africa into the United States, an asylum for fugitive slaves from the neighbouring states, and a port for smuggling of every kind. An establishment of a similar nature had previously been formed on an island in the gulf of Mexico, on the coast of Texas; which was also a rendezvous for smugglers. Privateers were also equipped here, which gave great annoyance to the commerce of the United States. These marauders were found, however, to be merely private adventurers, unauthorized by any government; and the United States sent out a force, which took possession of the islands, and soon put a stop to their ilicit trade. . . .

1818. During the year 1818, the United States became engaged in a war with the Seminole Indians, who occupied the lands lying on the confines of the United States and Florida; the greater part, however, lying within the dominions of the king of Spain. Outlaws from the Creek nation, negroes who had fled from their masters in the United States, and the Seminole Indians, had united in committing depredations upon the lives and property of the citizens of the United States. For many months, the southern frontier was exposed to savage and bloody incursions; and the most horrid massacres had become so frequent, that the inhabitants were obliged to flee from their homes for security. The hostile spirit of the Indians was strengthened by Arbuthnot and Ambrister,[51] two English emissaries, who had taken up their residence among them, for the purposes of trade. They were also incited by one Francis, whom they regarded as a prophet. In December, 1817, a detachment of forty men, under the command of Lieut. Scott, was sent to the mouth of the river Appalachicola, to assist in removing some military stores to fort Scott. The party in returning, were fired upon by a body of Indians, who lay in ambush upon the bank of the river, and six only escaped. Lieut. Scott was one of the first who fell. Notwithstanding the offenders were demanded by Gen. Gaines,[52] to commanding officer on that frontier, the chiefs refused to deliver them up to punishment. Gen. Jackson, with a body of Tennesseans, was now ordered to the protection of the southern frontier. In several skirmishes with the Indians, he defeated and dispersed them; and persuaded that the Spaniards were active in fomenting the Seminole War, and furnishing the Indians with supplies, he entered Florida, and took possession of fort St. Marks and Pensacola. He took as prisoners, Arbuthnot, Ambrister, and the Indian prophet, Francis.

A court martial was called, at which Gen. Gaines presided, for the trial of Arbuthnot and Ambrister. Arbuthnot was tried on the following charges;—"for exciting and stirring up the creek Indians to war against the United States and her citizens, he being a subject of Great Britain, with whom the United States are at peace." Second, "for acting as a spy, aiding, abetting, and comforting the enemy, and supplying them with the means of war." He was found guilty of these charges, omitting the words, "acting as a spy," and sentenced to be hung. Ambrister was tried on similar charges, and sentenced to be shot.

The treaty between the United States and Spain, stipulated, that the Spanish should keep such forces as would enable them to restrain the hostilities of the Indians, inhabiting their colonies. It was the refusal of Spain to do this, which produced the necessity of carrying the war into its provinces. The massacres committed by the savages, left no alternative but to suffer the frontier settlements of Georgia to remain exposed to the mercy of those barbarians, or to carry the war into Florida. Pensacola and St. Marks were restored to Spain, by order of the president. In April of this year, the governor of Georgia received information that the Phlelemmes and Hoppones, tribes of Indians, had shown indications of a hostile disposition, and that several murders had been committed by them. He accordingly ordered Capt. Wright, with a company of militia, to go to the relief of the inhabitants in that part of the country. The Creeks were at this time friendly, and many of them assisted Gen. Jackson in the Seminole war. Notwithstanding this, Capt. Wright, instead of defending the frontier from the Phlelemmes, attacked the Cheraw village, which belonged to the Creeks. Their warriors being with Gen. Jackson, they were unable to defend the town, and Capt. Wright took possession of it, murdered many of the Indians, some of their women, and reduced their dwellings to ashes. This treatment enraged the Creeks, and it was expected that they would immediately retaliate. Measures were, however, taken by government, to redress the injuries inflicted upon them, and they became satisfied. It seemed doubtful whether Capt. Wright's proceedings arose from a misapprehension of the point of attack, or not. He was arrested by government, but escaped from prison. . . .

1819. This year, the Chickasaws ceded to the government of the United States, all their lands, west of the Tennessee river, in the states of Kentucky and Tennessee.

The condition of those tribes living within the territories of the United States, now attracted the attention of the government, and a humane policy dictated its measures. The sum of 10,000 dollars annually, was appropriated for the purpose of establishing schools among them, and to promote, in other ways, their civilization. By means of the missionary societies, already established in the United States, missionaries were supported among the Indians, and success, in many instances, crowned their efforts.

Alabama territory was this year admitted into the union of the states; and the territory of Arkansaw separated from Missouri territory.

On the 23d of February, 1819, a treaty was negotiated at Washington, between John Quincy Adams,[53] secretary of state, and the Spanish minister, by which Spain ceded to the United States, East and West Florida, and the adjacent islands. The government of the United States agreed to exonerate Spain from the demands which their citizens had against that nation, on account of injuries and spoliations; and it was stipulated that congress should satisfy these claims, to an amount not exceeding five millions of dollars. Three commissioners were to be appointed by the president, with the advice of the senate, to examine and decide upon the amount and validity of all claims included by the treaty. The contracting parties renounced all claims to indemnities for any of the recent acts of their respective officers in Florida. This treaty was ratified by the president and senate of the United States, and sent to Spain, but the king very unexpectedly refused to sanction it. Don Onis, the Spanish minister, was recalled, and another minister was sent to the United States, to make complaints of the unfriendly policy on the part of the American government, and to demand explanations respecting the imputed system of hostility on the part of the American citizens, against the subjects and dominion of the king of Spain. Explanations were made, and it was satisfactorily shown, by Mr. Adams, the secretary, that there had been no system of hostility pursued by the citizens of the United States. . . .

APPENDIX. A.

Many efforts to civilize the Indians have been made by the government of the United States; and these humane exertions have been ably seconded by pious and benevolent individuals; but apparently with little effect. What is known of the history of those tribes who inhabited the central and northern parts of the American Republic, exhibits them as a peculiar people, and shows that there are principles in their mental constitution, averse to civilization.[54] Although the Indians had for centuries, perhaps for thousands of years, been the sole lords of rich and extensive domains, affording many eligible and central situations, yet from authentic histories, we do not learn that they had any cities. Compared with other nations, the Indian scarce seems a gregarious animal. Other barbarians have, by degrees, seen the advantages of union; and hence have bartered their independence for security. Not so with the Indian. He is master of his own conduct; the avenger of his own wrongs. Even in war, he follows his leader only by his own choice. If it should be said that the comparative solitude in which he lives, is rather the necessary effect of the manner in which he procures his subsistence, than of his own voluntary selection—that his living in this state marks no peculiarity of his taste, but only his degree in the scale of civilization, other nations having gone through the same barbarous state before arriving at refinement—why then, it may be asked, when the pleasures and comforts of civilization are introduced, does he not manifest the same eagerness to possess himself of them, that other barbarians have hitherto manifested on like occasions? The savage tribes in the north of Europe were, at the period when history first presents them to our notice, in the same wandering unsettled state, in which the Indian tribes have been subsequently found; but as soon as these blood-hounds of war scented, from the south the distant cities and fields of civilization, they rushed towards them, drove off their possessors, and gladly abandoning their own inhospitable mountains, enjoyed the pleasures and learned the arts of civilized men. So far from this, the Indians, when civilization is brought to their door, flee from it. Their tribes, it is true, made war upon our forefathers; but it was to exterminate them, and to regain a soil which they regarded as belonging to them, and over which they wished again to roam uncontrolled; but in no instance did the Indian seek, like the European barbarian, to drive the white man from his dwelling, that he might have a more commodious one to inhabit himself. And now that these tribes have so long lived with a civilized people, they do not incline to mingle with them. The contrast between the character of the Indian and the negro, in this respect, shows still more plainly, that the former acts from his propensities rather than his situation. The negro, brought from the wilds of Africa, immediately acquires a taste for luxury, and gladly serves in the dwellings of the rich; but the Indian can rarely be thus tempted to forego his independence.

The Indians themselves appear to be impressed with the belief that they are, by nature, different men from the whites. It was related by a lady who had long lived near them, that a chief in her neighbourhood, had sent his son, for an education, to Dartmouth College. On his return to his paternal fields, he immediately reassumed the dress and ferocious manners of the Indians. On her noticing this circumstance to the father, "Hoh!" said the old Indian, "if you catch a young wolf, and shut him up in a pen, do you think, when you let him out, he will not catch lambs?"

That man is the same in all ages and in all climates, is doubtless a general truth, but it cannot be received without its limitations. When considering the bodily structure of different races, that anatomist would err, who should practise his profession, on the presumption that there were no differences,—and let us but open our eyes to the lights of history, and we shall be convinced that the politician would equally commit an error, who should proceed on the supposition that there are no original differences of mental constitution.

There is something melancholy in contemplating the fate of this people, when we look back to the time when they were lords of the soil of America, crowded, as they have been, further and further to the west: nor does their future prospect, unless some unforeseen change takes place, seem much more cheering. "By and by," says Mr. Moulton,[55] "they will have passed the Rocky Mountains, and in a few centuries scarcely a remnant will be seen, unless along the beach of the Pacific, the utmost boundary to which they can flee; where, as they gaze upon the illimitable expanse, and turn back to the country of their ancestors, they will mingle with the resounding surge the death song of departed nations."

We should hope that this mournfull image was rather the production of poetic fancy, than historic truth; nor have the considerations mentioned been brought forward to deter benevolent exertions in their favour; but in hopes that it may tend to make those exertions more effectual. The statesman, like the mechanician, must know in what element he is to operate, and what resistance he is to overcome. Taking for granted the absolute identity of their nature with ours, we have proceeded on the supposition that the perfection of their society and institutions must be the same as our own, and to this point have our exertions been directed. Allow that there is a difference in their mental, as well as physical formation—allow that it is as impossible for us to suppress their native independence, as it would be to sink their high cheek bones, or bend their erect and stately figures; that we can no more give them the tenderness of feeling, which makes us so dependent on each other, than we could impart to them the fair and roseate tints of our skin, or the softness of our hair; allow this, and it follows that the perfection of their nature, and consequently of their institutions, is something different from the perfection of ours. What is then the most perfect state of society in which the Indian can live? What advances has he made towards attaining it? What can we do to aid him in securing it? These are questions for the American statesman and philanthropist.

To the northwest lies one full quarter of North America, yet uninhabited except by savage tribes. In that region is room for the Indians to form themselves into a mighty nation. If their leaders could once receive a spirit of improvement, they could do what cannot be done by the whites; whom the Indians hate as usurpers of a soil which of right belongs to them, and despise as, on the whole, inferior to themselves. Such a spirit of improvement might lead them to profit by their past errors, to select such among our arts and sciences as are best fitted to their peculiar character, and finally to form themselves into a united people; never, it is true, possessing what we consider the refinements of society, but perhaps exhibiting traits of greatness of which we have little idea.

Explanatory Notes

CHAPTER 1: ANN ELIZA BLEECKER

1. *Burgoyne* John Burgoyne (1722–1792) led his troops in the Saratoga Campaign of the Revolution, which included the march through Tomhanick toward Albany. He surrendered in October 1777.
2. *based on real-life events* See chapter 3, "Posthumous Constructions: The Writings of Ann Eliza Bleecker and Margaretta Bleecker Faugeres," in Sharon M. Harris's *Resisting/Colonizers: Race, Class, and the Law in Eighteenth-century U.S. Women's Narratives* (forthcoming); a shortened version was presented at the MLA conference in San Francisco, December 1998.
3. *Mrs. C—— V——* Unidentified, but probably a member of the Van Wyck family.
4. *Penelope* In Greek mythology, the wife of Odysseus; in Homer's *Odyssey*, Penelope is renowned for her fidelity.
5. *French and Indian war* A series of wars between England and France in North America between 1689 and 1763, in which each European nation aligned itself with various Native American nations.
6. *Schochticook* Or "Schaghticoke," a region near Albany where the Bleecker and Knickerbocker families resided; named after the Native American nation, Schaghticoke.
7. *Ceres* Roman goddess of grain, a model of fertility and fecundity, but also known for her rites for the dead.
8. *Phosphor* Morning star.
9. *Lazarus* Jesus raised Lazarus from the dead.
10. *Flora* Roman goddess of flowers.
11. *Lot did from Sodom* To escape destruction, Lot fled the corruption and carnality of the city of Sodom.
12. *Tisiphone* In Greek religion, one of the Furies or goddesses of vengeance. She was the "blood avenger."

13. *Hermes* In Greek mythology, Hermes conducts souls into Hell.
14. *Cimmeria* An ancient city in the Crimea.

CHAPTER 2: MARGARETTA V.
BLEECKER FAUGERES

"The Hudson"

1. *Bastille Day* The Bastille was a prison in Paris with many political prisoners secretly imprisoned by the crown. On July 14, 1789, working-class protesters stormed the Bastille, making their gesture a symbol of resistance to tyranny during the French Revolution. After the war, Bastille Day became a national holiday in France.
2. *evergreens* "Cyprus, hemlock, firr and pine." [Faugeres's note]
3. *my current* "All the waters of Lakes George, Champlain and Ontario empty in the river St. Lawrence, except one small stream, which, running an opposite course, forms the Hudson." [Faugeres's note]
4. *Naïad* Nymph.
5. *Pomona* Ancient Italian goddess of fruit trees.
6. *fortress* "St. John's, besieged and taken by the American army under General Montgomery." [Faugeres's note]
7. *Montgomery* Richard Montgomery (1738–1775) served in several Revolutionary War battles; he died in an unsuccessful campaign to conquer Quebec.
8. *Allen* "Colonel Ethen [Ethan] Allen, who took Ticonderoga by surprise." [Faugeres's note.] Allen (1738–1789) led the Green Mountain Boys in the capture of Fort Ticonderoga.
9. *smooth lake* "Lake George." [Faugeres's note]
10. *marble bed* "Almost the whole bed of Lake George is a smooth WHITE rock." [Faugeres's note]
11. *M'Crea* "Near Fort-Edward the beautiful Miss M'Crea was cruelly murdered by Indians, who were sent by General Burgoyne to escort her to her lover, one of his officers, to whom she was to have been married in a few days." [Faugeres's note] Jane McCrea (c.1752–1777) became a symbol of the ruthlessness of British aggression, and her death galvanized patriot zeal for the war.
12. *thine eyes* "He died in 1792." [Faugeres's note]
13. *New Albion* New England.

14. *Gates* Horatio Gates (1728–1806), a Revolutionary War general who defeated Burgoyne in the Saratoga compaign.

15. *Cohoes* "Next to the Niagara the grandest falls on the continent, seventy feet high." [Faugeres's note]

16. *buck-wheat* "This grain, when in bloom, can be smelt at such a distance, and so rich is the scent, that it may be said, that,
    'Many a league,
    'Cheer'd with the grateful smell old HUDSON smiles.' "
    [Faugeres's note]

17. *Albania* Albany, New York.

18. *Esopus* "Esopus was burnt by the British in 1777. Besides this place and Hudson there are several towns and villages upon the river, viz. Red-Hook, Poughkeepsie, New-Windsor, Newburgh, New-Malborough, Fish-Kill, &c." [Faugeres's note]

19. *Arnold* Benedict Arnold (1741–1801), American general who committed treason.

20. *Andre* John André (1751–1780) plotted with Benedict Arnold to betray the American post at West Point.

21. *Wayne* Anthony Wayne (1745–1796), American general who captured the strategic city of Stony Point, New York, during the Revolution.

22. *Bellona* Roman goddess of war.

23. *Fleury* André Hercule Fleury, Cardinal de (1653–1743), French statesman and chief adviser to Louis XV.

24. *banner proud* "At the storming of Stony-Point Lieutenant Fleury struck the British standard with his own hand." [Faugeres's note]

25. *Tall mural rocks* "These rocks rise for many miles nearly perpendicular, some of them 600 feet." [Faugeres's note]

26. *Nassau's isle* "Commonly called Long-Island." [Faugeres's note]

27. *Two mighty rivers* "The HUDSON and the EAST-RIVER or SOUND, which meet at the south-west end of the city." [Faugeres's note]

28. *Clio* One of the Muses (patron goddesses of the arts); Clio was the muse of history.

"On seeing a Print, exhibiting the Ruins of the Bastille

1. *Gallia* France.

2. *AEolus* In Homer's *Odyssey*, he is the controller of the winds.

3. *Gauls* A variant of "Gallia," e.g., French people.

4. *Columbian* Common term for the United States of America.

5. *Fayette* Marie Joseph Paul Yves Roch Gilbert Motier, Marquess de La Fayette (1757–1834), a French general and supporter of the

American Revolution; he served in the Continental army as a major general. He would make a triumpant tour of the United States in 1824–25, long after Faugeres had died, fulfilling her prophecy of continued acclaim in America.

6. *Coriolanus* A fifth-century Roman tyrant; in return for supplying grain to the starving people, he insisted they abolish the people's tribunate, depriving them of any political voice.

CHAPTER 3: JUDITH SARGENT MURRAY

1. *Observations . . .* This four-part essay is included in *The Gleaner* (1798) as essay Nos. LXXXVIII through XCI, here indicated as Parts I through IV.

2. *The Equality of the Sexes* An essay by Murray, originally published in *The Massachusetts Magazine* in March–April 1790.

3. *"the Rights of Women"* Mary Wollstonecraft's highly influential *A Vindication of the Rights of Woman* (1792).

4. *Spartan women* The women of Sparta, an ancient Greek city renowned for its military power and discipline.

5. *Ottoman Empire* In 1526 the Ottoman Turks defeated the Hungarians; a series of wars followed in which the Turks came to dominate most of Hungary.

6. *Sibyls* Female prophets, according to mythology.

7. *Commodore Byron* Probably John Byron (1723–1786), British admiral who commanded a fleet in 1779 that was sent to relieve British forces in America.

8. *Plutarch* Greek essayist and biographer (c.46–c.120 A.D.); author of *Parallel Lives*, a study of Greek and Roman leaders.

9. *Descartes* René Descartes (1596–1650), French philosopher and scientist; he is best known for his cryptic philosophical assertion on the certainty of existence: "I think, therefore I am."

10. *Arria, the wife of Paetus* A Roman woman who killed herself in 42 A.D. as an example of courage for her husband, who had been condemned to death.

11. *Lady Jane Gray* Lady Jane Grey (1537–1554) was named Queen of England in 1553; her reign lasted only nine days, after which she was imprisoned and subsequently executed.

12. *Anna Askew* An English author (1521–1546) of poetry and an autobiography.

13. *Cranmer* Thomas Cranmer (1489–1556) was Archbishop of Canterbury under King Henry VIII of England.

14. *Jane of Flanders* Johanna of Flanders, who reigned from 1244 to 1278.
15. *Margaret of Anjou* Queen to Henry VI of England (1430–1482); she was politically active during the War of the Roses.
16. *Corde* Charlotte Corday (1768–1793) was a political activist during the French Revolution; she was executed for assassinating the Jacobin leader, Jean Paul Marat. See Sarah Pogson's *The Female Enthusiast* in this volume for a dramatic account of Corday's life.
17. *mother and wife of Coriolanus* Veturia and Volumnia, respectively. In the fifth century, they were the only people capable of convincing Coriolanus, the Roman leader, not to destroy Rome.
18. *Aspasia, of Miletus* A renowned philosopher (5th c. B.C.); Plato refers to her writings, but none are extant today.
19. *Hortensia* Known for a speech she gave (lst c. B.C.) protesting taxes to be assessed againt women's property; the taxes were intended to fund a war begun, as she noted, by men.
20. *Mrs. Roper* Margaret Moore Roper (1505–1544), an English translator and letter writer. Her father, Sir Thomas Moore (1478–1535), was an English statesman and author. His imprisonment was due to his religious stances against King Henry VIII, for which he was decapitated.
21. *Portia* A Roman woman (?–42 B.C.) recognized for her courage and her role as confidante to her husband, Brutus (85?–42 B.C.), a politician who was one of Caesar's assassins.
22. *Julia* Julius Caesar's daughter (?–54 B.C.). She negotiated peace between Caesar and her husband, Pompey, both rulers of Rome.
23. *Molfa Tarquinia* A member of the legendary Etruscan Tarquin family, which ruled Rome in the 6th c. and 5th c. B.C.
24. *Ferrara* A commonality in northern Italy.
25. *Artemisia, wife of Mausolus* An Asian princess (?–c.350 B.C.). She ruled Caria for three years after her husband's death.
26. *Victoria Colonna* An Italian poet (1490–1547).
27. *Mrs. Rowe* Elizabeth Singer Rowe (1674–1737), an English poet ("Philomela") and journalist who was a member of the Dissenters, a group seeking religious reform in England.
28. *Semiramis* Mythological queen of Assyria and founder of Babylon.
29. *Amalasuntha* (498–535), queen and regent of the Ostrogoths (Tuscany) from 526 to 534.
30. *Julia Mammaea* Regent of Rome during her emperor son Alexander Severus's minority. Both were assassinated in 235 A.D. in a military coup.
31. *Alexander Severus* Marcus Aurelius Severus Alexander (208–235)

ruled Rome from 222 to 235 A.D. An ineffectual ruler, his empire descended into civil strife.

32. *Zenobia* Queen of Palmyra (Syria) from 267 A.D. to 272 A.D.

33. *Longinus* A Greek literary critic (1st c. A.D.).

34. *Christina* (1626–1689) was renowned for her learning and was a patron of the arts; she reigned from 1632 to 1654.

35. *Corinna* A Greek poet (5th c. B.C.).

36. *Pindar* A Greek poet (c. 518–c. 438 B.C.).

37. *Sappho* A Greek poet from the Isle of Lesbos (7th–6th c. B.C.).

38. *Sulpicio* Sulpicia II (1st c. A.D.), a Roman poet.

39. *Dimitian* Emperor of Rome in the 1st c. A.D.

40. *Hypatia* A philosopher and teacher (370–415 A.D.); Socrates ranked her as the first among contemporary philosophers.

41. *Cassandra* Mythological prophet who was cursed by Apollo so no one would believe her prophecies.

42. *Homer, Virgil, and Dante* Homer (fl. 850? B.C.), Greek epic poet; Virgil (70–19 B.C.), Roman poet; Dante (1265–1321), Italian poet.

43. *Erasmus* Desiderius Erasmus (1466?–1536) was a Dutch priest, educator, and writer.

44. *The Seymours* Anne, Jane, and Margaret Seymour, all of whom were poets; in 1549 they collaborated on an elegy honoring the French author Marguerite de Navarre (1492–1549).

45. *Isabella of Rosera* Isabella I (1451–1504) was Queen of Castile from 1474 to 1504; she aided Columbus's first expedition.

46. *Scotus* John Duns Scotus (?–1308), a celebrated Franciscan scholastic philosopher.

47. *Mary Stuart, queen of Scotland*, was also a poet, essayist, and letter-writer (1542–1587).

48. *Issotta Nogarolla* An author of poetry, dialogues, and letters (1420?–1466).

49. *Tasso* Torquato Tasso (1544–1595) was an Italian poet and playwright.

50. *Modesta Pozzo* An Italian poet and playwright (1555–1592) who used the pen name "Moderata Fonte."

51. *Mary de Gournai* Marie Le Jars de Gournay (1566–1645) was a French editor and essayist; she wrote essays on the equality of the sexes.

52. *Guyon* Jeanne-Marie Bouvier de La Motte, Madam Guyon (1648–1717), was a French author of religious tracts.

53. *Anna Maria Schuman* Probably Anna Maria van Schurman (1607–1678), author of *The Learned Maid* (1659).

54. *Mademoiselle Scudery* Marie-Madeleine du Moncel de Martinval Scudéry (1607–1701) was a French author of letters and novels.

55. *Anna de Parthenay* A sixteenth-century French composer and poet.

56. *Catharine de Parthenay* (1554–1631) was a French translator and author of poetry, drama, and satire; married Viscount René de Rohan, Prince of Leon, in 1575.

57. *Renatus de Rohan* Louis René Eduoard, Prince and cardinal de Rohan (1734–1803), French church and political leader.

58. *Duke of Rohan* Henri, Duke de Rohan (1579–1638), French Protestant general.

59. *Mademoiselle le Fevre* Anne Lefebvre, Madame Dacier (1647–1720), was a French scholar, editor, translator, and pamphleteer.

60. *Maria de Sevigne* Marie de Rabutin-Chantal, marquise de Sévigné (1626–1696), was a French author of letters.

61. *Mary II. Queen of England* Mary Stuart (1662–1694); in 1689 she was proclaimed joint sovereign with her husband William III of Nassau, Prince of Orange (1650–1702).

62. *Countess of Pembroke* Mary Sidney (1561–1621), was a poet, patron, and editor.

63. *Anna Killigrew* Anne Killigrew (c. 1660–1685) was an English artist and poet.

64. *Anna Wharton* Anne Warton (1659–1685) was an English author of plays and poetry.

65. *Catharine Phillips* Katherine Philips (1631–1664) was an English author of poetry, plays, and letters, as well as a translator.

66. *Lady Burleigh . . . Sir Anthony Cook* Mildred Burghley; Anne Cooke, Lady Bacon (1528–1610), was an author of letters and a translator; Elizabeth Cooke, Lady Hoby and later Lady Russell (1529–1609), was an author of poetry and a translator; Katherine Killigrew; Sir Anthony Cooke (1504–1576), was a politician, scholar, and tutor to Edward VI.

67. *Duchess of Newcastle* Margaret Cavendish (1623–1673) was an English philosopher and author of poetry, biographies, and an autobiography.

68. *Lady Halket* Lady Ann Halkett (1623–1699) was an English teacher and author of memoirs.

69. *Lady Masham* Damaris Masham (1658–1708) was an English author of religious papers.

70. *Mary Astell* Astell (1666–1731) was a poet and author of letters and religious and political essays, especially critiques of women's social oppression.

71. *Lady Grace Gethin* An English author of essays (1676–1697).

72. *Xenophon* A Greek historian (c.430–c.355 B.C.).

73. *Mr. Congreve* William Congreve (1670–1729) was an English Restoration author of plays.

74. *Chudleigh . . . Montague* English authors: Mary, Lady Chudleigh (1656–1710) was an author of poetry and a critic of women's social oppression; Anne Finch, Countess of Winchilsea (1661–1720), was an author of poetry; "Monk," Mary Molesworth (?–1715), was an author of poetry; Catharine Bovey (or Boevey) (1669–1726) was a philanthropist; "Stella," Esther Johnson (1681–1728) was a companion of Jonathan Swift; Lady Mary Wortley Montague (1689–1762) was an author of letters and essays.

75. *Catharine Macaulay* (1731–1791), an English Whig radical, historian, and philosopher, and an advocate of women's education.

76. *Madame de Genlis* Stéphanie-Félicité du Crest de Saint-Aubin, comtesse de Genlis (1746–1830), was a French author of novels, memoirs, and dramas as well as educational tracts.

77. *Madame Roland* Manon Philipon, Madame Roland de La Platière (1754–1793), was a French author of letters, essays, and memoirs as well as a political activist.

78. *Barbauld . . . Wollstonecraft* English authors of renown: Anna Laetitia Barbauld (1743–1825), a poet and essayist; Anna Seward (1742–1809), a poet and novelist widely known as "The Swan of Lishfield"; Hannah Cowley (1743–1809), a poet and playwright; Elizabeth Inchbald (1753–1821), an actress and author of dramas, essays, and novels; Fanny (Frances) Burney (1752–1850), a novelist and memoirist; Charlotte Smith (1749–1806), a novelist; Ann Radcliffe (1764–1823), also a novelist; Jane Elizabeth Moore (1738–?), a poet and memoirist; Helen Maria Williams (1762–1827), a poet, novelist, and translator; and Mary Wollstonecraft (1759–1797), essayist and novelist. See the beginning of this essay for reference to her renowned feminist text, *A Vindication of the Rights of Woman*.

79. *Warren . . . Euphelia* American authors: Mercy Otis Warren (1728–1814) was a dramatist, poet, historian (see selection in this volume), and a friend of Murray's; "Philenia" was the pen name of Sarah Wentworth Morton (1759–1846), a poet and prose writer of considerable renown; "Antonia" and "Euphelia" are unidentified.

80. *Mr. Gleaner* The persona under which Murray wrote the essays published in *Massachusetts Magazine* and collected in the three-volume *The Gleaner*.

81. *panegyrist* Unidentified, although Murray herself could be the "panegyrist," considering how many personae she used in *The Gleaner*.

CHAPTER 4: HANNAH ADAMS

1. *Belknap* Jeremy Belknap (1744–1798), American historian and one of the founders of the Massachusetts Historical Society in 1791, he wrote a three-volume *History of New Hampshire* (1784–1792), among other texts.

2. *Trumball* Benjamin Trumbull (1735–1820) was a Congregational minister and author of *A Complete History of Connecticut* (1797).

3. *Ramsay* David Ramsay (1749–1815), a South Carolinian physician and historian, published *History of the Revolution of South-Carolina* (1785).

4. *Gordon* William Gordon (1728–1807), an English supporter of the American cause, came to the United States in 1770. He published *The History of the Rise, Progress and Establishment of the Independence of the United States of America* in 1788.

5. *Minot* George Richards Minot (1758–1802) was a Massachusetts jurist. In 1788 he published *The History of the Insurrection in Massachusetts in the Year 1786*, a harsh critique of Shay's Rebellion.

6. *Sullivan* John Sullivan (1740–1795), a general during the American Revolution, Governor of Massachusetts (1807–1808), and a historian of such texts as *History of Maine*.

7. *Morse* Jedidiah Morse (1761–1826), an American Congregational minister, was considered the "father of American geography." He wrote histories of New England and the American Revolution as well as *Geography Made Easy* (1784).

8. *intrepid conquerors* "See Robertson's *History of South-America*." [Adams's note.] William Robertson (1721–1793) was a Scottish historian; his *History of America* was published in 1777.

9. *Puritans* "Neal's *History of the Puritans.*—Belknap's *History of New-Hampshire*, Vol. I. p. 61, 62, 63." [Adams's note.]

10. *worship increased* "See Neal's *History of the Puritans.*" [Adams's note.]

11. *Mr. Robinson* John Robinson (1576?–1625) was an English nonconformist pastor; he settled in Holland in 1608. Though he desired to go to New England on the *Mayflower*, the majority of his congregation did not; he remained in Holland.

12. *the old world* "Prince's *Chronological History of New-England*, Vol. I. p. 82." [Adams's note.] Thomas Prince (1687–1758) was an American clergyman and historian. His *Chronological History* was published in two volumes (1736, 1755).

13. *obtained a patent* "Mather's *Magnalia*, Book I. p. 6." [Adams's

note.] Cotton Mather (1663–1728) published *Magnalia Christi Americana* in 1702, an ecclesiastical history of New England.

14. *final adieu* "*Prince's Chronology, Vol. I. p. 66.*" [Adams's note.]
15. *their former plan* "*Morton's New-England's Memorial, p. 13.*" [Adams's note.]
16. *this contract* The document they created was the Mayflower Compact. ·
17. *John Carver* (1576?–1621) came over on the *Mayflower* and was the first governor of Plymouth Plantation.
18. *their government* "*Mather, B. I. p. 8.*"[Adams's note.]
19. *native country* "*Morse's Geography, Vol. 1, p. 344.*" [Adams's note.]
20. *Tarrantenes . . . Penobscot* Native Americans of the Algonquian language family; during the Revolution they sided with the Americans.
21. *people perished* "*Gookins' Historical Collections, p. 148.*" [Adams's note.]
22. *Narraganset* Also of the Algonquian family, the Narragansetts were one of the largest and most powerful of the New England tribal societies, but they never recovered from their enormous losses in King Phillip's War.
23. *wasted and destroyed* "*Morton's Memorial. p. 18, 19, 20. Belknap's American Biography, Vol. I. p. 358.*" [Adams's note.]
24. *Port-Royal* A French settlement in southwestern Nova Scotia, founded in 1605.
25. *exertions and fatigues* "*Prince's Chronology, Vol. 1. p. 98.*" [Adams's note.]
26. *the subsequent year* "*Chalmer's Political Annals, p. 88.*" [Adams's note.]
27. *Massassoiet* Massasoit (1580?–1661) was a Wampanoag chief who signed a peace treaty with Governor John Carver in 1621.
28. *king of England* "*Mather, Book I. p. 10.*" [Adams's note.]
29. *Indian proprietors* "*Declaration respecting the proceedings of the government of Plymouth.*" [Adams's note.]
30. *assigned to each one* "*Hutchinson's History of Massachusetts Bay, Vol. II. P. 474.*" [Adams's note.] Thomas Hutchinson (1711–1780), a governor of Massachusetts (1769–1771), published the three-volume *History of the Colony of Massachusetts Bay* between 1764 and 1828.
31. *its support* "*Chalmer, p. 89.*" [Adams's note.]
32. *age, in which he lived* "*See Robinson's farewell charge to his flock, when embarking for America, in Neal's History of New-England, Vol. 1. p. 84.*" [Adams's note.]

33. *English claims* "*Mather, Book I. p. 12.*" [Adams's note.]

34. *Bradford* William Bradford (1590–1657), a Pilgrim historian and second governor of Plymouth Plantation.

35. *Winslow* Edward Winslow (1595–1655), governor of Plymouth Plantation in 1633, 1636, and 1644.

36. *their conduct* "*See an account of the church in Plymouth, in the Historical Collections for the year 1794. See also Dr. Robbins' anniversary Sermon preached in Plymouth, 1796.*" [Adams's note.]

37. *several towns* "*Hutchinson, Vol. II. p. 467. Chalmer, p. 88.*" [Adams's note.]

38. *Brownists* Followers of Robert Browne (c.1550–c.1633), a leader of the early English Separatists and considered the creator of the principles of Congregationalism.

39. *strictly Calvinian* "*Prince's Chronology, Vol. 1. p. 93.*" [Adams's note.]

40. *Massachusetts colony* "*Hutchinson, Vol. II. p. 478.*" [Adams's note.]

41. *Sir William Phips* (1651–1695), governor of Massachusetts, resisted French attacks during King William's War (1689–1697). When he became governor in 1692, at the height of the witch craze, he established a commission to try cases of alleged witchcraft.

42. *war with the eastern Indians* King Phillip's War (1675–1678), between the Narragansetts and the New England colonists.

43. *daughter and niece of Mr. Parris* Betty Parris and Abigail Williams, respectively. The Rev. Mr. Samuel Parris was minister at Salem Village and his contentious nature fueled the initial witchcraft charges.

44. *an Indian woman* Tituba, Samuel Parris's slave.

45. *number of the accused* "*Hutchinson, Vol. II. p. 25–29. Hale's Modest Inquiry into the Nature of Witchcraft, p. 22.*" [Adams's note.] The Rev. John Hale's *Modest Inquiry* recounts his involvement in and interpretation of the witchtrials.

46. *committed to prison* "*Hutchinson, Vol. II. p. 30. Hale, p. 26.*" [Adams's note.]

47. *Mr. Burroughs* Rev. George Burroughs, an opponent of Rev. Parris, was executed during the 1692 scourge.

48. *imagination increased* "*See Dr. Cotton Mather's Wonders of the Invisible World.*" [Adams's note.]

49. *the accused* "*Neal, Vol. II. p. 129; and Calef's More Wonders of the Invisible World, p. 185.*" [Adams's note.] Robert Calef (1648–1719) was a Boston merchant; in *More Wonders* (1700), he attacked Cotton Mather for his part in the witchcraft trials.

50. *their example* "*Hale, p. 33. Calef.*" [Adams's note.]

51. *sorcery, or enchantment* "Hutchinson, Vol. II. Calef, p. 133." [Adams's note.]

52. *complicated distress* "Blackstone, Vol. IV. p. 61." [Adams's note.] Sir William Blackstone (1723–1780) was a renowned English jurist and author of *Commentaries on the Laws of England* (1765–1769), the standard in English and U.S. law.

53. *Hon. William Stoughton* (c. 1630–1701) was lieutenant-governor of Massachusetts from 1692 until his death; he presided at the Salem witch trials.

54. *pious liberality* "Clark's Letters, p. 18." [Adams's note.]

55. *every county town* "Morse's Geography, Vol. I. p. 458." [Adams's note.]

56. *Mr. Davenport* John Davenport (1597–1670), English minister and founder of the colony at New Haven, Connecticut.

57. *governor Hopkins* Stephen Hopkins (1707–1785) was a chief justice of Rhode Island (1751–1754, 1773) and served nine terms as governor of the colony.

58. *to this day* "Stiles' History of the Judges, p. 40." [Adams's note.] Ezra Stiles (1727–1795), American theologian, historian, and president of Yale from 1778 until his death. He published *History of Three of the Judges of King Charles I* in 1794.

59. *September, 1717* "See a particular account of Yale college in the appendix to Holmes' Life of President Stiles." [Adams's note.]

60. *Governor Yale* Elihu Yale (1649–1721), founder of Yale College, was a governor of the English East India Company.

61. *Yale college* "Holmes' Life of President Stiles, p. 386." [Adams's note.]

62. *ninety students* "Manuscript of the late President Stiles." [Adams's note.]

63. *the appellation* "Life of President Stiles, p. 391." [Adams's note.]

64. *Connecticut hall* "Ibid." [Adams's note.]

65. *churches of Connecticut* "Manuscript of the late President Stiles." [Adams's note.]

66. *towards each other* "Trumbull." [Adams's note.]

67. *Colonel Heathcote* Probably a reference to Caleb Heathcote (1666–1721), merchant and mayor of New York City from 1711 to 1713. An ardent supporter of the Anglican Church, he led five missionary journeys into Connecticut and established new congregations in the region.

68. *Rev. Mr. Johnson* Samuel Johnson (1696–1772), American clergyman and philosopher, was educated at Yale and was the first president of

what is now Columbia University. Earlier, he had been a missionary for the Society for the Propagation of the Gospel and established the first Anglican Church in Connecticut.

69. *to succeed Mr. Pigot* "Trumbull." [Adams's note.]

70. *Mr. Clark* John Clarke (1609–1676) was a founder of Rhode Island and, in 1639, joined William Coddington in founding Newport, Rhode Island. He was a physician and minister of the Seventh Day Baptist church.

71. *Mr. William Hifcex* "Callender, p. 65." [Adams's note.]

72. *governor Coddington* William Coddington (1601–1678) was a founder of Rhode Island. When Newport and Portsmouth were united under one government in 1640, Coddington was elected governor. He resisted joining Roger Williams's settlement at Providence; after long patent battles, the two colonies were combined in 1652.

73. *end of the island* "Morse, p. 446." [Adams's note.]

CHAPTER 5: MERCY OTIS WARREN

1. *Thomas Hutchinson, Esq.* was governor of Massachusetts from 1771 to 1774.

2. *John Adams* (1735–1826) argued against British control of America and signed the Declaration; he was second president of the United States.

3. *Nimrod* In the Bible, Nimrod is the "first on earth to be a mighty man" (Gen. 10:8–12). Assyria became known as the land of Nimrod.

4. *house of Brunswick* Ruling dynasty of the free state of Brunswick in Germany.

5. *aceldama* The field Judas bought with the money paid him for betraying Christ.

6. *Augustus* First Roman emperor (63 B.C.–14 A.D.).

7. *Nero* Roman emperor from 54–68 A.D.

8. *Mr. Bernard* Sir Francis Bernard (1712–1779), colonial governor of Massachusetts from 1760 to 1769.

9. *Machiavellian policy* Niccolò Machiavelli (1469–1527) was an Italian statesman and political philosopher. In his famous text *The Prince* (1532), he describes the ideal leader as amoral and tyrannical, though his other works suggest his interest in republican values.

10. *Edward the sixth* Reigned from 1547 to 1553.

11. *Mr. Hume* A reference to David Hume's *The History of England Under the House of Tudor* (1709); see especially II:505–509.

12. *Dalrymple* Probably a reference to Captain Hugh Dalrymple; under Burgoyne, he was convoy commander and leader of the Brunswick troops.

13. *Boston Gazette* The *Gazette* was known for its arguments in favor of civil liberty. James Otis, John Adams, and many other leaders of the Revolution published in its pages.

14. *Mr. Otis* James Otis (1725–1783), Warren's brother and a leader of the opposition to British rule in America. Otis had struggled with mental illness before being struck on the head by the British officer in 1769. Thereafter, he had only rare moments of lucidity.

15. *resignation of office* "Office of judge advocate in governor Bernard's administration." [Warren's note.]

16. *Richard Henry Lee, Esq.* (1732–1794) was a Revolutionary War leader and signer of the Declaration of Independence.

17. *John Dickinson* (1732–1808), Revolutionary leader from Pennsylvania.

18. *Penn* William Penn (1644–1718), English Quaker and original proprietor of Pennsylvania.

19. *Butler* John Butler (1728–1796) fled to Canada at the beginning of the Revolution and formed Butler's Rangers, which included Loyalists and Native Americans. He led the Rangers in the Wyoming Valley of Pennsylvania in 1778.

20. *colonel Donnison* Possibly William Donneson, in the Rhode Island Artillery Regiment from 1777 to 1778.

21. *their bloody hands* "The transactions at Wyoming are recorded above, agreeably to the most authentic accounts at the time." [Warren's note.]

22. *colonel Clark* George Rogers Clark (1752–1818) was a hero of the American Revolution. In 1774, he served as captain in Lord Dunmore's War against the Ohio Indians, and in the 1780s he led expeditions against the Shawnee and the Wabash Indians.

23. *governor Hamilton* "Governor Hamilton was afterwards captured by Clark." [Warren's note.]

24. *Brandt* Joseph Brandt was a Mohawk chief who was instrumental in the Iroquois's decision to side with the British in the Revolution.

25. *arts and sciences* "By the testimony of British writers, this description is not exaggerated. See their registers and histories." [Warren's note.]

26. *conquest of the savages* "See general Sullivan's account of this expedition on the public records, dated Sept. 30, 1779." [Warren's note.] Sullivan's report was first published in the *Maryland Journal and Baltimore Advertiser* on October 19, 1779.

27. *Pickens, Van Schaick* Andrew Pickens (1739–1817) was a general during the American Revolution and participated in the frontier wars against the Cherokee in 1761. Goose Van Schaick (1730?–1789) had participated in the French and Indian Wars and, as a colonel in the Revolutionary War, led the successful siege against the Onondaga in 1779.

28. *a gentleman* "A young American officer of great sensibility and penetration, who fell at the battle at the Miamis, one thousand seven hundred and ninety-one." [Warren's note.] She is referring to her son, Winslow Warren, who fought against the Indians in Ohio.

29. *to a friend* "This original letter was to James Warren, esquire, speaker of the assembly of Massachusetts, March the thirty-first, one tousand seven hundred and seventy-nine" [Warren's note]. James Warren (1726–1808) was her husband.

30. *part to the whole* "See Lessons to a Prince, by an anonymous writer" [Warren's note.] Probably David Williams's *Lessons to a Young Prince on the Present Disposition in Europe to a General Revolution*, 6th ed. (1791).

31. *Otis, Dickinson, Quincy* "The characters of Dickinson and Otis are well known, but the early death of Mr. *Quincy* prevented his name from being conspicuous in the history of American worthies. He was a gentleman of abilities and principles. . . . The writings of the above named gentlemen, previous to the commencement of the war, are still in the hands of many" [Warren's note].

32. *Ludlow* Edmund Ludlow (c.1617–1692), a radical republican who supported Parliament in opposition to the Royalists during the English Civil Wars.

33. *Sydney* Sir Philip Sydney (1554–1586), English author of *Arcadia* (1590).

34. *Milton* John Milton (1608–1674), renowned English Puritan poet.

35. *Harrington* James Harrington (1611–1677), English political philosopher.

36. *Locke* John Locke (1632–1704), renowned English philosopher and author of *Two Treatises on Civil Government* (1680).

37. *judge Blackstone* Sir William Blackstone (1723–1780), renowned for organizing English law in *Commentaries on the Laws of England* (1765–69), which influenced the formation of U.S. laws.

38. *The ignorance* "Some of them indeed were artful and shrewd, but most of them were deluded and persuaded to attempt, by resistance to government, to relieve themselves from debts which they could not pay, and from the hand of tax-gatherers, who had distrained in some instances to the last article of their property" [Warren's note].

39. *myrmidons* Loyal followers, especially subordinates who carry out orders unquestioningly.

CHAPTER 6: SARAH POGSON

1. *Charlotte Corday* (1768–1793) was a sympathizer with the Girondists, a group of moderate republicans in the French Revolution. The Girondists split with the more radical Jacobins. Jean-Paul Marat was a supporter of the Jacobins and opposed the Girondists. In 1793, Corday stabbed Marat to death while he was bathing. She was arrested and executed.
2. *Jean-Paul Marat* (1743–1793) was a physician and political activist. He founded the journal *L'Ami du peuple* in 1789, in which he ardently attacked those in power.
3. *his bath* To avoid capture by those in power, Marat sometimes had to hide in the sewers of Paris, which caused him to develop terrible skin diseases. Bathing was the only relief.
4. *ignis fatuus* A deceptive goal or hope.

CHAPTER 7: SARAH PIERCE

1. *Catharine Beecher* (1800–1878), American educator and writer, founded the Hartford Female Seminary in 1823.
2. *Harriet Beecher Stowe* (1811–1896) was an extraordinarily successful writer with influential novels such as *Uncle Tom's Cabin* (1852).
3. [*B.C. 898*] This and subsequent bracketed dates are Pierce's notations.

CHAPTER 8: HANNAH MATHER CROCKER

1. *able commentator* "Lord Coke." [Crocker's note.] Sir Edward Coke (1552–1634) was an English judge and political leader.
2. *Arius* 4th c. theologian who denied Jesus's divinity.
3. *Demothenes* (385?–322 B.C.) was an Athenian orator and statesman.
4. *Zenomia* Zenobia (?–post-272) was queen of Palmyra, ruling as regent for her son, the titular prince. A brilliant but ambitious ruler, she called her son emperor and produced coinage in his name, which led Emperor Aurelian to attack Palmyra and take her prisoner.

5. *Aurelian* (212?–275) was Roman emperor from 270 to 275.

6. *Rapin* Paul de Rapin de Thoyras (1661–1725), a French soldier and historian, spent seventeen years writing the eight-volume *Histoire d'Angleterre* (1724).

7. *Rennes* A city in northwest France.

8. *Mr. Ascham* Roger Ascham (1515–1568) was an English scholar and author; he began tutoring Elizabeth I in 1548. He was later Queen Elizabeth's secretary (1558–1568).

9. *Dr. Fuller* Thomas Fuller (1608–1661) was an English clergyman and author of such texts as *The Church History of Britain* (1655).

10. *Cornelia* flourished in the 2nd c. B.C. She was the Roman daughter of general Scipio Africanus the Elder and mother of the Gracchi. Though extremely wealthy, she asserted the only "jewels" she valued were her sons.

11. *Semphronia*, or Cornelia, the matron Cornelia's daughter, married Scipio Africanus the Younger.

12. *the second Scipio Africanus*, or Scipio Africanus the Younger (c.185–129 B.C.) was a Roman general.

13. *Tiberius and Caius* Tiberius and Gaius, known as the Gracchi.

14. *Valerius Maximus* Gaius Galerius Valerius Maximinus (?–313) was a Roman emperor from 308 to shortly before his death.

15. *Xantippe*, the wife of Socrates, flourished in the 5th c. B.C.

16. *Madam Maintenon, Madam de Severns and Madam Chapon* Françoise d'Aubigné, marquise de Maintenon (1635–1719) was a French noblewoman.

17. *independence of the female sex* In 1798, William Godwin published a memoir about Wollstonecraft which revealed that he and Wollstonecraft had lived together and had children without benefit of marriage. Though many advocates of women's rights continued to acclaim Wollstonecraft's *Vindication*, they often distanced themselves from her radical life choices.

18. *Oberach, queen of Otheite* Possibly a reference to queen of Otaheite, the former name of Tahiti.

19. *Miss H. More* Crocker dedicated her book to Hannah More (1745–1833), an English religious writer.

20. *Morton* Sarah Wentworth Morton (1759–1846), a poet, opposed her family's Loyalist inclinations during the Revolution, pronouncing herself a Patriot.

21. *Mrs. Washington* Martha Dandridge Washington (1731–1802) lived with her husband during the brutal winter at Valley Forge.

22. *Mrs. Jackson* During the Revolution, Andrew Jackson's spouse nursed American prisoners in South Carolina.

23. *Fabius* (?–203 B.C.) was a Roman general who was best known for his battle against Hannibal (247–183 B.C.), a Carthaginian general.

24. *Pandora* In Greek mythology, Pandora was given every grace of beauty and goodness by the gods, but was also given a box and warned not to open it. When she did open it, plagues were sent out to the world, with only Hope left to comfort humanity.

CHAPTER 9: ANNE ROYALL

1. *Gen. Andrew Lewis* During the Battle of Point Pleasant in Lord Dunmore's War (1774), Lewis joined Dunmore in aggression against the Shawnee Indians of Kentucky. The Shawnees' defeat completed the colonists' conquest of the area.

2. *Col. John Stewart* was superintendent of Indian affairs for the southern department. Though suspected of inciting Native Americans to participate in the war, he advised they remain neutral, fearing an uprising would benefit the colonists.

3. *Major Thomas Tolly . . . Wm. Hammond* In 1729, when Baltimore was incorporated as a city, Major Thomas Tolley, William Hamilton, William Buckner [sic], Dr. George Walker, Surveyor Richard Gist [sic], Dr. George Buchanan, and William Hammond were named the first commissioners of the city.

4. *Mr. Carrol* Charles Carroll (1737–1832) was a Revolutionary war leader from Maryland who signed the Declaration of Independence. His family estate was Carrollton Manor, a ten-thousand-acre tract.

5. *Gen. Striker* General John Striker resisted the British invasion in the Battle of Baltimore.

6. *Lord Baltimore* George Calvert, the 3rd Lord Baltimore, was proprietor of Maryland, arriving in 1661.

7. *Yoamancos* The Yaocomicoes entered into a treaty with Lord Baltimore in 1634.

8. *Patuxent* Indians were peaceful until the outbreak of attacks between colonists and Patuxents in 1639.

9. *Sir John Harvey* was royal governor of Virginia in the early 1620s, and Lord Baltimore's constant antagonist. Lord Baltimore feared Harvey would overthrow the Maryland Colony.

10. *Chesterfield* Philip Dormer Stanhope, 4th earl of Chesterfield (1694–1773), English statesman and author, was noted for his wit and oratory skills.

11. *DeWitt Clinton* (1769–1828) was mayor of New York City from 1803 to 1815; he was recognized for his advocacy of public education, development of the city, and care for the poor.

12. *the Clintons ... De Witt family* The renowned families of New York state, many of whom could trace their families to the original European settlers of the region. The most powerful family was the Van Rensselaers, one of the founding patroon families of Dutch New York. Stephen Van Rensselaer (1764–1839) was the reigning patroon when Royall visited Albany.

13. *Mrs. Grant* Anne MacVicar Grant (1755–1838) was a widely recognized memoirist, travel writer, and poet, including *Memoirs of an American Lady* (1808).

14. *Colonel Philip Schuyler* (1733–1804) moved to the rank of general during the Revolution. Like the Van Rensselaers, the Schuylers were one of the dominating colonial New York families.

15. *Thomson* James Thomson (1700–1748), a British poet, was best known for his four-part blank verse poem *The Seasons* (1726–1730).

CHAPTER 10: EMMA WILLARD

1. *Elizabeth Cady Stanton* (1815–1902) was one of the foremost leaders of the nineteenth-century women's suffrage movement.

2. *Republic of America* "We use the term Republic of America, in the same manner as we would that of the Republic of Colombia. We conceive that America is as much a distinctive appellation of the one country, as Colombia is of the other. . . . In fact, the style assumed, at the declaration of independence, is not the United States merely, but the 'United States of America;' and it may be fairly presumed that the term America is used in the same manner as in the expression, 'the United States of Holland,' or 'the United States of Mexico,' and that we may, except in formal state papers, abbreviate, and use only the last word. . . ." [Willard's note].

3. *General Thomas* Brigadier General John Thomas, a physician and veteran of the French and Indian Wars, was named commander of rebel forces in Canada in 1775.

4. *Gen. Clinton* George Clinton (1739–1812) became New York State's first governor, serving from 1777 to 1795; he was vice president of the United States from 1805 to 1812.

5. *Sir Peter Parker* (1721–1811) was a British admiral who assisted in the capture of New York during the Revolution.

6. *Gen. Gage* Thomas Gage (1721–1787), a British general, served as

governor of Massachusetts from 1774 to 1775; his attempts to enforce the Intolerable Acts led to the beginning of the American Revolution via the battles at Lexington and Concord.

7. *Gen. Carleton* Guy Carleton (1734–1808) was the British governor and commander of Quebec in the early years of the Revolution.

8. *Gen. Thompson* General William Thompson and two thousand men were sent by Gen. Sullivan to attack Trois Rivières on the St. Lawrence River, in an attempt to stop Burgoyne's advancement in Canada. He was taken captive.

9. *Col. Bedel* Timothy Bedel (?–1787) was colonel of the New Hampshire Rangers in 1775–76 and colonel and brigadier general of the Vermont Militia from 1777–87.

10. *Captain Foster* Possibly Ezekiel Foster, captain and later major of the New Jersey Militia (1777–79).

11. *Maj. Sherburne* Edward Sherburne (?–1777), major and aide-de-camp to Gen. Sullivan.

12. *Gen. Frazer* Possibly Col. Simon Fraser who, with St. Leger, had overwhelmed Gen. Thompson's detachment.

13. *Philips* Major General William Philipps was a British commander who fought at the battle of Ticonderoga.

14. *German baron Reidesel* fought with Gen. Burgoyne at Saratoga.

15. *Lord Cornwallis* Charles Cornwallis, first Marquess (1775–1805), led the British forces during the Revolution.

16. *Gen. Vaughn* Major General Sir John Vaughan was sent with two thousand soldiers to assist Burgoyne, but he arrived to late to assist.

17. *Gen. Lee* Charles Lee (1731–1782) was captured in 1776 by the British. He provided them with a plan to defeat the Americans, who were unaware of his treasonous acts when he rejoined General Washington's troops in 1778.

18. *Gadsden* Christopher Gadsden (1724–1805) was a Revolutionary War leader from Charleston and delegate to the First and Second Continental Congresses.

19. *Moultrie* William Moultrie, governor of South Carolina and a major-general in the Revolutionary War.

20. *Thomas Paine* (1737–1809) was an ardent supporter of the American Revolution. His pamphlet "Common Sense" (1776) argued for separation from England.

21. *General Prescott* William Prescott (1726–1795) was a British soldier who gained renown at the Battle of Bunker Hill, and he participated in the Saratoga Campaign.

22. *Colonel Barton* William Barton (1748–1831) is best known for his daring capture of British Brigadier General Prescott in July 1777.

23. *Powel* Brigadier General Henry W. Powell joined Burgoyne in Montreal early in the campaign.

24. *Brigadier General Specht* Johann Friedrich von Specht, like Reidesel, supported Burgoyne as he invaded New York.

25. *Col. St. Leger* Barry St. Leger (1737–1789) commanded British and Native American troops in the Saratoga Campaign. After taking Fort Stanwix (later Fort Schuyler), he was forced to retreat when his frightened troops deserted.

26. *Sir John Johnson* (1741–1830) was a Loyalist during the Revolution and fled to Montreal. He was unsuccessful in uniting settlers and natives in the Mohawk area. He was with St. Leger in the Saratoga Campaign.

27. *Col. Gansevoort* Peter Gansevoort (1749–1812) is best known for turning back General St. Leger at Fort Stanwix, halting St. Leger's support of Burgoyne in New York.

28. *Gen. Herkimer* Nicholas Herkimer (1728–1777), New York militia brigadier general, led troops to Fort Stanwix to support the resistance against St. Leger.

29. *Col. Willet* Marinus Willett (1740–1830) was part of the American forces at Fort Ticonderoga and a leader among New York's Sons of Liberty, and he joined Montgomery in the invasion of Canada during the Revolution.

30. *Lieut. Stockton* Richard Stockton (1730–1781) signed the Declaration of Independence as a delegate from New Jersey. Captured by the British in 1777, he died from harsh treatment in prison.

31. *Gen. St. Clair* Arthur St. Clair (1743–1818) abandoned Fort Ticonderoga without a fight but in a court martial in 1778 was exonerated.

32. *Colonel Francis* Colonel Ebenezer Francis headed the Eleventh Massachusetts Continentals.

33. *Col. Warner* Seth Warner (1743–1784) was a leader of the Green Mountain Boys; he and John Stark achieved a victory at Bennington in 1777.

34. *Gen. Gates* Horatio Gates (1727–1806) replaced Schuyler when he was removed from his command at Fort Ticonderoga and was successful in the Saratoga Campaign.

35. *Lincoln* American troops at Charleston under Major General Benjamin Lincoln surrendered to Sir Henry Clinton in 1780.

36. *Morgan* Daniel Morgan (1736–1802), known for commanding companies of Virginia sharpshooters, fought at Saratoga.

37. *Kosciusko* Thaddeus Kosciusko (1746–1817) fought for the colonists in the Revolution; when he returned to Poland, he campaigned for the independence of his homeland.

38. *Lieut. Col. Baum* Friedrich Baum fought with the British in the Battle of Bennington (1777).

39. *Gen. Stark* John Stark (1728–1822), commander of the New Hampshire militia, helped defeat the British in the battle of Bennington (1777).

40. *Col. Breyman* Lieutenant Colonel Heinrich Christoph Breymann also fought with the British in the Battle of Bennington.

41. *Col. Warner* Under Colonels Allen and Warner's command, these makeshift troops captured Fort Ticonderoga in 1775 and gained victory at Bennington in 1777.

42. *taken prisoners* "After the battle of Bennington, the Hessian prisoners were carried into the village, and distributed into public buildings and out-houses. The meeting house was filled to crowding. The next day, an alarm was suddenly given to the women of the village, to take their children and flee. The Hessians, it was said, were rising on their guard. They were rushing in all directions out of the meeting house. The guard fired, and killed five of them. But the fears of the inhabitants were suddenly changed to compassion. The galleries were giving way. In danger of being crushed to death, the unfortunate men rushed out, and met the fire of a guard, who could not understand from their foreign speech, their explanation of the disorder. This anecdote was related to me by a venerable matron, then a young lady and an inhabitant of Bennington" [Willard's note].

43. *Maj. Ackland* Probably Major John Dyke Acland, leader of a battalion of grenadiers picked for their notable height, who fought at Boucherville on the St. Lawrence and at Saratoga.

44. *earl of Balcarras* Alexander Lindsay, earl of Balcarras, led troops in Montreal and at Saratoga under Burgoyne.

45. *Gen. Poor* Brigadier General Enoch Poor of New Hampshire fought under Philip Schuyler.

46. *General Jackson* Andrew Jackson (1767–1845) defeated the Creek Indians in the War of 1812, for which he was promoted to major general. In 1818 he led the attack on the Seminoles in Florida, taking Pensacola, which created disputes with Spain and England. "Old Hickory" was considered a hero by many in his time, but today is recognized for his ruthless actions against Native Americans.

47. *society for colonizing the free blacks* The American Colonization Society was founded in 1817, with the goal of removing freed African Americans to Africa.

48. *Mr. Madison* A Revolutionary War leader, James Madison (1751–1836) was fourth president of the United States (1809–1817).

49. *James Monroe* Monroe succeeded Madison as president, serving from 1817 to 1825.

50. *Daniel D. Tompkins* (1774–1825) was a member of the Jeffersonian Republican Party, and Monroe's vice president from 1817 to 1825.

51. *Arbuthnot and Ambrister* Alexander Arbuthnot and Robert Ambrister were British subjects who supported the Seminoles. Jackson hanged them for their actions.

52. *Gen. Gaines* Edmund Pendleton Gaines (1777–1849) served under Andrew Jackson in the Creek and Seminole campaigns.

53. *John Quincy Adams* (1767–1848), son of Abigail and John Adams, served as secretary of state under President Monroe from 1817 to 1825. He succeeded Monroe in the presidency for one term.

54. *averse to civilization* "These remarks are not intended to include the Cherokees" [Willard's note].

55. *Mr. Moulton* William Moulton (1731–1805) rose to the rank of general in the American Revolution. He successfully withstood Sir Peter Parker's attack on Charleston. He wrote a two-volume *Memoirs of the Revolution* (1802).

FOR THE BEST IN PAPERBACKS, LOOK FOR THE

In every corner of the world, on every subject under the sun, Penguin represents quality and variety—the very best in publishing today.

For complete information about books available from Penguin—including Penguin Classics, Penguin Compass, and Puffins—and how to order them, write to us at the appropriate address below. Please note that for copyright reasons the selection of books varies from country to country.

In the United States: Please write to *Penguin Group (USA), P.O. Box 12289 Dept. B, Newark, New Jersey 07101-5289* or call 1-800-788-6262.

In the United Kingdom: Please write to *Dept. EP, Penguin Books Ltd, Bath Road, Harmondsworth, West Drayton, Middlesex UB7 0DA.*

In Canada: Please write to *Penguin Books Canada Ltd, 10 Alcorn Avenue, Suite 300, Toronto, Ontario M4V 3B2.*

In Australia: Please write to *Penguin Books Australia Ltd, P.O. Box 257, Ringwood, Victoria 3134.*

In New Zealand: Please write to *Penguin Books (NZ) Ltd, Private Bag 102902, North Shore Mail Centre, Auckland 10.*

In India: Please write to *Penguin Books India Pvt Ltd, 11 Panchsheel Shopping Centre, Panchsheel Park, New Delhi 110 017.*

In the Netherlands: Please write to *Penguin Books Netherlands bv, Postbus 3507, NL-1001 AH Amsterdam.*

In Germany: Please write to *Penguin Books Deutschland GmbH, Metzlerstrasse 26, 60594 Frankfurt am Main.*

In Spain: Please write to *Penguin Books S. A., Bravo Murillo 19, 1° B, 28015 Madrid.*

In Italy: Please write to *Penguin Italia s.r.l., Via Benedetto Croce 2, 20094 Corsico, Milano.*

In France: Please write to *Penguin France, Le Carré Wilson, 62 rue Benjamin Baillaud, 31500 Toulouse.*

In Japan: Please write to *Penguin Books Japan Ltd, Kaneko Building, 2-3-25 Koraku, Bunkyo-Ku, Tokyo 112.*

In South Africa: Please write to *Penguin Books South Africa (Pty) Ltd, Private Bag X14, Parkview, 2122 Johannesburg.*